# Anna Olson's
# Baking Wisdom

Cranberry, Orange &
Hazelnut Crostata (p. 149)

# Anna Olson's
# Baking Wisdom

**THE COMPLETE GUIDE: EVERYTHING YOU NEED TO KNOW
TO MAKE YOU A BETTER BAKER (WITH 150+ RECIPES)**

appetite
by RANDOM HOUSE

Library and Archives of Canada Cataloguing in Publication is available upon request.
ISBN: 978-0-52-561097-7
eBook ISBN: 978-0-52-561098-4

Photography by Janis Nicolay
Prop styling by Catherine Therrien
Design by Emma Dolan
Printed in China

Published in Canada by Appetite by Random House®,
a division of Penguin Random House Canada Limited

www.penguinrandomhouse.ca

10 9 8 7 6 5 4 3 2 1

appetite
by RANDOM HOUSE

Penguin
Random House
Canada

To family, and the wisdom we
share and receive within it.

# Contents

# Introduction

Baking could easily be assumed to be simple. After all, with a recipe in hand, you have a list of ingredients and their measurements followed by step-by-step instructions. What else could you possibly need for a successful bake? And yet we've all eaten a dessert or pastry that didn't look or taste as we expected.

That's because baking isn't just following instructions; it's a journey and an exploration. Every recipe has a learning curve, even if you've made it repeatedly over the years. At first you might find yourself saying, for example, "Now I know I have to let my melted chocolate cool a little before adding it to my brownie batter, to prevent it from splitting"; or "The next time I make choux paste, I will make sure I let the hot batter cool for a minute longer before I add the eggs." It's not that you're changing the recipe, it's that you're beginning to understand the details needed to get a perfectly delicious and delightful-looking baked good. Those moments of comprehension and bits of knowledge, gained through repeated baking, are what I call "baking wisdom" and they enhance your baking and empower you as a baker.

I've created this book to pass along the baking wisdom I have acquired over the years through education, experience, repetition, research, your questions and a whole mess of mistakes in the kitchen. (I never regret a baking failure; I embrace it as an opportunity to get to know my ingredients and methods better so that I can manage and fix future problems.)

Whether this is your very first baking cookbook or you're a seasoned baker with baking wisdom of your own, I am confident you will find something worth exploring here. I am constantly learning, and while I'm thrilled to be sharing the knowledge I have at this moment, I will continue to challenge myself, listen to the wisdom of others and try new things.

I hope you'll take some time to read the information that precedes the recipes. There I share lots of insight about ingredients, methods and baking in general, not just about the recipes in this book. I discuss how protein, fat, starch, sugar, acidity and salt work in baking, so you'll have a better understanding of why ingredients behave the way they do. Each recipe references these sections and others from the front of the book. Listed as Bites of Wisdom, they highlight further reading that specifically applies to each recipe to enhance your understanding of the process before you bake.

I have also included tips within the recipe methods to answer questions you may have while carrying out each step. My hope is that these will spark a few "aha" moments, or at least prevent disasters. (If you do have a problem, don't worry. I have a whole section devoted to how to fix common baking problems after they've happened; see p. 55.)

Each chapter in *Baking Wisdom* is centred on a type of baking. The recipes within each chapter are grouped by commonly shared technique or principle, and in some cases you'll see how a foundation recipe can be added to and changed for different uses.

For each recipe, I've listed the preparation time, which begins after your ingredients are prepped and measured, unless otherwise noted, and the cook time, which includes time on the stovetop and in the oven.

The complexity of each recipe is identified as Simple, More Involved or Complex to give you an idea about the time and tools needed. These tags indicate which recipes involve many steps, with cooling or chilling in between, and which ones can be mixed, baked and eaten in a hurry. Know that Simple recipes can be made by experienced bakers and Complex ones by new bakers.

Bonus Bakes throughout the book are variations on the recipe they accompany. Use them to get adventurous, change your flavours and find new ways to apply what you've just learned.

My hope is that you'll use the baking wisdom I've shared plus your own discoveries to dive into these recipes with more confidence and take even more pleasure in your baking. Then you can pass along your own baking wisdom to others.

—Anna

# Baking Ingredients

Compared to cooking, baking uses a relatively small number of key ingredients. But consider the impressive number of methods you can apply and styles of baking you can create with these ingredients. The key, when the ingredient list is so simple, is to use the best and most appropriate items you can to get the best results.

In this chapter, I talk you through the ingredients every baker should have in their fridge or pantry. I've organized this information alphabetically rather than by importance—although butter does appear at the top of the list, an ingredient that I value greatly! I've also given advice on storing your ingredients, on the ideal temperatures when using your ingredients, and recommendations for how to substitute certain ingredients depending on different dietary needs—or simply because you've been caught in a pinch without something, and you really want to start baking!

# Glossary of Ingredients

Ingredients are the foundation of every recipe. Use good-quality foods to get great-tasting baked goods. The ingredients listed below are used often throughout this book, and I've provided little bites of wisdom about each of them, including storage tips, so you can choose the ones that are right for your budget, needs, tastes and baking frequency. Ingredients specific to a single recipe are talked about in more detail in that recipe. You can pick up basic baking ingredients at your preferred local grocery store. However, online ordering now makes it possible to source specialty ingredients from farther afield. For example, you can choose your baking chocolate or vanilla extract based on quality or price instead of being limited to what is available in your hometown.

## Butter

I always use unsalted butter in baking because it is fresher and sweeter tasting, and I am then in control of the salt. When cooking, I use whichever is handy, salted or unsalted. In Canada, butter is made with an 80% fat content—this is fine for most baking, but for more butter-rich doughs like puff pastry or croissant, a fat content of 82% or 84% yields a tastier and flakier result. If higher-fat European or European-style butter (the fat content should be listed on the label) isn't available, create your own by combining Canadian butter and ghee or chilled clarified butter.

*See the Pearson Square equation (p. 72) to learn how to calculate how much Canadian butter and ghee you need to make your own higher-fat butter.*

When butter is specified to be at room temperature, 65°F to 68°F (18°C to 20°C) is the ideal range. I pull my butter from the fridge, cut it into pieces and let it sit for an hour. Try to avoid softening the butter in the microwave—the temperature will be uneven.

**Storing butter:** Unsalted butter will keep in the fridge for about 2 months or the freezer for about 3 months without absorbing odours or compromising taste.

## Chocolate & Cocoa Powder

*Couverture chocolate* is also known as baking chocolate, and it comes in squares, blocks or chips called callets. This chocolate has a higher cocoa butter content (32% to 39%) than eating chocolate or chocolate chips, and is designed to be melted and worked smoothly into cake batters, fillings and frostings. Chocolate chips, on the other hand, are designed to hold their shape when baked.

*In my recipes, I specify which type of chocolate is needed. Baking/couverture chocolate must always be weighed, whereas chocolate chips (but not baking callets) can be measured by volume.*

Chocolate is made from chocolate liquor, also called cocoa mass, and it's the paste made from fermenting and roasting cacao beans. That mass is separated into cocoa solids and cocoa butter, which are then blended together at a specific temperature along with sugar and sometimes milk, vanilla and emulsifiers like lecithin. The result is set into the chocolate bars we use for baking and eating.

The percentage listed on many chocolates tells you the quantity of cocoa liquor (cocoa mass). The higher the total quantity of cocoa solids and cocoa butter, the lower the quantity of sugar and other ingredients. Bittersweet chocolate gets its intensity because it has a higher proportion of the strong, bitter cocoa solids than semisweet. The percentage of cocoa in different types of chocolate can vary by country, but in general:

- Unsweetened: 85% and higher (up to 99%)
- Bittersweet: 60% to 75%
- Semisweet: 51% to 59%
- Milk: At least 20% cocoa solids in Europe (10% in the US), but 32% is ideal for baking and chocolate work
- White: At least 20% cocoa butter, but no cocoa solids and no more than 55% sugar

*Bittersweet and semisweet chocolate* are interchangeable in recipes, and the deciding factor should be taste. A recipe made using bittersweet will taste more intensely of chocolate and the bitterness may come through, while semisweet is a little milder and sweeter. Make the choice based on your audience—kids tend to favour semisweet chocolate. In this book, if a recipe benefits from using one over the other, I specify either semisweet or bittersweet. If not, I call for *dark chocolate* and you can choose whichever intensity you prefer.

Each type of chocolate melts and sets up differently and has its own sweetness and intensity. For this reason, dark, milk and white baking/couverture chocolate are not interchangeable in recipes. *Ruby and gold chocolate* are new to the market. Ruby chocolate is made from a special variety of cacao bean that when processed naturally produces a pink colour and mild berry-chocolate flavour. Gold chocolate is made by caramelizing the sugars and milk to make a gold-coloured and caramel-flavoured chocolate (similar to the Roasted White Chocolate Ganache, p. 92). Ruby and gold chocolate should be treated like white chocolate when tempering, and can be used in place of white chocolate in recipes where it is called for.

If any of your chocolate develops a dusty coating, called bloom, the chocolate has undergone a temperature change at some point and some of the cocoa butter in the chocolate has risen to the surface. The chocolate is still perfectly fine to use, bloom and all.

COCOA POWDER: This is the powder left after extracting most of the cocoa butter when cacao beans are processed. It has an intensely strong and bitter chocolate taste, and is unsweetened. The process of alkalizing cocoa powder—which neutralizes some of the acidity and mellows the flavour—is referred to as Dutch-process. This does not mean the cocoa powder is a better quality than natural cocoa powder, but it does mean it reacts differently with baking powder and soda, and the colour and chocolate intensity of your desserts may be different. If Dutch-process cocoa powder is not specified in my recipes, you can presume that either type of cocoa is fine.

**Storing chocolate & cocoa powder:** Keep your chocolate in a cool, dark place in airtight containers (use a separate one for each type of chocolate). Chocolate will keep for well over a year, provided it remains at an even 65°F to 68°F (18°C to 20°C). Never refrigerate or freeze chocolate unless it's in a dessert that must be chilled. Cocoa powder can be stored in an airtight container in the pantry for over a year.

## Citus

I love citrus desserts, and I make a point of always using fresh lemon, lime or orange juice. Lemon, lime and orange zest can be interchanged in most desserts, and lemon and lime juice can also be interchanged. To make its flavour pronounced enough in baking, orange juice needs extra acidity. If you're replacing lemon juice with orange juice in a recipe, use two-thirds orange juice and one-third lemon juice. For example, replace 1 cup (250 mL) lemon juice with ⅔ cup (160 mL) orange juice and ⅓ cup (80 mL) lemon juice.

*If you happen to buy lemons on sale or in bulk, you can zest them all at once and store the zest in a container in the freezer. You can then juice the lemons and freeze the juice in ice cube trays to have on hand. To use frozen zest, scrape it with a fork to pull away what you need.*

**Storing citrus juice & zest:** Freshly squeezed lemon juice will keep refrigerated for up to 3 days, but the zest will only retain its fresh flavour and brightness for a day.

## Eggs

I call for large eggs in all of my baking for a simple reason: their standard weight. A large egg in Canada weighs at least 56 g (just under 2 oz) and no more than 62 g (just over 2 oz), including the shell. The white accounts for two-thirds of the weight and three-quarters of the egg's volume, or 30 g (1 oz) by weight and 3 Tbsp (45 mL) by volume. The yolk weighs 18 to 20 g (0.6 to 0.7 oz) and is 1 Tbsp (15 mL) by volume.

*The weight of an egg can vary by a few grams, and generally this doesn't affect a recipe's outcome. (Macarons are the exception, and weighing the egg whites is essential.) If you have reserved egg whites, yolks or whole eggs already out of their shell, weighing them is easier than measuring by volume (egg whites can be very slippery!).*

The magic in an egg is in its physical makeup. The egg white consists of water, protein and minerals. The yolk is made up of water, fat and a little protein, in addition to vitamins and minerals. It's this combination of fat and protein that gives baked goods structure and volume. As a whole egg, the fat and protein together set cookie doughs, cake batters and cheesecakes, and can be whipped up with sugar for sponge cakes. Egg whites whip to enormous volumes because of the way their protein is arranged, making meringues the beautiful, voluminous creations they are. Egg yolks thicken and enrich custards like pastry cream and crème brûlée. For information on the function of proteins and fats in baking, refer to p. 65. For egg substitution options, see p. 15.

**Storing eggs:** Leftover egg whites or yolks can be refrigerated for 2 to 4 days. Egg whites can be frozen in an ice cube tray or small containers for up to 6 months. For egg yolks, stir in 1 tsp (5 mL) of sugar for every three egg yolks before freezing to prevent them from thickening, and freeze for up to 6 months. Thaw egg whites or yolks overnight in the fridge before using.

## Flours

Wheat flour is a cornerstone in our baking. There are three main types of white flour at our disposal.

BREAD FLOUR: Bread flour is milled from a hardy wheat and has a higher protein (gluten) content than other flours, which is why it is suited to bread making and is sometimes referred to as hard or strong flour. Structure develops when you knead a bread dough; it holds in the carbon dioxide that yeast produces, making your bread airy.

CAKE & PASTRY FLOUR: Cake & pastry flour is milled from a "softer" strain of wheat, has a lower protein content and is milled more finely, which is why it makes delicate cakes when called for.

ALL-PURPOSE FLOUR: This is, quite simply, a blend of the soft and hard wheat flours, which is why it's used in everyday baking like cookies and loaf cakes.

"00" FLOUR: This is an Italian white flour. Like all-purpose flour, it is a blend of soft and hard wheat flours, but it is more finely milled, which results in a stretchy and elastic dough that is perfect for pizzas. Baked goods using it have a chewy interior and a crisp exterior once baked.

WHOLE WHEAT FLOUR: Whole wheat flour is healthier than white flour because the wheat bran and germ, with their added fibre, are left in (or added back to) the milled flour. I use white flour a fair bit throughout this book, but if you wish to replace white flour with whole wheat in a recipe on your own, you can typically do this for only up to 50 percent of the flour called for in the recipe. Replacing more than half of the flour in a recipe compromises the taste and texture of the final product.

**Storing flour:** White flour (bread, cake & pastry, all-purpose and "00" flour) will keep in an airtight container for 6 months or more. Whole wheat flour lasts 3 to 6 months because the oils within the bran and germ of the whole grain can turn rancid. You can freeze flour, but it must be tightly sealed and you have to determine if the relatively inexpensive cost of flour is worth taking up the real estate in your freezer.

## Food Colouring

Added to cake batters, frostings, macarons, candies and chocolates, food colouring comes in three forms: liquid, paste (or gel) and powder. *Professional liquid colours* are more concentrated than the grocery store colours and give you the greatest control because they are less concentrated than paste or powder, but the liquid can interfere with macarons, candy and chocolate making because the recipes are moisture-sensitive. You can even buy white liquid colouring, which can neutralize an overtinted frosting or glaze. *Colour pastes* offer a lot of colour punch with less moisture and come in countless shades. *Colour powders* are now more widely available and are ideal for all needs, but

especially macarons, candy and chocolate work. A little goes a long way, so just add a touch when you begin tinting your batch of treats.

**Storing food colouring:** Liquid food colouring and colour powders will keep in a dark place at room temperature for up to 2 years. Colour pastes (or gels) can be stored the same way for up to a year (after a year, they can begin to dry out).

## Fruits, Dried

Dried fruits such as raisins, dried cranberries and dates are affordable and easy to find. Don't worry if a white dust develops at the edges of dried fruits, particularly on dates and figs; their sugars are simply rising to the surface, and the fruits are still fine to eat.

**Storing dried fruits:** Stored in an airtight container at room temperature, dried fruits will keep for more than 6 months. I don't bother freezing them.

## Fruits, Fresh & Frozen

How we treat and use fruits in baking really depends on the fruit itself.

APPLES: Apples for baking should be firmer and tarter than apples for eating fresh. Varieties such as Honeycrisp, Granny Smith, Crispin, Cortland, Spy and Spartan suit baked goods not only for their full apple flavour but also because they hold their shape after cooking.

BANANAS: Bananas mashed and used as part of a batter should be as ripe as possible—look for more brown spots than yellow space on the banana. You can freeze overripe bananas whole, in their peel. Thaw them on the counter in a bowl before peeling and mashing to use.

BERRIES: Use fresh berries in their peak season (this will vary depending on where you live) for the full tart/sweet balance. They are delicious in baked desserts, and their colour and visual appeal make them a beautiful part of a décor. Use frozen berries in baked goods (but not as décor) directly from the freezer or thaw and drain them first, depending on the recipe.

PEARS: Bartlett, Bosc and Anjou pears all suit baking. Most pears are poached or precooked before going into baked goods so that they retain their shape and colour. Use firm to semifirm pears for poaching; ripe pears can turn too soft on the outside and become misshapen after poaching.

STONE FRUITS (PLUMS, APRICOTS, CHERRIES): These fruits have a very short season in Canada, so treasure the fresh fruits when they are available. These can be purchased jarred or tinned in syrup out of season, and sometimes you may find them frozen and pitted.

**Storing fresh & frozen fruits:** Most fresh fruits should be refrigerated, but for how long depends on their moisture content. Soft, fragile fruits like berries keep loosely covered for 4 to 5 days, stone fruits for a week, and sturdy apples and pears for a few weeks. Bananas and pears will ripen if left at room temperature, and then chilling them halts this process. The peel on bananas will turn black once refrigerated, but the banana itself will not discolour.

Frozen fruits are often sold as IQF (which stands for individually quick frozen) so that berries and diced fruit pieces are not clumped together in a big block, but can be easily scooped or poured from their packaging for measuring. Frozen fruits should be measured while frozen, but used—frozen or thawed—as called for in the specific recipe. Frozen fruit will keep for 6 to 12 months in the freezer.

## Gelatin

In North America, unflavoured gelatin is normally sold in powder form, in 7 g packets (about 2 tsp). Because it is sold in a package by weight, you may find it easier and more precise to measure by weight, but volume measures are also provided in the recipes. In Europe and in professional kitchens, sheet gelatin is more commonly used because of its clarity and fine control in setting. Gelatin sheets are graded by their setting strength (not a quality grading); for silver or gold gelatin sheets, 1 sheet = 1 tsp gelatin powder.

Because this book is based on a great number of classic and French techniques, gelatin appears in many places to set mousses, creams and confections. Whether in powder or sheet form, all gelatin must be "bloomed" first. This means softening it in cold water before using. Soften powdered gelatin in a measurement of cold water specific to the recipe, but gelatin sheets can be softened in any amount of cold water, so long as the excess liquid is squeezed out before adding it to the recipe.

Gelatin is a collagen-based product and is not for vegans. For a substitution, please see p. 16.

**Storing gelatin:** If stored in a cool, dark and dry place, gelatin will keep indefinitely.

## Leaveners

The difference between great baking and a less successful product is often how airy and light it is. Whipped whole eggs or egg whites can be useful leaveners, but baking soda, baking powder and yeast have their own virtues.

BAKING SODA: This powdered leavener needs to be liquefied. When it reacts with an acid that has been worked into the dough or batter, carbon dioxide is released and expands the batter immediately, even before your goods go into the oven. (Once you mix your batter, get it into the oven soon!) Baking soda responds quickly but also expends itself quickly, so it is most often used on its own when the bake time is *short*, such as with cookies, or when the baking temperature is *hot*, such as with biscuits.

**Storing baking soda:** Baking soda is best if used in the first 3 months after opening. Transfer it to an airtight container. After 3 months, open the box or jar and use it as a fridge deodorizer, replacing your pantry container with a fresh batch.

BAKING POWDER: Baking powder is composed of baking soda, cream of tartar (an acid in powdered form) and usually cornstarch. Unlike baking soda, which reacts with an acid in the batter, baking powder contains an acid. When the baking powder is liquefied, the starch in the powder slows down the initial release of carbon dioxide, which is why baking powder reacts most powerfully after your cake is in the oven and the batter heats up, producing bubbles that give the cake a light and fluffy texture. Baking powder is essentially gluten-free; however, the starch component in it may not be. Certified gluten-free baking powder is available.

**Storing baking powder:** Baking powder will keep in the pantry until its expiry date.

*Why do some recipes call for both baking powder AND baking soda? Some recipes, especially cakes, call for baking powder and baking soda. The baking soda causes the cake batter to start rising immediately. When its lifting power begins to wind down, the baking powder kicks in, continuing to lift as the other ingredients transform and set as the cake bakes.*

YEAST: Yeast is a single-celled organism that lives naturally in the air and on surfaces everywhere. It feeds on sugars and produces carbon dioxide and alcohol. In wine making, the alcohol is kept in the liquid and the carbon dioxide blows off (except for sparkling wine). In baking, the carbon dioxide lifts bread doughs up and adds delectable flavour, and the alcohol cooks away when the bread is baked. I call for instant dry yeast in my bread recipes, which is easy and predictable to work with and does not need to be dissolved in liquid before using, as regular dry yeast does.

**Storing yeast:** Yeast in 2¼ tsp (7 g) packets can be stored in a cool, dark place until its expiry date. Yeast in a jar, once opened, should be refrigerated until its expiry date.

## Milk & Other Dairy

When baking with milk, I typically use 2%, though you can use 1% without compromising the recipe. I don't recommend baking with skim milk because its lack of milk fat makes it like baking with water. The same is true for fat-free yogurts and sour creams. Starches and gelatins are used to thicken these fat-free products, and these additives change texture when stirred or heated, so your baked goods could end up dry or crumbly. Use full-fat sour cream and yogurt in baking, unless otherwise specified.

Both evaporated milk and condensed milk start as fresh milk that is evaporated under pressure to halve its water volume. Sugar is added to this evaporated milk to make sweet and thick condensed milk. Both products are sold in tins but are used very differently in baking and in confectionery. They should never be interchanged.

**Storing milk & other dairy:** Always refrigerate and follow the best-before dates listed on your fresh dairy products. Cream and milk can be frozen for up to 2 months (allow space for the liquid to expand as it freezes), but once thawed, the fat may separate from the whey and the liquid may look curdled at first glance. Give the milk or cream a shake or whisk to reincorporate the fat. It may not be ideal for your coffee in the morning, but it is fine to use in baking. Unopened evaporated and condensed milk will keep until its expiry date. Once opened and transferred from the tin to an airtight container and refrigerated, evaporated milk will keep for up to 3 days and condensed milk for up to 14 days.

## Nuts & Seeds

Nuts figure prominently in classic French and other European baking recipes, so you will see them called for a fair bit throughout this book. Nuts do more than add flavour and crunch to a recipe—their oils add fat and, when ground, they can even replace flour. Nuts can often be interchanged in recipes; use their texture as your guide. Walnuts and pecans share a similar texture and fat content and so are interchangeable, as are almonds with hazelnuts. Unique nuts like pistachios or pine nuts have their own character, so a substitution isn't recommended. Seeds like sesame and poppy add their own texture and flavour to baking, and sunflower and pumpkin seeds can often be used in place of nuts if there is an allergy.

*Purchasing nuts and seeds already shelled is simplest, and I favour untoasted and unsalted so that I can control the flavours in the dish.*

When whole nuts or nut pieces are folded into the batter or filling of a recipe, they are often toasted first to intensify and almost sweeten their flavour. Heat releases their oils and gets rid of the slightly astringent taste of raw nuts, mellowing and sweetening them. Do not overlook this step! See How to Toast Nuts (p. 36) for the temperatures and times for different nuts. Ground nuts are rarely toasted before use because untoasted nuts are better at absorbing liquids and binding batters than toasted ones, which is why untoasted nuts are most often called for in recipes.

**Storing nuts & seeds:** Store raw or toasted nuts and seeds in airtight containers for up to 3 months, or freeze them for up to 6 months.

## Spices

Spices are a key baking ingredient. Cinnamon is a classic, with the supporting spices of ginger, nutmeg, cloves and allspice often blended into autumn and winter baked goods. Cardamom offers a citrus- and pepper-like kick to baking.

**Storing spices:** Store spices in an airtight container in a cool, dark place for up to a year. After a year, they will still be edible but their flavour may have faded. Do not refrigerate your spices—they lose their flavour faster and can pick up "fridge taste."

## Sugars & Syrups

Sugar does more than just add sweetness to a baked treat. It also adds moisture and structure. If you've ever tried to reduce the sugar in a recipe, you may have noticed that your baked goods become crumbly or dry. The recipes in this book call for an assortment of sugars, which are not always interchangeable. Depending on its use—baking or candy making—the sugar in a recipe may add a specific

flavour or help encourage browning, hold onto moisture, tenderize, leaven, stabilize or garnish to ensure a proper end product. Here is a Sugar 101:

GRANULATED SUGAR: This is the most common sugar in baking. Also known as sugar, table sugar or sucrose, it is white, generally affordable and available everywhere. Granulated sugar is made from fully refined beet or cane sugar, which is 50% glucose and 50% fructose, simple sugars that when bonded make sucrose, a complex sugar.

BROWN SUGAR: Granulated sugar that has molasses added to give it its brown colour and moist, sticky texture. Light brown (sometimes called golden) and dark brown sugars are fully refined. If you prefer a less refined sugar, try demerara in place of brown sugar. Turbinado sugar is an unrefined cane sugar; it is brown and has a dry texture like granulated sugar, but it is quite coarse and must be ground finer to use in baking recipes. Typically it is sprinkled on muffins or tarts to add sweetness and crunch.

ICING SUGAR: Also known as confectioner's sugar or powdered sugar. It is finely ground granulated sugar with up to 3% cornstarch added to prevent caking or clumping. It is not interchangeable with granulated sugar in baking recipes, since it dissolves at a different rate and with a different concentration of sweetness.

PEARL SUGAR: Compressed sugar granules that don't dissolve when baked. They are sprinkled on breads or pastries before baking for a little sweetness but mostly a decorative effect. Purchase them from European groceries or online.

**Storing dry sugars:** Sugar, like salt, is essentially a preservative and has no best-before date. You need to keep granulated sugar, icing sugar and brown sugar away from moisture (and critters), so store it in an airtight container. Icing sugar, because it is so finely ground, is more susceptible to absorbing moisture and after a few months, you may find that you need to sift it before using, even in recipes that don't call for sifting. To keep the natural molasses-based moisture in brown sugar, store it in an airtight container with a piece of terra cotta pottery.

INVERT SUGAR: Also called invert syrup, this is liquid sucrose to which an acid or an invert sugar has been added. The acid breaks down the sucrose into its two simple sugars, glucose and fructose. Invert sugars, such as honey, corn syrup and glucose syrup, don't crystallize when cooked, so caramels stay creamy and liquid and candies set and hold together properly. Adding a little lemon juice, vinegar or corn syrup to granulated sugar when cooking or caramelizing it prevents it from recrystallizing as it cooks.

CORN SYRUP: Made by breaking down the starches in corn into sugars. It comes in a clear form (sometimes called white syrup) and regular or golden corn syrup and is common in candy making and in baking. *Glucose syrup* is made from corn or wheat and is thicker and slightly less sweet than corn syrup. Corn syrup and glucose syrup are not interchangeable in candy making. Both give candies the right stretch or set when cooked but are rarely used in home baking.

HONEY: Made by honeybees from the nectar of flowers. 40% of honey's makeup is fructose and 30% is glucose, both simple sugars. The remaining 30% is water, pollen and minerals, plus trace amounts of sucrose, maltose and other complex sugars. Its distinctive taste can overwhelm a dish in large amounts, so you will often find it used with granulated sugar in baking and confections.

MAPLE SYRUP: A favourite sweetener in Canadian baked goods because of its distinctively mild caramelized taste with hints of fruit and nuts. The sap from maple trees is collected before the trees develop buds, and the sap is evaporated to produce maple syrup. It takes 10½ gallons (40 L) of sap to produce 4 cups (1 L) of maple syrup, and 60% to 66% of its final makeup is sucrose, a complex sugar.

Maple syrup is given one of three grades—golden (or light), amber and dark—based on how much light shines through the syrup. The golden and amber maple syrups are noticeably milder tasting because they are made from early-season maple sap. Dark syrup is made from later-season sap, and bakers often prefer it because of its more pronounced flavour.

MOLASSES: The liquid left after unrefined sugar is boiled down, crystallized and separated. It adds a deep caramel flavour and colour to baked goods along with a hint of bitterness. *Fancy molasses* is used in sweet recipes because of its mild flavour. *Blackstrap molasses* is boiled to intensify its colour and flavour and is used in modest amounts to colour and flavour breads. It is too strong for most desserts, and these styles are not interchangeable. Molasses does contain a little acidity, so it activates leaveners like baking soda in baking.

Storing liquid sugars: Honey can be stored in the pantry practically indefinitely, but you may find it crystallizes after a few months. This is not a sign of spoilage or an inferior product. To reliquefy your honey, immerse the jar, lid off, in a pot of hot water that comes up to the fill line and heat over low until liquefied again. Once opened, store your bottle of maple syrup in the fridge for up to 2 years. Molasses will keep in the pantry for up to 5 years.

## Vanilla

Vanilla is an aromatic and delectable flavour on its own, but it also enhances other flavours, which is why it appears in so many baking recipes. I favour pure vanilla extract, but it can be costly, so I call for it only when it is essential to the recipe. Vanilla bean paste is extract with the seeds left in, and it is attractive in recipes where you can see the vanilla speckled throughout. Vanilla beans need to be split open, the seeds scraped out and then the flavour extracted by heating the seeds in a liquid.

*Vanilla bean equivalents: 1 vanilla bean = 1 Tbsp (15 mL) vanilla bean paste or vanilla extract*

Storing vanilla: Good-quality vanilla extract comes in a dark glass bottle and should be stored in a cool, dark place.

# Temperatures

Cold? Room temperature? Slightly warmed? Knowing what temperature your ingredients should be for the best results in baking can be confusing. As a general rule, the butter is your guide to the temperature of other ingredients. Ingredients of a like temperature come together more smoothly, which is why if the butter is at room temperature, your eggs should be too. Conversely, if the recipe calls for the butter to be cold, then your eggs and other ingredients should be also. But use your judgement: small measures of milk, yogurt or sour cream shouldn't sit on the counter too long. Here is a guide to best letting your ingredients warm up from the fridge.

**BUTTER:** Pull a full pound from the fridge 2 hours before using or, for a quick fix, dice the butter, break it into pieces and set on a plate for 30 minutes. Do not soften butter in the microwave—it heats unevenly.

**CREAM CHEESE:** Dice the cream cheese, break it into pieces, place on a plate (cover it loosely with the wrapper to prevent drying) and let sit on the counter for 30 minutes.

**DAIRY:** Milk can be warmed to room temperature over low heat on the stovetop or in the microwave, but do not heat buttermilk or yogurt, as it may curdle.

**EGGS:** Immerse the whole eggs, in their shells, in a bowl filled with hot tap water for a few minutes. If heating five or more eggs, you may have to change the water and let them sit a little longer.

# Substitutions

An easy 1:1 substitution for common allergy- and dietary-sensitive ingredients like wheat flour, dairy, eggs or sugar would be absolutely wonderful, but the plain truth is that the recipe and its method have as much influence on what ingredient substitute might work best. Please note that while I use these substitutions regularly with my recipes, not all of the recipes in this book have been tested and verified using each of them. In many cases, other adaptations to the ingredient list or method are made to recipes to balance the change in ingredients, but on a simple level, these substitutions are a good starting point.

## Dairy Substitutes

BUTTER: Non-dairy butter products abound, so this is one of the easiest substitutions to make. There are good non-dairy baking "butters" on the market if you want to steer clear of vegetable shortening, the most common non-dairy fat. These can be used as a 1:1 replacement to butter in baking.

Virgin coconut oil is also a viable option, but keep in mind that it sets up more firmly than butter when chilled. It is also worth noting that coconut oil is 100% fat, whereas butter is 80% fat. So if you are using coconut oil in place of butter, particularly in a butter-rich recipe like pie pastry, reduce the coconut oil measurement by 20% by weight and increase the water by 20%.

CREAM: Non-dairy cream products can be used in place of whipping cream, or try coconut cream as a delicious alternative. For every ½ cup (125 mL) whipping cream needed, chill one tin of coconut milk. Once chilled, open the tin and spoon off the solidified coconut cream from the top (save the clear liquid separately). Keep the solid cream cold before whipping, and if it is semisolid and difficult to whip, add 1 to 2 Tbsp (15 to 30 mL) of the liquid to allow the coconut cream to expand as you whip it. You can store whipped coconut cream in the fridge, and unlike its dairy equivalent, it won't lose its volume over time.

MILK: Oat milk or almond milk are my preferred options for baking, as their texture and fat content mimic dairy milk best. Coconut milk (in Tetra-Paks, not tins) is also suitable, but rice milk is like skim milk; it is simply too thin and watery to work well in baking.

YOGURT, SOUR CREAM AND CREAM CHEESE: Many quality non-dairy yogurt, sour cream and cream cheese products make good substitutes for dairy in baking. Many are coconut, almond or soy based, so pick the style that suits you best, ensuring that it is as neutral tasting as possible. Some non-dairy yogurt and sour cream products are not as "sour" as their dairy counterparts, so I always stir in 1 tsp (5 mL) of lemon juice. Some non-dairy cream cheeses are designed more for spreading onto bagels than for baking, so seek styles that are suited for the task.

## Egg Substitutes

Commercial plant-based egg-substitute products are widely available now, so if you find one that suits the style of baking that you do, you should stick with it. Here are some other common substitution options.

FOR BASIC COOKIES, LOAF CAKES & MUFFINS: Soak 2 Tbsp (14 g) ground flaxseed in 3 Tbsp (45 mL) warm water for 2 minutes to replace 1 large egg. Do not use for custards, soufflés or sponge cakes.

FOR DELICATE CAKES, CHEESECAKES & ENRICHED BREADS: Use 2 oz (60 g) well-beaten silken or soft tofu to replace 1 large egg. Do not use for custards, soufflés or sponge cakes.

FOR WHIPPED EGG WHITES: For recipes calling for whipped egg whites, like cake batters, soufflés and meringues, use aquafaba, the liquid drained from a tin of chickpeas (unsalted is best). Measure 2 Tbsp (30 mL) aquafaba and ¼ tsp cream of tartar for 1 large egg white, then whip and use as per the recipe. Keep in mind that aquafaba takes a lot longer to whip than egg whites (up to 10 minutes or more). Where egg whites whip up because of their protein, aquafaba holds its volume due to the starch in the liquid. Added sugar stabilizes the aquafaba meringue so it behaves just like an egg-white one (and doesn't taste like chickpeas). Do not use for macarons (other elements of the recipe need altering), nougat or marshmallows.

## Flour Substitutes

Gluten-free baking blends are fairly widely available these days, and many are reliably good and yield tasty baked goods with nice texture and moisture. If you already have a preferred blend, use it 1:1 in place of wheat flour in my recipes as a starting point. If you do not have a blend of your own, use ⅔ cup (90 g) brown rice flour, ⅓ cup (55 g) tapioca starch and ½ tsp xanthan gum for every 1 cup (150 g) all-purpose flour.

Gluten-free flour is less effective in recipes for breads and pastries like puff and croissant doughs that traditionally rely on gluten (the method and ingredient list take more specialized tweaking), but it does work well in recipes where eggs figure prominently, such as sponge cakes and choux paste.

## Gelatin Powder or Sheet Substitutes

Use agar agar powder 1:1 in place of gelatin. Agar is a gelatinous algae-based product that thickens and sets custards and mousses very similarly to gelatin powder. The difference in using it is the technique. Like gelatin, agar agar powder still needs to be bloomed in cold water. It must also reach a full boil to activate (gelatin only needs to be melted into a warm liquid). So look at your recipe to see where you can add the agar agar so that it can cook. For example, when making Diplomat Cream (p. 98), you may need to add the agar to the milk with the egg yolks and other ingredients for the pastry cream so that it reaches a full simmer. Gelatin is added after the pastry cream comes off the heat.

## Nut Substitutes

When nuts are used as an add-in, such as the Walnut, Raisin & Chocolate Rugelach Tart (p. 140), nuts can be substituted with a seed like pumpkin or sunflower to replace the texture and taste. You can even get playful and use crushed pretzels in place of toasted almonds for the Almond Rochers (p. 351). Where nut replacements become more complicated is when they are ground and embedded within a dough or batter, like the Jam Almond Linzer Tart (p. 148). For recipes calling for ground almonds or ground hazelnuts in the batter or dough, I use 50% pumpkin or sunflower seeds and 50% all-purpose flour by weight, ground together to replace the nut flour.

## Spirit & Wine Substitutes

Spirits are a lovely way to add flavour and pizzazz to baking, but they are not essential. Spirits are usually added in small measure, 1 oz (30 mL) or less, so they can be replaced with something neutral like apple or orange juice in the same volume (the Almond Streusel, p. 82, is an exception). Wine adds acidity to baking and may be called for in larger amounts. In a pinch it can be replaced with apple juice or orange juice or even water with a splash of lemon juice.

## Sugar Substitutes

Sugars are the trickiest to replace, in my opinion, because they lend not only sweetness but also moisture and structure as your treats bake. That fact, combined with many people's need or choice to reduce or eliminate sugar, makes finding good substitutes a challenge. Like with dairy and eggs, many commercial sugar replacements are geared to baking, so if you find one that suits you, stick with it.

You can certainly play with the sweeteners in a recipe, but using different ones, reducing the amount of sugar or replacing it entirely will fundamentally transform a recipe. I can't guarantee the results, though the fun is in the playing! You may create something wonderful or learn something new. Avoid recipes with whipped egg whites, since sugar is critical to stabilizing egg whites in baking. The recipes in the confections chapter (p. 331) also will not adapt easily to sugar-free products except for the chocolate recipes, which can be made using sugar-reduced or sugar-free chocolates.

# In a Pinch

If you've run out of an ingredient or can't get to the store before it's time to bake, here are some quick fixes to get you through a recipe. While the original ingredient is always the best choice, these will deliver a comparable result in a pinch.

| Missing Ingredient | Quantity Needed | Substitute With |
| --- | --- | --- |
| BAKING POWDER | 1 tsp | ¼ tsp baking soda + ½ tsp cream of tartar |
| BROWN SUGAR | 1 cup (200 g) | Measure 1 cup (200 g) granulated sugar, remove 1 Tbsp (12 g) and replace with 1 Tbsp (16 g) fancy molasses |
| BUTTERMILK | 1 cup (250 mL) | 1 cup + 1 Tbsp (265 mL) lemon juice or vinegar or use 1 cup (250 mL) plain (1% or higher) yogurt (not Greek) or kefir |
| CAKE & PASTRY FLOUR | 1 cup (130 g) | Use "00" Italian flour or measure 1 cup (150 g) all-purpose flour, remove 2 Tbsp (18 g) and replace with 2 Tbsp (15 g) cornstarch |
| HALF-&-HALF CREAM | ½ cup (125 mL) | ¼ cup (60 mL) 2% milk + ¼ cup (60 mL) whipping cream |
| ICING SUGAR | 1 cup (130 g) | Grind 1 cup (200 g) granulated sugar + 1 Tbsp (8 g) cornstarch in a blender until fine |
| SOUR CREAM | ½ cup (125 mL) | ½ cup (125 mL) plain Greek yogurt (2% or higher) |

# Baking Tools

A s in cooking, having the right tools when baking makes the whole experience easier and more enjoyable, but it doesn't have to mean a huge financial commitment to get started. I've listed the essential baking tools you'll need for most recipes, followed by specialty items you might need to make a few of the recipes in this book. I've also included a section on how to properly prepare pans for baking. Many people rush this step, but greasing (or not greasing) a cake tin or baking tray can be the difference between baked goods that rise or brown evenly and treats that sink, crack or burn. Set yourself up for success!

# Glossary of Baking Tools

Depending on your baking commitment and interests (and the space you have to store things), here are lists of essential and specialty baking tools to suit your needs. Each section is organized alphabetically. The more speciality tools are recommended when you are diving deep into baking. I've listed them according to the type of baking they're most useful for. Most of these items can be purchased online at specialty cake and candy supply sites or at professional baking supply stores.

## Essential Baking Tools

**BAKING PANS:** After preheating the oven, you typically grease and/or line your baking pans before mixing any ingredients. The basic pans you'll need for baking include:

- Two metal baking trays (13 × 18 inches/33 × 46 cm is standard for a large tray, but any size will do if you are starting out or have a smaller oven)
- A 9-inch (23 cm) square metal pan
- Two round metal baking pans (8 inches/20 cm or 9 inches/23 cm)
- A loaf pan (typically 9 × 5 inches/2 L)
- A 12-cup muffin tin
- A 9-inch (23 cm) glass pie plate

*To check the size of your baking pans, measure the inside base of the pan. Pans can vary in the angles of their sides and their heights, but the base dimension will tell you if you have the correct size for your recipe. If you have a smaller oven, you may want to measure baking trays from their outside edge to make sure they can fit into your oven.*

What your baking pan is made of can sometimes affect how your recipes bake. *Metal* pans can be stainless steel (often coated with a non-stick silicone glaze) or aluminum. Stainless steel is more durable and scratch and dent resistant. Metal pans heat up quickly and cool down quickly, making them an ideal choice for predictable and controllable results. And metal conducts heat to the baked goods for even browning, though the ingredients in the recipe (sugar and fat) impact how much a recipe browns more than the colour of the metal. (Although it has been said that darker baking pans brown goods more because they absorb heat faster,

I have found the difference barely discernable compared to lighter-coloured pans.)

*Never use a knife or sharp cutting tool in direct contact with a metal pan. It can scar the coating of the pan and rust may develop, plus baked goods are prone to stick where there are scratch marks.*

*Tempered glass* is slower to heat than metal, but it holds and retains the heat for much longer. I prefer to bake pies in a glass plate because the heat retention really helps to set the crust, plus I can check the sides and bottom of my pie easily for doneness. Do not use glass pans for delicate items like lemon squares, which may soufflé and overbake on the outside edges. Additionally, glass pans often have softly curved edges that make portioning precise squares or slices a challenge. Like glass, *ceramic* heats up gradually and holds the heat so well that baked goods are at risk of overbrowning, but it makes an attractive serving dish. I like to bake tray cakes in ceramic pans. *Porcelain bakeware* is more heat and chip resistant than ceramic ware.

*Silicone* bakeware comes in an assortment of shapes, colours and sizes and it is flexible, so removing baked goods is easy. Unlike other pan materials, silicone does not conduct heat, so your baked goods won't develop a crust where they're in contact with the silicone and they won't brown very much unless you place the silicone pan on a metal baking tray. The metal will conduct heat through the silicone. I like silicone for baked goods that bake at a high temperature (so the oven heat can travel through the pan) or for candy making.

**CAKE WHEEL/TURNTABLE:** A cake stand that spins makes getting polished sides to your cake a breeze, and it elevates the cake, so you don't put your back out leaning too far over to decorate. In a pinch, a lazy Susan will work.

**COOLING RACK:** Once your treats come out of the oven, this slightly raised wire or non-stick grid allows air to circulate around baked goods so they cool down quickly, and you won't damage your countertops.

**ELECTRIC BEATERS:** A handheld set of beaters is relatively inexpensive and makes blending batters, whipping egg whites and whipping cream, or mixing frostings a breeze.

**FINE ZESTER:** This rasp-like tool, also known as a Microplane, makes zesting citrus a snap, pulling away only that flavourful outer surface and not the white, bitter pith beneath it. It is also fabulous for grating fresh ginger or, when called for, garlic cloves, and it is easy to clean.

**MEASURING CUPS & SPOONS:** Most bakers in North America measure by volume (cups and teaspoons). To measure all dry ingredients, use a set of measuring cups (1 cup, ½ cup, ⅓ cup and ¼ cup) and a set of measuring spoons for small amounts. Liquid ingredients or anything chopped or grated (apple, cheese) should be measured in a liquid measuring cup, often glass.

**MIXING BOWLS:** When it comes time to assemble your ingredients, an assortment of sizes will make blending pancake batters, cookie doughs and cake batters easy. The material is up to you: ceramic, glass, melamine or stainless steel—it's all the same. The only time stainless-steel bowls are preferred is when you might be melting chocolate or other ingredients over a pot of simmering water, so that the heat conducts quickly and then cools quickly once removed from the heat.

**OFFSET SPATULA:** This stepped metal lifter will become an extension of your hand as you bake. Use it to remove warm cookies from a tray, extract that perfect slice of cake from its whole or spread frosting or meringue with ease, whether smooth and flat or with dimples and swirls.

**OVEN & STOVE:** These kitchen tools may seem obvious, but learning to appreciate the type of heat source and fan you have will help to better control your cooking and baking.

All recipes in this book have been written with a conventional "still" oven, rather than a convection oven, in mind. The fan in a convection oven moves hot air, browning the surface and even causing leaveners to activate more quickly. The fan speed can cause baked goods to bake quickly on the outside, sometimes even before the centre has fully cooked. Newer convection ovens (within the last 5 years) often have a thermostat that adjusts the oven temperature to account for the fan speed. In general, if you are unable to shut off the fan, then reduce the oven temperature by 25°F (about 10°C). Before you start baking, check the actual temperature of your oven (see Oven Thermometer, below).

Stoves can be heated by electricity, which heats a coil or panel, or by gas or induction. Gas and induction heating are very responsive, so you can increase and decrease your heat source quickly to speed up or slow down cooking. Electric heat is much slower to respond, so you may have to lift or move your pots off the burner occasionally to control the timing and temperature of your items as they cook.

**OVEN THERMOMETER:** The first step in baking is usually to preheat your oven, and while you may set your oven to 350°F (180°C), it could be hotter or cooler than that temperature. To be sure you get predictable results when baking and cooking, get to know your oven by testing its temperature. Set a thermometer inside the oven to compare how close the actual heat is to the temperature you've set it to, so you can adjust accordingly. This step is essential for continued baking success.

**PARCHMENT PAPER:** This heatproof, greaseproof and moisture-resistant paper makes cleanup a breeze, and cakes and cookies come away from their pans easily. Parchment paper can be reused multiple times, especially when it lines baking trays. When a recipe calls for greasing and then lining the pan with parchment paper, the greasing is done just to get the parchment to stay in place while you scrape in your batter.

PIPING BAGS & TIPS: Disposable piping bags are the most common these days and are clean and easy to manage (many are recyclable and there are even biodegradable ones on the market). You don't need too many piping tips to begin with (large and small plain and star tips will get you started) and they are relatively inexpensive.

REMOVABLE-BOTTOM TART PAN: Like the springform pan of the tart world, this two-part pan makes it easy to pop a tart out for display, and the fluted edge adds visual appeal and strength to a delicate tart.

ROLLING PIN: A wooden rolling pin is preferred because it holds an even temperature and doughs don't tend to stick to it. If buying a new pin, try a French tapered rolling pin. It lacks handles, so when you roll, your hands rest on the pin over the dough, giving you a good sense of how the dough is rolling. The taper at each end allows you to angle the pin as you roll, so you can coax your desired shape and even thickness easily.

SCALE: A small digital scale makes measuring ingredients more precise. My recipes show metric measurements by weight in addition to imperial volume. Most of the world (North America excepted) measures by weight, and it is consistent, tidy and easy. Some ingredients, such as baking/couverture chocolate, need to be weighed, and once you try "scaling" your ingredients, you'll realize how easy it is. Most digital scales include a "tare" button that you can touch to reset to zero after each addition (no math required!) and can use to toggle between imperial and metric. I prefer a scale that measures to as small a measure as a single gram and with as few seams and crevices as possible so that flour doesn't build up there.

SIFTER: You can start with a simple fine-mesh strainer or go for a tamis, which has a flat sifting surface that can rest on a bowl or a sheet of parchment and hold a large volume of ingredients. Sifting aerates and combines your dry ingredients, so you end up with evenly textured baked goods.

SILICONE SPATULA: Popular for mixing ingredients by hand, this spatula's silicone head makes it heatproof, useful for stirring fillings and sauces when they are on the stove.

SPRINGFORM PAN: Essential for cheesecakes or for any cakes that have to set in a mold after assembly. The latch on the side of the pan releases the bottom plate and makes the cake easy to extract.

STAND MIXER: If you're baking regularly, the strong motor of a stand mixer takes the pressure off your electric beaters and frees you up as well. Most stand mixers come with three attachments: a dough hook for bread doughs; a paddle for cookie and pastry doughs and many cake batters; and a whip for sponge cakes, meringues and whipped cream.

WHISK: A wire whisk is the tool of choice to blend fluid ingredients by hand or add volume to ingredients like whipping cream or egg whites.

## Pies & Tarts

DOUGH CUTTER: This metal, straight-edged hand tool is also called a bench scraper. In addition to being a handy tool for dividing or cutting dough into portions, it is useful for cleaning the excess flour or stuck pieces of dough from your rolling surface before you wash it down with water.

FLAT SPATULA: Loosening the bottom of a tart from its base to slide it onto a platter is much easier using a flat spatula that's 8 inches (20 cm) or longer. With the tart resting on the counter, insert the side of the spatula under the edge of the crust. As you slowly rotate the tart pan, gently push the side of the spatula toward the centre of the pan to release the crust.

PIE WEIGHTS: When blind-baking a pie shell (p. 48), reusable pie weights keep the pastry in place as it bakes. Ceramic ball weights and a stainless chain are the most common inedible options if you've graduated from using dried rice or beans, and they can be washed and stored easily.

## Pastries

**LARGE ROLLING PIN:** While a French tapered rolling pin is suitable for common pie and tart doughs, the process of laminating doughs by rolling and folding them repeatedly in bigger batches can require a rolling pin with more heft. A heavy wooden rolling pin with the handles on the side gives you more leverage and surface area, ensuring that your lamination is level and easier to handle.

**PASTRY BOARD:** If you have a countertop with a bevel or pattern in it, rolling pastry evenly can be a challenge. A wooden pastry board has a lip to it, securing it to the edge of your counter and giving you plenty of space to roll. Wood is an ideal rolling surface because pastry doesn't stick to it (many bakeries will have a wooden "bench" for pastry and bread work).

**PASTRY WHEEL:** Portioning croissants or shaping puff pastry is easy and quick when using a pastry wheel, and it won't damage your work surface as a knife might. Many are two-sided, with a fluted wheel to add a pattern if you wish.

## Cakes

**CAKE BOARDS:** Simple cardboard rounds make it easy to lift cakes from your cake wheel to the fridge or from the fridge to your cake stand or platter.

**CAKE EDGER & CAKE COMBS:** The straight, right-angled side to a cake edger helps you to smooth frostings onto a cake easily and ensure the sides and top are straight and seamless as you rotate the cake on a turntable. In a pinch, a dough cutter will work, but a cake edger is thinner and longer. Cake combs are flat plastic or stainless-steel rectangles with pointed, angled or squared teeth. Holding them against the cake as you rotate it allows you to work a pattern into the frosting.

**SPECIALTY PIPING TIPS:** In addition to the staple plain, star and leaf tips, specialty tips allow you to get really creative in terms of patterns. The St. Honoré tip lets you pipe wave-like patterns of frosting or fillings, and Russian piping tips are large tips built to pipe a flower in a single press (note that your frosting needs to be as firm as manageably possible for the pattern to hold its shape).

## Custards & Creams

**BUTANE KITCHEN TORCH:** For home use, a small kitchen torch is handy for evenly caramelizing the top of your crème brûlées or browning your meringues.

**PORCELAIN SOUFFLÉ DISHES & RAMEKINS:** Porcelain bakeware is made using a finer clay product and is fired at a higher temperature than ceramics, making it less prone to cracking and chipping. It also tends to have a glossier look, which can make it more stain resistant.

## Confections

**ACETATE:** Usually sold in rolls, acetate plastic is available in various widths that are handy for setting chocolates and lining cake pans and molds. The surface of any chocolate resting on acetate as it sets will be smooth with a gorgeous shine. And the edges of any cake made in a pan lined with acetate, such as the Vanilla Pear Chiboust Torte (p. 235) or Torta Setteveli (p. 277), will be smooth and precise (parchment can pucker, making for an uneven look).

**CHOCOLATE & CANDY MOLDS:** Molds for candy and chocolate making come in many shapes and sizes, but it's the material that counts. Silicone molds work well for candy making because they resist heat and make it easy to extract the sweets after setting. They are less effective for making chocolate because you won't get a reflective shine on chocolates set in silicone molds.

**DIGITAL INSTANT THERMOMETER:** An instant-read thermometer that can handle high temperatures is essential in candy making and for tempering chocolate, because precise temperatures are critical. It is far safer and easier to use than the glass candy thermometer that latches onto the side of a pot and much less expensive than it used to be.

MARBLE BOARD: If you are table tempering chocolate, this tool is essential. Marble absorbs the heat of the chocolate, cooling it down as you spread it over the surface of the board. A glossy granite countertop will work as well.

POLYCARBONATE PLASTIC MOLDS: These are ideal for making bonbons. They are sturdy, and when polished they release chocolates with a gorgeous shine to them. You can buy cheaper, thinner clear plastic molds for chocolate, but they are good for only one or two uses since they scratch easily.

PUTTY KNIFE: This may seem a strange tool to suggest, but the thin metal of a medium-sized putty knife is the best tool for spreading and lifting chocolate when using the table-tempering method (p. 43). You can find putty knives in the paint-tool section of the hardware store.

## Cookies & Bars

ICE CREAM SCOOPS: Getting serious about cookie or cupcake baking or making truffles? Mechanical scoops, with their spring-release feature, are tidy and will ensure evenly sized cookies. A large scoop is best for muffins and cupcakes, a medium scoop for cookies, and a small scoop for mini muffins.

## Breads

BANNETON: Also called a proofing basket, a banneton is a coiled rattan, cane or other fibre basket that comes in an assortment of shapes. It controls the shape of your bread loaf as it goes through its second (final) proofing stage and can leave a lovely spiral pattern on the loaf. (If you don't want the pattern, use a removable linen liner.)

To use the banneton, shape the loaf and then set it into the well-floured basket so that the bottom side is facing up. Cover the basket and proof as per the recipe, then gently tip the proofed loaf onto the baking tray before baking. Do not wash the banneton; instead, brush out excess flour using a dry pastry brush. The linen liner can be washed. Do not put the banneton in the oven.

BREAD LAME: This sharp, thin razor cuts cleanly through proofed dough, allowing the bread to expand through the cuts in a controlled manner. Some bread lames have a curved blade, and you can get creative with the cuts, although a classic baguette is meant to have only five slashes, representing the five senses.

LINEN COUCHE: When covering bread as it rises, a square of natural unbleached and untreated linen—a couche—is ideal because the fabric is lint-free and has a tight weave that protects the dough from drying out but allows it room to rise. A clean tea towel will also work, but do not use terry towels—and if the tea towel isn't made of a tightly woven fabric, place a piece of plastic wrap loosely over the towel to keep the dough from drying out.

# Preparing Pans for Baking

Regardless of the pan material or non-stick finish, all baking pans should be greased and/or lined with parchment paper according to the recipe instructions.

## Greasing

Use soft butter or spray to evenly coat the pan with fat. Focus on the corners and edges, where baked goods are prone to sticking. If lining the pan with parchment paper, greasing holds the paper in place, so only a quick, light application is needed.

## Lining with Parchment Paper

Whenever possible, I line my baking pans with parchment paper. This keeps the pans in good condition, makes extracting the baked goods easy and cleaning up a snap. Lightly greasing a pan holds the paper in place, but cutting and trimming the parchment to fit the pan is key. Here are a few tips.

BAKING TRAY: Trim the parchment so it sits flat inside the bottom of the tray.

ROUND PAN: Trim the parchment so it fits snugly into the bottom of your pan. To cut a circle without using a marker to trace your pan (pen or pencil will not show on parchment), cut a square of parchment slightly larger than the diameter of the pan and fold it in half to form a rectangle. Fold the rectangle in half again to make a square. Fold one corner of the square up to its opposite corner to form a triangle, then repeat the fold with the opposite corners to create a smaller triangle (photo 1a). Find the centre fold (the point without any open edges). Invert your pan and place the centre point at the centre of the pan (photo 2a). Set the folded paper flat against the bottom of the pan, holding the widest part against the outside edge of the pan. Use scissors to cut an arc at that outside point. When you unfold the paper, it will be a circle that fits into the bottom of your pan (photo 3a).

SQUARE OR RECTANGLE PAN: Trim the parchment to fit the bottom and sides of the pan so you can easily remove your baked goods by lifting them out with the parchment paper. To cut a single piece of parchment that will fit the bottom and sides of the pan without wrinkles, cut a square or rectangle that's the same size as the bottom plus two sides of the pan. Fold this sheet into quarters (photo 1b). Where the open corners of the paper meet in a point, use scissors to make a cut the same size as the height of the pan (photo 2b). Open up the parchment, and as you press it into the pan, the notched edges will overlap into the corners, creating a good seal without wrinkling (photo 3b).

## Flouring

With wet batters such as cake batters, just greasing the pan won't prevent sticking on the sides, and lining the sides with parchment paper won't prevent the puckering that makes for an unevenly shaped cake (in rare cases, such as the Basque Cheesecake, p. 263, puckering is desirable).

To dust a pan with flour, first grease the bottom and sides of the pan evenly and line the bottom with parchment paper. Spoon a couple of tablespoons of flour into the pan. Lift the pan and hold it at an angle as you rotate it, tapping the flour to cover the sides completely. If flouring multiple pans, hold the first pan over the next one and tap any excess flour from the first pan into the second one. Repeat until all of your pans are floured.

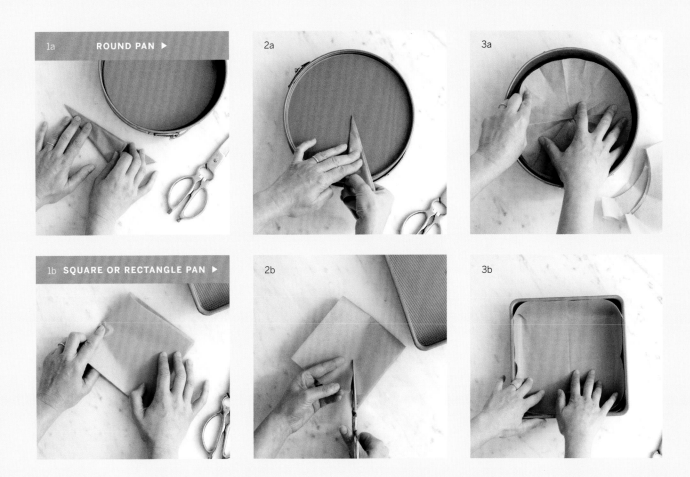

## Sugaring

Occasionally you need to coat the sides of a pan with sugar in place of flour; for example, if the recipe is flourless or if a slight crust is desired, such as for the Flourless Chocolate Torta Tenerina (p. 215). Use the same method as you would for dusting with flour, but use sugar instead. Keep in mind that any excess sugar will have come in contact with the greased sides of the pan, so reuse it only in basic baking, not for whipping with egg whites.

## When to Leave Pans Ungreased

In some cases, you actually want the batter to stick to the pan. Sponge cakes like the Chocolate Sponge Cake (p. 232) and Coconut Chiffon Cake (p. 236) "climb" up the side of the pan as they bake. Leaving the pans ungreased ensures that the batter doesn't rise and then slide down the sides and result in a domed cake.

A chiffon cake pan also needs to remain ungreased so you can invert the pan to cool the cake upside down. You don't want the cake to slide out by accident.

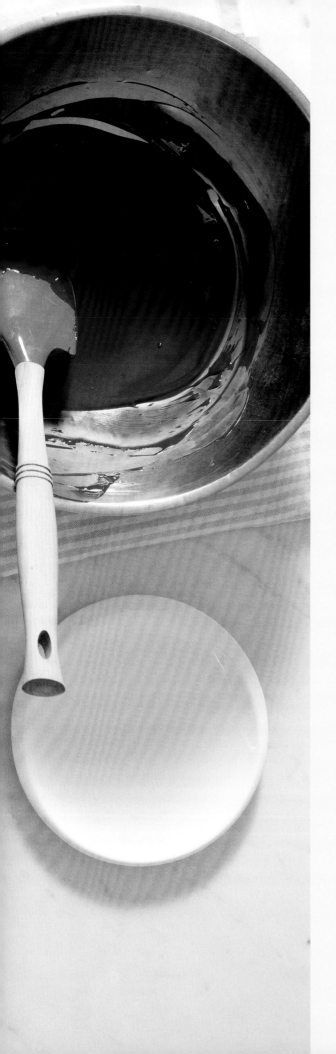

# Baking Actions & How-tos

While the proper ingredients and tools are critical to successful baking, your own actions are the catalyst that brings everything together; the way that ingredients are combined in a recipe determines a baked good's appearance, taste and texture. I like to think of the chemical processes that occur between ingredients and the physical changes they undergo as a result as the "baking actions."

In this chapter I describe what these baking actions entail so you know what is expected of you when reading the recipes. I also cover "How To's" extensively: from simple tips on separating eggs (p. 32) and advice on how to easily line your baking pans with parchment paper (p. 26), to extensive guidance on assembling a layer cake (p. 50), blind baking pie pastry (p. 48) and tempering chocolate (p. 42). This is followed by a section on fixing baking blunders, an important resource for bakers of all levels—even experienced bakers make mistakes—as knowing how to repair or recover from your missteps instills an impressive sense of confidence as you continue to bake.

# Glossary of Baking Actions

Here are some common baking actions that are used throughout the book. Take a moment to review these terms so that you can differentiate between them and anticipate the intended result.

**BEAT:** To mix vigorously using a wooden spoon, silicone spatula, electric beaters or stand mixer fitted with the paddle attachment. The goal is to combine the ingredients with speed and energy until evenly combined.

**BLEND:** To combine ingredients in the easiest way possible so they are homogeneous (no distinctly visible ingredients and no lumps). Similar to combining and mixing.

**CARAMELIZE:** To cook until rich amber or golden brown. This most commonly refers to cooking sugar between 320°F (160°C) and 350°F (177°C) to achieve a clear, rich brown colour. It also refers to caramelizing the top of pastries and cakes when baking so the sugars and proteins in the dough or batter produce a crust with a rich brown colour. Egg wash promotes the surface caramelization of baked goods.

**COMBINE:** To bring together ingredients evenly in the easiest way possible by stirring. Similar to blending and mixing.

**CREAM:** To press butter and sugar together along the side of a mixing bowl using a wooden spoon or spatula by hand, electric beaters or a stand mixer fitted with the paddle attachment until blended. The goal is to disperse the sugar evenly and aerate the butter to create structure so doughs and batters hold together when baked. Depending on the butter-to-sugar ratio, the creamed mixture may be smooth and fluffy (more butter) or dry and crumbly (more sugar).

**DOCK:** To pierce unbaked pastry, often in the bottom of a pie or tart pan, with a fork. This step allows the pastry to expand as it bakes, preventing big air pockets from developing or the pastry lifting from the base of the pan. These holes will not cause fillings to seep through.

**DUST:** To lightly coat a surface with flour or icing sugar. This commonly refers to a work surface that is sprinkled with flour before rolling pastry or bread doughs. It also refers to desserts that are sprinkled with icing sugar immediately before serving. The surface should always be dry (wet surfaces will dissolve any dusting) and, once dusted, should still be evenly visible.

**FOLD:** To gently combine an aerated ingredient (usually whipped egg whites or whipped cream) into a heavier base. Use a spatula and pull the heavier base batter from the bottom of the bowl. In a circular motion, pull it over the aerated addition, completing the circular motion back to the bottom of the bowl to repeat. This should be done in a gentle but quick fashion—the longer you spend folding, the more time the aerated element has to deflate. Rotate the bowl as you fold, and stop when the mixture is evenly combined.

GLAZE: To brush, dip or pour a thin coating of a sweet icing or clear jelly over a dessert. The function is to add sweetness, shine or visual appeal or to seal the dessert.

GREASE: To treat a baking pan with fat to prevent sticking. This can be with butter, oil or sprays. Even non-stick pans should be greased before baking. For more tips on greasing pans, see p. 26.

KNEAD: To continue working a dough after mixing to develop the proteins in the flour so the dough becomes elastic and taut. This can be done by hand, by stretching and reshaping the dough on a lightly floured surface, or by using a stand mixer fitted with the hook attachment, which pulls and stretches the dough against the side of the bowl.

LAMINATE: To work thin layers of butter in between a dough through repeated rolling and folding. This layering process produces a baked product that is flaky, with air between the layers. Through lamination, the butter sits in thin sheets between the dough. While the treat is baking, the butter melts and produces steam, which pushes up the dough around it, generating the flaky layers.

MIX: To bring ingredients evenly together by stirring in the easiest way possible. Similar to blending and combining.

PIPE: To use a piping bag with a shaped tip to push out batter, frosting or other pliable ingredients into a pattern or shape.

PROOF: To allow a yeasted dough to rise in a covered and protected environment. Proofing can happen steadily at room temperature or slowly if refrigerated. Proofing times can vary depending on the amount of yeast in the dough, the density of the dough or the desired finished texture and flavour of the risen dough.

SCORE: To make a small incision or mark on the surface of a dough or pastry with a knife. Breads are scored to break through the surface of the dough, but some pastries are scored on the surface to create a pattern (Galette des Rois, p. 176).

SIFT: To aerate and combine dry ingredients by letting them fall through a mesh sieve or other similar device. Gravity is the primary force, and the dry ingredients can be sifted over a bowl or onto a sheet of parchment paper, to then be added as needed.

STEEP/INFUSE: To transfer flavour to a liquid by heating gently. The original item can be removed after infusing if not consumable, and the original liquid should not reduce in volume.

STIR: To make or keep ingredients evenly combined by using a circular motion with a wooden spoon or spatula.

TEMPER: To control the temperature of ingredients as they are heated or when combining ingredients of different temperatures together. Tempering chocolate is the method of using temperature and motion to transform chocolate to a state that will set quickly (see p. 42), but tempering also applies to gradually adding a hot liquid to a cold one in a slow and steady motion to bring the two elements together smoothly. An example is adding eggs to hot milk or dairy when making a pastry cream (see p. 33).

WHIP: To aerate an ingredient by vigorously whisking by hand or using electric beaters or a stand mixer fitted with the whip attachment. If whipping by hand, push and pull the whisk in a lateral back-and-forth motion as you rotate the bowl. Do not push the whisk in a circular motion—that is closer to stirring and will take longer to aerate your ingredients.

WHISK: To use the wire tool of the same name to blend or aerate ingredients. Whisking can remove lumps from a liquid more quickly than stirring in some cases.

ZEST: To remove the outer layer of citrus to add it to baking. The coloured outer layer of citrus fruits contains the flavourful oils, but the white layer underneath (pith) is bitter, so stop zesting when the white pith becomes visible.

# Baking How-tos

This section explains some of the most common steps that bakers use. If you are new to baking, read this section to understand what's meant when you see these instructions in a recipe. If you are a seasoned baker, you may pick up a new tip or time-saving bit of wisdom.

## How to Separate an Egg

There are a few ways to separate an egg yolk from the white. My preferred method is still the one taught to me by my mom and grandma: tipping the yolk from shell to shell. Here is how.

1. **If possible, start with a cold egg,** which is easier to separate than a warm one. When separating an egg that's at room temperature, be gentle.

2. **Have ready a clean bowl,** but do not use the edge of the bowl to crack the egg. Instead, give the egg one clean crack on a flat surface like a countertop (photo 1). You'll get a nice straight line of a crack in the shell with fewer jagged edges and tiny chips that can easily get pulled into the bowl or batter.

3. **Hold the egg over your clean bowl** (or the bowl of ingredients you are adding it to). Carefully break the egg open and hold one half upright so that the yolk stays in it. Let gravity do its work and let the egg white fall away from the yolk to the bowl (photo 2).

4. **Carefully tip the yolk from one eggshell half to the other,** letting the excess white run off. Tip the egg yolk back to the other half again, if needed (photo 3). Reserve the yolk in another bowl.

# How to Temper Eggs

Making a custard often requires adding a hot liquid to whole eggs or egg yolks. The liquid needs to be added to the eggs gradually, otherwise the shock of the hot liquid could risk curdling or overcooking the egg. Tempering your eggs helps to ensure a smooth, silky custard. To temper eggs or egg yolks:

1. **Whisk the eggs or egg yolks** together in a small bowl, along with any sugar or other ingredients called for while your liquid heats.

2. **Slowly ladle or pour a little of the heated milk or cream** into the eggs while whisking them.

3. **Add a little more of the hot liquid** to the eggs while whisking them and continue until at least 50% of the liquid has been added (but you can add all of it if you wish).

    Now the tempered eggs and liquid can be added back to the pot or poured into dishes to bake (as in crème brûlée, pp. 310 to 315).

---

# How to Make & Use Egg Wash

An egg wash is a combination of egg and water or cream that's brushed on an unbaked pastry to add shine and promote an even browning during baking. The type of egg wash will determine the level of browning you get. Crispness is rarely a factor when adding an egg wash—it is about colour and shine only. Refrigerate unused egg wash in an airtight container for up to 2 days.

| Type of Egg Wash | How to Get It |
|---|---|
| **LIGHT EGG WASH** <br> (used for adding shine without extra browning) | Whisk one large egg with 2 Tbsp (30 mL) cold water. |
| **MEDIUM** <br> (the most commonly used) | Whisk one large egg with 1 Tbsp (15 mL) cold water. |
| **DARK** <br> (typically used only for puff pastry and croissants when a dark and intense shine is desired) | Whisk one large egg with 1 Tbsp (15 mL) whipping cream, or whisk two egg yolks with 1 Tbsp (15 mL) whipping cream. |

# How to Whip Egg Whites

The method for whipping egg whites seems relatively easy—whip them on high speed until the appropriate volume is reached—but it is rarely that simple. Successfully whipping egg whites can elude even an expert baker if they look away at the wrong moment. Here are a few tips to help you reach "peak perfection" every time.

1. **Start with a clean bowl.** Lightly moisten a paper towel with white vinegar or lemon juice and wipe your washed and dried bowl to remove any fat residue that might remain. Fat droplets will repel the air bubbles in the egg white and deflate them as it pushes them away, so your egg whites will never achieve full volume.

2. **Use room-temperature egg whites.** This tip is important for two reasons. At room temperature, the proteins in egg whites will stretch to a greater volume faster. More importantly, if adding sugar, the sugar will dissolve into the whites, building in structure as they whip.

3. **Add the sugar gradually.** Let your egg whites start building some volume before you begin adding your sugar, and when adding, slowly pour it in while you continue whipping. This allows the already added sugar a moment to dissolve before more is added.

4. **Watch your whites or reduce your speed.** Time passes very quickly while whipping egg whites, especially if no sugar is added. It's easy to pass your goal peak in a blink, so don't walk away. While whipping egg whites at the highest speed achieves volume quickly, lowering the speed by one level lengthens the time between soft, medium and stiff peaks without compromising the volume of the meringue.

5. **Read your peaks.** Whipped egg whites are identified by their volume, which is referred to as their peak. Recipes call for one of three levels of peak, depending on their intended use. Here's how to tell when you've reached the desired peak level; lift your beater and invert it and:

    *For soft peaks:* The peak of the whites has a full curl to it. The meringue should not drip off the beater at all.

    *For medium peaks:* The peak of the whites has a partial curl.

    *For stiff peaks:* The peak of the whites stands upright and has no curl at all.

*Glossiness when whipping egg whites results from the amount of sugar added, not the peak. Egg whites whipped without adding sugar have no glossiness, whip up exceptionally quickly and tend to have larger air bubbles than meringues with added sugar. The more sugar you add, the glossier the meringue, the longer the egg whites will take to whip up and the finer their bubble structure will be when whipped.*

6. **Don't overwhip.** Overwhipping egg whites happens to bakers of every expertise. See p. 55 for tips on how to fix overwhipped egg whites (good news: you don't have to throw them away and start again).

# How to Toast Nuts

Toasting nuts mellows any bitterness, heightens their aroma, deepens their flavour and builds in extra crunch. Nuts vary in size and texture, so their toasting times vary as well. The level of toasting is a matter of taste (and if I don't specify which level of toasting is ideal for a particular recipe, the choice is yours). In general: Use a light toast for recipes where the nuts may have an opportunity to toast further; use a medium toast to increase the crunchiness and intensify the nut flavour; and use a dark toast when the nuts are competing against other intense flavours, such as the hazelnuts with chocolate in the Torta Setteveli (p. 277). Note that coconut is not technically a nut, but it uses the same toasting method as tree nuts, so it's included here. I haven't included peanuts because most are sold pretoasted (or fried).

1. **Preheat the oven to 350°F (180°C).** If needed, separate the nuts by type (you don't want to mix walnuts, for example, with almonds or cashews).

2. **Spread the nuts in an even layer** on one or more parchment-lined baking trays and put them in the oven. The toasting times below are based on 1 to 2 cups (250 to 500 mL). Be sure to set your timer and check often, as nuts can turn from perfectly toasted to burnt very quickly. Give the nuts a stir once or twice partway through the cooking time. Remove from the oven and allow to cool.

3. **Once cool, remove the skins from hazelnuts** before using in baking—the skins are exceptionally bitter tasting and could ruin a delicious recipe. Pour the nuts into a colander set over a tray, bowl or sink and rub the nuts around. The holes of the colander will help loosen the skins and many will fall through. Pick out the peeled hazelnuts to use in your recipe.

*Light toasting is not recommended for hazelnuts, as it is insufficient to remove the skins easily.*

| Type of Nut or Coconut | Light Toast | Medium Toast | Dark Toast |
|---|---|---|---|
| **ALMONDS (WHOLE, WITH SKINS OR BLANCHED)** | 10 minutes | 12 minutes | 15 minutes |
| **ALMONDS (SLICED)** | 5 minutes | 7 minutes | 10 minutes |
| **ALMONDS (SLIVERED)** | 5 minutes | 8 minutes | 11 minutes |
| **CASHEWS** | 7 minutes | 9 minutes | 13 minutes |
| **HAZELNUTS (WHOLE, WITH SKINS)** | Not recommended | 15 minutes | 19 minutes |
| **HAZELNUTS (WHOLE, WITHOUT SKINS, BLANCHED)** | 10 minutes | 15 minutes | 19 minutes |
| **PINE NUTS** | 4 minutes | 6 minutes | 8 minutes |
| **PISTACHIOS** | 5 minutes | 7 minutes | 9 minutes |
| **WALNUTS & PECANS (HALVES)** | 8 to 9 minutes | 10 to 11 minutes | 12 to 13 minutes |
| **WALNUTS & PECANS (PIECES)** | 7 to 8 minutes | 9 to 10 minutes | 11 to 12 minutes |
| **COCONUT, UNSWEETENED** | 3 minutes | 5 minutes | 6 minutes |
| **COCONUT, SWEETENED** | 3 minutes | 4 minutes | 5 minutes |

# How to Cook & Caramelize Sugar

Sugar is an incredibly versatile ingredient. Beyond sweetening and adding moisture to baked goods, it can be melted and boiled to specific temperatures, which results in a clear sugar with varying states of set after cooling. When cooked until caramelized, sugar has a rich amber colour and its own delicious flavour profile and nutty sweetness.

As sugar boils, any added water evaporates and sugar can cook to well above 212°F (100°C), the boiling point for water. Once caramelization starts at 320°F (160°C), the sugar is 100% concentrated. The method for caramelizing sugar is quite simple: boil it over high heat, uncovered, until it becomes a rich amber colour. That said, plenty of little tips make this process seamless and consistent.

1. **Add your water first.** Most recipes call for a specific amount of water to be added to the pot when cooking sugar. It may be only a small amount, but because it fills the bottom of the pot, it helps to dissolve the sugar immediately and evenly when you first apply the heat.

2. **Add an acid.** Acids (lemon juice, white vinegar or cream of tartar) convert granulated sugar from crystallized sucrose to a liquefied invert sugar while cooking. The acidity ensures that the sugar remains clear and liquid as you cook it. Recipes in which corn syrup, honey or glucose cook with the sugar do not need an added acid since they are already invert sugars.

3. **Cook over high heat.** Sugar should cook as quickly as possible so that it doesn't cool at the edges, crystallize or go back to its granular state. The only time you cook at a lower heat is when other ingredients such as butter or cream are cooked with the sugar, in which case they protect it.

4. **Do not stir.** Unless butter, cream or other ingredients are also included, stirring can cause the liquid yet jagged sugar crystals to rebond and turn the pot of clear, liquid sugar into a cloudy, solidified mass. If one side of the pot seems to cook faster than the other, lift the pot and gently swirl it, but do not stir.

5. **Brush the sides of the pot with water.** As the liquid sugar boils over high heat and the water begins to evaporate, tiny sugar droplets may splash up onto the side of the pot. If these droplets cool ever so slightly and set, they will return to a crystallized state, and this process will spread like frost on a window through the entire pot of sugar. Brushing the sides of the pot with cool water, close to the top of the sugar but without letting the brush touch it, allows the water to run down into the pot, cleaning the sides as it falls. The excess water evaporates and will not affect your sugar at all.

6. **Use your thermometer.** Depending on what you are making, your sugar will need to cook to a specific temperature to give your confections or frostings the right set and structure.

You may hear terms like thread, soft ball, soft crack and hard crack used in reference to stages of cooked sugar. They describe the appearance of sugar when a small spoonful is dropped into a glass of ice water and then felt between your fingers. These terms were used before candy thermometers became available. These days, if needed, we can call for an exact temperature in a recipe rather than these general ranges, but we still use the "stages" to describe the type of set we expect after cooling. In the case of caramel, the firmness of the set of the sugar does not increase by degree, so it's simpler to assess by its amber colour—a lighter caramel will be milder tasting than a darker caramel, but the set will be the same. Below is a table of the most common stages of sugar cooking.

*If you are using an old family recipe for candy making that refers only to the descriptive stage of the sugar, use the middle of that temperature range listed below. For instance, if your grandmother's recipe for toffee calls for cooking the sugar to "hard ball," cook it to 247°F (119°C).*

| Temperature Range | Description | Uses (In This Book) |
|---|---|---|
| **223°F to 236°F** (106°C to 113°C) | Thread | Raspberry Jelly Candies (p. 336) |
| **234°F to 240°F** (112°C to 116°C) | Soft Ball | Pretty Lemon Meringue Tart (Italian meringue) (p. 130), Sea Salt Caramel Candies (p. 360), Maple Marshmallows (p. 369) |
| **244°F to 250°F** (118°C to 121°C) | Hard Ball | Peach Raspberry Salt Water Taffy (p. 339), Montélimar Nougat (p. 371) |
| **270°F to 290°F** (132°C to 143°C) | Soft Crack | Sponge Toffee (p. 363) |
| **300°F to 310°F** (149°C to 154°C) | Hard Crack | Sour Lemon Drops (p. 356), Cranberry Lollipops (p. 359), Candy Canes (p. 355), Buttercrunch Toffee (p. 364) |
| **320°F to 350°F** (160°C to 177°C) | Caramel | Mixed Nut Brittle (p. 352), Praliné Noisette (p. 85), Millionaire Tart (p. 139), Îles Flottantes (p. 318) |

# How to Melt Chocolate

Chocolate is a delicate ingredient that needs to be melted gently so the result is silky and smooth. If it's heated too quickly or at too high a temperature, the chocolate can seize or split, meaning the cocoa solids separate from the cocoa butter and you have to fix the problem (see p. 57) or start again. Here are some tips for melting chocolate successfully. I prefer to use the water bath method, as it allows you the best control over the heat.

1. **Fill a pot with no more than an inch (2.5 cm) of water** and place it on the stove. Set a metal bowl over the pot. The bowl should not touch the water, but it should fit securely over the pot so the steam can't escape and sit high enough that it can be easily held and lifted from the pot.

   *A metal bowl is best because the heat transfers quickly from the steam through the bowl to melt the chocolate and cools down quickly when removed from the heat. Glass holds the heat when removed from the heat, which can overheat your chocolate and make tempering it (p. 42) extremely difficult.*

2. **Heat the water over medium-low heat** until you see wisps of steam rise from the water but no bubbles break the surface. The gentle heat of the steam will melt the chocolate.

3. **Weigh the chocolate in the bowl** and place it over the water bath. Wait 30 to 45 seconds for the heat to reach the chocolate before stirring.

4. **Using a heatproof spatula, never a whisk, stir the chocolate** in a slow, circular motion and scrape the sides of the bowl often to keep the chocolate contained. Even a thin smear of chocolate left on the side of the bowl can overheat, increasing the risk that the chocolate will seize.

*Milk and white chocolate melt at 104°F (40°C) compared to dark chocolate, which melts at 113°F (45°C). Milk and white chocolate melt more quickly, but they also are more sensitive to heat and can split more easily because of their higher cocoa butter content. To prevent them from splitting, pull them off the heat before they have fully melted so they don't get too hot. Continue stirring the chocolate off the heat until smooth. Dark chocolate can remain on the heat until fully melted.*

5. **Condensation will form on the bottom of the bowl** while it sits over the water bath. To be sure the water droplets don't accidentally transfer to the chocolate, wipe the underside of the bowl with a tea towel when you remove the bowl from the heat. Water causes melted chocolate to become grainy.

6. **Always cool the chocolate** for about 10 minutes before using, unless the recipe specifies warm melted chocolate.

*Melting chocolate in the microwave is not ideal but it can be done. Use only medium heat and stir the chocolate every 10 seconds, even when it appears to be barely melted. Chocolate melted in the microwave can burn, and there is no recovering it once that has happened. Because of the frequent stopping and stirring, the microwave method of melting chocolate takes about the same amount of time as the water bath method, so there is really no advantage.*

# How to Temper Chocolate

Tempering chocolate is essential to have it set at room temperature with shine and a good "snap" when you take a bite. Mastering the skill of tempering chocolate can take a little practice through repetition. The process involves heating chocolate, cooling it while moving it and then reheating slightly to cause good crystallization, which binds and sets the chocolate. Without this tempering process, melted chocolate would take hours to set and it would have a dull, soft finish. The good news is that heating and cooling chocolate does not harm it, so if you do not successfully temper the chocolate on your first or even second try, you can reuse and retemper it as needed.

Seed tempering requires no tools beyond a bowl, a spatula and a thermometer, but it takes a little more active time stirring the chocolate to cool it. Table tempering is quicker but requires a marble or other smooth stone surface (your table) and putty knives to move the chocolate around the cool surface. Both methods are for 10 oz (300 g) dark baking/couverture chocolate (semisweet or bittersweet).

## Seeding Method

1. **Fill a pot with no more than an inch (2.5 cm) of water** and bring it to barely a simmer. Have ready an instant-read digital thermometer.

2. **Weigh 7 oz (210 g) chopped chocolate in a metal bowl** and place it over the water bath. Wait 30 to 45 seconds for the heat to reach the chocolate, then stir until it has melted and reaches 113°F to 122°F (45°C to 50°C) (photo 1). If it gets warmer than this, let it cool to below 113°F (45°C) and rewarm.

3. **Remove the bowl from the heat and stir in the remaining 3 oz (90 g) chocolate** (photo 2) to melt it, continuing to stir until the chocolate reaches 82°F (28°C) (photo 3). Return the bowl to the water bath and stir until the chocolate reaches 88°F to 90°F (31°C to 32°C)—this doesn't take long. The chocolate is ready to use and will set at room temperature with a nice satin finish.

## Tabling Method

1. **Have ready a marble board** (or a granite or other stone countertop; a stainless-steel counter will also do), two putty knives (or a palette knife and a bench scraper) (photo 1) and an instant-read digital thermometer.

2. **Fill a pot with no more than an inch (2.5 cm) of water** and bring it to barely a simmer.

3. **Place all of the chopped chocolate in a metal bowl** and place it over the water bath. Wait 30 to 45 seconds for the heat to reach the chocolate, then stir gently until it has melted and reaches 113°F to 122°F (45°C to 50°C).

4. **Remove the bowl from the heat** and pour two-thirds of the chocolate onto the marble board. Set the bowl with the remaining chocolate off to the side on a towel (away from the heat and not on the marble).

5. **Using two putty knives, spread the chocolate on the board into a thin layer** (photo 2). Then use your tools to push the chocolate back into the centre of the board, scraping your tools to clean them of the chocolate at each push (photo 3). Moving the chocolate on the cool marble will lower the temperature of the chocolate. Keep repeating this spreading and scraping in until the chocolate reaches 82°F (28°C).

6. **Stir the reserved chocolate and check the temperature:** it should be 104°F to 113°F (40°C to 45°C) and completely smooth. If the temperature goes higher, you must let it cool to below 104°F (40°C) and start again. Add the marble-cooled chocolate back to the bowl and stir for about 30 seconds. Check the temperature again: it should be between 88°F and 90°F (31°C and 32°C), which means it is "tempered." To double-check, dip a piece of parchment paper into the chocolate and set it on your marble board: it should start setting within a minute or two.

*Because of their higher cocoa butter, milk and sugar contents, milk, white and ruby chocolates temper at different temperatures than dark chocolate. The key temperatures are:*

- *Heat the chocolate to 104°F to 113°F (40°C to 45°C).*
- *Cool the melted chocolate to 81°F to 82°F (27°C to 28°C).*
- *Temper the chocolate to 84°F to 86°F (29°C to 30°C).*

1 TABLING METHOD ▶

# How to Roll Pastry Doughs

Rolling a pastry dough to line a pie plate or tart pan or to cut and bake on its own can be done confidently with a few guiding tips. The nature of the pastry dough helps to determine the best method for rolling. Below are tips to help with every step of the rolling process, no matter what type of pastry you're working with. Remember two key points:

**FOR CLASSIC PIE PASTRY DOUGH AND SWEET PASTRY DOUGH:** Use the tapered end of a French rolling pin, if you have one, to *coax the pastry into a circle as you roll.* Roll in short strokes to prevent the pastry from baking unevenly or shrinking. And it's a good habit to flip the dough over halfway through rolling even if it shows no signs of cracking, just to spread out the pressure.

*Cracks in classic pie pastry have nothing to do with what you do or don't do while mixing or rolling the dough. They result* *simply because butter sets firmly once chilled. As the dough is rolled out, the butter gradually softens and the dough becomes more pliable. That's why cracks tend to develop earlier in the rolling process.*

**FOR PUFF PASTRY DOUGH:** *Keep your rolling motions square to the sides of the dough,* even if you are rolling and cutting out a circle, so the pastry rises level when it bakes.

| | Classic Pie Pastry | Sablé, Nut or Other Sweet Rolled Pastry | Puff Pastry |
|---|---|---|---|
| **WHEN TO ROLL** | Pull the dough from the fridge 20 to 30 minutes before rolling to soften the butter and make it easier to roll without compromising flakiness. If it is a hot or humid day, use the dough chilled, directly from the fridge. If making a **single-crust pie**, you will need one disc of dough; if making a **double-crust pie**, you will need two discs of dough. | Always use the dough chilled, directly from the fridge. | Always use the dough chilled, directly from the fridge. |
| **HOW TO PREVENT INITIAL STICKING AND CRACKING** | Lightly dust the work surface and top of the dough with flour before rolling. | Lightly dust the work surface and top of the dough with flour. Break the dough into two or three pieces (photo 1b) and knead gently for 30 seconds until soft and pliable. Kneading the dough at this stage helps to redistribute the sugar and makes the dough easier to roll. Stack the pieces on top of each other and knead until just combined before rolling. | Lightly dust the work surface and top of the dough with flour before rolling. To avoid compressing the layers, use a sharp chef's knife to cut and portion the dough as directed by the recipe. |

|  | Classic Pie Pastry | Sablé, Nut or Other Sweet Rolled Pastry | Puff Pastry |
|---|---|---|---|
| **HOW TO ROLL EVENLY** | Using a rolling pin, start in the centre of the dough and roll back and forth 2 inches (5 cm) (photo 1a) to start. Slowly extend the length of the roll. To keep the shape and an even thickness, never roll over the edge of the dough. | Start in the centre, rolling back and forth 2 inches (5 cm) to start. Slowly extend the length of the roll (photo 2b). To keep the shape and an even thickness, never roll over the edge of the dough. | Using a rolling pin, start in the centre of the dough and roll back and forth 2 inches (5 cm) to start. Slowly extend the length of the roll. To keep the shape and an even thickness, never roll over the edge of the dough. If you're working with a thick piece of puff pastry and it feels as if it is stretching more than rolling, place it on a baking tray and chill for 20 minutes, then go back to rolling. |
| **HOW TO PREVENT CRACKS** | Flip the dough over, redust the work surface with flour and reroll (photo 2a). | Flip the dough over, redust the work surface with flour and reroll. | Puff pastry will not crack. |
| **HOW TO FIX LARGE CRACKS** | Pinch the dough together with your fingers and keep rolling. Small cracks around the edges are to be expected. | See how to prevent initial sticking and cracking (above). | n/a |
| **HOW TO PREVENT STICKING WHILE ROLLING** | Rotate the dough 90 degrees after a few strokes and dust the work surface and top of the dough as needed. | Rotate the dough 90 degrees after a few strokes and dust the work surface and top of the dough as needed. If the dough starts to stick too much to the rolling surface, chill it for 10 minutes to set up the butter a touch; no need to reknead again. | Rotate the dough 90 degrees after a few strokes and dust the work surface and top of the dough as needed. |
| **WHAT THICKNESS TO ROLL** | Roll to ¼ inch (6 mm) thick, starting at the centre and rolling out. Never roll the full diameter of the pastry. | Roll to ¼ inch (6 mm) thick, starting at the centre and rolling out. Never roll the full diameter of the pastry. | Roll the pastry to just shy of ¼ inch (6 mm) thick and at least an inch (2.5 cm) bigger all around than you need. |
| **HOW TO PREVENT STICKING TO THE PIE PLATE OR PAN** | Dust the pie plate or tart pan with a little flour; do not grease it. | Dust the bottom of a removable-bottom tart pan with a little flour; do not grease it. | n/a |
| **HOW TO TRANSFER THE DOUGH TO THE PIE PLATE OR PAN** | Carefully slide your hands under the dough and lift it gently into place, or roll the dough onto your rolling pin, carry the pin to the pie plate or pan and unroll the dough into place. | Carefully slide your hands under the dough and lift it gently into place (photo 3b), or roll the dough onto your rolling pin, carry the pin to the pan and unroll the dough into place. | Carefully slide your hands under the dough and lift it gently into place. |

|  | Classic Pie Pastry | Sablé, Nut or Other Sweet Rolled Pastry | Puff Pastry |
|---|---|---|---|
| **HOW TO KEEP THE DOUGH FROM SHRINKING IN THE PIE PLATE OR PAN** | Gently press the pastry into the pie plate or pan and let it relax into the sides (photo 3a); resist pushing the dough toward the top edge of the plate, which might cause the dough to shrink after baking. Instead, push the pastry down into the bottom edge. Trim away the rough edges, leaving an inch (2.5 cm) of pastry overhanging. | Lift the pastry up and gently press it into the edges of the pan; resist immediately pushing the rounded dough into the bottom edge of the pan, which might cause the dough to shrink after baking. Instead, carefully push the pastry into the fluting and down into the bottom edge of the pan before trimming the rough edges (photo 4b). | n/a |
| **HOW TO TRIM THE DOUGH** | If lining **a fluted tart** pan, trim the pastry at the top edges. If you roll your pin over the top of the pan to do this, be sure to press the dough into the fluted sides of the pan again.<br><br>If baking **a single-crust pie**, tuck the overhanging edge under and pinch the edges to create a pattern and adhere it to the pie plate (photos 4a, 5a and 6a).<br><br>If baking **a double-crust pie**, place the top crust over the filled pie. Trim the top edge of the pie to just over ½ inch (1.2 cm) past the pie plate and pinch the two crusts together. | Hold the pastry in place and run your thumb around the top edge. Or use your rolling pin to roll over the top of the pan, which will cut it like a knife (photo 5b). Trim away and discard the excess, then press the pastry back into the sides of the pan to prevent tiny air pockets from forming at each flute. (photo 6b) | To avoid compressing the layers, use a sharp chef's knife to trim the edges so they are clean and precise. Discard the excess dough. |
| **HOW TO PREPARE THE DOUGH FOR BAKING** | Chill the dough in the pie plate or pan for 20 minutes or up to 1 day. | Chill the dough in the pan for at least 30 minutes. You can dock the pastry, if needed, before or after chilling. | Chill the dough in place for at least 30 minutes. |

1a **CLASSIC PIE PASTRY** ▶

2a

3a

4a

5a

6a

1b **SABLÉ PASTRY** ▶

2b

3b

4b

5b

6b

# How to Blind-bake Pie Pastry

In some cases, you'll need to prebake your pie pastry in part or in full before filling it and completing your recipe. Knowing when, why and how to do this will result in pies that are perfectly cooked every time.

Blind-baking involves faking a filling. If you were to place an unfilled pie shell into the oven, the sides would slip down the pie plate and the bottom pastry would bubble up, leaving no space for the filling and losing all of its shape. By weighing down the pie pastry with foil and weights, the pastry stays in place.

Before covering the how-to of blind-baking, here are the different stages of prebaking your pie pastry.

NO PREBAKING: If the pie spends 50 minutes or more in the oven, you do not need to prebake the pastry because it will fully cook along with the filling. Fruit pies and the Leek & Crème Fraîche Flamiche (p. 112) are examples.

PARTIALLY BLIND-BAKED PASTRY: If the pie has a filling that cooks in less time than the pie pastry, you need to partially bake the pastry first. You don't want to fully bake it because then you risk overbaking it, especially the edges. Quiches are an example.

FULLY BLIND-BAKED PASTRY: If the pie has a filling that does not get cooked in the oven, the pastry needs to be fully baked and cooled before being filled in order to stay crisp and flaky. Brushing the hot pie shell creates a seal, helping to prevent the filling from seeping into the crust and making it soggy. The Chocolate Hazelnut Cream Pie (p. 127) is an example.

1. **Roll out the pie dough** on a lightly floured surface into a circle just under ¼ inch (6 mm) thick. Trim away any large pieces of dough from the edge and tuck and pinch the edges in a pattern. Alternatively, trim the pastry to the outside edge of the pie plate and press in place. Cut out shapes from the excess pastry, moisten with water and press gently along the top edge of the pastry. Dock the bottom of the pie shell with a fork. Chill the pastry shell for at least 30 minutes (up to a day).

*When trimming the outside edge of your pie shell, take the time to press the pastry onto the top lip of the pie plate to keep it in place.*

2. **Preheat the oven** to 375°F (190°C).

3. **Weight the pie shell.** Place two sheets of aluminum foil over the pie shell, gently covering the outside trim. Use pie weights, dried rice or dried beans (about 2 cups/500 mL) and pour these on top of the foil, spreading them out to the edges.

4. **Bake the pie for 20 minutes.** Carefully remove the foil together with the pie weights (this is why you double up on the foil).
   *For a partially baked pie shell:* Return the pan to the oven to bake for 10 minutes more, until the edges of the pastry are light brown and the bottom of the pastry appears dry but still pale.
   *For a fully baked pie shell:* Return the pan to the oven for 18 to 20 minutes, until the edges of the pastry are golden brown and the bottom of the pastry is lightly browned.

5. **Brush the pie shell**, hot from the oven, with lightly whisked egg white.

6. **Cool the pie shell** in its pan on a rack before filling.

# How to Bake Sweet Pastry Dough

Sweet dough made with sugar and egg yolks is softer than pie or puff pastry dough and will absorb the filling if not prebaked, even if it will be baked when filled. Here are a few tips for prebaking sweet dough with confidence.

1. **Dock the dough before baking.** Good news! Sweet dough does not need to be blind-baked (lined with foil and weighted). Simply piercing the pastry in the bottom of the tart pan with a fork (docking) allows the pastry to expand as it bakes so air pockets or bubbles don't form in your tart shell. These holes will close up during baking, so there is no need to fear that your filling will leak through.

2. **Chill your tart shell before baking.** This step ensures that the sides of your tart shell will stay in place and not sink toward the bottom. Bake the tart shell directly from the fridge.

3. **Let your tart shell cool completely before adding any filling.** A warm tart shell is prone to absorbing moisture and then losing its strength and crispness.

4. **Brush the pastry with egg white after prebaking.** The egg white serves as a seal to help your pastry stay crisp longer after filling. The protein in the egg cooks from the heat of the pastry, creating a barrier.

# How to Portion Unbaked Batters & Doughs

Precisely portioned batters and doughs are a satisfying sight for home bakers and they're essential for professional bakers. Here are the best ways to ensure precise shape and size for different types of baked goods.

**CAKE BATTERS:** For cakes of three layers or less, you can simply "eyeball" the amount of batter you'll need for each layer. To be more precise, weigh the batter as a whole and divide it by the number of layers you need. That will give you the weight for each layer. Then place a cake pan on the scale, hit tare to set it to zero and pour in enough batter to equal the weight of one layer. Repeat with the remaining batter.

If the cake batter is very fluid or the cake has many layers (like Esterházy Torte, p. 273), use either the weight method for portioning or measure the batter by volume and then pour it into the pans. Be very gentle when portioning sponge batters because every excess scrape, stir and pour can deflate the whipped eggs a little.

**PIPED BATTERS & DOUGHS:** Piping precise macarons, éclairs and profiteroles is a combination of practice and good tools. When starting out, it's a good idea to use silicone baking mats with macaron-sized patterns printed on them or your own template drawn onto parchment paper. With repetition, you will become faster and more accurate and can skip the templates.

**DROP COOKIES & MUFFINS:** Use an ice cream scoop to portion cookie doughs onto baking trays and muffin or cupcake batters into the holes of a muffin tin. Dip the scoop fully into the batter and scrape the flat side of the scoop onto the edge of the bowl to remove any excess, then drop the scoopful onto the tray or into the muffin cup. Repeat with the remaining batter.

**BREAD DOUGHS:** To casually divide bread dough, shape the dough into a cylinder. Use a dough cutter to divide the dough in half. Then divide each half in half. If you want 12 portions, cut each quarter into three even pieces, giving you a dozen in total.

For a more precise method, use a scale. Weigh the entire piece of dough and divide that number by the number of portions you need. That will give you the weight for each portion. Then use a dough cutter to cut a piece of dough. Weigh it, and cut away any excess or add more dough as needed.

# How to Assemble a Layer Cake

The satisfaction that comes from presenting a layer cake for a special occasion results as much from its assembly as it does from the delicious interior or colourful or creative decorating. Assembling a layer cake that is straight and level is as important to its look as any finishing touches. Here are some tips to help you.

1. **Have everything ready and at the correct temperature.** A still-warm cake will melt a frosting, or a too-chilled frosting will spread unevenly and tear the cake. Follow the recipe recommendations carefully.

2. **Level your cakes.** None of the cake recipes in this book will require you to trim a domed top from your cake, but some cake recipes (including some cake mixes) may produce cake layers with a peak or dome, which makes layering them difficult. Use a serrated knife to trim off the domed top. Start from the outside of the cake and rotate the cake as you cut inward; this will help you trim the cake with a level top, compared to cutting it horizontally from one side to the opposite side.

3. **Spread the frosting from the centre.** When stacking layers, dollop the frosting onto the centre of the cake (photo 1) and use an offset spatula to push the frosting to the outside of the top of the cake as you turn or rotate it (photo 2, 4, 5). Try to avoid lifting the spatula, to prevent pulling crumbs up with the frosting, but instead smooth and spread in a fluid motion. Push the frosting over the outside edge of the cake, which will make frosting the sides easier.

4. **Check the cake is level at each layer.** Squat down so the top of the cake is at eye level and turn the platter or cake wheel to ensure the cake is level. If not and the top layer has no frosting yet, you can gently press down on the higher side (photo 3, 6). If the cake already has frosting, add a little extra to the lower side. Also check that the cake is not leaning to one side. If so, use your offset spatula and gently press onto the leaning side to realign it. If the cake seems fragile and leans again as soon as you return to frosting it, realign it again and then chill it for 30 minutes to set the frosting before you continue.

5. **Frost the top and then the sides.** After all of the layers have been stacked, dollop a generous amount of frosting on the top of the cake (photo 7) and use the same technique as frosting the stacked layers to frost the top (photo 8). It is easier to pull away excess frosting from a covered cake than it is to add more, as each contact with the bare cake surface provides an opportunity for crumbs to pull away from it and mix into the frosting. Once the top is frosted, you can use a large piping bag to pipe frosting onto the sides (a quick way to get the frosting onto the cake) and then use an offset spatula to spread the frosting so the sides are fully covered (photo 9).

6. **Smooth the sides.** To create perfectly smooth sides, use a dough cutter (p. 23) or cake edger (p. 24). Holding the tool at a 45-degree angle against the side of the cake, rotate the cake while you hold the tool in place (photo 10). This may push some frosting to the top edge of the cake, so use your offset spatula to pull that frosting inward from the outside edge toward the centre of the cake; this will create a crisp top edge to the cake. Smooth the top of the cake with your offset spatula (photo 11). If you wish to add sprinkles or use a cake comb to create a pattern in the frosting, do it while the frosting is still soft.

7. **Chill before decorating.** Before adding any piping, drips or other decorating details (photo 12), chill the cake for a full 2 hours. This sets the interior of the cake so it won't shift while you decorate.

# How to Use Piping Bags & Tips

Piping bags are used for more than just adding decorative details to desserts. They are a way to pipe batters and doughs with precision or to fill small pans like mini-muffin tins quickly and tidily. Here are some guiding tips for using your piping bags and tips.

**HOW TO INSERT A TIP:** Snip an opening in the point of the piping bag so that the tip will fit in, with half of it peeking through the hole, including any tip detail, like the points of a star tip. Some place the tip into the bag before snipping an opening, but cutting around the piping tip to open the bag can scratch the tip.

**HOW TO USE A COUPLER:** a coupler is a two-piece insert that allows you to change piping tips on a filled piping bag easily (very handy if decorating with many colours and tips). Snip an opening in the point of the piping bag and drop in the base of the coupler. Place a tip onto the outside of the coupler and secure in place by threading on the ring. Fill the piping bag and use as you wish. To change piping tips, unthread the ring, remove the tip and replace with a different one, securing with the ring.

*If you have a fluid filling, batter or icing, it can be frustrating to fill the piping bag only to have the contents drip or leak out. To prevent this, give the piping bag a twist just above the piping tip and push the twist into the piping tip (photo 1). This now plugs the opening of the piping bag. You can then fill, and when you are ready to pipe, untwist the bag to release the seal and pipe away (photo 5).*

**HOW TO FILL A PIPING BAG:** Open the piping bag and fold the top over about halfway down. Hold the piping bag with your hand cupped in a C shape so that the folded bag rests on the C of your hand (photo 2). Spoon the filling into the bag; the spatula can be scraped on the edge of your piping bag–covered hand if the filling is stiff (photo 3). Once filled, unfold the piping bag. If the filling hasn't settled into the base of the piping bag, set the bag on your counter and use a dough cutter or offset spatula to gently push the filling toward the base of the piping bag (this way filling won't leak out the top or be left unused) (photo 4). Twist the piping bag at the top, where the filling ends (photo 5).

**HOW TO HOLD A PIPING BAG:** Place the curve of your dominant hand between your thumb and forefinger over the twist at the top of the filled piping bag. Use this hand to hold the piping bag and apply pressure, controlling the flow of the filling. Use the forefinger of your non-dominant hand to guide the piping bag at the tip (photo 6).

*Avoid squeezing a piping bag from the middle or placing your whole hand around it as you work, because the heat of your hand could warm or even melt the filling.*

**HOW TO PIPE:** Hold the piping tip as far above the cake or tray as you wish the full shape of the piped details to be. For example, if you want star-tip piped dots that sit ½ inch (1.2 cm) high, the end of the piping tip should be ½ inch (1.2 cm) from the cake. Press the filling from the top of the bag with as even a pressure as possible, then stop and lift the tip up and away quickly to break the connection. Piping choux paste, frosting and cream is best done holding the tip at a 45-degree angle from the cake or tray, but fluid items like macaron batter are best piped straight down at a 90-degree angle from the tray.

**HOW TO CREATE BASIC TIPS & PATTERNS:** Get playful with your tips. Between the shape of the tip and the texture of your frosting, you can really get creative. Use a leaf tip to pipe petals or even a basket weave pattern, and even a plain or star tip can take on different looks. Pictured (photo 7) are some basic patterns (from top left to bottom right: leaf tip, petal tip, leaf tip, star tip, star tip, plain tip).

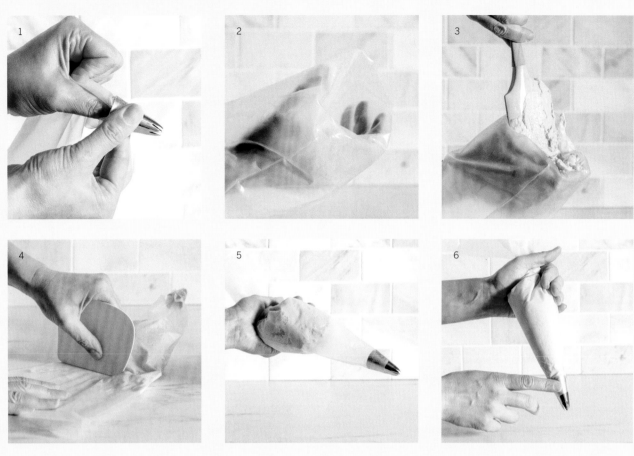

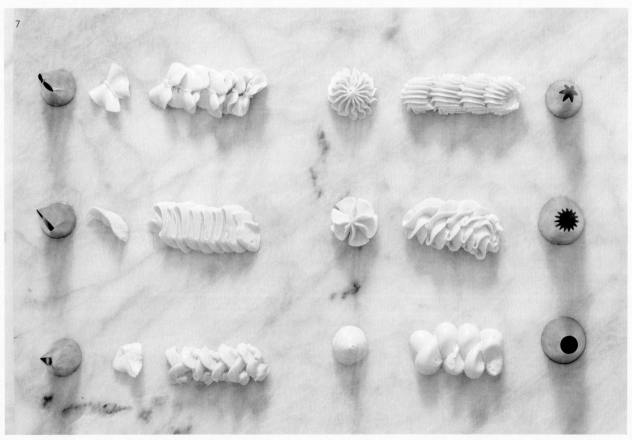

# How to Make a Parchment Paper Cone for Piping

When you need to drizzle, pipe or write with melted chocolate or glaze with precision, try using a parchment paper cone. It is small and nestles into the palm of your hand so it feels like using a pen. Here's how to make your own cone.

1. **Cut a square of parchment paper at least 10 inches (25 cm) across.** Fold the paper in half diagonally to form a right-angle triangle, then cut along the fold. Reserve one triangle for another use, or make a second cone for later use.

2. **To form the cone,** bring the two points at the ends of the longest side to meet the point at the right angle, curling and overlapping them to create a cone shape (photo 1). The centre of the longest side (opposite the right angle) will be the tip of the parchment cone. Wiggle the corners to tighten up the tip of the cone so liquids won't leak out (photo 2), then fold over the top edge where the points meet twice, to hold the cone in place (photo 3).

3. **To fill the cone, set it in a water glass.** Spoon the filling into the open end of the cone, then flatten the top of the cone and fold it over again to secure the filling.

4. **To use the cone, wrinkle and shape it to fit into your hand.** Snip the tip of the cone slightly and test your piping on a clean plate. If the results look good, go ahead and decorate your baked goods.

# Fixing Baking Blunders

Every baker will experience mistakes and pitfalls as they bake; it's an expected and accepted part of the baking process (not just the learning process—pros make mistakes too). The aim of this section is to help you repair mistakes so you don't end up feeling you've wasted time or ingredients. Although many of these fixes are for a specific problem, a few can apply to your next bake if the baked good in front of you is not what you'd expected.

## How to Repair Overwhipped Egg Whites

Everyone accidentally overwhips their egg whites at least once, but the good news is that there's an easy solution to fix them, even if you've added sugar. Here's what you need to know.

**WHAT DO THEY LOOK LIKE?** Instead of being fluffy, smooth and billowy, overwhipped whites look rough and craggy, like sea foam on the beach. Overwhipped whites with sugar may lose some of their shine (photo 1).

**WHY SHOULDN'T YOU USE THEM?** Because they have been stretched to their maximum volume, the whipped egg whites have no more room to grow. If they're folded into a batter, once they go into the oven the air within the bubbles expands and breaks the egg white surrounding it. The result is a cake or soufflé that does not rise much in the first place or immediately collapses when it comes out of the oven.

**HOW CAN YOU FIX THEM?** Once you realize that you've overwhipped your egg whites, stop whipping and let the egg whites sit in the bowl for 5 to 10 minutes (photo 2). Because they are stretched to beyond their capacity to hold in air, they will start collapsing. If you see liquid egg whites starting to pool at the bottom of the bowl or the whites break down and lose volume when you stir them up, repair them by whipping again (even if your sugar has been added) on medium speed. Whip them to the point you passed the first time around (photo 3).

*Remember, the more sugar you added to the egg whites, the longer they'll take to whip, but they reach a fuller volume and are more difficult to overwhip than egg whites whipped without sugar.*

# How to Repair Overwhipped Cream

Whipping cream, too, can quickly go from perfectly whipped to overwhipped. Just because you went a little too far on the whipping doesn't mean the cream is ruined. Here's how to tell if you're on your way to being a pioneer, making butter by hand, and how to bring your cream back to whipped heavenliness.

**WHAT DOES IT LOOK LIKE?** When you whip cream, the fat within it starts to coalesce, spreading around the air bubbles added through whipping and trapping the air within (photo 1). When cream begins to overwhip, the fat bonds together more closely and starts to force the air out. The cream will lose its smooth look, become a little rougher and change from soft white to a slightly butter-yellow colour (photo 2).

*If you were to continue whipping the cream, you would make butter. In 15 to 20 minutes (more quickly in a food processor), the fat in the cream will fully separate from the whey and you will have butter. If you then squeeze the butter between your hands in a bowl of ice water to push out as much remaining water as you can from the fat, you will have a butter you can spread onto your freshly baked bread. I do not recommend using the butter for baking, since the butter-fat content can be inconsistent.*

**WHY SHOULDN'T YOU USE IT?** Overwhipped cream is in the early stages of separating, meaning the fat is separating from the water and protein (whey) in the cream. If folded into a mousse, the overwhipped cream will be harder to incorporate and may deflate. More importantly, it will taste greasy if used in a mousse or to top a cake or tart.

**HOW CAN YOU FIX IT?** Once you notice that you've gone too far with your cream, stop the mixer and add 2 Tbsp (30 mL) unwhipped whipping cream for every 1 cup (250 mL) cream you are whipping; whisk this in by hand. The liquid cream will dissolve the bonded fat globules; this will smooth out the cream and no further whipping may be required. If the cream appears too soft, continue to whip by hand or on low speed to return it to a soft peak but not agitate the fat any further (photo 3).

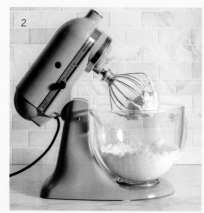

# How to Repair Seized Chocolate

Chocolate is a fragile baking ingredient, and even with best practices it can sometimes seize or split. Here is how to recognize and repair the problem.

**WHAT DOES IT LOOK LIKE?** Seized chocolate will lose its shine and develop a grainy texture, and you may even see fat (cocoa butter) pulling away from the thick grainy mass.

**WHY DID THIS HAPPEN?** When chocolate on its own is melted and somehow comes in contact with water droplets, it seizes. This can happen through the steam of the water bath when melting the chocolate, or if there is even a droplet of water on a tool.

*Chocolate can be overheated, which is why it should always be melted using a metal bowl and a water bath, not microwaved. Melt it to no more than 123°F (50.5°C). Overheated chocolate will lose its shine and become thick, but you will not see the fat separation.*

*Remove overheated chocolate from the heat immediately and add a little more unmelted chocolate to bring its temperature down. If you don't see the chocolate return to a smooth, glossy state, add 1 Tbsp (15 mL) vegetable oil (for amounts of 3 oz/90 g of chocolate or greater) and gently stir in. If using the chocolate for tempering, make sure the chocolate cools to below 113°F (45°C) before you restart the tempering process. It can be used in baking, but reweigh the chocolate if you added extra to the bowl to correct the overmelting.*

**WHY SHOULDN'T YOU USE IT?** You will find seized chocolate impossible to work with if making chocolate confections like bonbons because it won't become smooth again. If used in baking, it could force other fats to separate in the batter or frosting, and your baked cakes or brownies might seem dry and crumbly and the frosting would be coarse and grainy.

*Overheated chocolate could become "shocked" by colder ingredients being added to it and then seize the batter or frosting.*

**HOW CAN YOU FIX IT?** If you are melting the chocolate for a batter, mousse, frosting or filling, remove the bowl of chocolate from the heat and add a few drops of tepid water to the centre of the seized chocolate. Use a spatula (never a whisk) and slowly and gently stir at the centre point where the water was added. This will begin to rebond the cocoa butter to the cocoa solids and you will see the chocolate smooth out. Widen your stirring circle and the chocolate will correct itself; it should be used immediately in your recipe, since setting and remelting may cause it to split again (now that water has been added, albeit intentionally). This trick is not recommended when melting chocolate to temper for coating or confectionery work, since getting a proper temper will be next to impossible.

# How to Repair Curdled Cake Batter

Mixing ingredients together at a like temperature will help prevent a cake batter from splitting or curdling, as will adding eggs one at a time. However, when you are combining different ingredients, the curdling can still happen. Here's how to recognize and repair the issue.

**WHAT DOES IT LOOK LIKE?** The batter will not be smooth, and lumps of the butter/sugar mixture will be visible.

**WHY SHOULDN'T YOU BAKE IT?** Because of the uneven fat distribution of the batter, the cake will not have as strong a structure as a smooth batter. It may not rise enough and the result may be a dry and crumbly cake texture.

**HOW CAN YOU FIX IT?** If your batter begins to curdle, stop adding the eggs. Instead, add 2 to 3 Tbsp (18 to 24 g) of flour from the recipe (not extra flour) and stir in. This will smooth out the batter so you can go back to adding the eggs and mixing.

---

# How to Repair Overproofed Bread Dough

Perhaps your kitchen is warmer than you thought, or you lost track of time, but now your dough is at risk of being overproofed. Is all that effort, time and patience wasted? Not at all, and here's what you can do.

**WHAT DOES IT LOOK LIKE?** Instead of delicate air bubbles in your very risen dough, you may see large air pockets or a loose, spongy texture. The centre of your dough may have even collapsed on itself and could be sunken in the middle.

**WHY SHOULDN'T YOU BAKE IT?** If your dough is over-proofed during the final rise before baking and you bake it, the dough will quickly deflate, the crust will not brown and the texture of the bread will seem stale even though it's freshly baked. This is because the yeast fully expended itself prior to baking and the proteins in the flour can no longer hold all of the carbon dioxide that the yeast generated.

**HOW CAN YOU REPAIR IT?** There are a few solutions to choose from, depending on the timing and the state of your dough.

*If the overproofing happens during the first rise,* in the bowl, punch the dough down to let the yeast go to work again and the dough will rise up.

*If the overproofing happens during the second rise,* when the bread is already shaped, knock down the dough, reshape it and let it rise again, setting a timer to the time stated in the recipe.

*If you really forgot about the dough for either proof* and the dough was left to rise for double the time or longer than it should have, knead a little more yeast, water and flour into the dough to give the new yeast something to feed on. The dough should recover and you can continue the rising time as per the recipe.

# How to Troubleshoot Other Common Baking Issues

Even when following a recipe to the letter, your baked goods may not come out perfectly or perfectly beautiful, although they may still be delicious and enjoyable to eat. Here are some common signs that a problem occurred, and while there may not be an immediate fix to the issue in the moment, you'll know what happened and why so you can prevent or avoid it next time.

## Pastry

| Issue | What Could Have Caused It? | For Next Time . . . |
|-------|---------------------------|---------------------|
| **SHRINKS WHEN ROLLED** | Dough not being rested/chilled enough after making. If the dough resists rolling at the start of the rolling process, the proteins may not have had enough time to relax. If it shrinks back for a second or third rolling, chill or set the dough aside for 15 to 20 minutes to rest before rerolling the scraps. | Give your dough at least two hours to chill and rest after making it, or make it a day ahead. |
| **SHRINKS WHEN BAKED** | Dough not being rested/chilled enough after rolling and before baking, so the proteins in the flour have not had enough time to relax. <br><br> Pie crust not being weighted down enough while blind-baking. Without enough weight to hold the pastry in place, the crust will slide down the side of the pie plate. | Give the rolled pastry a minimum of 30 minutes to chill after rolling, with 1 to 2 hours being ideal. The pastry can rest in the fridge for up to a day loosely covered before baking. <br><br> Use at least 8 oz (240 g) of weight to hold the pastry in place. This is just over a cup of uncooked rice or dried beans. |
| **CRUMBLES AFTER BAKING** | Too little fat or too much flour being added, making for a dry pastry that does not have enough moisture to bond together during baking. | Measure carefully and try to not to excessively flour your work area when rolling out the pastry. |
| **TOUGH AFTER BAKING** | Too much water or overhandling. The flour absorbs the water, bonding the proteins in the flour and resulting in a "tight" or tough pastry. | Measure carefully and avoid over-handling the pastry with bare hands. If it is a warm day or you have warm hands, you can chill the dough part way through rolling to make it easier to handle and less prone to toughening. |
| **PUFF PASTRY DOESN'T PUFF** | Oven not being hot enough or dough not being chilled before baking. The dough needs to quickly go from cold to hot so that the butter within it melts and produces steam early on in baking, pushing up the layers of flour around it before the flour sets. | Let your oven preheat thoroughly and chill the rolled puff pastry for at least 30 minutes, but ideally 1 to 2 hours before baking. |
| **BUTTER LEACHES OUT** | Oven not being hot enough. The butter melted out before it had a chance to develop steam to push up the layers. <br><br> Underproofing (in croissants). The underproofed dough is too dense and won't expand quickly enough in the oven, so the butter is forced out. | Preheat your oven for longer. <br><br> When proofing the croissants, consider the ambient temperature in your kitchen and how cold your freezer is; if thawing from frozen, extra time may be needed. |

# Cakes

| Issue | What Could Have Caused It? | For Next Time . . . |
|---|---|---|
| **DENSE, HEAVY TEXTURE** | Undermixing. If moist yet dense, the batter didn't have enough structure to hold in the air.<br><br>Oven being too cool. The oven was not fully preheated. | Make sure batters are fully combined and well-mixed until homogeneous.<br><br>Check the oven temperature or allow more time to preheat. |
| **DOMED TOP** | Overmixing. The proteins in the flour were developed too much, or you added slightly too much flour. | Try cutting the butter into the dry ingredients and then adding liquids, or mix the batter on a lower speed when adding the flour. |
| **TUNNELS (AIR POCKETS)** | Overmixing. The proteins in the flour were developed too much, so the air produced by the leaveners had to force itself through the batter, creating tunnels. | Dense cake batters are more prone to this, compared to sponge cakes. Mix the batter on a lower speed and stop mixing when the batter is an even consistency. |
| **SPLITS ON TOP** | Oven being too hot. The batter set on the outside before the inside had finished rising, pushing the underbaked batter through the top and splitting the cake. (Note that splits are expected and accepted in loaves like banana bread or pound cake because of the size of the pan and the volume of batter.) | Use an oven thermometer to monitor your oven temperature, adjusting accordingly. |
| **SINKS IN THE CENTRE** | Oven not being hot enough or the temperature fluctuating. | Use an oven thermometer to track the temperature in your oven, adjusting accordingly. |

# Breads

| Issue | What Could Have Caused It? | For Next Time . . . |
|---|---|---|
| **DOESN'T BROWN ON TOP** | Underproofing. The yeast has not broken down the sugars in the flour enough, so there is not enough to brown on the surface.<br><br>Overproofing. The yeast has used up all the sugars in the flour, so there is nothing left to caramelize on the surface. | Consider the ambient temperature of your kitchen as well as the temperature of your ingredients. If both are very cool, you may need to add proofing time. If it is very warm (and especially if it is humid), you may wish to reduce the proofing time. |
| **DOESN'T RISE ENOUGH AFTER BAKING (BUT ROSE FINE WHEN PROOFING)** | Oven not being fully preheated before baking. The yeast gives its final lift to bread when it first goes in the oven, so it needs that blast of heat before the heat ultimately kills it.<br><br>Overproofing. The yeast is fully expended so has no more carbon dioxide to produce. | Give your oven extra time to preheat and use an oven thermometer to track it, adjusting accordingly.<br><br>Consider the ambient temperature of the kitchen and possibly reduce the proofing time if it is warm and/or humid. |

| Issue | What Could Have Caused It? | For Next Time . . . |
|---|---|---|
| **RISES TOO QUICKLY ON THE COUNTER** | Too much yeast or the ambient temperature being too warm. | Refrigerate the dough for an hour or up to 10 hours to slow the fermentation. |
| **DOESN'T RISE ENOUGH ON THE COUNTER** | Ingredients being too cold. | Yeast needs to be at room temperature to activate, so give the dough extra time to warm up. |
| **DENSE, HEAVY TEXTURE** | Oven not being hot enough. Without a blast of heat to give the yeast its final push to produce carbon dioxide, the yeast simply dies without generating enough air volume in the bread.<br><br>Overproofing. The yeast fully expended itself before going into the oven, so it cannot produce any more carbon dioxide. | Give your oven extra time to preheat and use an oven thermometer to track it, adjusting accordingly.<br><br>Consider the ambient temperature of the kitchen and possibly reduce the proofing time if it is warm and/or humid. |

# How to Save Overbaked Baked Goods

It is so easy to let time to escape us when we are busy baking, even with a timer set. For those occasions when your treats bake past the moment of perfection, here are some simple fixes to rescue them—and your pride, too.

| What Are You Baking? | Can You Fix It? |
|---|---|
| **COOKIES** | If they're overbrowned but not burnt, dust with icing sugar.<br><br>If they've baked unevenly on the tray (some too dark, some undercooked), rotate the pans halfway through baking. |
| **NUTS** | If only some are overtoasted (e.g., those on top or around the edges of the baking tray), discard the burnt ones and use the rest. |
| **CAKES** | Even if the outside seems overbaked, the inside is often fine. Use a serrated knife to shave away the overbaked parts. If the cake can't be trimmed, dust with icing sugar. |
| **PASTRY CREAM** | While fresh off the heat, pour the overcooked pastry cream into a blender or food processor and purée. Immediately push the mixture through a strainer and cool. |
| **CHEESECAKE OR PUMPKIN PIE** | If you find cracking when these come out of the oven, wait 10 minutes, then run a palette knife around the inside edge of the pan to loosen the sides. As the cake cools, it should contract from the sides (and not the centre) to close the crack. Alternatively, cover with a topping like Chantilly cream to cover it. |

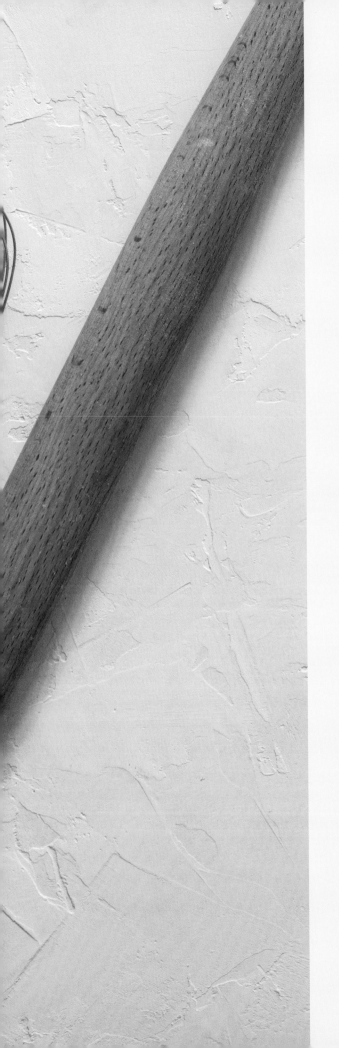

# Baking Science & Other Baking Wisdom

If you've ever been curious about the science behind baking, including the function of certain ingredients in baking, and what happens when your batters and doughs are placed into the oven, this is the section for you. There's even a bit about how to adapt recipes to baking at higher altitudes.

And if science isn't your thing, you will want to know how to easily portion and store your goods once you've baked them. Proper storage can be the difference between treats that stay fresh and ones that quickly become dry and stale. And when you finally get a moment to tackle that kitchen sink full of dishes, here are some hints to make cleaning up less arduous.

# How Ingredients Work in Baking

Understanding the function of specific ingredients will help you make sense of why they are used and why they are combined in a certain order. With these fundamentals, you can better "read" your baking to prevent a mistake before it happens or fix it if it already has. Understanding the science behind baking is mostly about understanding how these ingredients behave when in contact with each other.

## How Protein Works in Baking

Proteins are a part of the makeup of flour, dairy and eggs, and while their primary function in baking is to set through heating, the way they behave in contact with other ingredients can vary. Here are some interesting considerations.

FLOUR PROTEINS: Called gluten, these proteins are weakest when flour is first milled. The freshly milled proteins need a little time for oxygen to develop them (in case you are grinding your own flours). Glutens need to be hydrated and exercised to bond together and give baked goods (breads especially) strength to hold the carbon dioxide that yeast produces or the gases generated by baking powder or soda. Fat and sugars interfere with gluten development, which is why cakes and cookies are tender.

MILK PROTEINS: The proteins in milk don't coagulate with heat, which is why eggs and starch are added to custards to thicken them. Acid will coagulate the proteins in lower-fat dairy products (anything less than 30% fat, so milk and half-&-half cream); Crème Fraîche (p. 94) is a perfect example. The skin that forms on heated milk is the result of whey proteins that float to the top. If you don't catch it before fully forms, remove the skin as it will not dissolve back into the milk.

EGG PROTEINS: Egg whites are primarily made of protein and water, and egg yolks are protein and fat with a little lecithin (which helps to make custards smooth), so the temperatures at which whites and yolks set are different. Keep this in mind when making custards. In the oven, the egg protein strands unwind about halfway through baking and then reset into a gel in the presence of the other ingredients. This gel traps the air created by leaveners and makes for a light-textured cake. The proteins in egg whites hold volume when air is whipped into them, and adding sugar makes this easier.

**Cooking Temperatures for Eggs**
Egg white: Thickens at 145°F (63°C) | Sets at 150°F (65°C)
Egg yolk: Thickens at 150°F (65°C) | Sets at 158°F (70°C)
Whole egg: Sets at 158°F (70°C)
Cooked custards: Set at 160°F (71°C)

## How Fat Works in Baking

We all know that fat—solids like butter or coconut oil, or liquids like vegetable oil—makes baked goods delicious. This is in part because butter starts to melt at 68°F (20°C) and is fully liquefied between 90°F and 95°F (32°C and 35°C), so it literally melts in our mouth. But fat also has specific effects when combined with other ingredients in baking. Fat interferes with the water absorption of proteins in flour, slowing the gluten development, which leads to flaky pastry and tender, delicately textured cakes. Fat also protects the proteins in dairy when heated and in the presence of acidity, provided the cream is 30% butter fat or higher. When fat is beaten or creamed with sugar, it gives batters and dough structure and volume so that cakes and cookies hold their shape and volume when baked.

Fat works to the detriment of the proteins in egg whites when adding volume is the goal. If a droplet of fat (residual fat from the bowl or a drop of egg yolk) gets into egg whites when they're being whipped, the fat repels the protein and causes the air bubbles to break and collapse, deflating your meringue.

## How Starch Works in Baking

Starch is found in wheat flour and other grains, and it is used as an ingredient on its own (cornstarch is most common) to thicken and set batters and custards. This is why, when replacing wheat flour in gluten-free baking, a substantial amount of the substitute needs to be a starch. Starch also protects the proteins in custards from overcoagulating, helping to keep them from curdling. Heat transforms starch, a type of carbohydrate, during baking so it is easily digestible and releases its nutrients. This is why we always need to cook flour.

## How Sugar Works in Baking

Beyond the obvious sweetness that sugar adds to a recipe, it also adds moisture to cakes and cookies. Brown sugar and honey are hygroscopic—they pull moisture to themselves, which is why cookies and cakes made with them stay softer and even fresher longer. Sugar also slows the setting of starch, which is why cakes with a lot of sugar take longer to set up. Sugar also prevents protein strands in flour from meshing, keeping baked goods tender and custards smooth and silky.

## How Acidity Works in Baking

Acids such as lemon juice, molasses, buttermilk, yogurt and sour cream play a big role in baking. When in contact with the proteins in flour, such as when making pie pastry, adding a little acidity causes the protein strands (gluten) in the flour to relax and stretch without breaking, making the dough easy to roll, less prone to shrink when baked and tender to eat. Acidity speeds up the coagulation of egg proteins but keeps them from bonding too tightly, making for tender cakes and smooth custards (think Tart Lemon Curd, p. 100). In candy making, acidity breaks down sucrose into glucose and fructose, turning granulated sugar into an invert syrup that won't crystallize when cooked (the secret to a soft-centred butter tart). And acidity slows the browning caused by oxidization when fresh fruits like apple and pear slices are exposed to air.

## How Salt Works in Baking

Salt heightens sweetness in baked goods and desserts and reduces bitterness, which explains why we love salted caramel so much. In bread making, salt is critical to gluten formation as the dough rises, although it slows the fermentation process. And be sure salt doesn't come directly in contact with liquefied yeast when you start to mix your doughs. In direct contact, salt can kill yeast.

# How Baking Bakes

The process of working your ingredients together and their proportions will determine what happens when you are no longer in charge, that is to say, once they go into the oven. Learning what to expect when goods bake and why will empower you as a baker.

## How Pastry Bakes

BUTTER MELTING: A hot oven (375°F/190°C or higher) is key for the butter to melt while the glutens in the flour start to set, so that they hold the butter in. A lower-temperature oven could cause the butter to leach out, resulting in a flat, dense pastry.

BUTTER LIQUEFYING: As the butter continues to melt and the proteins in the flour set further, the 20% of the butter that is liquid turns into steam. The power of the evaporating steam pushes up the flour around it, making for a flaky pastry. Puff pastry, which has been repeatedly rolled and folded, has more and finer layers, while pie pastry has a rougher yet palatable flakiness. This is why a metal or, better yet, a glass pie plate is optimal for baking pastry, to maximize the heat contact.

FLOUR SETTING AND CARAMELIZING: When the pastry begins to brown, this is a sign of the Maillard reaction in which proteins and sugars crash together at the high temperature of the pastry, producing new flavours and aromas. Without this browning effect, the pastry would taste flat and flavourless.

COOLING: Setting the cooling pastry—especially croissants and puff pastry—on a wire rack allows cool air to circulate around it. This prevents condensation from forming on the tray, and in the case of a pie, the cooling air under the pan cools the crust faster so the moisture from the filling won't seep through.

## How Cake Bakes

When making a cake, we can have confidence that the ingredients have been properly measured and mixed (we can control this stage), but once that cake goes into the oven, it's all up to the oven and science to turn a sloppy raw batter into a fluffy, moist cake in just a short time. (No wonder kids love to pull up a stool in front of the oven and watch things bake. It's like magic!)

Here is what is happening while your cake bakes.

INITIAL RISING: The baking powder and baking soda start generating bubbles within the batter, which pushes it upward. The bubbles from any whipped eggs or egg whites expand from the heat of the oven as the batter warms. There is even a second rise if baking powder is used, since baking powder often has a double activation. As the batter heats up further, water within the batter produces steam, which further expands the bubbles, giving the cake even more rise.

SETTING: At the halfway point, the egg proteins unwind and reset themselves in a gel that, in combination with the other ingredients, starts to set the cake batter. At the same time, the starches in the flour absorb any remaining water and this creates and sets the delicate crumb structure of the cake.

BROWNING: The sugars and proteins in the batter start to interact at the now-higher temperature of the cake and begin to brown (called the Maillard reaction). This chemical reaction browns the top of the cake and develops delicious aromas and flavour as the sugars caramelize. Any remaining water escapes and the egg proteins shrink just a little, which is why cakes will often pull away from the edge of the pan slightly.

COOLING: Cakes need to cool in their pans on a rack for at least 15 to 20 minutes. Hot from the oven, the molecules of the now-baked cake are still very active from heat and the cake is exceptionally fragile. As the cake cools a little and the molecules slow down, it becomes less fragile and should be carefully tipped out or removed from the pan so it can cool completely on the rack. If left in the pan to cool (unless the recipe specifies otherwise, such as with tray cakes), the sides and bottom of the cake in contact with the pan will develop condensation since the moisture can't escape, and this can make the surface of the cake sticky and difficult to frost.

## How Bread Bakes

You've mixed and kneaded your bread dough, patiently waited for it to rise, shaped it and then patiently waited again for it to rise. After this investment of time, you now relinquish control of the process and the oven takes over, turning that risen dough into a beautifully golden brown and aromatic loaf of bread. So what happens to your bread as it bakes?

HEATING: A fully preheated oven is essential for circulating hot air around the dough (with or without a convection fan) in order to coax the best rise and crust development for your bread. The air circulating within the body of the oven is slightly cooler than the air near the walls of the oven, which explains why some breads, like the Farmhouse Oat & Whole Wheat Loaf (p. 410), are baked in an enamel pot—this becomes an oven within your oven and the metal of the covered pot conducts heat closer to the loaf of bread.

STEAMING: As the dough heats, the water and alcohol generated by the yeast turn to steam and evaporate. Carbon dioxide gas bubbles are produced by this steam, and puff up your loaf. A thin liquid film around each gas bubble dries and sets as the bread bakes.

SETTING: Any remaining moisture is absorbed by the starch, and the gluten in the flour tightens, binding with the starch, building structure into the bread so that it holds its shape. After the internal temperature of the bread reaches 155°F (68°C) the structure building is complete and the loaf won't rise any further.

BROWNING: The outer surface of the bread continues to dry as it bakes, sealing in the moister centre of the bread. In addition to the surface drying, once the bread itself reaches a temperature of 250°F (121°C) the proteins and sugars begin to crash together, transforming the surface to give it a deliciously golden or brown colour and a caramelized taste.

COOLING: The doneness of bread is checked by knocking on the bottom of the loaf. A hollow sound indicates that the moisture has cooked out of the bread and it is finished baking. Removing the bread from its tin immediately after it comes out of the oven ensures that the crust will stay intact—if left in the tin, the bread will develop condensation and the crust will soften. The molecules in still-hot bread are very active when the loaf is fresh from the oven; slicing when still hot will compress the loaf and make it dry out faster once it does cool. While it is hard to resist, try to let your freshly baked loaf of bread cool for at least 30 minutes before slicing.

# How High Altitude Affects Baking

The principle behind baking at high altitude—above 1,000 metres (3,280 feet)—is relatively simple, but adjusting recipes for this environment is a little trickier.

## Why Does Altitude Matter?

In a nutshell, the farther from sea level you get on this beautiful planet, the lower the air pressure will be. In baking, this means less resistance when things bake and water boiling and converting to steam at a lower temperature.

Cookies and pastries are less susceptible to these effects because they contain less water content and bake for less time, but cakes are definitely affected. At high altitudes, baking powder, baking soda and yeast expand more quickly because of less pressure and before the proteins and starches in baked goods set (see How Cake Bakes, p. 69), so the air bubbles they create collapse, causing cakes to sink or be heavy or dense. Water evaporates faster too, before starches and proteins have set, resulting in dry or heavy cakes. Here are some adaptations to help balance your baking with a higher altitude.

TEMPERATURE: Increase your oven temperature by up to 25°F (10°C). The proteins and starches will set sooner, trapping the air produced by your leaveners or eggs.

TIME: Decrease your baking time by 15% to balance the higher oven temperature.

LEAVENERS: Decrease your leaveners by 15% to slow the production of air bubbles early in the baking process.

LIQUIDS: Increase your liquids by 1 to 2 Tbsp (15 to 30 mL) for a cake, muffin or loaf batter to allow for the quicker liquid evaporation.

# How to Make High-fat Butter for Baking:

## Ghee and the Pearson Square

Canadian butter has a standardized butter-fat content of 80%, yet butter-rich recipes like croissants and puff pastry benefit from a higher-fat butter, ideally 82% to 84% butter fat. So what is a Canadian to do if buying imported or high-fat butter isn't an option? The answer is to use ghee (or clarified butter) and the Pearson Square.

First, the ghee. It is clarified butter containing 100% butter fat and no milk solids. It is used in Indian cooking because it can tolerate high temperatures. You can also buy and use vegetable ghee, made from emulsified and hardened vegetable oil, but it may lack a butter flavour. You can purchase ghee in most grocery stores or make your own by clarifying butter.

1. Melt butter in a saucepan over low heat, transfer it to a container and chill until cold.

2. Remove the solid butter mass (the ghee) and discard the milky liquid.

Second, the Pearson Square equation. It allows you to easily figure out how much ghee and how much 80% butter-fat Canadian unsalted butter to use in a recipe to make 84% butter. (It works for other recipes and ratios as well, such as how much milk plus whipping cream to replace half-&-half cream.)

1. Draw the square on the opposite page.

2. Place the desired fat content in the centre of the square (A).

3. Record the regular butter-fat content in the top left corner (B).

4. Record the ghee butter-fat content in the bottom left corner (C).

5. Subtract the smaller of A or B from the larger and record in the bottom right corner (D): 84 − 80 = 4.

6. Subtract the smaller of A or C from the larger and record in the top right corner (E): 100 − 84 = 16.

7. Read across the square to determine the parts per item: Butter = 16 parts (E = 16) and Ghee = 4 parts (D = 4).

8. Find the total sum (F) of parts (D) + (E): 4 + 16 = 20.

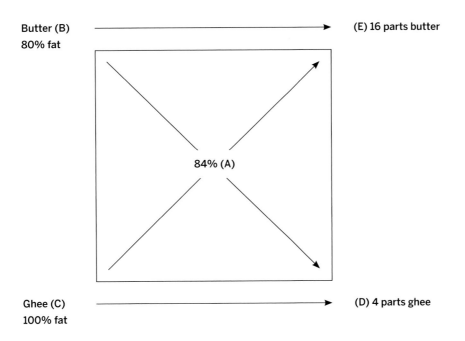

Butter (B)
80% fat

(E) 16 parts butter

84% (A)

Ghee (C)
100% fat

(D) 4 parts ghee

To apply this calculation to a specific recipe, you need to know the total amount of butter the recipe calls for. As an example, the Puff Pastry Dough (Inverted Method) (p. 162) calls for 805 g total. So the total weight (G) is 805 g.

1. Divide the total weight (G) of butter needed by the total parts (F) to obtain the weight of a single part (H): 805 g/20 = 40.25 g (G/F = H).

2. Multiply the weight of a single part (H) by the number of parts of butter (E): 40.25 g × 16 = 644 g butter (H × E = J), and the number of parts of ghee (D): 40.25 g × 4 = 161 g ghee (H × D = K).

3. To make 805 g of 84% butter, combine 644 g of regular butter and 161 g of ghee (G = J + K).

# When the Baking Is Done

Your treats are cooling or chilling and you're feeling pleased. Here's some baking wisdom to help you complete your baking project with a satisfied smile.

## Portioning Baked Goods

You've gone to a great effort to make your whole baked goods look delicious, and you'll want them to look just as lovely once they're cut into squares or slices. Here are a few tips for portioning different goodies.

PIES & TARTS: Serve baked pies in their pie plate, but you can slide tarts onto a serving platter. If serving a crowd (at least half the pie/tart, or more), cut the pie/tart in half. Then divide the half into wedge portions using a chef's knife. Repeat each cut to make sure it is fully cut through. (If you're cutting through layers of cream and fruit, you may need to wipe your knife between cuts.)

*If you prefer to cut slices one at a time, cut the first slice so that the two angled cuts meet and cross over each other in the centre by a little. The first slice is the most difficult to remove, and this little crossover ensures the first slice will have a nice point to it when removed.*

Before serving individual pieces, have your serving plates at hand. Slide an angled pie lifter under the pie/tart, loosening it if it's still in the pan, and lift straight up.

CAKES: If you are serving the entire cake, or most of it, cut it in half and then into quarters (follow the face of a clock, making a cut from 12 to 6 and then from 9 to 3). Each quarter can then be portioned into three or four slices more manageably. If serving smaller portions of a cake to a large crowd, cut the cake in parallel slices an inch (2.5 cm) across, regardless of whether the cake is round or square. Gently let each slice fall before cutting the next, and portion that slice into single servings of the desired size and repeat. You can get up to 28 servings from an 8-inch (20 cm) round cake.

CHEESECAKES: Cut one slice of cheesecake at a time. Pre-portioning the whole cake tends to make a mess because the soft-textured slices may fuse back together before you can get them to the plate. To cut the cheesecake cleanly, dip a chef's knife in a pitcher of very hot tap water for about 30 seconds to warm it through. Dry the knife and make your first cut. Dip the knife back into the water to rewarm it and clean it, then wipe dry and repeat. The re-dippings into the hot water will take less time than the initial dip into the water.

BARS: Using the parchment paper, remove the complete uncut item from the pan and lift it onto a cutting board. Peel away and discard the parchment from the sides of the pan. Determine if you want to trim away the outside edges of your baked good (some like the end pieces best).

Before making any cuts, use a ruler to measure and then use a knife to make a mark at each cut point on all four sides of the square or rectangle. For best results, begin by cutting the item in half. (You'll get straighter cuts by working with smaller pieces.) Using a sharp chef's knife, cut through one of the centre marks and then straight down. Portion the bars from each half and then cut the half in half again, making four quarters. For 36 small squares, each quarter can now be easily portioned into nine by cutting it into thirds in each direction, or you can portion into rectangular bars or other shapes. What counts is that portioning is more manageable when working from a smaller piece.

# Storing Baked (& Unbaked) Goods

Whether you have leftover birthday cake from a party, are planning for an upcoming dinner party or are getting ahead on holiday baking, knowing what can be made ahead and frozen before or after baking is very helpful. In general, I find 3 months is the ideal frozen life of unbaked and baked items. After 3 months, baked goods may get freezer burn (white patches or markings) on the surface or start absorbing odours and flavours from other goods in the freezer. Baked items that do not freeze well include baked or assembled pies and tarts, custards, chocolates and confections. Store these items as noted in the method of individual recipes.

Here are tips to guide you through the general ins and outs of storing baked goods.

**PIES:** Unbaked fruit pies can be frozen, but it's not ideal. If you do freeze them, bake the pie straight from the freezer at 425°F (220°C) for 15 minutes and then reduce the temperature to 375°F (190°C) and continue to bake for 50 to 60 minutes. You may have to cover the edge of the pie with foil to protect it from overbaking due to this additional bake time.

**PASTRIES:** Unbaked pie pastry, sweet dough and puff pastry freeze very well. Wrap them well and thaw in the fridge overnight before using. Unbaked croissants freeze very well. Thaw them on a baking tray on the counter, but add an extra 90 minutes to the proof time called for, or thaw overnight in the fridge and follow the regular proof time.

You can freeze delicate baked pastries made using puff pastry, but they are very fragile. If freezing, wrap them but take care not to stack other items on top of them, even after they are completely frozen. Baked croissants can be frozen and then thawed on the counter and reheated in a 325°F (160°C) oven for a few minutes to crisp up the outside.

**CAKES:** Some cake batters can be frozen, as long as the batter doesn't contain whipped eggs or whipped egg whites. Pack the batter in an airtight container or resealable bag and freeze. Thaw fully in the fridge, then beat the batter by hand to smooth it out. Transfer to your pans and bake for 2 to 5 minutes longer than the suggested bake time to balance out the chilled temperature of the batter. Even cheesecake batter can be frozen; thaw it completely in the fridge and mix on low speed before baking.

You can also freeze baked but unfrosted cake layers, even sponge cakes. Wrap each layer separately before freezing, and thaw on the counter before frosting. I don't recommend freezing fully assembled cakes before they have been presented for their special moment, but leftover cake can be wrapped well and frozen. Do not stack other items on the cake, as it may not freeze firmly. Leftover cheesecake can be frozen and thawed in the fridge.

**COOKIES:** Unbaked cookie doughs freeze far better than baked cookies; they take up less room in the freezer, aren't as fragile and are easy to thaw and bake. Label all frozen cookie doughs with the name, portion instructions and bake time and temperature so you don't have to refer to the recipe later. The way you freeze your cookie doughs depends on the style of cookie dough.

*For drop cookies,* scoop, freeze on a tray or plate and then pack into an airtight container. This way you can pull out just two or three cookies to bake to order, or the whole batch to bake at once. The portions of dough can thaw on the baking tray until ready to bake. *For cut-out or sliced cookie doughs,* freeze into discs to be rolled or logs to be sliced after thawing. Thaw in the fridge overnight before preparing to bake. *For batters, such as for Classic Florentine Cookies (p. 394),* pour into an airtight container and freeze well. Thaw in the fridge overnight before preparing to bake. *Delicate batters and meringue batters,* such as macaron batter, do not freeze well since they are meant to be baked immediately after making.

If you want to freeze your baked cookies, those with a low sugar content (such as Walnut Snowball Cookies, p. 386) freeze better than very sweet cookies. Crisp, sweet cookies like Classic Florentine Cookies (p. 394) will become sticky and soft once thawed. It is best to freeze cookies without icing sugar dusting or icing; these, too, will melt or soften once thawed.

**BREAD:** Unbaked yeast doughs freeze very well because the yeast goes dormant. It's best to make the dough and let it go through its first rise, shape it, fill it if called for and then freeze. Thaw the dough in the fridge overnight to slowly bring the yeast back to life as the dough thaws. After thawing, let the bread proof on the counter as instructed in the recipe before baking.

Wrap baked breads well and freeze, then thaw on the counter before using. Warming the thawed bread in a 325°F (160°C) oven will freshen it up and bring back the crust if it had one when freshly baked.

## Cleaning Up

Washing up after a baking project comes with the territory—unfortunately there is no way to avoid it—but here are a few tips to make cleaning even the stickiest messes easier. Knowing what can be put into the dishwasher and what needs to be washed by hand is important to ensure that your baking pans and tools last a long time. The chemicals and high temperatures used in machine-washing dishes can pit or break down non-stick finishes and warp wood or some plastics. Use the following list as a guide.

HAND-WASH: Non-stick metal baking pans; aluminum baking pans and tools; wooden rolling pins and boards; tools with wooden handles; plastic mixing bowls; piping bags and tips; tools with ball bearings or movable parts (such as a pastry wheel); marble boards and tools; mixer attachments with aluminum (such as whips).

MACHINE-WASH: Glass pans and bowls; stainless-steel pans, bowls and tools; ceramic or porcelain pans, dishes or bowls; silicone baking pans; enamel-coated or stainless-steel mixer attachments.

WASHING PIPING BAGS & TIPS: Fabric, silicone and even single-use plastic piping bags can be washed and reused. Remove the piping tips and soak the bag in hot soapy water, then rinse and wash the bag. It's especially important to wash away any fat residue so that if you use the bag for a meringue, the meringue won't collapse in the bag while piping. Turn the bag inside out to dry, and you can even wipe the bag with a paper towel dampened with a little white vinegar to remove any oil residue.

Soak piping tips in a dish with hot soapy water and then rinse. Refill the dish a few times with fresh soapy water. If washing a number of tips at once, pour the soaked tips into a strainer and rinse them well under hot running water. Let the tips air-dry completely before packing away.

CLEANING FLOURED OR SUGARED SURFACES: Adding water immediately to a floured or sugared counter after rolling pastry or decorating cookies makes for a sticky mess. Use a dough cutter or even an offset spatula to scrape away as much of the flour or sugar as possible before wiping down with warm soapy water.

WASHING POTS WITH CARAMELIZED SUGAR: To avoid frustration, soak pots and tools set with caramelized sugar; never try to scrub them. With a few repeated soaks in hot water, caramelized sugar will melt off any surface. If there is an excessive amount of caramelized sugar stuck in your pot, fill the pot with water and bring it to a simmer over high heat; the caramel will dissolve into the hot water. For pots with other foods burnt or stuck onto them, add 2 Tbsp (30 mL) baking soda to 4 cups (1 L) water and boil for 3 to 4 minutes to loosen the burnt bits, then rinse and wash.

Essentials

# Recipes at a Glance

These basic recipes are used to make numerous baked goods throughout the book. Many can be prepared well ahead of time, so they are at hand when you need them. They are also great stand-alone recipes to serve alongside your treats. These recipes include fillings, toppings, sauces and other elements to make a dessert more interesting in flavour, texture and décor.

## Nut Fillings & Toppings

Nuts are an integral part of baking, but these recipes help make nuts a real star in your baking, whether making mixing easier (Tant pour Tant, p. 82) or as a sparkling sprinkle on top of a dessert (Praliné Noisette, p. 85).

- **Tant pour Tant**  page 82
- **Almond Streusel**  page 82
- **Marzipan**  page 85
- **Praliné Noisette**  page 85

## Fruit Fillings & Toppings

While fresh fruit can look lovely to top a cake or tart, cooked fruits can add gorgeous colour and complexity to dessert. These are staples I always have on hand.

- **Maple Caramelized Apples**  page 86
- **Spiced Plums**  page 86
- **Poached Pears**  page 88

## Caramel & Chocolate Sauces & Fillings

These make-ahead recipes take a step out of baking. Having them on hand means you'll be ready to assemble or plate your baked delights that much sooner.

- **Salted Butter Caramel Sauce**  page 89 (and pictured opposite)
- **Dulce de Leche**  page 90
- **Chocolate Fudge Sauce & Filling**  page 91
- **Roasted White Chocolate Ganache**  page 92

## Creams & Custards

Whipped, soured or cooked into a custard, cream and milk transform into delicious additions to your baking.

- **Crème Fraîche**  page 94
- **Chantilly Cream**  page 95
- **Vanilla Pastry Cream**  page 96
- **Mousseline Cream (Crème Mousseline)**  page 97
- **Diplomat Cream (Crème Diplomat)**  page 98
- **Chiboust Cream (Crème Chiboust)**  page 99
- **Tart Lemon Curd**  page 100

**MAKES:** 4 cups (520 g)

**PREP TIME:** under 5 minutes

❗ **SIMPLE**

**USED IN:**

*Almond Pâte Sablée (Almond Sweet Dough), p. 129*

*Summer Fruit Frangipane Tart, p. 133*

*Galette des Rois, p. 176*

*Lemon Bostock Bread Pudding, p. 326*

*Macarons, p. 390*

**INGREDIENTS**

**2 cups + 3 Tbsp (260 g)** ground almonds

**2 cups (260 g)** icing sugar

# Tant pour Tant

Although its name may seem mysterious, *tant pour tant* is French for "so much for so much" and it is simply equal amounts by weight of icing sugar and ground almonds pulsed together. This blend becomes the base for so many desserts, from an Almond Pâte Sablée to a frangipane filling, but it is the key to smooth-topped Macarons (p. 390). This ingredient is now a staple in my pantry.

1. **Pulse the almonds and icing sugar** together in a food processor until well combined.

**Store in an airtight container for up to 3 months.**

---

**MAKES:** about 4 cups (1 L)

**PREP TIME:** under 10 minutes
**COOK TIME:** 25 minutes

❗ **SIMPLE**

**USED IN:**

*Blueberry & Greek Yogurt Breakfast Galette, p. 118*

*Lemon Crunch-&-Cream Tray Cake, p. 258*

*Creamy Mascarpone Mousse, p. 296*

*Almond Streusel Jam Squares, p. 398*

**INGREDIENTS**

**¾ cup (90 g)** ground almonds

**½ cup (75 g)** all-purpose flour

**⅓ cup (70 g)** packed light brown sugar

**½ tsp** ground cinnamon

**5 Tbsp (75 g)** unsalted butter, cool and cut into pieces

**1 Tbsp (15 mL)** rum, kirsch or other unsweetened spirit

# Almond Streusel

An unbaked streusel topping recipe is treated like an ingredient in a baker's repertoire. Before baking, it can be used to top muffins, loaves or fruit pies, or it can become a fruit crisp or even jam square. Baked, it adds crunch to a bowl of ice cream or it can be sprinkled between cake layers with frosting.

1. **For prebaked streusel, preheat the oven** to 325°F (160°C) and line a baking tray with parchment paper.

2. **Mix the streusel ingredients.** Combine the ground almonds, flour, brown sugar and cinnamon in a mixing bowl or the bowl of a stand mixer fitted with the paddle attachment. If mixing by hand, use a pastry cutter to work in the butter until a fine crumble, or mix on low speed. Add the rum or other spirit and continue to mix until the streusel just begins to bind and hold in larger clumps. Use immediately as is, store in an airtight container and refrigerate for up to 3 weeks, or bake and use.

*Adding spirits lends a bit of flavour and helps to preserve the unbaked streusel in the fridge longer. Once baked, the alcohol evaporates, leaving the streusel crunchy. For an alcohol-free version, replace the 1 Tbsp (15 mL) spirits with 1 Tbsp (15 g) butter.*

3. **Bake the streusel.** Spread the streusel onto the baking tray and bake for about 25 minutes, stirring once halfway through baking, until golden brown. Place the tray on a wire rack and let the streusel cool completely.

**Store baked streusel in an airtight container for up to 4 weeks.**

**MAKES:** about 1 lb (450 g)

**PREP TIME:** 20 minutes
**COOK TIME:** 5 minutes

**⸙ SIMPLE**

**USED IN:**
*Gingerbread Petits Fours, p. 223*
*Swedish Semlor, p. 428*
*Holiday Stollen, p. 431*

**INGREDIENTS**

1¾ cups (210 g) ground almonds

1 cup (200 g) granulated sugar

¼ cup (75 g) honey

2 Tbsp (30 mL) water

1 tsp pure almond extract (optional)

# Marzipan

This sweet, pliable almond confection can be used in many ways. I prefer to make my own because I can be assured of its freshness and control how much almond extract I want to add, if any.

1. **Place the ground almonds** in a food processor.

2. **Place the sugar, honey and water in a small saucepan** over high heat and stir until it just reaches a boil and the sugar has completely dissolved. With the food processor running, pour in the hot syrup. Add the almond extract, if using, and blend until the marzipan comes together.

3. **Shape the marzipan** into a log while it's still warm and wrap well in plastic wrap. Let sit at room temperature to cool until you are ready to use it.

   **Store well wrapped in the pantry for up to a month or freeze for up to 3 months. Thaw on the counter before using.**

**MAKES:** about 2 cups (300 g)

**PREP TIME:** 10 minutes
**COOK TIME:** 10 minutes

**⸙ SIMPLE**

**BITES OF WISDOM:**
*How to cook & caramelize sugar (p. 38)*

**USED IN:**
*Roasted White Chocolate & Pumpkin Pie, p. 124*
*Chocolate Hazelnut Cream Pie, p. 127*
*Individual Peanut Butter Paris-Brests, p. 199*
*Torta Setteveli, p. 277*
*Îles Flottantes, p. 318*

**INGREDIENTS**

2 Tbsp (30 mL) water

1 tsp lemon juice or white vinegar

½ cup (100 g) granulated sugar

2 cups (270 g) whole hazelnuts, toasted and peeled (see How to Toast Nuts, p. 36)

# Praliné Noisette

As an ingredient, these caramelized hazelnut pieces elevate a recipe to something special, and as a garnish, they add a sweet crunch and golden sparkle to many desserts. You can also vary the nuts: make praliné amandes using 2 cups (320 g) whole blanched, toasted almonds or praliné arachides using the same volume measurement of roasted peanuts.

1. **Line a baking tray with parchment paper** or a silicone baking mat.

2. **Caramelize the sugar.** Measure the water and lemon juice (or vinegar) into a saucepan, then add the sugar. Bring to a boil over high heat without stirring, and boil, uncovered, until the sugar reaches 240°F (116°C) on a candy thermometer.

3. **Add the hazelnuts.** Remove the pot from the heat, stir in the hazelnuts to coat them and then return the pot to the heat (still on high). Continue to cook, stirring, until the sugar turns a rich amber colour. Quickly scrape the hazelnuts onto the baking tray and spread them out as much as you can. Cool the tray on a wire rack completely before using.

   *Don't worry if the sugar crystallizes when you add the nuts—it's the temperature shock. Once returned to the heat, the sugar will melt and liquefy again.*

4. **Chop the praliné** by hand for larger pieces or pulse in a food processor for a finer praliné.

   **Store praliné noisette in an airtight container in the pantry for up to 6 weeks.**

**⏲ SIMPLE**

SERVED WITH:

*Maple Pumpkin Scones, p. 161*

INGREDIENTS

2 Tbsp (30 g) butter

2 cups (350 g) peeled and diced apples

3 Tbsp (45 mL) maple syrup

¼ tsp ground cinnamon

# Maple Caramelized Apples

A cooked fruit filling is perfect when you need the filling to stay in place and not drip, like in fruit-filled brioches or Danishes. The maple caramelized apple filling is great in pies or tarts too (triple the recipe), or as a side for other desserts or a sauce for waffles or pancakes.

1. **Cook the apples.** Heat a large sauté pan over medium-high and melt the butter. Add the apples and stir often, cooking until they begin to soften and start to sizzle, about 4 minutes.

2. **Add the spices.** Add the maple syrup and cinnamon and continue to cook for 5 minutes, stirring often, until most of the liquid evaporates but there is enough to coat the apples. Remove the apples from the heat to cool, then chill until ready to use.

*Add ½ cup (50 g) fresh or frozen cranberries and 1 Tbsp (15 mL) extra maple syrup for an apple-cranberry filling.*

**The filling will keep in an airtight container in the fridge for up to 3 days.**

---

MAKES: about 4 cups (1 L)

PREP TIME: 10 minutes
COOK TIME: 20 minutes

**⏲ SIMPLE**

USED IN:

*Apple, Spiced Plum & Cranberry Pie, p. 116*

*Blueberry & Greek Yogurt Breakfast Galette, p. 118*

*Creamy Mascarpone Mousse, p. 296*

INGREDIENTS

2 lb (900 g) Italian prune plums, or red or black plums

½ cup (125 mL) water

1 orange

1 lemon

3 whole star anise

1 tsp ground cinnamon

½ tsp ground cloves

½ tsp ground allspice

1½ cups (300 g) granulated sugar

# Spiced Plums

I make big batches of these cooked plums when Italian or German prune plums are in season, but any type of plum will work. I've nicknamed these "breakfast plums" because I love spooning a few and the spiced syrup over my oatmeal on cold mornings.

1. **Prep and simmer the plums.** Wash the plums and cut them in half, removing the pits. If the plums are large, cut the halves into quarters or sixths and place them in a saucepan. Add the water. Cut the orange and lemon in half, squeeze the juice into the pot and drop in the halves. Add the star anise, cinnamon, cloves and allspice and bring to a full simmer, uncovered, over medium heat, stirring occasionally.

*Red or black plums break down more when cooking and have more water in them than prune plums. You may need to cook them for an additional 15 minutes to thicken the mixture.*

2. **Add the sugar.** Once the plums reach a full simmer, add the sugar and continue to simmer for about 15 minutes, until the plums are tender yet still hold their shape. Remove the pan from the heat and let cool to room temperature. Remove the citrus halves and star anise before packing the plums into a jar.

**Store spiced plums in an airtight container in the fridge for up to 3 months.**

**MAKES:** 4 pears (8 halves)

**PREP TIME:** under 10 minutes
**COOK TIME:** 20 minutes

**SIMPLE**

**USED IN:**
*Vanilla Pear Chiboust Torte, p. 235*
*Poires Belle Hélène with Chocolate Crémeux, p. 317*

### INGREDIENTS

4 firm yet ripe Bartlett or Bosc pears

2 cups (400 g) granulated sugar

2 cups (500 mL) water with **2 Tbsp (30 mL)** lemon juice or **2 cups (500 mL)** dry white wine

# Poached Pears

Pears are such an elegant fruit to bake with because of their rounded shape and delicate fruit flavour. Raw pears are rarely used in baking because they discolour easily and break down messily. Poaching pears sets the colour and shape, and the poaching liquid provides a little extra flavour.

1. **Prepare the pears and the poaching liquid.** Peel the pears, cut them in half and scoop out the core with a melon baller or teaspoon. Bring the sugar and water with lemon juice (or the white wine) to a simmer in a medium saucepan over medium-high heat.

   *If you know how you will be using your pears, tailor the poaching liquid to coordinate. For example, if making the Vanilla Pear Chiboust Torte (p. 235), add the seeds from half of a vanilla bean to the syrup.*

2. **Add the pears to the liquid** and reduce the heat if necessary to get a gentle simmer. Cover the surface of the liquid with a piece of parchment cut to fit inside the pot, and top with a small plate or lid to keep the pears under the surface of the liquid.

3. **Poach the pears** for about 20 minutes, until they are tender when pierced with a fork or skewer. (If the pears are on the firmer side, let them poach for another 10 minutes to soften them.) Remove the pot from the heat to cool, then transfer the pears and the liquid to a bowl to chill until ready to serve.

   **Store in an airtight container in the fridge for up to 5 days.**

**MAKES:** about 3 cups (750 mL)

**PREP TIME:** under 10 minutes, plus chilling

**COOK TIME:** 8 minutes

**⚑ SIMPLE**

**BITES OF WISDOM:**

*How to cook & caramelize sugar (p. 38)*

**SERVED WITH OR IN:**

*Caramelized Pineapple Tart with Coconut Chiboust, p. 136*

*Chocolate Soufflé, p. 303*

*Butter Ganache Bonbons, p. 346*

**INGREDIENTS**

¼ cup (60 mL) water

**2 cups (400 g)** granulated sugar

**1 tsp** white vinegar or lemon juice

**1 cup (250 mL)** whipping cream

**½ cup (115 g)** unsalted butter, cut into pieces

**2 tsp** flaked sea salt

# Salted Butter Caramel Sauce

There is caramel sauce, and then there is salted butter caramel sauce. The latter has a deeper, richer flavour and a thicker set than a cream-only caramel sauce, and when softened slightly has the perfect consistency for creating those appealing drips that cascade off the top of a cake or surprise you inside a chocolate bonbon.

1. **Caramelize the sugar.** Measure the water and then the sugar and vinegar (or lemon juice) in a medium saucepan and bring to a full boil over high heat without stirring. Continue to boil the sugar, occasionally brushing down the sides of the pan with water (to prevent the sugar from crystallizing), until the sugar turns an even amber colour.

2. **Stir in the cream and butter.** Remove the pot from the heat and add the cream all at once, whisking to combine (1) (watch out for steam—the caramel will bubble up too). Add the butter a few pieces at a time, whisking until it melts in (2). Stir in the sea salt (3), cool to room temperature and then chill for at least 2 hours before using.

**Store in an airtight container in the fridge until the best-before date of your cream.**

**MAKES:** one 10 oz (300 mL) tin

**PREP TIME:** under 5 minutes, plus chilling
**COOK TIME:** 3 hours

**⁎ SIMPLE**

**USED IN:**
*Chocolate Peanut Butter & Dulce de Leche Lava Cakes, p. 226*
*Alfajor Cheesecake, p. 267*
*Banoffee Crème Brûlée, p. 313*
*Alfajores, p. 389*

**INGREDIENTS**

1 (10 oz/300 mL) tin sweetened condensed milk

# Dulce de Leche

This thicker version of caramel—a combination of milk sugars and sugar rather than simple caramelized sugar—gives dulce de leche its own intense flavour personality. It is immensely popular in South America, where two styles are commonly sold. The softer, lighter-coloured dulce de leche is for spreading on toast. The thicker, darker style is used to fill cakes and pastries.

1. **Prepare the condensed milk for cooking.** Peel the label from the tin and place the tin, unopened, in a deep pot. Fill the pot with water so that the tin is covered by at least 2 inches (5 cm).

   *For safety reasons, be sure to keep the water level well above the top of the tin at all times to prevent the tin from leaking or even exploding. Check the pot often during cooking and top up the water when needed.*

2. **Simmer the milk.** Bring the water to a simmer, uncovered and over medium heat, so that bubbles gently break the surface of the water. Continue to simmer, uncovered, for 3 hours for a thick dulce de leche (2 hours for a lighter, thinner dulce de leche sauce).

   *If you have a silicone trivet or mat to place in the bottom of the pot, it will prevent the mildly annoying rattle that the tin makes as it simmers away.*

3. **Cool the tin.** Remove the pot from the heat and use tongs to lift the tin out onto a rack to cool. Cool the tin, unopened, on the counter for 2 hours and then chill for at least 4 hours before opening.

   **Store the dulce de leche in the fridge for up to a month once opened and up to 3 months if unopened.**

**MAKES:** about 3 cups (750 mL)

**PREP TIME:** under 10 minutes, plus chilling
**COOK TIME:** 8 minutes

**SIMPLE**

**USED IN:**
*Chocolate Peanut Butter Cream Cake,*
*p. 253*

**INGREDIENTS**

1 cup (250 mL) whipping cream

½ cup (60 g) Dutch-process cocoa
powder

½ cup (100 g) granulated sugar

¼ cup (50 g) packed light brown sugar

¼ cup (60 mL) white corn syrup

6 oz (180 g) dark baking/couverture
chocolate, chopped

¼ cup (60 g) unsalted butter

1 tsp vanilla extract

½ tsp fine salt

# Chocolate Fudge Sauce & Filling

The versatility of this chocolate sauce makes it an essential if chocolate desserts are your specialty. Use it warm as a sauce or at room temperature as a filling or frosting to spread or pipe. Once chilled, it sets up with the texture of a chocolate truffle-style ganache.

1. **Cook the sauce base.** Bring the cream, cocoa powder, granulated sugar, brown sugar and corn syrup to a simmer over medium heat, whisking often, until smooth.

2. **Add the remaining ingredients.** Stir in the chocolate and butter and return to a simmer while whisking constantly. Stir in the vanilla and salt and remove from the heat. Cool to room temperature and then chill for at least 4 hours before using.

   **Store in an airtight container in the fridge for up to 3 weeks or the best-before date of your cream, whichever is sooner.**

**PREP TIME:** under 15 minutes
**COOK TIME:** 1 hour

❙ **SIMPLE**

**USED IN:**
*Roasted White Chocolate & Pumpkin Pie, p. 124*

*Butter Ganache Bonbons, p. 346*

**INGREDIENTS**

**8 oz (240 g)** white baking/couverture chocolate, chopped

**½ cup (125 mL)** whipping cream

# Roasted White Chocolate Ganache

Commercially made "gold" or caramel chocolate is starting to appear in specialty stores, but making your own isn't terribly difficult. White chocolate is oven baked to caramelize the sugars within, giving the chocolate a caramelized taste and a rich brown colour. Adding cream turns it into a versatile ganache that can be used as an ingredient in baking or chocolate making.

1. **Preheat the oven** to 250°F (120°C).

2. **Melt and roast the chocolate.** Place the chopped chocolate into a 9-inch (23 cm) glass pie plate or ceramic dish of similar size. Roast the chocolate, uncovered, for 1 hour, stirring every 15 minutes. The chocolate will become a light caramel colour.

   *While roasting, chocolate naturally goes through an amazing transformation. It may almost appear to seize. Keep stirring for about a minute every 15 minutes, and by the time the hour is up and the cream is added, it will reach a smooth, silky consistency.*

   *Here are the visual cues at each 15-minute mark:*

   *After 15 minutes: Chocolate is fluid once stirred. Press out any lumps with a spatula (1).*

   *After 30 minutes: Chocolate is beige on the surface, is darker underneath once stirred and has lost its shine. Stir the chocolate very well. It will be tight at first but will smooth out to become spreadable (but not fluid) (2).*

   *After 45 minutes: Chocolate is similar to how it was at 30 minutes, but darker and tighter and grainier. Stir for a full minute to make it smooth.*

   *After 1 hour: Chocolate is very tight and grainy. Keep stirring. The chocolate will become smooth and spreadable, and the shine will return (it will look like melted peanut butter, shown in the photo on the opposite page).*

3. **Make the ganache.** Heat the cream in a small saucepan over medium heat to just below a simmer. Remove the pan from the heat and scrape in the roasted white chocolate, whisking gently until smooth and well combined. The ganache will have the same colour and texture as a caramel sauce. Cool the ganache to room temperature and then chill until ready to use.

   *Heated, the ganache becomes a luscious sauce with the silkiness of a chocolate sauce but the flavour of a caramel sauce.*

**Store ganache in an airtight container in the fridge until the best-before date on the cream you used.**

**MAKES:** just under 1 cup (250 mL)

**PREP TIME:** under 5 minutes (make a day ahead), plus resting

❚ SIMPLE

**INGREDIENTS**

**1 cup (250 mL)** whipping cream

**1 Tbsp (15 mL)** buttermilk or fresh lemon juice

# Crème Fraîche

Crème fraîche is a high-fat soured cream made from whipping cream. It has 30% fat content and milder flavour compared to regular full-fat sour cream, which is 14% fat content and tangy, makes it a great addition to raw desserts and for whipping. Crème fraîche is delicious served in place of clotted cream with Classic English Scones (p. 158) and jam, or alongside sweet desserts like Sticky Toffee Date Loaf (p. 211).

1. **Sour the cream.** Stir the cream and buttermilk (or lemon juice) together, place in a glass pitcher or bowl and cover. Set the pitcher into a larger bowl and fill the larger bowl with hot tap water up to the line of the cream. Let sit on the counter for 24 to 36 hours.

   *I find I get a tighter set to the crème fraîche using buttermilk, but don't go and buy a large carton of buttermilk just for this 1 Tbsp (15 mL) when lemon juice also works.*

2. **Check and chill the crème fraîche.** Lift the glass pitcher or bowl out of the water and look to see if there is liquid separated and sitting at the bottom. If not, let the pitcher sit out for another 12 hours (not in a water bath this time). Do not stir. Chill the pitcher for 3 hours, then spoon off the crème fraîche without stirring in the whey. Chill until ready to use.

   *You can discard the whey or use it in place of buttermilk in a recipe. Keep it in an airtight container in the fridge for no more than 2 to 3 days.*

   *If you are making the crème fraîche in wintry, dry weather, it can take almost 2 days to sour compared with under 24 hours on a hot, humid summer day. The key is to not stir in the liquid that naturally separates—this way you'll have a thick, rich crème fraîche after it has chilled.*

**Store in an airtight container in the fridge until the best-before date of the whipping cream.**

**MAKES:** about 2 cups (500 mL)

**PREP TIME:** under 5 minutes

❗ **SIMPLE**

**BITES OF WISDOM:**
*How to repair overwhipped cream (p. 56)*

**INGREDIENTS**

1 cup (250 mL) whipping cream

1 Tbsp (8 g) instant skim milk powder (optional)

1½ Tbsp (12 g) icing sugar

½ tsp vanilla extract or vanilla bean paste

# Chantilly Cream

This is the fancy name for whipped cream that has been lightly sweetened and flavoured with a hint of vanilla. Chantilly cream is immensely versatile, as the long list of recipes where it is used indicates.

1. **Whip the cream** and skim milk powder, if using, by hand or with beaters on high speed until it holds a soft peak.

   *Use the skim milk powder if you are whipping the cream ahead of time. It stabilizes the whipped cream so that it holds its shape for hours (whereas regular whipped cream will start to deflate within a few hours).*

2. **Whip in the icing sugar and vanilla** and chill until ready to use.

   **Store in an airtight container in the fridge for up to 2 days.**

# Vanilla Pastry Cream

Vanilla is the basic flavouring for this foundation custard recipe, but it can easily take on other flavours. Even if you are changing the flavour of your pastry cream, leave the vanilla in the recipe to round out the taste.

**MAKES:** about 3 cups (750 mL)

**PREP TIME:** under 10 minutes, plus chilling
**COOK TIME:** 10 minutes

❗ SIMPLE

**BITES OF WISDOM:**
*How to temper eggs (p. 33)*

**USED IN:**
*Diplomat Cream, p. 98*

*Chiboust Cream, p. 99*

*Chocolate Hazelnut Cream Pie, p. 127*

*Esterházy Torte, p. 273*

*Pineapple & Pink Peppercorn Pavlova, p. 322*

**INGREDIENTS**

⅔ **cup (140 g)** granulated sugar

¼ **cup (30 g)** cornstarch

**2 cups (500 mL)** 2% milk

**6** large egg yolks

¼ **cup (60 g)** unsalted butter, cut into pieces

**2 tsp** vanilla extract

1. **Combine the ingredients.** Whisk the sugar and cornstarch together in a large saucepan, then whisk in the milk, followed by the egg yolks. Place the butter and vanilla in a medium heatproof bowl and set a strainer on top.

   *The traditional method for making custard involved heating the milk, then slowly adding it to the yolks, sugar and cornstarch (a step called tempering) before returning it to the heat to cook quickly. This more contemporary method—combining all of the ingredients except the butter and vanilla in the pot—allows the mixture to heat up gradually. As you whisk the pastry cream, you can easily feel when it begins to thicken and avoid overcooking.*

2. **Cook the pastry cream.** Bring the milk mixture to a full simmer at just above medium heat while whisking constantly (but not vigorously) until it begins to bubble and is very thick, about 10 minutes. Pour the custard through the strainer, using the whisk to push it through. Remove the strainer and whisk the custard in the bowl until the butter has melted.

   *If you do accidentally overcook your custard (it will look lumpy or curdled), there is a fix. Pour the hot custard into a blender, or use an immersion blender, and purée on high speed for 10 seconds. Immediately strain the custard over the butter and then continue.*

3. **Cool and chill.** Place a piece of plastic wrap directly on the surface of the custard, let cool on the counter for an hour and then refrigerate for at least 2 hours.

   **Store in an airtight container in the fridge for up to 5 days.**

**MAKES:** about 3 cups (750 mL)

**PREP TIME:** under 10 minutes, plus chilling
**COOK TIME:** 10 minutes

❗ **SIMPLE**
**USED IN:**
*Profiteroles au Craquelin, p. 193*

**INGREDIENTS**

⅔ cup (140 g) granulated sugar

¼ cup (30 g) cornstarch

2 cups (500 mL) 2% milk

6 large egg yolks

¾ cup (175 g) unsalted butter, divided, at room temperature and cut into pieces

# Mousseline Cream (Crème Mousseline)

This rich pastry cream thickened and enriched with additional butter holds its shape better than regular pastry cream when being piped or used as a filling. It makes a satisfying filling in smaller amounts, such as in Profiteroles au Craquelin (p. 193). One batch of this recipe can make up to three different flavours (see below).

1. **Combine the ingredients.** Whisk the sugar and cornstarch together in a large saucepan, then whisk in the milk, followed by the egg yolks. Place 6 Tbsp (90 g) butter in a medium heatproof bowl and set a strainer on top.

2. **Cook the pastry cream.** Bring the milk mixture to a full simmer at just above medium heat while whisking constantly (but not vigorously) until it begins to bubble and is very thick, about 10 minutes. Pour the custard through the strainer, using the whisk to push it through. Remove the strainer and whisk the custard in the bowl until the butter has melted.

3. **Cool and add more butter.** Let the pastry cream cool to just above room temperature (77°F/25°C). Using electric beaters or a stand mixer fitted with the whip attachment, beat the pastry cream on medium speed, add the remaining butter a little at a time, and stir in any flavourings (see below). Keep the cream covered or in an airtight container in the fridge until ready to use.

*Having the pastry cream just above room temperature is the key to working the added butter in smoothly. Too warm and the butter will melt. Too cool and the mousseline will not be smooth.*

**Store in an airtight container in the fridge for up to 5 days.**

**VARIATIONS**

**Tahini Mousseline:** Whisk **1 Tbsp (15 mL) tahini paste** and **two to three drops sesame oil** into 1 cup (250 mL) warm mousseline, and then chill.

**Lemon Mousseline:** Stir the **zest of two lemons** and **1½ Tbsp (22 mL)** cold milk into the still-warm mousseline, and then chill.

**Saffron Lemon Mousseline:** Stir **four to six saffron threads** into **1½ Tbsp (22 mL)** cold milk and let sit for 5 minutes. Stir the **zest of two lemons** and the saffron milk into the still-warm mousseline, and then chill.

**Matcha Green Tea Mousseline:** Whisk **1 tsp matcha green tea powder** into 1 cup (250 mL) still-warm mousseline and add **a drop or two of green food colouring** to brighten the green hue, and then chill.

**MAKES:** about 3 cups (750 mL)

**PREP TIME:** under 10 minutes, plus chilling

❦ **SIMPLE**

**USED IN:**
*Strawberry Chocolate Tart, p. 134*
*Caramelized Peach Mille-feuille, p. 181*
*Éclairs, p. 195*
*Individual Peanut Butter Paris-Brests, p. 199*

**INGREDIENTS**

2 tsp (7 g) gelatin powder

2 Tbsp (30 mL) cold water

1 recipe Vanilla Pastry Cream (p. 96), freshly made and still warm

1 cup (250 mL) whipping cream

# Diplomat Cream (Crème Diplomat)

This versatile pastry cream is airier than the original because of the whipped cream, and it sets well thanks to a little gelatin. Diplomat cream is ideal for holding piping detail or as a filling for cakes and tarts. Turn one batch into three different flavours (see below) for filling Éclairs (p. 195) or Individual Peanut Butter Paris-Brests (p. 199).

1. **Soften the gelatin.** Stir the gelatin powder with the cold water in a small dish and set aside.

2. **Add gelatin to pastry cream and cool.** Whisk the gelatin into the warm pastry cream, then place a piece of plastic wrap directly on the surface of the custard. Let cool on the counter until it reaches room temperature or just slightly warmer, about 90 minutes.

3. **Fold in the whipped cream and chill.** Using a whisk or a stand mixer fitted with the whip attachment, whip the cream until it holds a soft peak. Add to the cooled custard all at once and fold in until fully incorporated. Cover and refrigerate until set, at least 2 hours. The cream can also be made a day ahead.

**Store in an airtight container in the fridge for up to 3 days.**

**VARIATIONS**

The following flavour additions can each be integrated into a single recipe of the Diplomat Cream. Take note that the raspberry version has the flavouring added after the pastry cream has cooled, while the rest are added while the pastry is still warm.

**Raspberry:** Stir **1½ tsp freeze-dried raspberry powder** into the cooled pastry cream before you fold in the whipped cream. You can add **a few drops of pink food colouring** to heighten the pink colour.

**Pistachio White Chocolate:** Pulse **¼ cup (30 g) shelled pistachios** with **1 oz (30 g) white chocolate** until finely ground. Whisk this mixture into the still-warm pastry cream before cooling and folding in the whipped cream.

**Chocolate:** Stir **1½ oz (45 g) chopped dark baking/couverture chocolate** into the still-warm pastry cream before cooling and folding in the whipped cream.

**Peanut Butter:** Whisk **¾ cup (187 g) smooth peanut butter** into the still-warm pastry cream, after dissolving the gelatin into the cream. Cool to room temperature before folding in the whipped cream.

**Caramel:** Whisk **6 Tbsp (90 mL) Dulce de Leche** (p. 90) into 3 cups (750 mL) still-warm pastry cream, after dissolving the gelatin into the cream. Cool to room temperature before folding in the whipped cream.

**⫚ SIMPLE**

**USED IN:**

*Caramelized Pineapple Tart with Coconut Chiboust, p. 136*

*Vanilla Pear Chiboust Torte, p. 235*

## INGREDIENTS

---

**2 tsp (7 g)** gelatin powder

**4 Tbsp (60 mL)** cold water , divided

**½ recipe** Vanilla Pastry Cream (p. 96), freshly made and still warm

**3 large** egg whites, at room temperature

**½ cup (100 g)** granulated sugar

# Chiboust Cream (Crème Chiboust)

This pastry cream is lightened with an Italian meringue and set with a little gelatin for stability. It is so fluffy that it can be enjoyed even as a dessert on its own, poured into glasses and topped with fruit. Try flavouring the cream (see below) for desserts such as the Caramelized Pineapple Tart with Coconut Chiboust (p. 136).

1. **Soften the gelatin.** Stir the gelatin powder with 2 Tbsp (30 mL) of the cold water in a small dish and set aside.

2. **Add gelatin to pastry cream and cool.** Whisk the gelatin into the warm pastry cream, then place a piece of plastic wrap directly on the surface of the custard. Let cool on the counter until it reaches room temperature or just slightly warmer, about an hour.

3. **Make the Italian meringue.** Using electric beaters, whip the egg whites at high speed until foamy. Set aside. Bring the sugar and the remaining 2 Tbsp (30 mL) of water (it does not have to be cold) to a full boil over high heat without stirring. Boil until the sugar reaches 240°F (116°C)—this takes only a minute. With the beaters whipping the egg whites at high speed, carefully pour the hot sugar into the bowl, letting the sugar run down the inside of the bowl into the whites. Continue to whip the whites until they hold a stiff peak but are still warm.

   *Letting the hot sugar run down the inside of the bowl rather than pouring it directly into the egg whites prevents it splashing.*

4. **Fold the meringue into the cooled pastry cream** in two additions, folding gently but well after each one.

   **If using the chiboust cream in another recipe, use immediately, otherwise store in an airtight container in the fridge for up to 3 days.**

### VARIATION

---

**Coconut Lime:** Prepare a ½ recipe of pastry cream as directed in the recipe (p. 96), but use **1 cup (250 mL) coconut milk** in place of the 2% milk and add the **zest of 1 lime** to the pot before heating. You can add **½ tsp coconut extract** in addition to the vanilla extract to bolster the coconut flavour.

**MAKES:** about 1½ cups (375 mL)

**PREP TIME:** 15 minutes, plus chilling
**COOK TIME:** 7 minutes

**❗ SIMPLE**

**BITES OF WISDOM:**
*Glossary of ingredients—Citrus (p. 6)*

**USED IN:**
*Lemon Crunch-&-Cream Tray Cake, p. 258*

*Lemon Bostock Bread Pudding, p. 326*

*Pink Lemonade Eton Mess, p. 328*

**INGREDIENTS**

½ cup (125 mL) fresh lemon juice

⅔ cup (140 g) granulated sugar

1 large egg

3 large egg yolks

1 Tbsp (15 mL) finely grated lemon zest

2 tsp cornstarch

½ cup (115 g) unsalted butter, cut into pieces

¼ cup (60 mL) sour cream or Crème Fraîche (p. 94)

# Tart Lemon Curd

The combination of ingredients makes a citrus curd unique. While eggs thicken the curd and give it its yellow colour, butter sets the curd once chilled and makes it smooth and rich tasting. This pucker-worthy version is sweet enough to spread on Classic English Scones (p. 158), yet adds an assertive tartness to desserts like the Lemon Crunch-&-Cream Tray Cake (p. 258).

1. **Cook the curd.** Whisk the lemon juice, sugar, egg, egg yolks, lemon zest and cornstarch together in a medium saucepan. Add the butter and place the pan over medium heat, whisking constantly until the curd thickens slightly and just begins to show signs of starting to bubble, about 7 minutes. The curd should coat the back of a spoon but it will remain fluid.

   *Acid ingredients like the lemon juice and lemon zest make it harder for the proteins in eggs to bond and coagulate, which is why you can fully cook the curd without actually curdling the eggs.*

2. **Cool and chill the curd.** Remove the curd from the heat and whisk in the sour cream (or crème fraîche). Transfer the curd to a container to cool to room temperature. Cover the container and chill until set, at least 3 hours.

   *Adding the sour cream off the heat stops the curd from cooking by cooling it down a little.*

   **The curd will keep in an airtight container in the fridge for up to 10 days or frozen for up to 3 months.**

# Pies & Tarts

# Recipes at a Glance

Whoever came up with the expression "easy as pie" clearly had never baked a pie. For many people, "easy" is not the word to describe the process. That's why I think it fitting to start by mastering the two most-used types of pastry: classic pie dough and pâte sablée. In addition to these doughs, I've designed a nut-based pastry dough that works well for European-style tarts.

The foundation for any pie is its crust, and I have divided the chapter according to the different types of pastry dough so you can see the wide variety of fillings and techniques you can use with each one. From these basic doughs, the world of savoury and sweet recipes awaits.

## Savoury and Sweet Pies

Who doesn't love pie? A classic crust is endlessly versatile, enclosing savoury fillings in quiches and pot pies as well as sweet fillings in rustic galettes and decadent cream pies. Pie pastry is buttery and flaky, its neutral taste doesn't detract from the taste of the pie as a whole, and it has the strength to hold up under wet ingredients like fruit, egg or custard fillings.

Classic pie dough can seem daunting because people are often taught how to make it in negatives: don't let the butter get warm, don't add too much water, don't overmix the dough. So what happens? We don't make it! I prefer to teach in positives, giving you wiggle room on the temperature, adding my special ingredients to ensure the dough won't be tough and giving you tried and tested precise measurements so you won't have to guess how much water to add. The result: perfect pie dough every time.

## Sweet Tarts

Sweet tarts are more delicate and decorative than pies. Their complexity comes from layering a sweet pastry crust with a filling and often a topping. Pâte Sablée is my go-to sweet dough for tarts. The fine grind of icing sugar, cake & pastry flour or ground almonds, and egg yolks in place of whole eggs make for a pastry that is easy to mix and roll and holds its shape when baked. It is also substantial enough to bear the weight of rich fillings, and it slices easily without crumbling.

I have two options: my long-time favourite classic pâte sablée and a traditional almond pâte sablée. Both yield a crisp yet tender and sweet crust, and they are interchangeable as the base for all of the sweet tart recipes. Making pâte sablée is similar to making cookie dough, but my recipe calls for a cooked egg yolk in addition to the raw. The almond pâte sablée is slightly less sweet than the classic pâte sablée but just as easy to make, and ground almonds keep the pastry delicate and crisp. After working the butter into the flour, the dough can be rolled without cracking.

## Linzer Tarts & Crostatas

Both are filled tarts, but the first is from Austria and the second from Italy. A Linzer tart often has a criss-cross pattern to its top crust, whereas the top crust of a crostata can be criss-cross, fully covered or even open. Once you master this recipe, you can vary the flavours of the filling and the style of the top crust.

**Foundation: Classic Pie Dough**
Page 108

**Bacon, Beer & Mushroom Quiche**
*(plus Bonus Bake: Spinach, Chevre,
Olive & Lemon Quiche)* Page 111

**Leek & Crème Fraîche Flamiche**
*(plus Bonus Bake: Ham & Caramelized
Onion Flamiche)* Page 112

**Seafood Chowder Pot Pie**
Page 114

**Apple, Spiced Plum & Cranberry Pie**
*(plus Bonus Bake: Blueberry, Raspberry
or Cherry Pie)* Page 116

**Blueberry & Greek Yogurt Breakfast
Galette** Page 118

**Fresh Strawberry Pie with Hibiscus**
Page 120

**Brown Butter Pecan Pie**
Page 123

**Roasted White Chocolate &
Pumpkin Pie** Page 124

**Chocolate Hazelnut Cream Pie**
Page 127

SWEET TARTS ▶

**Foundation: Pâte Sablée**
(Sweet Dough)  Page 128

**Foundation: Almond Pâte Sablée**
(Almond Sweet Dough)  Page 129

**Pretty Lemon Meringue Tart**
Page 130

**Summer Fruit Frangipane Tart**
*(plus Bonus Bake: Prune & Armagnac
Frangipane Tart)*  Page 133

**Strawberry Chocolate Tart**
Page 134

**Caramelized Pineapple Tart with
Coconut Chiboust**  Page 136

**Millionaire Tart**
Page 139

**Walnut, Raisin & Chocolate
Rugelach Tart**  Page 140

**Rhubarb Cheesecake Tart**
*(plus Bonus Bake: Strawberry
Cheesecake Tart)* Page 143

LINZER TARTS & CROSTATAS ▶

Foundation: Crostata/Linzer Dough
Page 146

**Jam Almond Linzer Tart**
Page 148

**Cranberry, Orange & Hazelnut Crostata**
Page 149

**Pear, Blue Cheese & Pistachio Crostata**
Page 151

**MAKES:** enough for one 9-inch (23 cm) double-crust pie

**PREP TIME:** 10 minutes, plus chilling

⏸ **SIMPLE**

**INGREDIENTS**

2½ cups (375 g) all-purpose flour

1 Tbsp (12 g) granulated sugar

1 tsp fine sea salt

3 Tbsp (45 mL) vegetable oil

1 cup (225 g) cool unsalted butter, cut into pieces (does not have to be ice cold)

¼ cup (60 mL) cool water

2 tsp white vinegar or fresh lemon juice

# Classic Pie Dough

An all-butter pie dough delivers a rich taste and a tender flakiness to any pie, savoury or sweet. This is my staple pie dough that I have been using for at least 10 years, ever since I discovered that adding a little oil before the butter protects the flour and that the butter does not have to be ice cold, contrary to popular belief.

1. **Combine the dry ingredients** by stirring the flour, sugar and salt in a large bowl. Add the oil. Using a pastry cutter, electric beaters or a mixer fitted with the paddle attachment, blend until the flour looks evenly crumbly.

   *Adding a little vegetable oil to the flour before adding the butter is another secret for tender and flaky pie dough. The oil coats the flour so that it won't overhydrate when the water is added. Too much water develops the protein in the flour, which is why a crust becomes tough or shrinks when it bakes.*

2. **Add the butter** and cut in until the dough is rough and crumbly but small pieces of butter are still visible.

   *I have found that working with cool—but not ice-cold—butter is easiest. Pull your butter from the fridge about 30 minutes before making your dough and it will cut into the flour quickly and more evenly.*

3. **Add the liquids.** Place the water and vinegar (or lemon juice) in a small bowl, stir together and then add all at once to the flour mixture, mixing just until the dough comes together. Shape it into two discs, wrap well and chill until firm, at least 1 hour. Turn to p. 44 for how to roll pastry doughs.

   *While butter is ideal, if you prefer to use vegetable shortening, omit the oil and increase the added water to 7 Tbsp (105 mL). This balances the fat-to-water ratio, since butter is 80% fat and shortening is 100% fat.*

   **If you are not making a pie immediately, refrigerate the dough, well wrapped, for up to 2 days, or freeze it for up to 3 months. Thaw it overnight in the fridge before rolling.**

**MAKES:** one 9-inch (23 cm) quiche
**SERVES:** 8

**PREP TIME:** 30 minutes
**COOK TIME:** 1 hour

🍴 **MORE INVOLVED**

BITES OF WISDOM:
*How to roll pastry doughs (p. 44), How to blind-bake pie pastry (p. 48)*

## INGREDIENTS

3 strips thick-cut bacon (about **4 oz/120 g**)

**1 cup (125 g)** finely diced onions (1 medium onion)

**1 cup (100 g)** coarsely grated carrots (1 medium carrot)

**4 oz (125 g)** sliced cremini or button mushrooms

**¾ cup (175 mL)** wheat beer

**½ tsp** fine salt

**¼ tsp** finely ground black pepper

**¼ tsp** ground nutmeg

**2** large eggs

**½ cup (125 mL)** whipping cream

**⅓ cup (80 mL)** half-&-half cream

**½ recipe** Classic Pie Dough (p. 108), rolled to 9 inches (23 cm), then partially blind-baked (see p. 48) and cooled

**1 cup (110 g)** grated Emmenthal or Gruyere cheese

## BONUS BAKE

### Spinach, Chevre, Olive & Lemon Quiche

For a lighter, summery quiche: Replace the bacon, onion, carrot, mushrooms and cheese with **1 lb (450 g) frozen spinach**, thawed, drained and excess water squeezed out. Stir **one clove of finely minced garlic** and the **zest of one lemon** into the spinach and arrange on the bottom of the pie shell. Sprinkle **½ cup (90 g) pitted kalamata olives** and **4 oz (120 g) crumbled fresh goat cheese** overtop, then pour over the egg mixture and bake as above.

# Bacon, Beer & Mushroom Quiche

While a quiche is known as a savoury tart made up of an egg filling with added ingredients, this version is more like a lot of tasty fillings bound with a little egg. The bacon, mushrooms and cheese are bolstered by adding onions and carrots, and the wheat beer brings all the flavours together without being overly rich or heavy.

1. **Preheat the oven** to 400°F (200°C). Line a plate with paper towel.

2. **Prepare the filling.** Slice the bacon into lardons (narrow strips). In a large sauté pan over medium heat, cook the bacon until crisp, stirring often. Transfer the bacon to the lined plate to drain. Reserve 2 Tbsp (30 mL) of the bacon fat from the pan and discard the rest. Add the onions, carrots and mushrooms and sauté over medium heat, stirring often, until the onions appear translucent, about 8 minutes. Add the beer, salt, pepper and nutmeg and simmer the vegetables until all of the liquid has evaporated, about 8 minutes. Remove the pan from the heat to cool to room temperature.

3. **Whisk the eggs** well and then whisk in the whipping and half-&-half creams.

   *Whisk your eggs very well before adding any liquids to ensure the eggs are well blended. This is an all-around good habit, even when making something as simple as scrambled eggs.*

4. **Assemble the quiche.** Line a baking tray with parchment paper and place the partially blind-baked pastry shell on top (still in its pan). Sprinkle the cooled vegetables over the bottom of the pie, then sprinkle with the bacon, followed by the cheese. Carefully pour the eggs into the pastry, giving them time to cascade and fill in between the vegetables, bacon and cheese. The quiche will not be filled to the top of the pan, but the eggs will expand as the quiche bakes.

5. **Bake the quiche** for 15 minutes, then reduce the oven temperature to 350°F (180°C) and continue to bake for about 20 minutes more, until the quiche is set and golden brown.

6. **Cool the quiche** in its pan on a rack for at least 15 minutes before slicing to serve warm.

   **The quiche can also be baked a day ahead and chilled, then rewarmed for 20 minutes in a 350°C (180°C) oven.**

**MAKES:** one 9-inch (23 cm) tart
**SERVES:** 8

**PREP TIME:** 30 minutes
**COOK TIME:** 70 minutes

🍴 **MORE INVOLVED**
**BITES OF WISDOM:**
*How to roll pastry doughs (p. 44)*

### INGREDIENTS

3 large leeks

3 Tbsp (45 g) butter

½ cup (125 mL) dry white wine

¼ cup (37 g) all-purpose flour

½ cup (125 mL) Crème Fraîche (p. 94)

½ cup (125 mL) 2% milk

½ tsp fine salt

¼ tsp ground black pepper

¼ tsp ground nutmeg

1 large egg

2 large egg yolks

1½ cups (165 g) coarsely grated Gruyere cheese

1 recipe Classic Pie Dough (p. 108), chilled

Medium egg wash (see p. 33)

### BONUS BAKE

### Ham & Caramelized Onion Flamiche

For a heartier flamiche made with caramelized onions, melt **1 Tbsp (15 g) butter** in a large sauté pan over medium heat and add **3 cups (375 g) sliced cooking onions**. Cook for 5 minutes, stirring often, then reduce the heat to medium-low and continue cooking, stirring often, until the onions begin to turn golden brown, about 25 minutes. Deglaze the pan with the white wine in step 2 and continue preparing the flamiche as above, **adding 1 cup (100 g) diced, cooked ham** when you add the cheese.

# Leek & Crème Fraîche Flamiche

What is a flamiche? While it is a close cousin to the quiche, the flamiche hails from the Picardy region of France, close to the Belgian border. While variations do have an open top, the traditional flamiche has a pastry top covering its savoury filling, which is made up of soft, buttery leeks and Gruyere cheese. It can be enjoyed warm, at room temperature or chilled. The flamiche can be picked up and eaten with your hands, so it can be served in slivers as a starter or packed for a lunch or a picnic.

1. **Prepare the leeks.** Trim away the ends and dark green parts of the leeks. Cut each leek in half lengthwise, then cut into ¼-inch (6 mm) slices. Place in a colander and rinse and drain well.

2. **Cook the leek filling.** Melt the butter in a large sauté pan over medium heat and add the leeks. Cook, stirring often, until softened completely, about 15 minutes. Add the white wine and continue to cook until all liquid has evaporated. Add the flour and stir constantly until the flour just begins to pull at the bottom of the pan, about 3 minutes. Stir in the crème fraîche and milk and stir until the liquid starts to bubble at the edges. Remove the pan from the heat and stir in the salt, pepper and nutmeg. Let the mixture cool for 15 minutes. Whisk the egg and egg yolks together in a small dish, then stir this mixture and the cheese into the leeks.

*Whereas a quiche relies on the combination of eggs and cream to set it, a flamiche uses a béchamel sauce enriched with a little egg for its set. The sauce makes a flamiche velvety and delicious at any temperature, while a quiche is best enjoyed warm.*

3. **Preheat the oven** to 400°F (200°C) and place a 9-inch (23 cm) removable-bottom tart pan on a parchment-lined baking tray.

4. **Roll out the first disc of pie dough** on a lightly floured surface to a circle that is just under ¼ inch (6 mm) thick. Dust the bottom of the pan with flour and line it with the pastry, trimming away any excess dough and pressing it in the fluted edge to secure it in place. Spoon the cooled leek filling into the pan and spread to level.

5. **Roll out the second disc of pie dough** to the same size and thickness. Cut an opening in the centre using a small cookie cutter, or use a pair of scissors to cut decorative notches around the pastry. Place this pastry on top of the leek filling and trim away the edges by pressing down on the fluted tart shell edge. Brush the top of the flamiche with egg wash.

6. **Bake the flamiche** for 10 minutes, then reduce the oven temperature to 375°F (190°C) and continue baking for 35 to 40 minutes, until the crust is a rich and even golden brown.

7. **Serve the flamiche** warm, at room temperature or chilled.

**The flamiche will keep, loosely covered, in the fridge for up to 3 days.**

MAKES: two 9-inch (23 cm) pies
SERVES: 8 (per pie)

PREP TIME: 1 hour
COOK TIME: 1¾ hours

‼️ COMPLEX

BITES OF WISDOM:
*How to roll pastry doughs (p. 44)*

### INGREDIENTS

**Filling:**

3 strips thick-cut bacon (about **4 oz/120 g**), diced

1 medium onion, peeled and diced small

2 stalks celery, diced small

1 medium carrot, peeled and diced small

¼ cup (37 g) all-purpose flour

½ lb (225 g) russet or Yukon Gold potato (**about 2 medium**), peeled and diced small

3 cups (750 mL) chicken stock

½ cup (125 mL) dry white wine

2 tsp celery salt or Old Bay seasoning

1 tsp chopped fresh thyme

3 bay leaves

Pinch of cayenne

Pinch of sweet paprika

1 cup (175 g) fresh or frozen corn kernels

1 lb (450 g) peeled and deveined shrimp, cut into bite-sized pieces, if necessary

8 oz (240 g) crab meat (two 4 oz/120 g tins or equivalent)

5 oz (150 g) salmon fillet, cut into bite-sized pieces

5 oz (150 g) frozen or tinned clam meat, thawed and drained

1 cup (250 mL) whipping cream

Salt and pepper

**Assembly:**

1 recipe Classic Pie Dough (p. 108), chilled

1 recipe Classic English Scone dough made with ½ cup (125 mL) finely chopped chives or green onions (p. 158)

Milk, for brushing the scones

# Seafood Chowder Pot Pie

A good bowl of seafood chowder packed with a mix of seafood and fish along with bacon, potato and sometimes corn is a real treat. This pot pie takes all that chowder goodness and delivers it in a pastry crust. What takes it over the top is the chive biscuit topping, made from my Classic English Scones recipe (p. 158). Because making the filling, pie dough and scones is a bit of a project, make two pot pies at the same time. The second pot pie can be frozen before baking, or plan to serve both to a larger crowd. To save a bit of time, make the scone dough up to a day ahead and chill until ready to use. I cut eight teardrop-shaped scones for each pie, arranging them so that each scone marks one portion.

1. **Prepare the bacon.** Line a plate with paper towel. In a large sauté pan over medium heat, cook the bacon until crisp, stirring often. Transfer the bacon to the lined plate to drain. Reserve 2 Tbsp (30 mL) of the bacon fat from the pan and discard the rest.

2. **Prepare the vegetables and sauce.** Add the onions, celery and carrots to the pot and sauté, stirring often, until the onions are translucent, about 5 minutes. Add the flour and cook, stirring constantly, until the flour begins to stick a little to the bottom of the pot, about 4 minutes. Add the potatoes, stock and wine, followed by the celery salt (or Old Bay), thyme, bay leaves, cayenne and paprika. Increase the heat to medium-high to bring the filling to a simmer and thicken the sauce. Once the sauce starts to bubble, reduce the heat to medium-low and simmer, uncovered and stirring occasionally, until the potatoes are tender, about 20 minutes.

3. **Cook the seafood in the sauce.** Increase the heat to medium and add the corn, shrimp, crab meat, salmon, clam meat and whipping cream. Stir as the sauce returns to a simmer and the seafood cooks through, about 5 minutes. Add back the cooked bacon. Season to taste with the salt and pepper and remove from the heat to cool before chilling completely. This seafood filling can be prepared a full day in advance of assembling the pies.

4. **Preheat the oven** to 375°F (190°C). Pull the pie dough from the fridge 30 minutes before rolling. Dust two 9-inch (23 cm) pie plates with flour. Have ready a 2½-inch (6.5 cm) cookie cutter.

5. **Roll the pie pastry.** Lightly flour a work surface. For each pie, roll out a disc of pastry to a circle that is just under ¼ inch (6 mm) thick. Line each pie plate with pastry. Trim and cinch the edges of the pastry to create a fluted pattern.

6. **Fill and finish assembling.** Ladle the chilled seafood filling into the pie shells. Using your hands, flatten the scone dough to ½ inch (1.2 cm) thick and cut shapes from the dough with the cookie cutter. You can collect the scraps, flatten again and cut more shapes until all of the dough has been used. Arrange the scones on top of the filling, leaving a little space between them, and brush the tops with a little milk.

*You can freeze assembled, unbaked pies for up to 3 months. Wrap them well in plastic. Thaw the pie for 24 to 36 hours in the fridge before baking.*

7. **Bake the pies.** Place the pot pies onto baking trays and bake for 60 to 70 minutes, until the filling is bubbling at the edges and the scones and pastry are a rich golden brown. Let the pies cool for 20 minutes before serving.

*A baked and chilled pie can be reheated in a 300°F (150°C) oven for 50 minutes before serving.*

**MAKES:** one 9-inch (23 cm) pie
**SERVES:** 8 to 10

**PREP TIME:** 25 minutes, plus cooling
**COOK TIME:** 75 minutes

🍴 **MORE INVOLVED**

**BITES OF WISDOM:**
*How to roll pastry doughs (p. 44),*
*Portioning baked goods (p. 74)*

## INGREDIENTS

1 recipe Classic Pie Dough (p. 108),
chilled

**3 cups (400 g)** peeled and sliced baking
apples (**about 3** apples), such as
Honeycrisp, Spartan or Crispin

**1 cup (100 g)** fresh or frozen, thawed
cranberries

**1 cup (250 mL)** Spiced Plums (p. 86)

**⅔ cup (140 g)** granulated sugar

**½ tsp** ground cinnamon

**2 Tbsp (12 g)** regular rolled oats

Medium egg wash (see p. 33)

## BONUS BAKE

### Blueberry, Raspberry or Cherry Pie

To make a summer fruit pie with
a cooked filling, bring **4 cups (1 L)
fresh or frozen blueberries,
raspberries or pitted cherries** and
**1 Tbsp (15 mL) lemon juice** to
a simmer in a small saucepan over
medium heat, stirring once or twice.
Add **1 cup (200 g) granulated sugar**
and continue to simmer, stirring occasionally, until the fruit breaks down
a little, under 10 minutes. **Whisk
3 Tbsp (24 g) cornstarch** with **¼ cup
(60 mL) cold water** and stir into the
simmering fruit, stirring until the
mixture thickens and bubbles, about
a minute. Remove the pan from the
heat and cool the fruit. Chill the filling
and then follow the pie assembly
instructions above and bake.

# Apple, Spiced Plum & Cranberry Pie

An apple pie is a staple recipe, but now and again you want to give your
classic apple pie a little flair, especially around holiday time. Adding spiced
plums and cranberries lends a sparkle of bright colour and an aromatic
spice flavour, and the pectin in cranberries helps set the filling so you get
clean slices every time. Customize the top crust of your pie according to
your mood: fully covered, lattice or decorated with pastry cut-outs.

1. **Preheat the oven** to 375°F (190°C). Pull the pie dough from the fridge
   30 minutes before rolling. Dust a 9-inch (23 cm) pie plate with flour and place
   it on a baking tray lined with parchment paper.

   *As the pie bakes, the bottom crust absorbs the flour that was sprinkled on the
   bottom of the pie plate, making it easier to remove clean slices because the
   pastry won't stick to the bottom. This is preferred over greasing the pie plate,
   which could cause the pastry to slide down the pan as it bakes.*

2. **Toss the apples, cranberries and spiced plums together** (including any
   plum liquid) in a large bowl. Stir in the sugar and cinnamon.

3. **Roll out the first disc of dough** on a lightly floured surface to a circle just
   less than ¼ inch (6 mm) thick. Line the pie plate with the pastry, leaving the
   edges untrimmed. Sprinkle the oats over the pastry and then spoon the fruit
   into the crust.

   *The oats on the bottom piece of pastry absorb the fruit juices as the pie bakes,
   which helps to prevent a soggy bottom to your pie. The oats also completely
   disappear as they thicken up those juices.*

4. **Roll out the second disc of dough** to the same thickness. You have a few
   top-crust options:

   *Whole crust:* **Place the sheet of rolled pastry over the fruit filling and use
   scissors to snip openings in the top crust to allow steam to escape.** Pinch
   the top and bottom layers of the pastry together, trim away large overhanging
   pieces and tuck and crimp the outside edge.

   *Lattice top:* **Use a knife or pastry wheel to cut long strips** about ½ inch
   (1.2 cm) wide (you should have between 12 and 16 strips). Place half of the strips
   parallel to each other over the fruit, leaving ½ inch (1.2 cm) between them.
   Starting at one edge, gently lift alternating strips of pastry, folding them halfway
   back. Set a new strip of pastry beside the folds and perpendicular to them. Unfold
   the original strips over the newly laid one. Lift the opposite alternating strips and
   fold them back as far as they can go (to the edge of the newly laid strip). Set
   a second perpendicular strip beside the first one and then unfold the original ones.
   Repeat this technique, moving first toward one side of the pie shell and then the
   other, until the lattice is complete. Trim away the excess pastry and gently press
   the outside edge of the top and bottom crusts together to secure in place.

*Cut-outs:* **Trim and crimp the outside edge of the pie pastry.** Use a small cookie cutter or an assortment of sizes to cut out pieces of pastry and arrange these over the fruit to cover at least 75% of it. Gently press the edges of any shapes that overlap the bottom crust, to seal the edges.

5. **Brush the top pastry with egg wash and bake** the pie for about 75 minutes, until the fruit is bubbling and the pie is a rich golden brown.

6. **Cool the pie** on a cooling rack for at least 2 hours before serving, or chill to serve cold.

The pie will keep, loosely wrapped, in the fridge for up to 2 days.

**MAKES:** 1 large galette
**SERVES:** 6 to 8

**PREP TIME:** 25 minutes
**COOK TIME:** 40 minutes

 SIMPLE
**BITES OF WISDOM:**
*How to roll pastry doughs (p. 44)*

### INGREDIENTS

½ **recipe** Classic Pie Dough (p. 108), chilled

½ **cup (125 mL)** plain Greek yogurt (any fat content)

2 **Tbsp (37 g)** liquid honey, plus extra for drizzling

2 **tsp** finely grated lemon zest

1 large egg yolk

1½ **cups (190 g)** fresh blueberries

Medium egg wash (see p. 33)

# Blueberry & Greek Yogurt Breakfast Galette

This fruit pie has a rustic look because the pastry half-covers the fruit in overlapping folds. Although it makes a delicious dessert, I like to serve the galette as a breakfast or brunch pastry. It is made with no refined sugar and only a touch of honey. If you prefer individual galettes, divide the dough into six pieces and then roll and fill them as below.

1. **Preheat the oven** to 375°F (190°C). Pull the pie dough from the fridge 30 minutes before rolling. Line a baking tray with parchment paper. Dust a work surface with flour.

2. **Roll out the dough** on a lightly floured surface to a circle just less than ¼ inch (6 mm) thick and about 16 inches (41 cm) across. Carefully lift the pastry onto the prepared baking tray and leave it untrimmed.

   *If making individual galettes, it's OK if your rolled-out pastry pieces overlap on the baking tray. Just make sure you have space to add the yogurt and blueberry fillings to each one.*

3. **Fill the galette.** Combine the Greek yogurt with the honey and lemon zest, then whisk in the egg. Dollop the yogurt in the centre of the dough and spread it out to about 6 inches (15 cm) across. Sprinkle the blueberries over the yogurt (1). Fold the edges of the pastry over the filling in five to six folds (2, 3). Brush the top of the pastry with egg wash.

   *You can substitute any tender, fresh fruit for the blueberries: raspberries, blackberries, strawberries and diced rhubarb, peeled and diced peaches or even Spiced Plums (p. 86). Fresh fruits hold their shape better for this simple galette; they let off less liquid, allowing the filling to hold its shape well and not seep through the pastry.*

   *To dress up this galette, sprinkle with ¼ cup (60 mL) unbaked Almond Streusel (p. 82) before baking.*

4. **Bake the galette** for about 40 minutes, until the pastry is a rich golden brown.

5. **Cool the galette** on a rack for at least 30 minutes. Serve warm or at room temperature, drizzled with honey.

   **The galette will keep, wrapped in plastic, in the fridge for up to 2 days.**

**MAKES:** one 9-inch (23 cm) pie
**SERVES:** 8

**PREP TIME:** 20 minutes, plus chilling
**COOK TIME:** under 10 minutes

🍴 **MORE INVOLVED**

BITES OF WISDOM:
*How to roll pastry doughs (p. 44), How to blind-bake pie pastry (p. 48)*

### INGREDIENTS

**Filling:**

**6 cups (1 kg)** fresh strawberries, divided

**¾ cup (150 g)** granulated sugar

**3 Tbsp (24 g)** cornstarch

**1 cup (250 mL)** brewed hibiscus tea, cooled to room temperature

**Assembly:**

**½ recipe** Classic Pie Dough (p. 108), rolled to 9 inches (23 cm), then fully blind-baked (see p. 48) and cooled

**1 recipe** Chantilly Cream (p. 95)

# Fresh Strawberry Pie with Hibiscus

This fruit pie is all about fresh, ripe strawberries. Here they are paired with floral and tart hibiscus and topped with Chantilly cream. The acidity of the hibiscus complements the berries' sweetness, and this is now a new summer classic for me.

1. **Prepare the strawberries.** Hull the strawberries, then purée 1 cup (165 g) to make ½ cup (125 mL) strawberry purée. Set aside the rest.

2. **Make the sauce.** Whisk the sugar and cornstarch together in a small saucepan. Whisk in the strawberry purée followed by the hibiscus tea. Set the saucepan over medium-high heat and bring the sauce to a simmer, whisking constantly until it thickens and begins to bubble, about 4 minutes. Transfer the sauce to a bowl to cool, then chill for at least 1 hour before assembling.

   *Be sure the tea is at room temperature before whisking it into the strawberry mixture. Hot liquids added to a starch will immediately lump up, but cool or cold ones won't.*

3. **Finish the filling.** Slice the remaining strawberries into a large bowl (1) and toss with the chilled sauce. Spoon this filling into the prepared pie shell (2).

4. **Decorate.** Dollop and spread the Chantilly cream over the filling or pipe the cream onto the pie as you wish (3). Chill until ready to serve.

   **This pie is best enjoyed the day it is made, but it will keep in the fridge for a day.**

**MAKES:** one 9-inch (23 cm) pie
**SERVES:** 8 to 10

**PREP TIME:** 25 minutes, plus chilling
**COOK TIME:** 50 minutes

🍴 **MORE INVOLVED**
**BITES OF WISDOM:**
*How to roll pastry doughs (p. 44), How to toast nuts (p. 36), Storing baked (& unbaked) goods (p. 74)*

**INGREDIENTS**

½ **recipe** Classic Pie Dough (p. 108), chilled

½ **cup (115 g)** unsalted butter

1 **cup (200 g)** packed dark brown sugar

½ **cup (125 mL)** maple syrup

¼ **cup (60 mL)** corn syrup

¼ **cup (60 mL)** whipping cream

2 **tsp** lemon juice or white vinegar

1 **tsp** vanilla extract

½ **tsp** fine salt

3 large eggs

1½ **cups (150 g)** pecan halves, lightly toasted

# Brown Butter Pecan Pie

I am quite picky when it comes to pecan pie. I prefer a pie that is not too sweet and has an even balance of syrupy filling and nuts—too much of one or the other and I'm thrown off balance. Rich and nutty, the brown butter in this filling lends so much flavour and enhances the toastiness of the pecans.

1. **Prepare the pastry.** On a lightly floured work surface, roll out the pastry to a circle just under ¼ inch (6 mm) thick. Dust the bottom of a 9-inch (23 cm) glass pie plate with flour and line it with the pastry. Trim, tuck and crimp the edges of the pastry shell and chill for at least an hour.

   *Although the liquid filling suggests this recipe should be made using a partially blind-baked pie shell, an unbaked one works perfectly. The pastry still crisps up, and the filling really holds the pastry in place nicely.*

   *For a pecan tart, use a 9-inch (23 cm) round fluted pan with a removable bottom.*

2. **Preheat the oven** to 400°F (200°C).

3. **Brown the butter.** Melt the butter in a saucepan over medium-high heat and let it cook, stirring occasionally, until the bubbling subsides and the butter itself turns a rich nutty colour, about 5 minutes. Set aside to cool for 10 minutes.

   *Dark sediment will settle to the bottom of the pan as the brown butter cools. Provided they have not turned black (in which case they may taste bitter), these caramelized milk solids can be stirred into the filling with the butter. If they have turned black, pour the brown butter through a coffee filter or fine strainer to remove them.*

4. **Make the filling.** Whisk the brown sugar, maple syrup, corn syrup, whipping cream, lemon juice (or vinegar), vanilla and salt together until well combined. In a separate bowl, whisk the eggs, then add them to the sugar mixture and whisk until blended. Pour in the brown butter and whisk well. Toss in the pecans, stirring to coat them completely, and pour the filling into the pie shell.

   *Not only does the lemon juice balance the sweetness of the filling, it also helps to prevent the sugar from crystallizing so that your filling stays smooth and syrupy. This is also the secret to a syrupy, smooth butter tart filling.*

5. **Bake the pie** on a baking tray for 10 minutes, then reduce the oven temperature to 375°F (190°C) and bake for another 30 to 35 minutes, until the pie filling starts to soufflé around the outside edge. The centre will still be jiggly. Cool the pie on a rack to room temperature before serving.

   **The pie should be refrigerated after a day. It will keep, loosely wrapped in plastic, for up to 3 days.**

**MAKES:** one 9-inch (23 cm) pie or fluted tart
**SERVES:** 8

**PREP TIME:** 15 minutes, plus chilling
**COOK TIME:** 40 minutes

🍴 **MORE INVOLVED**
**BITES OF WISDOM:**
*How to roll pastry doughs (p. 44), How to blind-bake pie pastry (p. 48)*

### INGREDIENTS

½ **recipe** Classic Pie Dough (p. 108), rolled to 9 inches (23 cm), then partially blind-baked (see p. 48) and cooled

**Pumpkin filling:**

1½ **cups (375 mL)** pure pumpkin purée

½ **cup (125 mL)** whipping cream

½ **cup (125 mL)** Roasted White Chocolate Ganache (p. 92), at room temperature

¼ **cup (50 g)** packed light brown sugar

¾ **tsp** ground cinnamon

½ **tsp** ground cardamom

½ **tsp** ground ginger

¼ **tsp** ground cloves

1 large egg

3 egg yolks

**Roasted white chocolate cream:**

½ **cup (125 mL)** Roasted White Chocolate Ganache (p. 92)

¾ **cup (175 mL)** whipping cream

Praliné Noisette (p. 85), for décor (optional)

# Roasted White Chocolate & Pumpkin Pie

This contemporary take on a classic pumpkin pie is velvety and smooth with the addition of Roasted White Chocolate Ganache (p. 92). It is used both in the pie filling and as part of the cream topping and provides a caramel flavour that partners perfectly with spices and pumpkin. Prepare the full ganache recipe so you have enough for both uses in this recipe.

1. **Preheat the oven** to 350°F (180°C). Place the blind-baked pie shell on a baking tray (still in its pan).

   *For a traditional pie, you can blind-bake the pastry in a 9-inch (23 cm) pie plate. For a different look, use a 9-inch (23 cm) round fluted tart pan with a removable bottom. Both hold the same volume of filling.*

2. **Prepare the filling.** Whisk the pumpkin purée with the whipping cream, roasted white chocolate ganache, brown sugar, cinnamon, cardamom, ginger and cloves. Whisk in the whole egg and egg yolks.

3. **Bake the pie.** Pour the filling into the pie shell and bake for about 40 minutes, until the filling is set when the pie plate is shaken. Cool to room temperature and chill for at least 2 hours before topping.

   *Partially blind-baking the pie shell before filling means the bake time is focused on getting the perfect set to the filling, knowing that the pie pastry will be fully baked and crisp beneath it.*

4. **Make the roasted white chocolate cream.** If the roasted white chocolate ganache is not at room temperature (smooth and almost fluid), warm it over low heat on the stove, while stirring, or microwave for 10 to 15 seconds and then stir. Using electric beaters or a stand mixer fitted with the whip attachment, whip the cream and white chocolate ganache until the chocolate cream holds a peak when the beaters are lifted.

   *Whenever using a microwave to melt chocolate, set the heat to medium and stir every 10 seconds to ensure the chocolate (or ganache, in this case) does not burn.*

   *Use this delicious roasted white chocolate cream to top other autumn desserts such as the Apple, Spiced Plum & Cranberry Pie (p. 116), Sticky Toffee Date Loaf (p. 211) or the "Bonus Bake" Pumpkin Apple Shortcakes (p. 161).*

5. **Decorate.** Spoon the chocolate cream into a piping bag fitted with a large star tip and pipe a "rope" design around the outside edge of the pumpkin filling. Sprinkle with praliné noisette, if using. Chill until ready to serve.

**The pie will keep, loosely wrapped in plastic, in the fridge for up to 3 days.**

**MAKES:** one 9-inch (23 cm) pie
**SERVES:** 8 to 10

**PREP TIME:** 35 minutes, plus chilling

🍴 **MORE INVOLVED**
**BITES OF WISDOM:**
*How to roll pastry doughs (p. 44), How to blind-bake pie pastry (p. 48), How to toast nuts (p. 36)*

**INGREDIENTS**

**Filling:**

**1 cup (135 g)** toasted and peeled hazelnuts

**4 oz (120 g)** dark baking/couverture chocolate, chopped

**¼ cup (60 g)** unsalted butter, at room temperature

**2 tsp** vanilla extract

**1 recipe** Vanilla Pastry Cream (p. 96), freshly prepared and still warm

**Assembly:**

**½ recipe** Classic Pie Dough (p. 108), rolled to 9 inches (23 cm), then fully blind-baked (see p. 48) and cooled

**1 recipe** Chantilly Cream (p. 95)

**¼ cup (40 g)** chopped Praliné Noisette (p. 85) (optional)

# Chocolate Hazelnut Cream Pie

A cream pie has a rich custard filling with a Chantilly cream topping. Chocolate and hazelnut are a classic flavour pairing whose rich chocolate and nutty flavours make a sumptuous cream pie. To elevate this pie, sprinkle with a hazelnut praliné noisette.

1. **Make the chocolate hazelnut paste.** Pulse the toasted hazelnuts, chocolate, butter and vanilla in a food processor until it forms a thick paste. The hazelnuts don't have to be finely ground.

   *As the food processor blends the ingredients, the friction of its high-speed blade partially melts the chocolate. It's not quite silky smooth like the popular commercial chocolate hazelnut spreads, but adding a few tablespoons of vegetable oil will smooth it out enough to use as a spread for toast, crepes and other desserts. Refrigerate in an airtight container for up to 1 month.*

2. **Make the filling.** Stir the chocolate hazelnut paste into the warm pastry cream, whisking gently until the chocolate has melted. Transfer the filling to a bowl, cover the surface directly with plastic wrap and let cool to room temperature before chilling completely, at least 2 hours.

   *For a bigger hazelnut kick, stir 2 Tbsp (30 mL) hazelnut liqueur into the filling along with the hazelnut paste.*

3. **Assemble the pie.** Stir the chilled chocolate filling to loosen it slightly and spoon into the pie shell, spreading it evenly. Dollop and spread the Chantilly cream over the filling or pipe the cream onto the pie as you wish. Sprinkle with praliné noisette, if using. Chill the pie until ready to serve.

**The pie will keep, loosely wrapped in plastic, in the fridge for up to 3 days.**

INGREDIENTS

½ cup + 2 Tbsp (145 g) unsalted butter, at room temperature

½ cup + 2 Tbsp (80 g) icing sugar, sifted

1 large hard-boiled egg yolk

1 large egg yolk

½ tsp vanilla extract

1¾ cups (230 g) cake & pastry flour, sifted

¼ tsp fine salt

# Pâte Sablée (Sweet Dough)

This recipe has been my staple sweet dough for tarts for years. It is tender, yet strong enough to hold moist fillings without breaking down. Adding a cooked egg yolk to the dough may seem strange, but it makes the pastry easier to handle and results in fewer cracks as you roll it.

1. **Beat the butter and icing sugar** together in a large bowl until smooth.

2. **Add the eggs.** Push the hard-boiled egg yolk through a sieve into a separate bowl and stir the raw egg yolk and vanilla into it. Add to the butter mixture and stir until blended.

3. **Add the flour and salt** to the butter mixture and stir until blended.

4. **Chill the dough.** Shape the dough into a disc (it will be very soft), wrap in plastic and chill until firm, about 2 hours. Turn to p. 44 for how to roll pastry doughs.

**You can prepare the dough ahead of time and freeze, well wrapped in plastic, for up to 3 months. Thaw in the fridge before using.**

**MAKES:** pastry for two 9-inch (23 cm) tart shells

**PREP TIME:** under 15 minutes, plus chilling

❗ SIMPLE

## INGREDIENTS

2¼ cups (337 g) all-purpose flour

1 cup (130 g) Tant pour Tant (p. 82)

¼ cup (30 g) ground almonds

½ tsp fine salt

1 cup (225 g) unsalted butter, at room temperature

3 large egg yolks

# Almond Pâte Sablée (Almond Sweet Dough)

This sweet dough is a newer addition to my repertoire. I use this dough interchangeably with the Pâte Sablée (p. 128), but it is a touch more delicate because of the ground almonds. If using with wet fillings, such as the Pretty Lemon Meringue Tart (p. 130), plan to serve your tart within a day so the filling doesn't seep through.

1. **Mix the dry ingredients.** Combine the flour, tant pour tant, ground almonds and salt with a wooden spoon in a mixing bowl or in a stand mixer fitted with the paddle attachment.

2. **Add the butter.** Using electric beaters or the mixer on low speed, blend until rough, crumbly and no large pieces of butter are visible.

3. **Add the egg yolks** and continue to mix on low speed until the dough comes together.

4. **Chill the dough.** Shape the dough into two discs, wrap well in plastic and chill for at least 2 hours before using. Turn to p. 44 for how to roll pastry doughs.

*This recipe makes enough dough for two large tart shells. If you won't need both shells, either freeze the second disc of dough or halve this recipe. You'll need 1½ egg yolks for half the recipe. To do this, separate your yolk into a small dish, whisk it lightly and then measure 1 Tbsp (15 mL) yolk to equal half of a yolk. Use the remaining tablespoon of egg yolk as an egg wash.*

**The dough can be frozen, well wrapped in plastic, for up to 3 months. Thaw in the fridge before using.**

**MAKES:** one 9-inch (23 cm) fluted tart
**SERVES:** 8 to 10

**PREP TIME:** 35 minutes, plus chilling
**COOK TIME:** 15 minutes

### ₮₮₮ COMPLEX

**BITES OF WISDOM:**
*How to roll pastry doughs (p. 44), How to bake sweet pastry dough (p. 49), How to whip egg whites (p. 34)*

## INGREDIENTS

**Filling:**

¾ cup (150 g) granulated sugar

¼ cup (30 g) cornstarch

Finely grated zest of **2** lemons

**1 cup (250 mL)** 2% milk

¼ cup (60 mL) Crème Fraîche (p. 94) or full-fat sour cream

**5** large egg yolks

⅔ cup (160 mL) fresh lemon juice

**Assembly:**

**1 recipe** Pâte Sablée (p. 128 or 129), rolled to 9 inches (23 cm), baked (see p. 49), brushed with egg white and cooled

**Italian meringue:**

**3** large egg whites, at room temperature

¾ cup (150 g) granulated sugar

**3 Tbsp (45 mL)** water

# Pretty Lemon Meringue Tart

In North America, lemon meringue pie is made with pie dough and a tart lemon filling that is more pudding than custard. It is most often topped with a common or French meringue. The European version uses a sweet pastry crust and a creamy yet still tart lemon curd filling. It is topped with either a Swiss or Italian meringue that is sweet and stable and does not risk weeping, melting or changing shape. This tart is a more European version that looks very polished and patisserie-worthy.

1. **Make the filling.** Whisk the sugar, cornstarch and lemon zest together in a medium saucepan. Whisk in the milk, crème fraîche (or sour cream) and egg yolks. Don't worry if the mixture does not blend smoothly at this point. Bring the filling to a simmer over medium heat, whisking constantly, until it thickens and bubbles break the surface, about 6 minutes. Remove the pan from the heat and whisk in the lemon juice. Transfer the filling to a bowl, place a sheet of plastic wrap on the surface of the filling to prevent a skin from forming and cool to room temperature, about 1 hour. Pour the filling into the cooled tart shell and chill for at least 1 hour and up to 4 hours.

   *The lemon curd in this recipe sets a little more firmly than my Tart Lemon Curd (p. 100). The sour cream sets the curd with the acidity of the lemon juice, making it more stable. (By nature, cornstarch breaks down in the presence of acidity, which is why traditional lemon meringue pie has a puddle of liquid in the pie plate the next day, but this version stays intact.)*

2. **Make the meringue.** Use electric beaters to whip the egg whites until they are frothy, then set aside. In a small saucepan, bring the sugar and water to a full boil over high heat. Without stirring, boil until the mixture reaches 240°F (116°C) on a candy thermometer; this happens quickly. Immediately remove the pan from the heat. With the beaters set at high speed, slowly pour the sugar down the side of the bowl into the egg whites. Whip the whites until they hold a stiff peak but are still warm, about 90 seconds.

   *Do not add the sugar directly to the egg whites while whipping them, to avoid splashes.*

3. **Pipe the meringue.** Dollop and spread the meringue over the lemon filling or pipe the meringue onto the tart as you wish (1). Use a butane kitchen torch to brown the meringue (2, 3) or bake the tart for 3 to 4 minutes in a 450°F (230°C) oven. Chill the tart for at least 2 hours before serving.

   *Because an Italian meringue is fully cooked, the top is browned only for visual effect. The browning can be skipped. This meringue holds piping details well, so get creative. It will stay in place and won't separate from the lemon curd, which is a risk of a traditional lemon meringue pie.*

**This tart is best served the day it is made, but it will keep well once cut, with the exposed portion loosely covered in plastic, in the fridge for up to 2 days.**

**MAKES:** one 9-inch (23 cm) tart
**SERVES:** 8 to 10

**PREP TIME:** 15 minutes, plus cooling
**COOK TIME:** 40 minutes

🍴 **MORE INVOLVED**
**BITES OF WISDOM:**
*How to roll pastry doughs (p. 44), How to bake sweet pastry dough (p. 49)*

## INGREDIENTS

**1 recipe** Pâte Sablée (p. 128 or 129), rolled to 9 inches (23 cm), baked (see p. 49), brushed with egg white and cooled

**Frangipane:**

**½ cup (115 g)** unsalted butter, at room temperature

**2 cups (260 g)** Tant pour Tant (p. 82)

**2 Tbsp (18 g)** all-purpose flour

**2 large eggs**

**1 tsp** vanilla extract

**½ tsp** almond extract (optional)

**Assembly:**

**2 cups (500 mL)** summer fruits, such as rhubarb, raspberries, blueberries, plums, apricots and/or peaches, pitted or cut as needed

Icing sugar, for dusting

## BONUS BAKE

### Prune & Armagnac Frangipane Tart

The Breton dried-fruit variation of this tart is delicious in winter. Soak **1½ cups (260 g) pitted prunes** in **2 Tbsp (30 mL) Armagnac** in a covered bowl for an hour. Nestle the soaked prunes into the frangipane, brushing any remaining Armagnac on top, and bake as above. Serve at room temperature with a dollop of **Crème Fraîche** (p. 94).

# Summer Fruit Frangipane Tart

This summer tart celebrates fresh fruits at their peak of ripeness. Frangipane, like marzipan, is made with almonds, but it is used as a soft and sliceable filling rather than an icing or confection. Here it expands around the fresh fruits as the tart bakes, absorbing excess juices and forming a lovely yet thin crust on top that matches the soft texture of the cooked fruit once sliced. The texture of frangipane can vary depending on how it's used, which is why this recipe differs from the more structured one in my Galette des Rois (p. 176).

1. **Preheat the oven** to 350°F (180°C) and place the baked, cooled tart shell in its pan onto a baking tray.

2. **Make the frangipane.** Beat the butter and tant pour tant until well combined. Add the flour and beat in. Add the eggs one at a time, beating well after each addition, switching to a whisk for easier blending. Whisk in the extracts. Pour the frangipane into the tart shell.

3. **Arrange the fruits** nicely on top of the frangipane, but there is no need to press them in. As the tart bakes, the frangipane will expand around the fruits but won't hide them.

   *When arranging berries or diced rhubarb (1-inch/2.5 cm pieces), leave a little space between them. Cut stone fruits like apricots and plums in half, pit them and place them flat side down. Cut peaches into large slices, arranging them on their side around the tart.*

4. **Bake the tart** for about 40 minutes, until the frangipane is set and turns an even golden brown on top. Let cool on a rack before dusting with icing sugar to serve.

   **This tart is best enjoyed at room temperature but will keep, loosely covered, in the fridge for up to 3 days.**

**MAKES:** one 9-inch (23 cm) tart
**SERVES:** 10 to 12

**PREP TIME:** 15 minutes, plus chilling
**COOK TIME:** 3 minutes

🍴 **MORE INVOLVED**

**BITES OF WISDOM:**
*How to roll pastry doughs (p. 44), How to bake sweet pastry dough (p. 49), How to melt chocolate (p. 41)*

**INGREDIENTS**

**1 oz (30 g)** dark baking/couverture chocolate, chopped

**1 recipe** Pâte Sablée (p. 128 or 129), rolled to 9 inches (23 cm), baked (see p. 49), brushed with egg white and cooled

**1 recipe** Chocolate Diplomat Cream (p. 98), chilled

**2 cups (330 g)** sliced fresh strawberries

**3 Tbsp (45 mL)** apricot jam or apple jelly

**¼ cup (30 g)** finely chopped shelled pistachios, for décor

# Strawberry Chocolate Tart

This gorgeous fruit-covered tart is worthy of display in a glass patisserie case. Its sablé pastry crust is filled with a generous amount of rich Chocolate Diplomat Cream (p. 98) and topped with fresh strawberries.

1. **Brush the tart shell with chocolate.** Melt the chocolate over a hot water bath until fluid. Using a pastry brush, lightly coat the bottom and sides of the pastry shell. Chill the shell for 10 minutes.

   *Brushing the baked tart shell with egg white while hot protects it from moisture, but this chocolate layer protects it further and adds to the flavour of the tart. Make sure the chocolate layer is thin and even. If the chocolate is too thick, the tart shell will be difficult to slice cleanly.*

2. **Fill the tart.** Gently stir the chilled chocolate diplomat cream to soften it slightly. Spoon the filling into the chilled tart shell and, using an offset spatula, spread it into a dome shape. Arrange the sliced strawberries in a single layer on top of the diplomat cream to cover it as much as possible.

   *I slice my strawberries into circles, starting from the narrow tip and ending at the base, so they are easier to arrange on the tart. Of course, fresh raspberries would make a delicious alternative.*

3. **Glaze the tart.** Melt the apricot jam (or apple jelly) in a small saucepan over medium heat until smooth. Use a pastry brush to completely cover the tart with the glaze. Sprinkle chopped pistachios around the outside edge of the tart. Chill, uncovered, until ready to serve.

**The tart is best enjoyed the day it is assembled, but any remaining tart will keep loosely covered in the fridge for up to 2 days.**

**MAKES:** one 9-inch (23 cm) tart
**SERVES:** 8 to 10

**PREP TIME:** 25 minutes, plus chilling
**COOK TIME:** 15 minutes

🍴🍴🍴 **COMPLEX**

**BITES OF WISDOM:**
*How to roll pastry doughs (p. 44), How to bake sweet pastry dough (p. 49)*

**INGREDIENTS**

**Filling:**

1 tsp (3.5 g) gelatin powder

1 Tbsp (15 mL) cold water

3 Tbsp (45 g) butter

¼ cup (50 g) packed dark brown sugar

3 cups (450 g) diced fresh pineapple

½ cup (125 mL) Salted Butter Caramel Sauce (p. 89)

1 Tbsp (15 mL) rum

**Assembly:**

1 recipe Pâte Sablée (p. 128 or 129), rolled to 9 inches (23 cm), baked (see p. 49), brushed with egg white and cooled

1 recipe Coconut Lime Chiboust Cream (p. 99)

¼ cup (25 g) lightly toasted flaked coconut

# Caramelized Pineapple Tart with Coconut Chiboust

A pretty, tropically inspired tart is perfect for mid-winter when we need a taste of sunshine and, as it happens, tropical fruits are at their peak. The airy Chiboust Cream (p. 99), made using coconut milk and lime, rests lightly on the caramelized pineapple filling beneath. This dessert is definitely a dinner-party crowd-pleaser.

1. **Prepare the gelatin.** Sprinkle the gelatin powder over the cold water in a small dish, stir and set aside.

2. **Make the filling.** Melt the butter in a sauté pan over medium-high heat and add the brown sugar, stirring until the mixture begins to bubble, under a minute. Add the pineapple and cook, stirring often, until the liquid from the pineapple cooks out and the syrup reduces almost to its original volume, about 8 minutes. Stir in the caramel sauce and rum, return to a full simmer and cook for about another 5 minutes, until the syrup begins to thicken and the colour darkens a little. Remove the pan from the heat and stir in the gelatin. Let the filling cool almost to room temperature.

3. **Fill and chill the tart.** Pour the cooled pineapple filling into the pastry shell (1) and chill for at least 1 hour (2).

4. **Finish the tart.** Spread the coconut lime chiboust cream over the chilled filling, creating a dome (3). Sprinkle with coconut and chill for at least 2 hours before serving.

This tart is best served the day it is made, but it will keep well once cut, with the exposed portion loosely covered in plastic, in the fridge for up to 2 days.

**MAKES:** one 9-inch (23 cm) fluted tart
**SERVES:** 8 to 10

**PREP TIME:** 20 minutes, plus cooling and chilling
**COOK TIME:** 15 minutes

### ¡¡¡ COMPLEX
**BITES OF WISDOM:**
*How to cook & caramelize sugar (p. 38),*
*How to bake sweet pastry dough (p. 49),*
*Portioning baked goods (p. 74)*

## INGREDIENTS

### Caramel:

**1 tsp (3.5 g)** gelatin powder

**1 Tbsp (15 mL)** cold water

**2 Tbsp (30 mL)** water

**½ cup (100 g)** granulated sugar

**3 Tbsp (60 g)** glucose syrup

**¾ cup (175 mL)** whipping cream

**¼ cup (60 g)** unsalted butter

**1 tsp** flaked sea salt, plus extra for sprinkling

### Assembly:

**1 recipe** Pâte Sablée (p. 128 or 129), rolled to 9 inches (23 cm), baked (see p. 49), brushed with egg white and cooled

### Chocolate ganache:

**8 oz (240 g)** dark baking/couverture chocolate, chopped

**2 Tbsp (40 g)** glucose syrup

**1¼ cups (310 mL)** whipping cream

**¼ cup (60 g)** unsalted butter, cut into pieces

# Millionaire Tart

Just like a millionaire bar, this tart has a sweet pastry base, a caramel filling and a rich chocolate topping, but it is served as an elegant plated dessert. Getting the two fillings to match in terms of set and sliceability requires a little gelatin in the caramel and glucose syrup in both. Corn syrup or other liquid sugars in place of the glucose will not work—and you definitely want to follow the proportions below so the chocolate and caramel melt in your mouth at the same rate.

1. **Soften the gelatin** in a dish with the 1 Tbsp (15 mL) cold water and set aside.

2. **Make the caramel.** Measure the 2 Tbsp (30 mL) water into a saucepan and then add the sugar and glucose syrup. Without stirring, bring the sugar to a full boil over high heat. Boil, occasionally brushing the sides of the pot with water at the boiling line to prevent crystallization, for about 4 minutes, until the sugar turns a rich amber colour. Remove the pan from the heat and carefully whisk in the cream in a steady stream (watch out for a burst of steam at first). Keep whisking until the caramel stops bubbling. Whisk in the softened gelatin, whisking until dissolved. Whisk in the butter followed by the sea salt. Set the caramel aside to cool for about 30 minutes.

   *Both corn and glucose syrups are invert sugars that don't crystallize, so they add a smooth texture to caramels and candies and prevent graininess when cooking. You can use glucose in place of corn syrup in recipes, but not the other way around. Corn syrup has a higher water content, which can affect the way confections, including this caramel, set.*

3. **Fill and chill the pie shell.** Pour the cooled caramel into the baked tart shell. Chill for another 30 minutes.

4. **Make the ganache.** Have the chocolate and glucose syrup ready in a bowl. In a small saucepan, bring the cream and butter to a full simmer over medium heat. Pour this mixture over the chocolate, letting it sit for a minute. Gently whisk the cream and chocolate together until smooth.

5. **Finish and chill the tart.** Pour the ganache over the now-chilled caramel layer and refrigerate the tart for a full 2 hours. Sprinkle with a little sea salt and serve.

   *It's best to sprinkle the flaked sea salt onto the tart after it has had time to set. If the chocolate ganache is still somewhat warm or unset, the salt may partly dissolve on top of the tart.*

   **Store the tart, uncovered, in the fridge until serving. Once cut, loosely cover the exposed portion and store in the fridge for up to 3 days.**

**MAKES:** one 9-inch (23 cm) tart
**SERVES:** 8 to 10

**PREP TIME:** 30 minutes, plus cooling
**COOK TIME:** 40 minutes

⫷ **MORE INVOLVED**
**BITES OF WISDOM:**
*How to bake sweet pastry dough (p. 49),*
*How to toast nuts (p. 36)*

## INGREDIENTS

**Filling:**

½ cup (100 g) packed dark brown sugar

½ cup (125 mL) maple syrup

¼ cup (60 mL) corn syrup

2 large eggs

2 tsp lemon juice or white vinegar

2 tsp vanilla extract

2 tsp ground cinnamon

¼ cup (60 g) unsalted butter, melted
(still warm is OK)

**Assembly:**

1 recipe Pâte Sablée (p. 128 or 129),
rolled out to 9 inches (23 cm), baked
(see p. 49), brushed with egg white
and cooled

1½ cups (150 g) toasted walnut pieces

1 cup (150 g) raisins

1 cup (175 g) semisweet chocolate chips

# Walnut, Raisin & Chocolate Rugelach Tart

I love a good rugelach. Perfectly bite-sized with a crispy pastry rolled around a tender, sweet filling, it's a contrast of textures and flavours. This tart has a soft, sweet filling (almost like a butter tart) that's packed with ingredients often found in a rugelach: walnuts, raisins and a bit of chocolate. This tart is waiting for a big scoop of ice cream.

1. **Preheat the oven** to 350°F (180°C).

2. **Make the filling.** Whisk together the brown sugar, maple syrup, corn syrup, eggs, lemon juice (or vinegar), vanilla and cinnamon by hand until well combined. Whisk in the melted butter.

   *It's the cinnamon in combination with the nuts and dried fruits that really gives this tart its rugelach-like taste.*

3. **Fill the tart.** Place the chilled tart shell on a baking tray. Sprinkle the walnuts, raisins and chocolate chips over the bottom of the shell, then pour the filling overtop.

   *Feel free to switch up the tart fillings—try pecan pieces in place of walnuts, dried cranberries in place of raisins and white chocolate chips in place of semisweet.*

4. **Bake the tart** for 35 to 40 minutes, until the centre is set when you gently jiggle the pan. Completely cool the tart in its shell on a rack and serve at room temperature.

   **The tart will keep, loosely covered, in the fridge for up to 3 days. Bring it back to room temperature before serving.**

**MAKES:** one 9-inch (23 cm) tart
**SERVES:** 8 to 10

**PREP TIME:** 40 minutes, plus chilling
**COOK TIME:** 40 minutes

### ⑪⑪⑪ COMPLEX

**BITES OF WISDOM:**
*How to bake sweet pastry dough (p. 49),*
*Portioning baked goods (p. 74)*

## INGREDIENTS

**1 recipe** Pâte Sablée (p. 128 or 129),
rolled to 9 inches (23 cm), baked
(see p. 49), brushed with egg white
and cooled

**Poached rhubarb:**

**16 oz (450 g)** fresh rhubarb stalks,
leaves trimmed

**1 cup (200 g)** granulated sugar

**1 cup (250 mL)** water

**1** vanilla bean or **1 Tbsp (15 mL)** vanilla
bean paste

**Cheesecake filling:**

**1 (8 oz/250 g)** pkg cream cheese,
softened

**6 Tbsp (90 g)** granulated sugar

**1 Tbsp (8 g)** cornstarch

**1 tsp** vanilla bean paste or vanilla extract

**1 tsp** finely grated lemon zest

**1** large egg

**1** large egg yolk

**6 Tbsp (90 mL)** sour cream

**Glaze:**

**¼ cup (60 mL)** apple jelly or apricot jam

# Rhubarb Cheesecake Tart

I have been making this tart for years (decades, even), but it has never made it into a cookbook. Once you try the delicately poached rhubarb spiralled in little rosettes overtop a creamy cheesecake filling, you'll make this springtime recipe a staple.

1. **Preheat the oven** to 350°F (180°C). Place the baked, cooled tart shell in its pan onto a baking tray.

2. **Poach the rhubarb.** Trim the rhubarb just enough to fit into a 9 × 13-inch (23 × 33 cm) pan, trying to leave the pieces as long as possible. Place the sugar and water into a small saucepan. Scrape the seeds of the vanilla bean into the pot (or add the vanilla bean paste) and bring to a simmer over high heat, stirring occasionally. Pour the hot syrup over the rhubarb, cover the pan with foil (or a lid) and bake for 15 minutes. Immediately uncover the pan and let the rhubarb cool in the syrup to room temperature (1). Leave the oven on.

   *I prefer hothouse rhubarb for this recipe because of its tenderness, intensely pink colour and thin stalks. Field rhubarb is just as tasty, but the stalks may be thicker, in which case you should slice each one lengthwise into ½-inch-wide (1.2 cm) wide pieces and add 5 minutes to the poaching time.*

   *The poaching liquid from the rhubarb is absolutely delicious and a beautiful pink. You can use it to sweeten your iced tea or cocktails, or reduce it to a glaze to drizzle over ice cream or sweeten up fresh berries and cream.*

3. **Make the cheesecake filling.** Using electric beaters or a stand mixer fitted with the paddle attachment, beat the cream cheese on medium-high speed until fluffy. Add the sugar in two additions, beating well and scraping the bowl after each one. Beat in the cornstarch, vanilla and lemon zest. Add the egg and mix on medium-low speed until combined. Add the egg yolk and sour cream, again beating on medium-low speed. Scrape the filling into the tart shell and spread to level it, if needed. The filling will fill the tart shell halfway.

4. **Bake the cheesecake filling** for about 20 minutes, until it no longer jiggles when the pan is gently tapped. Cool the tart on a rack to room temperature and then chill for at least 2 hours.

*CONTINUES*

## Strawberry Cheesecake Tart

Is rhubarb unavailable or are you short of time to poach it? Turn this recipe into a fresh strawberry cheesecake tart. **Double the recipe for the cheesecake filling** (so it fills the tart shell completely) and bake for 30 minutes. After cooling and chilling, arrange **sliced fresh strawberries** on top, glaze and chill.

5. **Assemble the rhubarb "rosettes."** Gently lift a rhubarb stalk out of the syrup and place on a cutting board. If the rhubarb is wider than 1 inch (2.5 cm), use a paring knife to cut it in half lengthwise. Spiral the soft piece of rhubarb around itself; it will be just under 2 inches (5 cm) across (2). Use a spatula to lift the rhubarb onto the cheesecake filling, barely touching the outside edge of the tart. Repeat with the remaining rhubarb stalks, arranging the spirals closely together as you cover the entire cheesecake filling with rosettes.

*Work slowly and carefully to make sure you cover the filling completely. The poached rhubarb is delicate, so once you lay a spiral down, you want to avoid moving it again.*

6. **Glaze the tart.** In a small saucepan, melt the apple jelly (or apricot jam) over medium heat until it has liquefied. Gently brush onto the rhubarb (3). Chill the tart until ready to serve.

**The tart will keep, uncovered, in the fridge, but once cut, the exposed portion can be loosely covered and refrigerated for up to 3 days.**

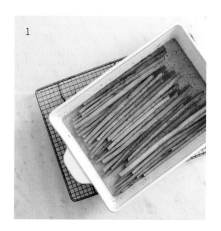

**MAKES:** enough dough for one 9-inch (23 cm) tart
**SERVES:** 8

**PREP TIME:** under 15 minutes, plus chilling

**SIMPLE**
**BITES OF WISDOM:**
*Glossary of ingredients—Nuts & seeds (p. 11)*

## INGREDIENTS

**Crostata dough:**

¾ cup (175 g) unsalted butter, at room temperature

½ cup (100 g) granulated sugar

2 tsp finely grated lemon or orange zest

1 tsp vanilla extract

2 large egg yolks

1⅓ cups (200 g) all-purpose flour

1 cup (120 g) ground almonds, ground hazelnuts or ground pistachios

½ tsp baking powder

¼ tsp fine salt

**Linzer topping:**

1 large egg

2 Tbsp (18 g) all-purpose flour

# Crostata/Linzer Dough

This dough is made like a rolled cookie dough: by creaming butter and sugar, adding egg yolks and then dry ingredients. Once chilled, the dough is easy to roll to line your tart pan. And if you add an egg to a bit of the dough, you'll get an even softer dough that can be piped on top of your jam filling for a Linzer tart.

1. **Cream the butter, sugar and zest** together by hand or using electric beaters on medium speed until smooth and fluffy. Beat in the vanilla and egg yolks until combined.

*You can tailor the citrus zest and nuts to individual recipes. In this chapter, refer to the specific recipes for details.*

2. **Add the dry ingredients.** Whisk the flour, ground nuts, baking powder and salt in a separate bowl and add to the batter, stirring until well combined.

*If you're grinding whole nuts for this recipe, place the 120 g of nuts (or volume equivalent, which may vary by nut) in a mini chopper or food processor with ½ cup (75 g) flour and pulse until finely ground. The flour will absorb the nut oils so you don't turn the nuts into a paste.*

*Few pastry dough recipes call for baking powder, but a crostata/Linzer dough is an exception. As the filled crust bakes, it expands a little, filling in gaps and giving itself more of a presence against the fruit filling.*

3. **For a crostata,** divide the dough into two discs, wrap and chill for at least 1 hour.

4. **For a Linzer tart,** weigh out 7 oz (210 g) of the freshly made dough and place in a small bowl. Add the egg and flour and stir well until the dough becomes a thick paste. Reserve at room temperature if using within 2 hours. If not, chill and then pull from the fridge an hour before using. Shape the remaining dough into a disc, wrap and chill for at least an hour.

**You can prepare the dough ahead of time and freeze, well wrapped in plastic, for up to 3 months. Thaw in the fridge before using.**

Jam Almond Linzer Tart
(p.148)

**MAKES:** one 9-inch (23 cm) tart
**SERVES:** 8

**PREP TIME:** 20 minutes
**COOK TIME:** 30 minutes

⑃ SIMPLE
**BITES OF WISDOM:**
*How to roll pastry doughs (p. 44)*

**INGREDIENTS**

---

**1 recipe** Crostata/Linzer Dough (p. 146), made using almonds and lemon zest and with the Linzer topping

**1¼ cups (310 mL)** jam or fruit preserves

Icing sugar, for dusting

*Photo on p. 147*

# Jam Almond Linzer Tart

The beauty of the original Linzer tart (or torte) is its simplicity. The tender almond pastry surrounds a sweet jam of any flavour, although raspberry or apricot are the favoured classics. It is typically served on its own without a sauce, or with whipped cream.

1. **Preheat the oven** to 350°F (180°C). Dust the bottom of a 9-inch (23 cm) removable-bottom tart pan with flour and place on a baking tray.

2. **Knead the first disc of crostata dough** on a lightly floured surface to soften it a little, then roll it into a disc about ¼ inch (6 mm) thick. Line the tart pan with the pastry, trimming away any excess. If you have any extra dough, roll it into a disc and place at the bottom of the pastry shell. It bakes into the bottom crust, adding substance (and preventing waste).

3. **Stir the jam to loosen it** and spread over the bottom of the tart shell.

   *The quality of the jam counts in this simple tart. Make sure it has a good set to it; a runny jam will seep into the pastry, blurring the distinction between the pastry and the filling.*

4. **Pipe the Linzer top layer.** Spoon the soft Linzer dough into a small piping bag fitted with a ¼-inch (6 mm) plain tip. Pipe dots of the batter of different sizes on top of the tart, leaving plenty of space in between the dots. For a more traditional look, pipe a criss-cross pattern on top of the filling.

   *Leave lots of space between your piping lines or patterns. This soft Linzer dough expands almost three times its width as it bakes, filling in many gaps.*

   *The jam filling and piped patterns will not fill the full volume of the tart, but as it bakes, the Linzer dough expands and the tart will bake up level with the top edge of your pan.*

5. **Bake the tart** for 25 to 30 minutes, until an even golden brown on top. Cool the tart completely in its pan on a rack, then carefully remove from the pan to serve at room temperature. You can also serve the tart chilled: refrigerate for 2 hours in the pan before removing to dust with icing sugar and serve.

**The tart will keep, loosely covered, in the fridge for up to 3 days.**

**MAKES:** one 9-inch (23 cm) tart
**SERVES:** 8

**PREP TIME:** 25 minutes
**COOK TIME:** 45 minutes

**⌘ MORE INVOLVED**
**BITES OF WISDOM:**
*How to roll pastry doughs (p. 44)*

## INGREDIENTS

**4 cups (400 g)** fresh or frozen cranberries

**1½ cups (300 g)** granulated sugar

**1** navel orange

**1 tsp** ground cinnamon

**2 Tbsp (30 mL)** brandy or orange liqueur (optional)

**1 recipe** Crostata/Linzer Dough (p. 146), made using ground hazelnuts and orange zest

Medium egg wash (see p. 33)

*Photo on p. ii–iii and p. 107*

# Cranberry, Orange & Hazelnut Crostata

Both cranberries and hazelnuts have a lot of flavour, so they partner wonderfully in this crostata. Adding orange zest to the pastry and the filling really gives this dessert a holiday flair.

1. **Make the cranberry filling.** Place the cranberries and sugar in a large saucepan over medium heat. Finely grate the zest of the orange into the pot, cut the orange in half, squeeze its juice into the pot and then toss both halves in as well. Add the cinnamon and bring this mixture to a simmer, stirring often. Simmer the cranberries until they have popped, about 15 minutes. Remove from the heat, stir in the brandy or orange liqueur (if using) to cool and remove and discard the orange halves. Chill the filling completely before using.

   *Frozen cranberries don't set up as firmly as fresh cranberries, so if using frozen, cook down the sauce an extra 3 to 5 minutes, stirring often.*

2. **Preheat the oven** to 350°F (180°C). Dust the bottom of a 9-inch (23 cm) removable-bottom tart pan with flour and place on a baking tray. Lightly dust a work surface with flour.

3. **Knead the first disc of crostata dough** on the floured surface to soften it a little, then roll it into a disc about ¼ inch (6 mm) thick. Line the tart pan with the pastry, trimming away any excess.

4. **Spoon the cranberry filling** into the tart pan and spread it to level.

5. **Knead the second disc of crostata dough** to soften it and then roll it into a circle just over 10 inches (25 cm) across. Use a small cookie cutter to cut out a few shapes (the cut-outs will reveal the filling beneath). Carefully lift the pastry and place it on top of the jam filling. Trim away any excess at the edges and brush the crostata with the egg wash.

   *Get creative with your cut-out shapes and patterns. You can even arrange the cut-out shapes on top of the tart, adhering them with a little egg wash.*

6. **Bake for 25 to 30 minutes,** until an even golden brown. Cool the crostata completely in its pan on a rack, then carefully remove from the pan to serve at room temperature. You can also serve the tart chilled: refrigerate for 2 hours in the pan before removing to dust with icing sugar and serve.

**The tart will keep, loosely covered, in the fridge for up to 3 days.**

**MAKES:** one 9-inch (23 cm) tart
**SERVES:** 8

**PREP TIME:** 20 minutes
**COOK TIME:** 35 minutes

⟊ **MORE INVOLVED**
**BITES OF WISDOM:**
*How to roll pastry doughs (p. 44)*

## INGREDIENTS

**4 oz (120 g)** creamy blue cheese

**⅓ cup (80 mL)** sour cream

**1** large egg

**3 Tbsp (56 g)** liquid honey

**1 tsp** chopped fresh thyme

**1 recipe** Crostata/Linzer Dough (p. 146),
made using pistachios and 2 tsp
chopped fresh thyme in place of
citrus zest

**4 halves** Poached Pears (p. 88)

Medium egg wash (see p. 33)

# Pear, Blue Cheese & Pistachio Crostata

This elegant tart is perfect served as a cheese course after dinner or for those with less of a sweet tooth. The pear and blue cheese partner wonderfully with the rich pistachio crust, and the fresh thyme in the crust brings the savoury and sweet worlds together in each bite.

1. **Make the filling.** Beat the blue cheese with the sour cream, egg, honey and thyme—the mixture does not have to be perfectly smooth. Set aside.

   *Depending on the blue cheese you use, the filling may be thick or somewhat fluid. Regardless, the cheese filling will set just fine.*

2. **Preheat the oven** to 350°F (180°C). Dust the bottom of a 9-inch (23 cm) removable-bottom tart pan with flour and place on a baking tray. Lightly dust a work surface with flour.

3. **Knead the first disc of crostata dough** on the floured surface to soften it a little, then roll it into a disc about ¼ inch (6 mm) thick. Line the tart pan with the pastry, trimming away any excess (1).

4. **Fill the tart.** Spread or pour the blue cheese filling over the bottom of the tart shell. Slice each of the pear halves into four wedges and arrange over the filling (2).

5. **Knead the second disc of crostata dough** to soften it, then roll it into a circle just over 10 inches (25 cm) across. Use a small cookie cutter to cut out a few shapes (the cut-outs will reveal the filling beneath). Carefully lift the pastry and place it on top of the filling. Trim away any excess at the edges (3) and brush the crostata with the egg wash.

6. **Bake for 30 to 35 minutes,** until golden brown—the crostata will brown more at the outer edges compared to the centre. Let the crostata cool completely in its pan on a rack, then carefully remove from the pan to serve at room temperature. You can also serve the tart chilled: refrigerate for 2 hours in the pan before removing.

   **The tart will keep, loosely covered, in the fridge for up to 3 days.**

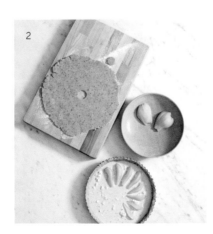

Pastries

# Recipes at a Glance

Eating pastries is truly an experience of the senses: the gorgeous sight of a flaky creation, the crackle as you break into a crispy croissant, the aroma of butter as you bring it to your mouth, the flaky and airy layers that melt on your tongue and the salty, buttery richness of pastry melding with a sweet or savoury filling. In a word: perfection.

In this chapter, I start simple with scones, which may seem like an odd fit, but my technique for flattening the butter into the dough between your palms was inspired by the more involved technique of laminating puff pastry and croissants. Lamination involves folding and flattening butter and flour layers, making them thinner and more delicate with each fold. When baked, the thin sheets of butter melt and produce steam, which pushes up the layers of flour, separating them from each other and crisping them into a flaky, airy and tender pastry. Making these laminated doughs takes time and patience, but this fundamental technique is worth mastering. Lastly comes choux paste, which is the exception to most typical pastry rules: this warm paste of a dough is piped. Just like other pastries, the result is a light-as-air vessel that is crying out for a creamy filling.

## Scones

Well-made scones have a hint of flakiness like pastry, so they easily break in half for buttering, and a cake-like quality that gives them a soft, light centre. Scones are best enjoyed the day they are baked or, even better, fresh from the oven. Making scones is quick, so they are a good starting point if you are new to making pastry.

## Puff Pastry

Versatile and easy to handle, puff pastry is a laminated butter-rich dough that bakes up to a light, flaky and tender pastry. Here I've provided two recipes for making puff pastry from scratch. The inverted method follows the more traditional technique of making a stretchy dough and working in a block of butter through repeated folds. With the quick method, the base dough is made similarly to pie dough but with more butter, so you can get to folding the pastry sooner.

The inverted method makes for a pastry with more even and delicate layers, but the quick pastry delivers a satisfying result in a little less time. Both pastries can be filled with a wide range of savoury and sweet fillings. Use either recipe or even a good-quality store-bought puff pastry in any of the recipes that call for puff pastry.

## Croissants

Yeast is the secret ingredient in croissants. Like puff pastry, it's a laminated butter-rich dough. The flour layer is called the détrempe (the "sodden"), which is the softer, wet yeast dough. The butter layer is the beurrage (the "buttering"). The slow introduction of the fermented yeast dough and the block of butter, through folding, produces the tender and flaky pastry we have come to love as the cornerstone of French baking. This process cannot be rushed, so give yourself plenty of time.

## Choux Paste

Pâte à choux, or choux paste, is one of the first doughs you learn to make in cooking school, perhaps to appreciate that it is the exception to every pastry and baking rule. Whereas most doughs are mixed, chilled and then rolled, choux paste is stirred into a thick paste on the stove, eggs are added gradually, and finally the warm paste is piped into shapes. The final result: airy, hollow shapes that offer plenty of space for a creamy filling and imaginative décor. The three most common baked styles are profiteroles (round cream puffs), éclairs (elongated filled pastries) and Paris-Brests (rings). Add the next level of texture and visual interest by adding a craquelin topper to any of theses styles.

**Classic English Scones**
Page 158

**Maple Pumpkin Scones**
*(plus Bonus Bake: Pumpkin Apple Shortcakes)* Page 161

**Foundation: Puff Pastry Dough (Inverted Method)** Page 162

**Foundation: Puff Pastry Dough (Quick Method)** Page 164

**Pissaladière**
Page 167

**Potato Tarte Tatin**
Page 168

**Salmon & Spinach Wellingtons**
Page 171

**Tarte Fine aux Pommes (Thin Apple Tart)** Page 172

**Mincemeat Dartois**
Page 174

Pastries    **155**

**Galette des Rois**
Page 176

**Strawberry Ricotta Napoleons**
Page 178

**Caramelized Peach Mille-feuille**
Page 181

CROISSANTS ▶

Foundation: Classic Croissant Dough
Page 182

**Classic Butter Croissants**
Page 185

**Almond Croissants** (*plus Bonus Bake: Ham & Cheese Croissants*)  Page 186

**Pains au Chocolat**
Page 188

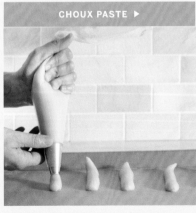

CHOUX PASTE ▶

Foundation: Choux Paste
Page 189

**Chouquettes**
Page 190

**Profiteroles au Craquelin**
Page 193

**Éclairs**
Page 195

**Individual Peanut Butter
Paris-Brests** Page 199

**MAKES:** 10 scones

**PREP TIME:** 15 minutes
**COOK TIME:** 15 minutes

▮ **SIMPLE**
**BITES OF WISDOM:**
*Temperatures (p. 14)*

## INGREDIENTS

2 cups (300 g) all-purpose flour

3 Tbsp (37 g) granulated sugar

4 tsp baking powder

½ tsp salt

6 Tbsp (90 g) unsalted butter, cold

⅔ cup (160 mL) 2% milk, plus extra for brushing

1 large egg

# Classic English Scones

My good friend Courtney has a Sunday morning tradition of making scones for her family. For something as basic as a scone, the recipe needs to be simple enough that it is easy to repeat and commit to memory within a few bakes. These are best served warm from the oven with butter and jam, or with clotted cream and jam if you are dressing them up.

1. **Preheat the oven** to 400°F (200°C) and line a baking tray with parchment paper.

2. **Combine the dry ingredients.** Stir the flour, sugar, baking powder and salt together in a mixing bowl. Use a box grater to grate in the cold butter. Use a pastry blender or two knives to work in the butter a little further, then switch to your hands, rubbing the mixture between your palms to flatten out the butter pieces. When you no longer feel round pieces of butter, you can stop.

3. **Combine the liquids and add to the flour.** Whisk the milk and egg together and add all at once to the flour. Stir until the liquid isn't running but the dough still has not come together. Tip everything out onto a work surface and bring the dough together by flattening and folding the dough over itself, scooping up the rogue crumbs and flour and working them in as you flatten and fold.

*Flattening and folding the shaggy dough as you bring it together is the key to building in flakiness. With each flattening and folding, you are building in thin sheets of butter, which will melt, produce steam and push away the flour around them, making for a flaky yet tender scone.*

4. **Portion the scones.** Flatten out the dough with your hands to ¾ inch (2 cm) thick. Use a 2½-inch (6.5 cm) round cutter to cut out scones. Reshape any scraps of dough and keep cutting out scones until all of the dough has been used. Place on the baking tray, leaving 2 inches (5 cm) between each scone. Dip your fingers in milk and pat the tops.

5. **Bake the scones** for 12 to 15 minutes, until golden brown on the top and bottom. Let the scones cool for at least 10 minutes on a rack. Scones are best enjoyed the day they are baked.

*These scones are a perfect match for butter or clotted cream and jam to serve with tea, but they are delicate enough to double as a base for berry shortcake. Split the scone in half and place the bottom on a plate. Top with a dollop of Chantilly Cream (p. 95) and fresh berries and cover with the remaining half of the scone. Dust with icing sugar and serve.*

**You can freeze unbaked scones, well wrapped, for up to 3 months. Thaw in the fridge overnight before baking fresh the next day.**

**MAKES:** 12 medium scones

**PREP TIME:** 18 minutes
**COOK TIME:** 15 minutes

❙ SIMPLE

**BITES OF WISDOM:**
*Temperatures (p. 14)*

## INGREDIENTS

2¼ cups (337 g) all-purpose flour

1 Tbsp (9 g) baking powder

1 tsp ground cinnamon

½ tsp ground ginger

¼ tsp ground cloves

¼ tsp ground allspice

¼ tsp salt

½ cup (115 g) unsalted butter, cold

¾ cup (175 mL) pure pumpkin purée

½ cup (125 mL) maple syrup

1 large egg

**Glaze:**

1 cup (130 g) icing sugar, plus extra for dusting

2 Tbsp (30 mL) maple syrup

2 Tbsp (30 mL) water

1 Tbsp (15 g) unsalted butter, melted (still warm)

## BONUS BAKE

### Pumpkin Apple Shortcakes

Shortcake doesn't have to be limited to strawberries! Try this version to end an autumn supper. Split each scone in half horizontally and place the bottom portions on individual plates. Using **one recipe of Roasted White Chocolate Ganache (p. 92)**, dollop or pipe ganache onto the bottom half of each scone. Spoon warmed **Maple Caramelized Apples (p. 86)** overtop so that they cascade down onto the plate. Set the top of each scone over the filling and dust with icing sugar. Serve immediately.

# Maple Pumpkin Scones

These scones are slightly softer and cakier than Classic English Scones (p. 158) because of the moisture from the pumpkin. With their spices and maple glaze, they are a wonderful teatime treat or gift to bring to a friend.

1. **Preheat the oven** to 400°F (200°C) and line a baking tray with parchment paper.

2. **Combine the dry ingredients.** Stir the flour, baking powder, cinnamon, ginger, cloves, allspice and salt together in a mixing bowl. Use a box grater to grate in the cold butter. Use a pastry blender or two knives to work in the butter a little further, then switch to your hands, rubbing the mixture between your palms to flatten out the butter pieces. When you no longer feel round pieces of butter, you can stop.

   *If you don't have all of the spices in the recipe, you can use 2 tsp pumpkin pie spice mix in their place.*

3. **Combine the liquids and add to the flour.** Whisk the pumpkin purée, maple syrup and egg together and add all at once to the flour. Stir until the liquid isn't running but the dough still has not come together. Tip everything out onto a work surface and bring the dough together by flattening and folding the dough over itself, scooping up the rogue crumbs and flour and working them in as you flatten and fold (this action builds in flakiness).

4. **Portion the scones.** Divide the dough into two pieces and flatten each one with your hands to ¾ inch (2 cm) thick. Cut each piece of dough into six wedges. Place on the baking tray, leaving 2 inches (5 cm) between each scone.

5. **Bake the scones** for 12 to 15 minutes, until golden brown on the top and bottom. Let the scones cool for 30 minutes on the tray on a rack before glazing.

   *This recipe makes wedge-shaped scones, but you can use a 2½-inch (6.5 cm) round or square cutter if you wish.*

6. **Make the glaze.** Whisk the icing sugar, maple syrup, water and butter together to make a thick glaze that runs off your whisk in a slow stream. Use a pastry brush to glaze the scone all over (or use a whisk to drizzle it over the scones), then place on a rack to set for 30 minutes.

**You can freeze unbaked scones, well wrapped, for up to 3 months. Thaw in the fridge overnight before baking fresh the next day.**

**MAKES:** about 3 lb (1.4 kg) dough

**PREP TIME:** 45 minutes, plus chilling

🍴 **MORE INVOLVED**

**BITES OF WISDOM:**
*Temperatures (p. 14), How to make high-fat butter for baking: Ghee and the Pearson Square (p. 72)*

**INGREDIENTS**

**Détrempe:**

**4 cups (600 g)** all-purpose flour

**1 cup (250 mL)** cool water

**½ cup + 1 Tbsp (130 g)** unsalted butter, at room temperature

**1 Tbsp (12 g)** granulated sugar

**2 tsp** salt

**1 Tbsp (15 mL)** lemon juice or white vinegar

**Beurrage:**

**3 cups (675 g)** unsalted butter, at room temperature

**1 cup (150 g)** all-purpose flour

# Puff Pastry Dough (Inverted Method)

This non-traditional technique for making classic French puff pastry ensures a remarkably flaky and tender puff pastry that rises evenly and rolls out easily. Whereas a traditional puff pastry is made by wrapping a block of butter (beurrage) with a flour/water dough (détrempe) and then folding them together, this recipe does the reverse. It is no more challenging than the traditional way but yields more consistent results. This recipe makes enough for an assortment of baked items. If you have more than you need, freeze the excess dough for later use. Simply thaw it in the fridge before rolling and using.

1. **Prepare the détrempe.** Fit a stand mixer with the dough hook attachment and blend all of the ingredients together on low speed. Once blended, increase the speed one level and mix for 4 minutes. Shape the dough into an 8-inch (20 cm) square, wrap and chill for at least 30 minutes or up to 2 hours.

2. **Prepare the beurrage.** Beat the butter with the flour in a stand mixer fitted with the paddle attachment until smooth. Line an 8-inch (20 cm) square pan with plastic and scrape the butter into the pan, spreading it to level (it will be soft). Chill until it is the same consistency as the détrempe—this could take 30 to 90 minutes. If the beurrage sets firmly or you are making it well ahead, let it soften to just cooler than room temperature.

   *Butter in Canada is 80% milk fat (butter fat), with the remaining 20% being milk solids and water. In Europe, butter is often 82% or 84% butter fat, making for richer, flakier pastries. You can find this higher-fat butter in Canada, or you can create your own 84% blend. For information on high-fat butter and how to calculate its fat content using the Pearson Square, see p. 72.*

3. **Laminate the layers for the first time.** (1) Dust a work surface and a heavy rolling pin well with flour. Place the beurrage onto the work surface. Using the rolling pin, roll the beurrage into a rectangle about 9 × 16 inches (23 × 41 cm). Lift the beurrage occasionally to ensure it isn't sticking to the work surface (after the first roll, it does not stick at all). Place the détrempe in the centre of the beurrage (2) and fold the beurrage over to completely envelop the détrempe (3, 4). Roll the dough out to a rectangle 10 × 20 inches (25 × 50 cm), dusting the dough and the work surface with flour as needed. Use a pastry brush to dust off any excess flour, then fold the pastry into thirds (5, 6). Rotate the dough 90 degrees and repeat rolling the dough to a 10 × 20-inch (25 × 50 cm) rectangle, brushing it off and folding into thirds again. Wrap the dough and chill for a minimum of 2 hours or up to 1 day.

4. **Laminate the layers a second time.** On a lightly floured work surface, roll the dough again into a 10 × 20-inch (25 × 50 cm) rectangle, brush off any excess flour and fold into thirds. Rotate the dough 90 degrees, repeat the rolling and folding and chill for a minimum of 2 hours or up to 1 day.

5. **Do a final fold.** On a lightly floured work surface, roll, brush and fold the dough into thirds, then rotate the dough 90 degrees and roll, brush and fold into thirds a final time (7, 8, 9). Wrap the dough again and chill for at least 2 hours before using.

**The puff pastry dough can keep, well wrapped in plastic, in the fridge for up to 4 days. Alternatively, portion and freeze the dough for up to 3 months. Thaw in the fridge before using.**

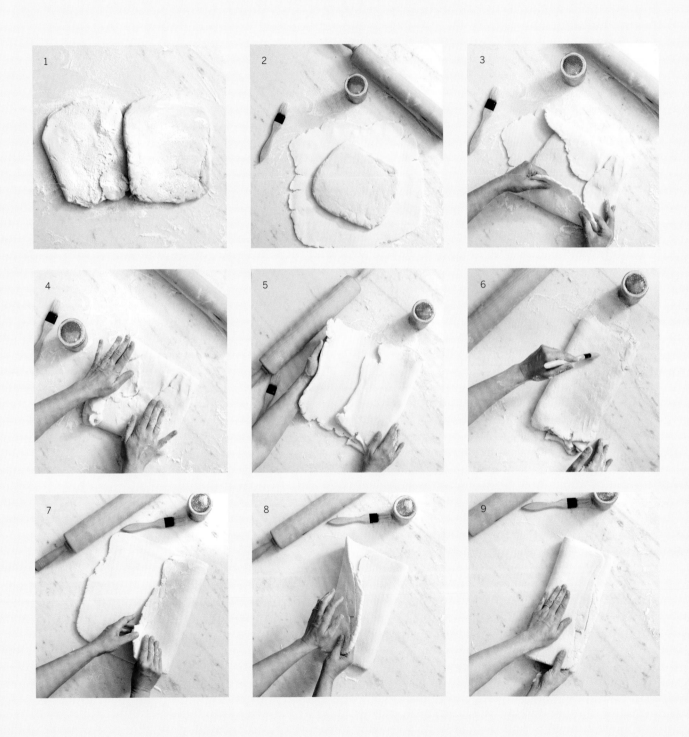

FOUNDATION RECIPE

**MAKES:** just over 2.2 lb (1 kg) puff pastry dough

**PREP TIME:** 30 minutes, plus chilling

**⁏⁏ MORE INVOLVED**
BITES OF WISDOM:
*How to make high-fat butter for baking: Ghee and the Pearson Square (p. 72)*

## INGREDIENTS

**3 cups (450 g)** all-purpose flour

**1 Tbsp (12 g)** granulated sugar

**2 tsp** fine salt

**2 Tbsp (30 mL)** vegetable oil

**2 cups (450 g)** unsalted high-fat butter (ideally 82% to 84%), cold, cut into 1-inch (2.5 cm) pieces

**¾ cup (175 mL)** cool water

**1 Tbsp (15 mL)** white vinegar or lemon juice

# Puff Pastry Dough (Quick Method)

The first part of this technique for making puff pastry will remind you of making pie pastry, but with more butter. Because the butter is worked right into the dough sooner, it shortens the rolling and folding process and allows you to double up on the folds at each stage after resting. But don't let the word "quick" fool you—you still need to leave at least an hour between each set of folds to allow the dough to relax.

1. **Combine the dry ingredients and oil.** Mix the flour, sugar and salt in a large bowl. Add the oil. Using a pastry cutter, electric beaters or a mixer fitted with the paddle attachment, blend until the flour looks evenly crumbly.

   *Just like my Classic Pie Dough recipe (p. 108), I coat the flour with oil before adding the butter and liquids. This protects the flour from overhydrating and toughening up when the water is added.*

2. **Add the butter** and cut in until the dough is rough and crumbly, yet pieces of butter are still visible.

   *Because this dough goes through repeated foldings, having plainly visible pieces of butter is acceptable before adding the liquids. The folding (laminating) process will flatten the butter pieces into thin sheets, ensuring a flaky pastry.*

3. **Add the liquid.** Mix the water and vinegar (or lemon juice) together, then add all at once to the flour mixture. Mix just until the dough comes together. Shape into a rectangle (the dough will seem rough and shaggy), wrap well and chill for an hour before rolling (1).

4. **Laminate the layers for the first time.** Dust a work surface and a heavy rolling pin well with flour. Roll the dough into a 10 × 20-inch (25 × 50 cm) rectangle, brush off excess flour (2) and fold into thirds (3, 4). Rotate the dough 90 degrees and repeat rolling the dough to a 10 × 20-inch (25 × 50 cm) rectangle. Brush off any flour, then fold into a book fold. Wrap and chill the dough for at least an hour (and up to a day).

   *See p. 165 for images on each of the folding (laminating) techniques and steps.*

5. **Roll and fold the layers a second time.** On the floured work surface, roll the dough into a 10 × 20-inch (25 × 50 cm) rectangle, brush off excess flour and fold into thirds. Rotate the dough 90 degrees, repeat the rolling and then fold into a book fold (p. 165). Wrap and chill the dough for at least an hour (and up to a day).

6. **Do a final fold.** On a lightly floured work surface, roll, brush and fold the dough into thirds, then rotate the dough 90 degrees and roll, brush and fold into a book fold a final time (5, 6, 7). Wrap the dough again and chill for at least 2 hours (up to a day) before using.

   **The puff pastry dough can keep, well wrapped in plastic, in the fridge for up to 4 days. Alternatively, portion and freeze the dough for up to 3 months. Thaw in the fridge before using.**

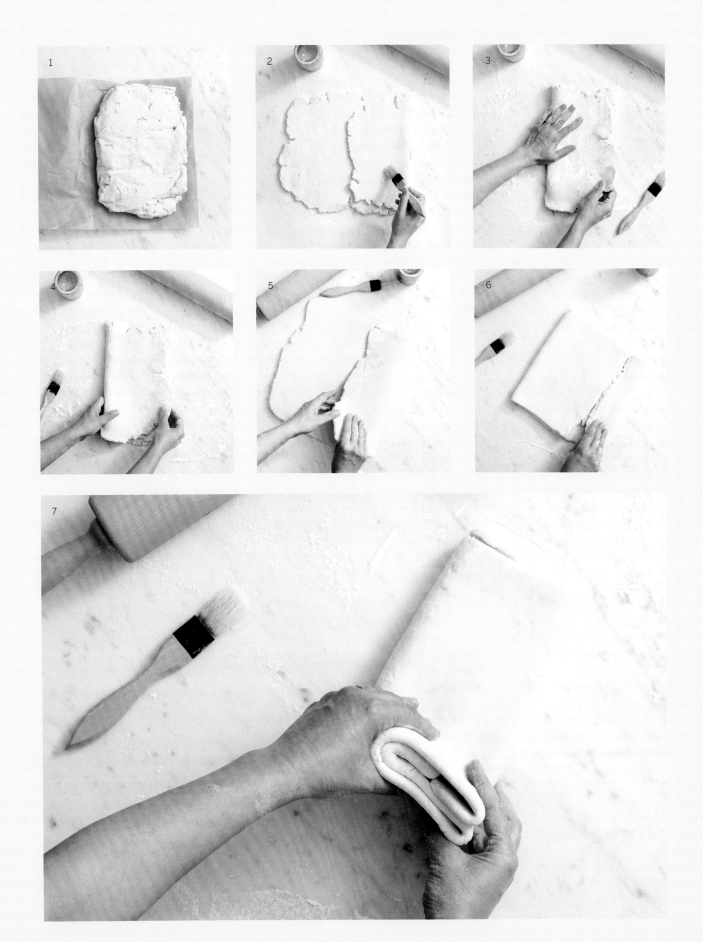

**MAKES:** one 10-inch (25 cm) tart
**SERVES:** 6 to 8

**PREP TIME:** 20 minutes
**COOK TIME:** 70 minutes

**❚ SIMPLE**
**BITES OF WISDOM:**
*How to roll pastry doughs (p. 44)*

**INGREDIENTS**

**3** medium cooking onions

**2 Tbsp (30 mL)** extra-virgin olive oil

**4** cloves garlic, minced

**2 tsp** herbes de Provence

**½ tsp** ground black pepper

**½ cup (125 mL)** dry white wine

**½ lb (225 g)** Puff Pastry Dough (p. 162 or 164) or store-bought all-butter puff pastry

**20 to 25** salted anchovy fillets

**25** pitted Niçoise or kalamata olives

# Pissaladière

The traditional Provençal tart is made with a pizza-like yeast dough and is topped with olives, onions and anchovies, but it can also be upscaled using puff pastry as the base, as I've done here. A pissaladière is perfect with an aperitif—a salty, flavourful bite to enjoy with a glass of chilled rosé wine.

1. **Caramelize the onions.** Peel the onions and slice them thinly. Heat the olive oil in a large sauté pan over medium heat for a minute, then add the onions. Cook them down, stirring often, until softened and translucent, about 20 minutes. Add the garlic, herbes de Provence, and black pepper and cook for another 20 minutes, adding white wine in splashes occasionally to loosen the caramelized bits at the bottom of the pan, until the onions are a rich golden brown. Transfer the onions to a dish to cool completely before using, or chill until ready to assemble the tart.

   *If you don't have herbes de Provence, add 1 tsp dried thyme, 1 tsp dried oregano and two bay leaves to the onions (remove the bay leaves before baking the tart).*

   *Instead of using anchovy fillets, you can stir 1 Tbsp (15 mL) anchovy paste into the caramelized onions right before taking them off the heat.*

2. **Preheat the oven** to 400°F (200°C) and line a baking tray with parchment paper.

3. **Roll out the puff pastry** on a lightly floured surface to a 10-inch (25 cm) square. Place the puff pastry on the tray and dock it with a fork.

4. **Arrange the toppings.** Spread the cooled caramelized onions over the pastry almost right to the edges. Arrange the anchovy fillets over the onions in a criss-cross pattern, or as you wish, leaving space in between them. Dot the tart with the olives.

5. **Bake the pissaladière** for about 30 minutes, until the pastry is an even rich golden brown when lifted from the tray. Cool for at least 20 minutes before slicing into little squares to serve. Serve warm or at room temperature.

   **After serving, the pissaladière will keep, well wrapped, in the fridge for up to 3 days. To rewarm it, place on a baking tray and heat for about 10 minutes in a 350°F (180°C) oven.**

MAKES: one 9-inch (23 cm) tart
SERVES: 6 to 8

PREP TIME: 12 minutes
COOK TIME: 45 minutes

♦ SIMPLE
BITES OF WISDOM:
*How to roll pastry doughs (p. 44)*

**INGREDIENTS**

½ lb (225 g) Puff Pastry Dough (p. 162 or 164) or store-bought all-butter puff pastry

1 lb (450 g) russet potatoes (about 2 medium)

3 Tbsp (45 g) butter, divided

2 tsp extra virgin olive oil

Pinch of fine salt

# Potato Tarte Tatin

This buttery, crispy potato tart is inspired by the classic apple tarte tatin, where apples are baked in a skillet with the pastry on top and then inverted to serve. This potato version layers thin potato slices in a skillet in the fashion of pommes Anna (definitely not named after me), and then the puff pastry is laid on top to bake. The potatoes crisp up in the pan, and the puff pastry has the freedom to puff up. Once inverted, this gratifyingly flaky tart is perfect next to slices of roast beef or chicken and all of their lovely juices, or as an appetizer with smoked salmon and sour cream.

1. **Preheat the oven** to 375°F (190°C).

2. **Roll out the puff pastry** on a lightly floured surface to a circle just over 10 inches (25 cm) across and just under ¼ inch (6 mm) thick. Trim to a 10-inch (25 cm) circle, dock with a fork and place on a plate to chill while preparing the potatoes.

3. **Prepare the potato layer.** Peel the potatoes and slice to ⅛ inch (3 mm) thick (use a mandoline if you have one). Heat a 9-inch (23 cm) ovenproof skillet or pan over medium-high heat and add 2 Tbsp (30 g) butter and the olive oil. Swirl to coat the pan and overlap the potato slices as you fan them to cover the bottom of the pan. Sprinkle lightly with salt and repeat with any remaining potato slices. Dot the top with the remaining 1 Tbsp (15 g) butter. Place a piece of parchment on top of the potatoes and transfer the pan from the stove to the oven. Bake until the potatoes are tender when pierced with a knife, about 15 minutes.

   *If you don't have a 9-inch (23 cm) skillet, melt the butter and then arrange the potatoes in a 9-inch (23 cm) glass pie plate instead.*

4. **Bake the puff pastry.** Remove the pan from the oven, remove the parchment cover and place the chilled puff pastry on top of the potatoes. Return the pan to the oven and bake for about 30 minutes, until the pastry is a rich golden brown. Let the tarte tatin cool in the pan for 10 minutes, then cover with a serving platter and carefully invert the pan and the platter. Cut into wedges and serve warm.

   *Before inverting your potato tarte tatin, run a small knife or palette knife around the outside edge of the tart to loosen any potato that may have stuck to the pan.*

   **The tarte tatin is best served freshly baked, but any remaining will keep, loosely wrapped, in the fridge for up to 3 days. Rewarm for 10 minutes in a 350°F (180°C) oven before serving.**

**MAKES:** 4 pastries

**PREP TIME:** 20 minutes, plus chilling
**COOK TIME:** 20 minutes

❗ SIMPLE
**BITES OF WISDOM:**
*How to roll pastry doughs (p. 44)*

**INGREDIENTS**

1 Tbsp (15 g) butter

1½ lb (675 g) fresh whole spinach leaves
or 1 lb (450 g) frozen and thawed
chopped spinach

2 cloves garlic, minced

Salt and pepper

20 oz (600 g) Puff Pastry Dough (p. 162
or 164) or 4 sheets (900 g) store-
bought all-butter puff pastry

4 (5 oz/150 g) skinless salmon fillets

Medium egg wash (see p. 33)

# Salmon & Spinach Wellingtons

Classic beef Wellington is a dish made by wrapping a portion of beef tenderloin in puff pastry with a mushroom filling in between. With this salmon and spinach version, the assembly process is simplified and each diner will have their own individual pastry.

1. **Prepare the spinach.** Melt the butter in a large sauté pan over medium-high heat and add the spinach. Sauté until wilted (if using fresh) and any excess liquid has evaporated. Add the garlic and season to taste with salt and pepper. Let the spinach cool completely, then chill before assembling the Wellingtons.

   *If you use fresh spinach, choose a large-leaf variety, which has a little more structure and flavour, instead of baby spinach.*

2. **Preheat the oven** to 400°F (200°C) and line a baking tray with parchment paper.

3. **Assemble the Wellingtons.** If using homemade puff pastry, divide the dough into four portions and roll out each one into an 8-inch (20 cm) square. If using store-bought sheets of prerolled pastry, trim each piece to an 8-inch (20 cm) square. Divide half of the spinach among the pastry squares, mounding it in the middle (1). Lightly season the fish and place a fillet on top of the spinach. Spoon the remaining spinach on top of the fish. Bring the corners of the pastry together, pinch the seams to seal the parcels and place, seam side down, on the baking tray (2). You can assemble the Wellingtons up to 6 hours ahead and chill before baking.

4. **Finish the Wellingtons.** Brush each Wellington with the egg wash. Use the back of a paring knife to mark a pattern on top of each parcel, but do not cut through the pastry (3).

5. **Bake for 20 minutes,** until the pastry is a rich golden brown. Serve immediately.

**The Wellingtons are best hot from the oven right after baking. Leftovers can be reheated for 15 minutes in a 325°F (160°C) oven.**

**MAKES:** one 8-inch (20 cm) tart
**SERVES:** 6

**PREP TIME:** under 15 minutes
**COOK TIME:** 35 minutes

🍴 **SIMPLE**
**BITES OF WISDOM:**
*How to roll pastry doughs (p. 44)*

**INGREDIENTS**

½ lb (225 g) Puff Pastry Dough (p. 162 or 164) or store-bought all-butter puff pastry

1 large or 2 small baking apples, such as Honeycrisp, Granny Smith or Cortland

3 Tbsp (45 g) butter, melted, divided

3 Tbsp (37 g) granulated sugar, divided

¼ cup (60 mL) apple jelly or apricot jam

# Tarte Fine aux Pommes (Thin Apple Tart)

The simplest desserts sometimes show off the complexity of puff pastry best. This French tart is a sheet of puff pastry topped with a single overlapping layer of thinly sliced apples basted with butter and sprinkled with sugar. The apples caramelize at the edges and the result is uncomplicated and entirely satisfying.

1. **Preheat the oven** to 400°F (200°C) and line a baking tray with parchment paper.

2. **Roll out the puff pastry** on a lightly floured surface to a circle about 9 inches (23 cm) across and just under ¼ inch (6 mm) thick. Use a plate or bowl to trace and cut a disc of pastry 8 inches (20 cm) across. Place on the baking tray and dock the pastry with a fork (1).

3. **Assemble the tart.** Peel the apples, cut in half and core. Cut the apples into slices about ⅛ inch (3 mm) thick. Arrange the apples over the puff pastry, overlapping them in a single layer that reaches almost to the outside edge of the pastry. Brush the apples with half of the butter (2) and sprinkle with half of the sugar (3).

*If you have a mandoline, use it to get thin, even slices. Thick slices weigh down the puff pastry and will result in a heavy, dense crust instead of light, crisp pastry.*

4. **Bake the tart** for 10 minutes, brush it with the remaining butter and sugar, and return to the oven to bake for 20 to 25 minutes more, until the puff pastry is golden brown at the edges. The butter and sugar may caramelize a little, adding a nice crunch once cooled.

5. **Cool and glaze the tart.** Let the tart cool on its tray on a rack for 15 minutes. Melt the apple jelly (or apricot jam) in the microwave or in a small saucepan over medium heat and use a pastry brush to apply a thin layer to the apples. Serve warm or at room temperature.

**The tart will keep, loosely covered, in the fridge for up to 3 days.**

MAKES: one 4 × 10-inch (10 × 25 cm) tart
SERVES: 8

PREP TIME: 30 minutes, plus chilling
COOK TIME: 35 minutes

🍴 MORE INVOLVED
BITES OF WISDOM:
*How to roll pastry doughs (p. 44),*
*Glossary of ingredients—Pearl sugar*
*(p. 12)*

### INGREDIENTS

**Mincemeat:**

1 apple or pear

¾ cup (112 g) raisins

¼ cup (35 g) dried cranberries

2 Tbsp (10 g) finely chopped crystallized ginger

¼ cup (60 mL) orange marmalade

¼ cup (60 mL) maple syrup

2 Tbsp (25 g) packed dark brown sugar

¾ tsp ground cinnamon

¼ tsp ground allspice

¼ tsp ground nutmeg

2 Tbsp (30 mL) brandy or rum

¼ cup (27 g) slivered or sliced almonds

**Assembly:**

1 lb (450 g) Puff Pastry Dough (p. 162 or 164) or store-bought all-butter puff pastry

Medium egg wash (see p. 33)

Turbinado or pearl sugar, for sprinkling

# Mincemeat Dartois

A dartois is a rectangular filled puff pastry tart with slits cut into the top layer of pastry to reveal the filling and let steam escape as it bakes. A dartois can be very rustic and approachable or very polished and professional. This recipe uses a spiced mincemeat filling, making it a nice dessert to end a holiday meal or add to an assortment of desserts for a larger group. Dress up individual portions with a scoop of vanilla ice cream or a dollop of Crème Fraîche (p. 94).

1. **Make the mincemeat.** Peel the apple (or pear) and use a box grater to coarsely grate it into a saucepan. Add the raisins, dried cranberries, ginger, marmalade, maple syrup, brown sugar, cinnamon, allspice and nutmeg and bring to a simmer over medium heat, stirring often. Simmer for about 15 minutes, reducing the heat if the sauce begins to stick, until the apple (or pear) cooks into the filling (it will no longer be clearly visible). Remove the mincemeat from the heat and stir in the brandy (or rum) and the almonds. Cool to room temperature and then chill completely before using. You can prepare the mincemeat up to a week in advance.

   *This mincemeat recipe makes 1½ cups (375 mL) of filling. Double the recipe to make enough filling for a traditional two-crust mincemeat pie. Follow the assembly and baking instructions for the Apple, Spiced Plum & Cranberry Pie (p. 116).*

2. **Preheat the oven** to 400°F (200°C) and line a baking tray with parchment paper.

3. **Roll out the puff pastry** on a lightly floured work surface to a rectangle just over 8 × 10 inches (20 × 25 cm) and just under ¼ inch (6 mm) thick. Trim the edges to straighten, then cut the pastry in half to make two 4 × 10-inch (10 × 25 cm) pieces (1).

4. **Assemble the dartois.** Place one piece of pastry on the baking tray. Dock the pastry with a fork and brush the outside edge with water. Spoon the mincemeat over the pastry, leaving a clear ½-inch (1.2 cm) edge uncovered on all sides. Use a paring knife or pastry wheel to cut slits into the second sheet of pastry, about an inch (2.5 cm) apart (2). Carefully lift the pastry up and place over the mincemeat filling, letting the slits open. Line up the edges of the top and bottom pieces of pastry and press down gently to secure them (3).

5. **Brush the top** of the dartois with egg wash and sprinkle with sugar.

6. **Bake the dartois** for about 30 minutes, until the pastry is an even rich golden brown. Let the pastry cool on the tray on a rack for at least 1 hour before slicing to serve. Serve warm or at room temperature.

   The dartois is best enjoyed the day it is made, but the unbaked dartois can be wrapped well and frozen for up to 3 months. Thaw overnight in the fridge before baking. Reheat for 10 minutes at 350°F (180°C) before serving. Once served, remaining dartois will keep, loosely wrapped, in the fridge for up to 3 days.

**MAKES:** one 9-inch (23 cm) dessert
**SERVES:** 8

**PREP TIME:** 25 minutes
**COOK TIME:** 35 minutes

❗ **SIMPLE**
**BITES OF WISDOM:**
*How to roll pastry doughs (p. 44)*

### INGREDIENTS

**1 lb (450 g)** Puff Pastry Dough (p. 162 or 164) or store-bought all-butter puff pastry

**1⅔ cups (215 g)** Tant pour Tant (p. 82)

**6 Tbsp (90 g)** unsalted butter, at room temperature and cut into pieces

**1** large egg

**½ tsp** vanilla extract

**½ tsp** almond extract

**1** whole almond, candied cherry or small cookie

**¼ cup (27 g)** toasted sliced almonds

Medium egg wash (see p. 33)

# Galette des Rois

This "cake of kings" is a traditional French dessert made to celebrate the Epiphany, the 12th day of Christmas. In the spirit of the three Magi bringing gifts to the baby Jesus, a little gift or surprise is hidden in this frangipane-filled puff pastry dessert, and whoever finds it is named queen or king for the day. Instead of the original bean (fève) or trinket, in this dessert the fève is a whole almond, candied cherry or small cookie, so it's OK if it is bitten into.

1. **Preheat the oven** to 400°F (200°C) and line a baking tray with parchment paper.

2. **Roll out the puff pastry.** If using a block of homemade puff pastry, cut it into two squares. On a lightly floured surface, roll out the first square to a circle just over 9 inches (23 cm) across and just over ¼ inch (6 mm) thick. Cut out a 9-inch (23 cm) circle and dock with a fork. Place the piece of pastry on a plate and refrigerate while you roll out the second piece of puff pastry to the same thickness and cut to the same size. Do not dock this piece. Chill both pieces of pastry while preparing the filling.

   If using store-bought puff pastry, cut each ½ lb (225 g) sheet into a 9-inch (23 cm) circle. Dock one circle with a fork and chill both pieces while you prepare the filling.

3. **Make the filling.** Using a mini chopper or food processor, pulse the tant pour tant with the butter until combined. Add the egg and the vanilla and almond extracts and pulse to a thick but relatively smooth paste.

   *Be sure to blend the butter and tant pour tant before adding the egg. If you try to blend all of the ingredients at once, you may find the filling leaks out from the pastry as it bakes.*

4. **Assemble the galette.** Remove the pastry discs from the fridge and place the docked piece onto the baking tray. Spread the filling overtop, mounding it so the filling has a dome shape and leaving ¾ inch (2 cm) around the edge. Press the almond, cherry or cookie into the filling (1) (but not into the centre). Brush the visible pastry edge with water. Sprinkle the toasted almonds on top and place the second disc of pastry overtop, letting it gently stretch to cover the filling and meet the edge of the base pastry piece.

5. **Crimp and decorate the galette.** Use your finger to crimp the edges of the pastry to seal the galette, or use a tool to create a decorative pattern (2). Brush the entire surface of the galette with egg wash. Use a paring knife to mark a pattern into the pastry, taking care not to cut through it (3). When you've completed the pattern, cut three or four slits toward the top of the galette to allow steam to escape.

6. **Bake the galette** for about 35 minutes, until it is a rich golden brown. Cool the pastry on the tray on a rack. Slice and serve at room temperature.

   **The galette will keep, wrapped in plastic, in the fridge for up to 3 days. To serve, reheat at 325°F (160°C) for about 15 minutes to crisp up the pastry and serve at room temperature.**

**MAKES:** 6 individual desserts

**PREP TIME:** 20 minutes
**COOK TIME:** 25 minutes

❘ SIMPLE
BITES OF WISDOM:
*How to roll pastry doughs (p. 44)*

**INGREDIENTS**

---

**Pastries:**

½ lb (225 g) Puff Pastry Dough (p. 162 or 164) or store-bought all-butter puff pastry

Medium egg wash (see p. 33)

**Filling:**

½ cup (125 mL) whipping cream

¼ cup (32 g) icing sugar, plus extra for dusting

¼ cup (60 g) mascarpone cheese or softened cream cheese

1 Tbsp (15 mL) finely grated orange or lemon zest

¼ tsp ground nutmeg

1 cup (225 g) creamy ricotta cheese

2 cups (330 g) sliced fresh strawberries

# Strawberry Ricotta Napoleons

A napoleon and a mille-feuille are virtually the same dessert of layered pastry and filling, but a napoleon is an individual pastry whereas a mille-feuille is a larger, more structured version that is sliced into portions after assembling (see Caramelized Peach Mille-feuille, p. 181). These strawberry ricotta napoleons are perfect for a dinner party because you can bake the individual puff pastry layers, make the ricotta filling and slice the strawberries in advance, then assemble the desserts just before serving.

1. **Preheat the oven** to 400°F (200°C) and line a baking tray with parchment paper.

2. **Roll out the puff pastry** on a lightly floured surface to an 8 × 12-inch (20 × 30 cm) rectangle. Trim away the rough edges so that you are left with a more precise 8 × 10-inch (20 × 25 cm) rectangle. Use a pastry wheel or knife to cut into six 3-inch (7.5 cm) squares. Place on the baking tray and dock the pastries with a fork. Brush the pastries with egg wash and bake for about 25 minutes, until puffed and a rich golden brown on top. Cool the pastries on the tray on a rack until ready to assemble. (You can bake the pastry a day ahead and store on the counter in an airtight container.)

3. **Make the filling.** Whip the cream by hand or with electric beaters until it holds a soft peak. Whip in the icing sugar and chill until ready to use. Place the mascarpone (or cream cheese), citrus zest and nutmeg in a medium bowl. Vigorously beat by hand until the mixture is as smooth as it can be. Fold in the whipped cream and chill until ready to assemble the napoleons.

   *This filling is very much like a creamy cannoli filling. In that Italian dessert, tubes of crispy pastry are filled with a sweet ricotta cream that's sometimes studded with pistachios or chocolate. To make a cannoli-inspired napoleon, add a grating of dark chocolate to the filling.*

4. **Assemble the napoleons.** Split open each puff pastry square horizontally to create a top and bottom half. Place each bottom half on a dessert plate and dollop the ricotta on top. Spoon the strawberries over the ricotta and place the top half of the puff pastry square on top. Dust with icing sugar and serve.

   **The pastry squares can be baked up to a day ahead and stored in an airtight container on the counter.**

**MAKES:** one 4 × 12-inch (10 × 30 cm)
mille-feuille

**SERVES:** 6

**PREP TIME:** 40 minutes, plus chilling
**COOK TIME:** 40 minutes

**॥॥ COMPLEX**

**BITES OF WISDOM:**
*How to roll pastry doughs (p. 44)*

**INGREDIENTS**

**Caramelized peaches:**

**1 Tbsp (15 g)** unsalted butter

**10 oz (300 g)** frozen peach slices,
thawed and drained

**⅓ cup (70 g)** granulated sugar

**2 tsp** lemon juice

**Assembly:**

**1 lb (450 g)** Puff Pastry Dough (p. 162 or
164) or **2 (8 oz/250 g)** sheets frozen
puff pastry, thawed

**1 recipe** Caramel Diplomat Cream
(p. 98), chilled for at least 4 hours

Icing sugar, for dusting

# Caramelized Peach Mille-feuille

A mille-feuille is an assembled puff pastry dessert filled with a cream filling. Here the puff pastry layers are baked under a weight so they compress and caramelize, crisping up tremendously and browning the butter within the pastry. This flavour matches wonderfully with the caramelized peaches.

1. **Caramelize the peaches.** Melt the butter in a sauté pan over medium heat and add the peaches. Cook for about 5 minutes, stirring often, until any excess liquid has evaporated and the peaches start to brown slightly. Add the sugar and lemon juice and continue to cook, stirring often, until the juices begin to thicken and turn a burnt orange colour, about 5 minutes. Remove the pan from the heat to cool, then chill the peaches for at least 2 hours.

   *Peaches have a high water content, which can make them seem tasteless or watery in desserts. By cooking them down this way, you are assured of a concentrated peach flavour and no watery sauce. The caramelized sugar paired with the natural pectin in the fruit sets up the sauce.*

2. **Preheat the oven** to 400°F (200°C) and line a baking tray with parchment paper. Have a second baking tray of the same size on hand.

3. **Cut the pastry dough into three equal pieces.** On a lightly floured surface, roll out each piece to a rectangle about 5 × 14 inches (12.5 × 35 cm). If needed, stack the three pieces of dough and trim the edges so that they are all the same size (they will be closer to 4 × 12 inches/10 × 30 cm once trimmed). If using store-bought puff pastry, cut three rectangles each 4 × 12 inches (10 × 30 cm). Chill the dough for 15 minutes.

4. **Bake the puff pastry.** Place the three pieces of dough on the lined baking tray and dock with a fork. Place a second sheet of parchment paper over the pastry and place the second baking tray on top. Bake the pastry for 10 minutes, then add a heavy weight on top of the top baking tray (a cast-iron skillet, or even two bricks wrapped in foil) and bake for 10 minutes more. Remove the weights, the top baking tray and the parchment and bake for about 10 more minutes, until the pastry is a rich golden brown. Cool completely before assembling.

5. **Assemble the mille-feuille.** Trim the edges of the pastry if needed with a sharp chef's knife or a serrated knife. Place one of the pastry pieces on a platter or flat board. Spread or pipe half of the diplomat cream onto the puff pastry and spoon half of the peaches on top. Top with a second sheet of pastry and spread with the remaining half of the pastry cream followed by the peaches. Top with the third piece of pastry and press it down ever so gently. Chill for at least an hour or up to 1 day.

6. **Finish and serve.** Dust the top of the mille-feuille generously with icing sugar. Cut into six individual portions right before serving.

   **The mille-feuille can be prepared up to a day in advance and will keep, loosely wrapped, in the fridge for up to 2 days.**

**MAKES:** about 2.2 lbs (1 kg) of dough (enough for 30 croissants)

**PREP TIME:** 90 minutes, plus lots of chilling

### ††† COMPLEX

**BITES OF WISDOM:**
*How to make high-fat butter for baking: Ghee and the Pearson Square (p. 72)*

## INGREDIENTS

**Détrempe:**

3½ cups (525 g) all-purpose flour

1 cup (250 mL) water, at room temperature

½ cup (125 mL) 2% milk, at room temperature

5 Tbsp (62 g) granulated sugar

1 (2¼ tsp/7 g) pkg instant dry yeast

1¼ tsp fine salt

2 Tbsp (30 g) unsalted high-fat (82% to 84%) butter, at room temperature

**Beurrage:**

1¼ cups (285 g) unsalted high-fat (82% to 84%) butter, at room temperature

Dark egg wash (see p. 33)

# Classic Croissant Dough

Making croissants from scratch is a bit of a project, but a gratifying one when you finally tear into a warm, homemade croissant, watching the soft, buttery interior unravel while a cascade of crumbs crackle and fall from the exterior and land in your lap.

1. **Prepare the détrempe.** Line a baking tray with parchment paper and have ready a tea towel and some plastic wrap. Using a stand mixer fitted with the hook attachment, stir the flour, water, milk, sugar and yeast on low speed to blend, then add the salt. Increase the mixer speed by one level and knead for about 4 minutes, adding the butter midway through kneading—the dough should just clean the sides of the bowl. Shape the dough into a rectangle (it will be soft), place it on the lined baking tray and cover with the tea towel and then the plastic wrap. Let the dough sit out on the counter for 90 minutes, then chill for at least an hour or up to 8 hours.

   *Similar to making puff pastry, the fat content in your butter when making croissants really counts. Butter in Canada is 80% milk fat (butter fat), with the remaining 20% being milk solids and water. In Europe, butter is often 82% or 84% butter fat, making for richer, flakier pastries. You can find this higher-fat butter in Canada, or you can create your own 84% blend using the Pearson Square (p. 72) to calculate how to make the blend.*

2. **Prepare the beurrage.** Shape the butter into an 8-inch (20 cm) square. Chill until ready to use if preparing in advance, but pull from the fridge to soften. Ensure that the butter has the same resistance (is the same consistency) as the chilled dough. (They may not be the same temperature, but they should have the same "give.")

3. **Fold the beurrage into the détrempe.** On a floured work surface, turn out the chilled détrempe and roll out to a square about 14 inches (35 cm) across. Place the beurrage in the centre of the square, but rotated so that the points of the butter square fall at the middle of each flat side of the dough. Bring the corners of the dough together, wrapping the butter like an envelope, and gently pinch the edges (1, 2, 3). Roll the dough (4) out into a rectangle about 20 inches (50 cm) long, then fold the dough into thirds (5). Return the dough to the baking tray, cover with the towel and plastic wrap and chill for at least an hour and up to 8 hours.

4. **Continue folding and resting the dough.** Repeat rolling and folding the dough into thirds two more times, rotating the dough 90 degrees each time (6, 7, 8) before rolling and chilling the dough for at least an hour and up to 8 hours before each fold. Let the dough rest for at least 4 hours and up to 12 hours after the final fold before using (9).

Croissant dough does not need to be folded as many times as puff pastry. While both types of pastry use three steps of rolling and folding with rests in between, croissant dough is only folded once at each step whereas puff pastry is folded twice at each step. Puff pastry relies on the multiple folds to lift the pastry so it becomes flaky and layered as it bakes. Croissant dough contains yeast, which further pushes and separates the layers as they bake.

**You can make the croissant dough ahead of time, fold it and let it rise, then refrigerate wrapped in plastic, for up to 2 days. The dough can also be frozen for up to 3 months and thawed in the fridge for 24 hours before using.**

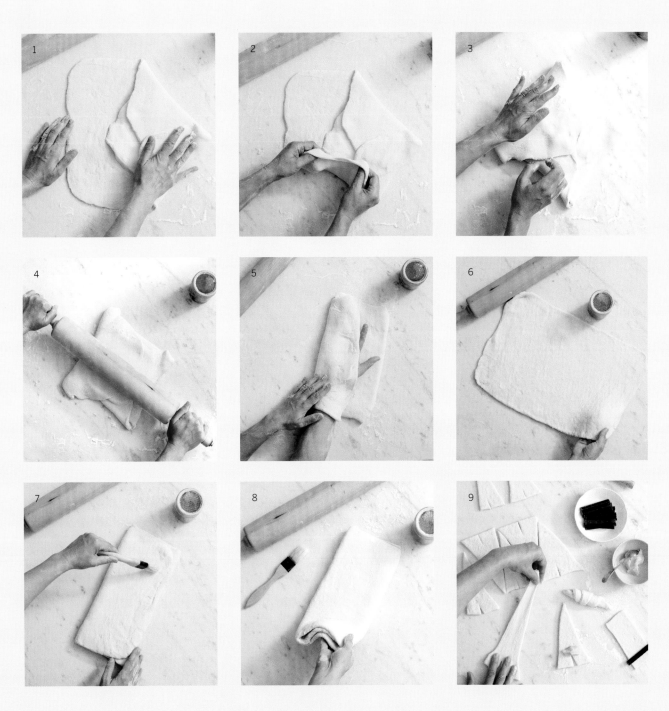

**MAKES:** 12 croissants

**PREP TIME:** 10 minutes
**COOK TIME:** 15 minutes

🍴 **MORE INVOLVED**
**BITES OF WISDOM:**
*How to roll pastry doughs (p. 44), How pastry bakes (p. 69)*

**INGREDIENTS**

**1 lb (450 g)** Classic Croissant Dough
   (p. 182)

Dark egg wash (see p. 33)

# Classic Butter Croissants

There is a satisfaction to the process of rolling out croissant dough, cutting it into triangles and rolling into that familiar croissant shape. There is even more satisfaction when you tear into a freshly baked croissant—flakes of crisp pastry go everywhere, and as you pull the croissant apart, the soft, buttery centre unravels so invitingly.

1. **Roll out the croissant dough** on a lightly floured surface to a rectangle about 12 × 16 inches (30 × 41 cm). Cut the dough in half horizontally to make two 8 × 12-inch (20 × 30 cm) rectangles. Cut six triangles, each 2 × 8 × 8 inches (5 × 20 × 20 cm), from each half.

2. **Shape the croissants.** Place each triangle with the short side parallel to the edge of the counter and the point facing away from you. Make a 1-inch (2.5 cm) notch on the short side of each triangle and roll up the croissant from this side. If you'd like a curved croissant (but see my note below), curve the croissant so that the point of the triangle is at the bottom and the two ends point up like a smile. Place on a parchment-lined baking tray, leaving at least 3 inches (7.5 cm) between each croissant. Cover with a tea towel and then plastic wrap. Let the croissants rise for 2½ hours.

   *Do not skimp on this long proofing time. After being in the fridge, the yeast has to "wake up" to really lift the croissants as the butter melts at the same time in the oven. If underproofed, the butter may leach out of the croissant as it bakes. The result will still be flaky, but the croissant will be quite dense and small.*

   *In France, some plain croissants have a curved shape and others are straight. The straight ones are all-butter croissants, and the curved ones indicate they are made with other fats (and are sometimes slightly less expensive).*

3. **Preheat the oven** to 375°F (190°C) and brush the croissants with the egg wash.

4. **Bake the croissants** for about 15 minutes, until a rich golden brown. Serve them warm from the oven or at least the day they are baked.

   **You can make the croissant dough ahead of time, fold it and let it rise, then cut and shape the croissants. Freeze the croissants on a baking tray, then pack them in an airtight container and freeze for up to 3 months. Thaw frozen croissants on the counter and, once thawed, proof for about 3 hours before baking.**

**MAKES:** 12 croissants

**PREP TIME:** 15 minutes
**COOK TIME:** 15 minutes

🍴 **MORE INVOLVED**

**BITES OF WISDOM:**
*Glossary of ingredients—Nuts & seeds (p. 11), How pastry bakes (p. 69)*

**INGREDIENTS**

¼ cup (30 g) ground almonds

3 Tbsp (37 g) granulated sugar

4 tsp (20 g) unsalted butter, at room temperature

Dash of almond extract (optional)

**1 lb (450 g)** Classic Croissant Dough (p. 182)

Dark egg wash (see p. 33)

Sliced almonds, for sprinkling

Icing sugar, for dusting

**BONUS BAKE**

## Ham & Cheese Croissants

For a savoury croissant, follow the same assembly method as above, but replace the almond filling with **2 Tbsp (14 g) grated Cheddar cheese** and **1 Tbsp (6 g) finely diced ham**. After brushing with egg wash, sprinkle the top of each croissant with **a little grated Cheddar** before baking.

# Almond Croissants

I have a sincere respect for the plain butter croissant, but when I am treating myself to a flavoured croissant, I will always pick an almond croissant. That soft almond paste filling and the crunchy, toasted almonds on top . . . mmm!

1. **Make the almond paste.** Stir the ground almonds, granulated sugar, butter and almond extract, if using, in a small bowl until evenly blended, then set aside.

2. **Roll out the croissant dough** on a lightly floured surface to a large square about 18 inches (46 cm) across. Cut the dough in half horizontally and then cut six triangles from each half.

3. **Fill and shape the croissants.** Make a 1-inch (2.5 cm) score on the short side of each triangle and drop a teaspoonful of the almond paste at the base of the score mark. Roll up the croissant from this side, tucking in the almond paste as you roll. Place the croissant (do not curve it) so the point of the triangle is at the bottom. Gently pinch the ends of the croissant down (to hold the almond filling in). Place on a parchment-lined baking tray, leaving at least 3 inches (7.5 cm) between each croissant. Cover with a tea towel and then plastic wrap. Let the croissants rise at room temperature for 2½ hours.

*When you start rolling each croissant, tuck the pastry around the almond paste a little to help prevent the filling from leaking out as it bakes.*

4. **Preheat the oven** to 375 °F (190°C). Brush the croissants with the egg wash and sprinkle with sliced almonds.

5. **Bake the croissants** for about 15 minutes, until a rich golden brown. Let them cool, then generously dust with icing sugar before serving. Serve warm from the oven or at least the day they are baked.

**You can make the croissant dough ahead of time, fold it and let it rise, then cut and shape the croissants. Freeze the croissants on a baking tray, then pack them in an airtight container and freeze for up to 3 months. Thaw frozen croissants on the counter overnight and, once thawed, proof for about 3 hours before baking.**

Pains au Chocolat (p. 188),
Almond Croissants (p. 186),
Classic Butter Croissants
(p. 185)

**MAKES:** 6 pastries

**PREP TIME:** 15 minutes
**COOK TIME:** 15 minutes

🍴 **MORE INVOLVED**

**BITES OF WISDOM:**
*Glossary of ingredients—Chocolate (p. 5),
How pastry bakes (p. 69)*

**INGREDIENTS**

**8 oz (240 g)** Classic Croissant Dough
(p. 182)

**1½ oz (45 g)** semisweet baking/
couverture chocolate (51% to 55%
cocoa), chopped, or **6 Tbsp (108 g)**
Nutella or other chocolate hazelnut
spread

Dark egg wash (see p. 33)

Turbinado sugar, for sprinkling

*Photo on p. 187*

# Pains au Chocolat

Pains au chocolat are easy to spot in a bakery because they're rectangular rather than crescent-shaped like croissants. No matter their shape, they are hard to resist with a cup of coffee or a glass of milk. Be sure to use the best-quality semisweet chocolate you can find or use dollops of hazelnut chocolate spread, if you prefer.

1. **Roll out the dough** on a lightly floured surface to a large square about 9 inches (23 cm) across. Cut the dough in half horizontally, then cut three rectangles from each half so that each rectangle is 3 × 4½ inches (7.5 × 11.5 cm).

2. **Fill the pastries.** Place 1 Tbsp (15 mL) chopped chocolate (or Nutella) at the end of a short side of each rectangle. Roll up the pains au chocolat from this side. Place seam side down on a parchment-lined baking tray. Press in the sides if needed to ensure each pastry is a rectangle. Leave at least 3 inches (7.5 cm) between the pastries. Cover with a tea towel and then plastic wrap. Let the pastries rise for 2½ hours.

   *In their pains au chocolat, bakeries use special chocolate batons that are about 44% cocoa, so richer than milk chocolate but not as strong or brittle as dark chocolate. Once baked, these chocolate batons stay soft even when cool. You can order batons online, but using a semisweet chocolate with 51% to 55% cocoa comes very close.*

3. **Preheat the oven** to 375°F (190°C). Brush the pastries with the egg wash and sprinkle with a little turbinado sugar.

4. **Bake the pains au chocolat** for about 15 minutes, until a rich golden brown. Allow them to cool a little before serving. Serve warm from the oven or at least on the day they are baked.

   **You can make the croissant dough ahead of time, fold it and let it rise, then cut and shape the pains au chocolat. Freeze them on a baking tray, then pack in an airtight container and freeze for up to 3 months. Thaw frozen pains au chocolat on the counter overnight and, once thawed, proof for about 3 hours before baking.**

# Choux Paste

The very light, egg-based choux pastry dough is flavour neutral, which makes it the perfect vehicle for all kinds of fillings and toppings. As you practise making choux paste, you'll be able to master fillings made with pastry cream (p. 96, 97, 98 and 99) at the same time.

**MAKES:** enough for 48 profiteroles, 24 éclairs or 6 individual Paris-Brests

**PREP TIME:** 15 minutes
**COOK TIME:** under 5 minutes

**SIMPLE**
**BITES OF WISDOM:**
*How protein works in baking—Flour proteins, egg proteins (p. 65)*

## INGREDIENTS

¾ **cup (175 mL)** water

¼ **cup (60 mL)** 2% milk

½ **cup (115 g)** unsalted butter

2 **tsp** granulated sugar

½ **tsp** fine salt

1⅓ **cups (200 g)** all-purpose flour, sifted

4 large eggs, at room temperature

1. **Cook the paste.** Bring the water, milk, butter, sugar and salt to a full simmer in a medium saucepan over medium-high heat. Reduce the heat to low and stir in the flour with a wooden spoon, stirring vigorously until the dough "cleans" the sides of the pot (no longer sticks). Scrape this mixture into a large bowl.

   *Be sure the flour has enough time over the heat to fully hydrate and cook. Although the mixture will come together quickly when you stir in the flour, give the paste a good minute on the stove so the proteins in the flour develop structure. As the choux paste bakes, it inflates and this structure helps to hold in the air, resulting in a light and airy pastry.*

2. **Cool the paste slightly.** Using electric beaters or a stand mixer fitted with the paddle attachment, beat the paste at medium speed for a minute or two to cool it a little.

   *While the choux paste is mixed and used warm, you do need to give it a little time to cool so the eggs don't cook as you add them. This time also allows steam to dissipate so that you don't have excess moisture, which could prevent your choux pastry from rising as it bakes. A minute or two of mixing is enough to cool the paste down and further develop the proteins in the flour.*

3. **Add the eggs.** Break the four large eggs into a bowl and whisk them just to blend a little. Add a third of the eggs to the flour mixture while beating at medium speed, and mix until blended, scraping down the sides of the bowl. Add the remaining eggs in two more additions, blending and then scraping the bowl after each addition, until you get a smooth paste.

   *Adding the eggs gradually is the key to a smooth paste. The first addition of eggs will turn the paste into a real mess, but keep mixing, stopping to scrape the bowl well. Once that first addition of the eggs is blended in, the remaining two additions are absorbed much more quickly than the first.*

**Use the choux paste while it is still warm. If baking in batches, the choux can be used even if it cools to room temperature, but it cannot be made more than 90 minutes ahead nor chilled before baking.**

**MAKES:** 48 profiteroles

**PREP TIME:** 10 minutes
**COOK TIME:** 25 minutes

**SIMPLE**

**BITES OF WISDOM:**
*How to use piping bags & tips (p. 52),*
*Glossary of ingredients—Pearl sugar*
*(p. 12)*

**INGREDIENTS**

**1 recipe** Choux Paste (p. 189), freshly
made and warm

Medium egg wash (see p. 33)

Pearl sugar, for sprinkling

# Chouquettes

These unfilled profiteroles topped with pearl sugar are easy, light little sweet treats to serve with coffee or tea. Chouquettes are often sold by the dozen or half dozen in French bakeries. Use this recipe to practise your piping skills before you get into fillings and fancier toppings.

1. **Preheat the oven** to 400°F (200°C) and line two baking trays with parchment paper.

   *Try dabbing a little choux paste in each corner of the baking tray before you set the parchment paper on top. It will hold the paper in place when you lift up your piping bag while piping the sticky choux paste into balls. Those little dabs of choux paste on the tray will cook and flake off easily when it's time to clean up.*

2. **Pipe the profiteroles.** Spoon the choux paste into a large piping bag fitted with a large star or plain tip. Pipe the paste into spheres about 1½ inches (4 cm) across, lifting up the piping bag and leaving 2 inches (5 cm) between each puff to allow for expansion. If your puffs have a point on top from lifting the piping bag, dip your finger in water and pat it down. Brush the profiteroles with the egg wash and sprinkle generously with pearl sugar.

   *When piping profiteroles, try to avoid spiralling upward as you pipe—this will result in a profiterole that isn't perfectly round. Dabbing your finger with water to pat down any peaks also helps with the precision of the shape.*

3. **Bake the profiteroles** for about 25 minutes, until a rich golden brown.

4. **Cool the profiteroles.** Tip the pastries onto a cooling rack to cool completely before serving.

   **The chouquettes will keep, wrapped well in plastic, at room temperature for 1 day or frozen for up to 3 months. Thaw on the counter before filling.**

**MAKES:** 48 profiteroles

**PREP TIME:** 35 minutes
**COOK TIME:** 35 minutes

╫╫╫ COMPLEX
**BITES OF WISDOM:**
*How to use piping bags & tips (p. 52)*

**INGREDIENTS**

**Craquelin:**

**5 Tbsp (75 g)** unsalted butter, at room temperature

**¼ cup (50 g)** packed light brown sugar

**¼ cup (50 g)** granulated sugar

**¼ tsp** vanilla extract

**½ cup + 2 Tbsp (93 g)** all-purpose flour

Food colouring (optional)

**Assembly:**

**1 recipe** Choux Paste (p. 189), freshly made and still warm

**1 recipe** Mousseline Cream (p. 97), flavoured if you wish

# Profiteroles au Craquelin

These eye-catching cream-filled profiteroles are topped with a thin biscuit wafer, a craquelin, which melts and then breaks into a crackle pattern as the choux paste expands and bakes. It adds a subtle sweetness but a delectable crunch to your profiteroles, a lovely contrast to the smooth pastry cream filling. For variety, follow the instructions on p. 97 to divide the filling and make three different flavours. (I coordinated my craquelin colours with the following three fillings (pictured): brown—Tahini Mousseline; yellow—Saffron Lemon Mousseline; green—Matcha Green Tea Mousseline.)

1. **Mix the craquelin dough.** If mixing by hand, cream the butter and sugars together until well combined. Stir in the vanilla. Add the flour and stir until the dough comes together. If using a small chopper or food processor, pulse the butter, sugars and vanilla together until combined, add the flour and continue to pulse until a dough forms.

2. **Colour the craquelin.** If colouring the craquelin, add a few drops to the batter and knead well to work it in. You can divide the dough into thirds and create different colours. If your choux pastries are not yet piped, shape the craquelin dough into a disc, wrap and refrigerate until ready to roll out thinly and use.

   *Uncoloured craquelin naturally bakes up a light golden brown that can cause subtle colour additions to be lost. Add an extra droplet of colour to balance the neutralizing effect of the brown sugar.*

3. **Roll out the dough.** Cut two sheets of parchment paper and place the craquelin dough between them. Using a rolling pin, roll them as thinly as possible, to ⅛ inch (3 mm). If you are not ready to cut the craquelin, freeze rolled sheets until ready to use.

   *A little goes a long way with this recipe, which makes about 9 oz (270 g) craquelin, or enough for 48 éclairs or 96 profiteroles. You can make it ahead, wrap well and chill for up to a week or freeze for up to 3 months. I stack my sheets of craquelin between layers of parchment paper and slip them into a resealable bag to freeze. Use it directly from the freezer.*

4. **Preheat the oven** to 350°F (180°C) and line two baking trays with parchment paper.

   *Profiteroles au craquelin are baked at a lower temperature than usual so the sweet craquelin pastry doesn't burn (burning coloured craquelin is especially disappointing). They also take a little longer to bake to allow for the profiteroles to inflate and then dry out enough that they won't collapse.*

5. **Pipe the profiteroles.** Spoon the choux paste into a large piping bag fitted with a large star or plain tip. Pipe the paste into shapes about 1½ inches (4 cm) across, lifting up the piping bag and leaving 2 inches (5 cm) between each puff to allow for expansion (1).

*CONTINUES*

6. **Top with craquelin.** Use a small cookie cutter to cut circles of the same diameter as the choux paste or slightly smaller (2), and gently set them on top of each profiterole (3, 4).

7. **Bake the profiteroles** for about 20 minutes, open the oven door for 15 seconds, then close and continue to bake for another 10 to 15 minutes, until the profiterole pastry (not the craquelin) is a rich golden brown.

*Opening the oven door at the 20-minute mark allows any built-up steam to escape, which helps the profiteroles to dry out a little faster.*

8. **Cool the profiteroles.** Tip the pastries onto a cooling rack to cool to room temperature before filling.

9. **Fill the profiteroles.** Spoon the mousseline cream into a piping bag fitted with a small plain tip or doughnut tip. Use a bamboo skewer to make a small hole in the bottom of each profiterole. Insert the piping tip and fill the profiterole until you feel resistance, then pull the tip out gently, wiping away any cream that might leak out. Chill the profiteroles until ready to serve.

**Filled profiteroles will keep, well wrapped, in the fridge for up to 2 days.**

**⦀ COMPLEX**

BITES OF WISDOM:
*How to use piping bags & tips (p. 52)*

**INGREDIENTS**

**Éclairs:**

**1 recipe** Choux Paste (p. 189), freshly made and still warm

**1 egg**, whisked well, for brushing (optional)

**Glaze (optional):**

**1½ cups (195 g)** icing sugar

**3 Tbsp (45 mL)** 2% milk

**1½ Tbsp (22 g)** unsalted butter, melted

**1 tsp** vanilla extract

Food colouring liquid, gel or paste (optional)

**Assembly:**

Sprinkles, for décor (optional) or icing sugar, for dusting

**1 recipe** Diplomat Cream (p. 98), flavoured if you wish

# Éclairs

Like profiteroles, éclairs can be filled so the pastry cream remains unseen until you take the first bite. I prefer a more decorative and showy style with a glazed and decorated top and a structured Diplomat Cream filling (p. 98) that visibly holds the pattern of the piping tip. For variety, I often divide the filling into three parts and make each one a different flavour, with a tinted vanilla glaze to match (or contrast). (I coordinated my glaze colours with the following three fillings (pictured on p. 197): pink—Raspberry Diplomat Cream; green—Pistachio White Chocolate Diplomat Cream; brown—Chocolate Diplomat Cream.)

1. **Preheat the oven** to 400°F (200°C). Trace two sets of parallel lines 4 inches (10 cm) apart onto two sheets of parchment paper. Turn the sheets upside down (marker lines face down) onto two baking trays.

   *Tracing lines onto your parchment helps you pipe with precision until you are practised enough to pipe consistently without them.*

2. **Pipe the éclairs.** Spoon the paste into a large piping bag fitted with a large plain tip. Pipe the choux paste in straight lines about ¾ inch (2 cm) wide, using the parallel lines on the parchment as a guide and leaving 2 inches (5 cm) between each éclair to allow for expansion (1). If your éclairs have a point on top from lifting the piping bag, dip your finger in water and pat it down (2).

   *As you are piping, use an even amount of pressure as you guide the choux paste into the éclair shape. Keep your piping tip at the same height from start to finish, with only a quick lift at the end when you finish each one. Changing the pressure or the height of the piping bag will change the width of the pastry, risking making your éclair bigger at one end or too narrow or too wide in the middle. Aim for evenly sized and symmetrical shapes.*

3. **Brush the éclairs** with the whisked egg (3).

5. **Bake the éclairs** without craquelin for 20 minutes, open the oven door for 15 seconds, then close and bake for another 10 to 15 minutes. For éclairs with craquelin, bake them for 35 to 45 minutes total, opening the oven door for 15 seconds after 30 minutes.

6. **Cool the éclairs.** Tip the éclairs onto a rack to cool completely before filling. Unfilled baked éclairs will keep, wrapped well in plastic, at room temperature for 1 day or frozen for up to 3 months before filling. Thaw on the counter before filling.

7. **Make the glaze (optional).** Whisk the icing sugar, milk, melted butter and vanilla together until smooth. Add food colouring if and as desired. Use immediately or cover the surface of the glaze directly with plastic wrap or parchment and use within 2 hours.

*CONTINUES*

## Éclairs au Craquelin

Just like the Profiteroles au Craquelin (p. 193), you can add that sweet crisp biscuit crackle of craquelin to the top of éclairs. Prepare **1 recipe of Craquelin (p. 193)** and using a small cookie cutter or a paring knife, cut into rectangles the same size as the éclairs (you can use a small cookie cutter or piping tip to trim the ends into semicircles) and gently set them on top of each unbaked pastry. Bake the éclairs for 35 to 45 minutes at 350°F (180°C), opening the door for 15 seconds after 30 minutes. Cool and fill the éclairs as instructed above, but do not glaze them, since the glaze does not stick well to the craquelin surface.

8. **Glaze the éclairs.** Set a wire rack over a baking tray and place the glaze in a shallow bowl. Using your fingers or tongs, dip the top of each éclair in vanilla glaze and place it glaze side up on the rack. Add sprinkles, if using, while the glaze is still wet. Let the éclairs dry for at least 2 hours. Alternatively, for a simpler version, do not glaze and the tops of the éclairs can be dusted with icing sugar (as pictured opposite).

9. **Fill the éclairs.** Spoon the diplomat cream into a piping bag fitted with a medium plain, star, petal or St. Honoré piping tip. Slice each éclair open horizontally to create a top and bottom half. Pipe the filling onto the bottom half of each éclair and gently place the glazed top onto the filling. Chill the éclairs until ready to serve.

**The éclairs will keep, well wrapped, in the fridge for up to 2 days.**

**MAKES:** 6 pastries

**PREP TIME:** 10 minutes
**COOK TIME:** 30 minutes
**BITES OF WISDOM:**
*How to use piping bags & tips (p. 52),*
*How to cook & caramelize sugar (p. 38)*

**INGREDIENTS**

**1 recipe** Choux Paste (p. 189), freshly
    made and still warm

**1** egg, whisked well, for brushing

**1 recipe** Peanut Butter Diplomat Cream
    (p. 98), chilled for at least 4 hours

**½ recipe** Praliné Noisette (p. 85), made
    with **1 cup (110 g)** salted roasted
    peanuts instead of hazelnuts

Icing sugar, for dusting

# Individual Peanut Butter Paris-Brests

The Paris-Brest pastry was created over 100 years ago in honour of the Paris–Brest–Paris long-distance bicycle race. Its ring shape was intended to represent a bicycle wheel and the pastry was meant to fuel the cyclists (there were no protein shakes 100 years ago!). This impressive dessert, which is often filled with a nut-flavoured cream—in this case, Peanut Butter Diplomat Cream (p. 98)—is as popular as ever. While a Paris-Brest may not be recommended as a post-workout snack, it is definitely a decadent dessert.

1. **Preheat the oven** to 400°F (200°C). Trace six 3½-inch (9 cm) circles onto a sheet of parchment paper. Turn the sheets upside down (marker lines face down) onto a baking tray.

    *Tracing circles onto your parchment helps you pipe with precision until you are practised enough to pipe consistently without them.*

2. **Pipe the rings.** Spoon the choux paste into a large piping bag fitted with a large plain or star tip. Pipe rings of choux paste following the traced lines, then pipe a second ring of paste inside the first rings. Pipe a third ring on top of the seam where the two bottom rings meet. Brush the Paris-Brests with the whisked egg.

    *Piping this third ring of choux paste on top of the first two gives the Paris-Brest rings their height as they bake.*

3. **Bake the pastry rings** for about 15 minutes, then reduce the oven to 375°F (190°C) and bake for another 12 to 15 minutes, until a rich golden brown.

4. **Cool the choux rings.** Let the pastries cool on the tray on a rack for 10 minutes, then gently lift them off the tray to cool completely on the rack before filling.

5. **Assemble the pastries.** Slice each choux ring in half horizontally to create a top and bottom half. Fit a large piping bag with a large star tip and fill it with the chilled peanut butter diplomat cream. Pipe generous dots of the cream onto the bottom half of each choux ring. Sprinkle the cream with the chopped peanut praliné. Set the top half of each choux ring on the filling and gently press it in place. Dust generously with icing sugar and chill until ready to serve.

**Assembled Paris-Brests will keep, well wrapped, in the fridge for up to 2 days.**

# Cakes

# Recipes at a Glance

Mastering the category of cakes is very different from mastering pastries. In the world of pastry, a few foundation doughs can turn into multiple desserts. Cakes, however, differ greatly by method, texture and assembly. While different cake styles often use similar ingredients, it is how they are treated and combined that produces such a wide variety of tastes and textures.

To help appreciate these differences, I've divided the chapter by cake style so you can see how various cake-making techniques and ways of assembling components are related, even though their flavours and textures may vary greatly.

## Loaf Cakes & Simple Cakes

These cakes are a perfect starting point for cake making. They take few tools, use the most basic of pans and don't involve fancy frostings or fillings. Simple cakes don't mean they're underwhelming—in fact, sometimes the best-selling cakes in a bakery are the simple ones. These familiar cakes are easy to make and bring instant comfort and joy.

## Petits Fours & Little Cakes

These bite-sized cakes are a good way to practise working with small proportions when baking, portioning and even decorating. Some of these cake batters, such as the London Fog Madeleines (p. 216) and Cannelés (p. 220), are relatively simple to mix, and following the method carefully will make the difference between flawless and failure.

## Warm Saucing Cakes

Warm cakes with the sauce built right in have a reputation for being simple to make, yet they are also a deliciously complex and decadent combination of a cake layer and a liquid layer. Think a rustic Warm Lemon Saucing Cake (p. 228) or a vintage chocolate lava cake. Saucing cakes are not overly complicated to make: larger versions rely on a fluid batter that separates into a moist cake on top and a sauce on the bottom as it bakes, and smaller lava cakes use timed baking to ensure a liquid centre. Virtually any flavour is possible.

## Sponge Cakes

All sponge cakes are a combination of separated or whole eggs whipped with sugar to give them volume and an airy texture. Well-made sponge cakes are anything but dry and flavourless, and they make a great foundation for other, more complex cakes. Master basic vanilla and chocolate sponges, then try the ethereally airy and soft Coconut Chiffon Cake (p. 236) or the intensely flavoured Matcha Swiss Roll with Raspberry Cream (p. 241). No matter which sponge you make, you will become adept at whipping eggs.

## Layer Cakes

The defining characteristic of layer cakes is their assembly: stacking multiple layers of a cake with a filling and frosting of complementary texture so that each bite delivers a balance of visual appeal, texture and flavour. The Black Velvet Chocolate Layer Cake (p. 247), for example, pairs a rich and dense cake with an equally dense filling. In contrast, the Chocolate Peanut Butter Cream Cake (p. 253) matches a fluffier chocolate cake with its almost mousse-like peanut butter cream filling. The most successful versions cut smoothly when sliced, and with every bite the flavours meld and melt in your mouth at the same rate. These decorative cakes have presence, which makes them perfect for special occasions when you want a wow factor.

## Tray Cakes

Larger-format cakes served in their baking pan, tray cakes can feed a crowd whether served in small slices at a gathering or dished up in full-sized portions for a dinner party. The method for mixing tray cake batters is similar to layer cakes, but they are faster to complete because they need no assembly. Tray cakes range from casual and colourful, like the Cranberry Cardamom Tray Cake (p. 257), to a little more elaborate, like the Lemon Crunch-&-Cream Tray Cake (p. 258), to the formal and fancy Chocolate Swirl Tray Cake with Decadent Marble Glaze (p. 261).

## Cheesecakes

Although cooking cheesecakes resembles cooking custards because both combine eggs and dairy, cheesecakes are more similar to cakes in their method and style of presentation. Cream cheese is the key ingredient in cheesecakes and contributes to their rich and creamy texture, but how they look and taste depends a lot on how the cream cheese is combined with other ingredients.

## European Tortes

Classic European tortes are unparalleled in their design, flavour and presentation. In many Central European languages, the word "torte" or "torta" means cake, often an elaborate combination of many cake layers and fillings. My own background is Eastern European (Slovak), so I feel a special connection to this style of cake, and over the years I have developed my own recipes for famous tortes like Sacher Torte (Austria), Dobos Torte (Hungary) and Opera Torte (France). Recently I have embraced lesser-known torte recipes inspired by my travels. Although many of these styles are new to me, they have been around for decades—or even a century or more. Give yourself time to make these tortes at home: the many steps and layers are not necessarily hard, and the results are well worth the effort.

## Savoury Cakes

Savoury breads, pastries and pies are common enough, but savoury cakes are a little outside of the typical bakery offering. In this chapter I present an upside-down cake, a savoury layer cake and a playful waffle cake. I hope you'll get adventurous and try one. Whereas sweet cakes rely on sugar to provide structure and keep them moist and tender, many savoury cake batters use cheese or extra liquid. And instead of vanilla or chocolate flavours, herbs and onions give savoury cakes a boost. Serve them as a side dish or as a celebration cake for anyone without a sweet tooth.

**LOAF CAKES & SIMPLE CAKES** ▶

**Hot Cross Muffins**
Page 208

**Sticky Toffee Date Loaf**
*(plus Bonus Bake: Sticky Toffee Loaf
Cake with Warm Toffee Sauce)* Page 211

**Quick Kefir Citrus Cake**
Page 212

**Flourless Chocolate Torta Tenerina**
Page 215

**PETITS FOURS & LITTLE CAKES** ▶

**London Fog Madeleines**
Page 216

**Brown Butter Cherry Financiers**
Page 219

**Cannelés**
Page 220

**Gingerbread Petits Fours**
Page 223

**WARM SAUCING CAKES** ▶

**Chocolate Peanut Butter & Dulce
de Leche Lava Cakes** Page 226

**Warm Lemon Saucing Cake**
Page 228

**Warm Bananas Foster Saucing Cake**
Page 231

SPONGE CAKES ▶

**Chocolate Sponge Cake** (*plus Bonus Bake: Vanilla Sponge Cake*) Page 232

**Vanilla Pear Chiboust Torte**
Page 235

**Coconut Chiffon Cake**
Page 236

**Ma Lai Go (Cantonese Steamed Sponge Cake)** Page 239

**Matcha Swiss Roll with Raspberry Cream** Page 241

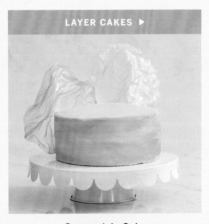

LAYER CAKES ▶

**Creamsicle Cake**
Page 245

**Black Velvet Chocolate Layer Cake**
Page 247

**White Velvet Layer Cake**
Page 251

**Chocolate Peanut Butter Cream Cake**
Page 253

TRAY CAKES ▶

**Cranberry Cardamom Tray Cake**
Page 257

**Lemon Crunch-&-Cream Tray Cake**
Page 258

**Chocolate Swirl Tray Cake with
Decadent Marble Glaze** Page 261

CHEESECAKES ▶

**Basque Cheesecake** (*Burnt Cheesecake*)
Page 263

**Alfajor Cheesecake**
Page 267

EUROPEAN TORTES ▶

**Medovik** (*Russian Honey Torte*)
Page 269

**Esterházy Torte**
Page 273

**Torta Setteveli**
Page 277

SAVOURY CAKES ▶

**Onion, Herb & Parmesan
Upside-down Cake** Page 281

**Nacho Cornbread Layer Cake**
Page 282

**Zucchini Cheddar Waffle Cake**
Page 285

**MAKES:** 12 jumbo muffins (tulip cups) or 24 regular muffins

**PREP TIME:** 20 minutes, plus setting
**COOK TIME:** 30 minutes

♪ SIMPLE

BITES OF WISDOM:
*How to make a parchment paper cone for piping (p. 54)*

### INGREDIENTS

2½ cups (375 g) all-purpose flour

2 tsp baking powder

1¼ tsp ground cinnamon

½ tsp baking soda

½ tsp ground allspice

½ tsp ground nutmeg

½ tsp ground cloves

¼ tsp fine salt

1 cup (200 g) granulated sugar

1 cup (250 mL) 2% milk

⅔ cup (160 mL) vegetable oil

2 large eggs

2 Tbsp (37 g) honey

Zest of 1 lemon

1 Tbsp (15 mL) fresh lemon juice

1½ cups (225 g) raisins or 1½ cups (240 g) currants

½ cup (70 g) dried cranberries

¼ cup (37 g) diced candied orange peel

**Glaze:**

1½ cups (200 g) icing sugar

1½ Tbsp (22 mL) water

½ tsp meringue powder (optional)

# Hot Cross Muffins

These fruit-laden muffins smell exactly like hot cross buns as they bake and taste just as satisfying, but with a fraction of the effort.

1. **Preheat the oven** to 375°F (190°C). Line a 12-cup muffin tin with extra-large paper liners (tulip cups) or line two 12-cup muffin tins with regular paper liners.

2. **Combine the dry ingredients.** Sift together the flour, baking powder, cinnamon, baking soda, allspice, nutmeg, cloves and salt in a large mixing bowl.

3. **Combine the liquids.** In a separate bowl, whisk the sugar, milk, oil, eggs, honey, lemon zest and juice together. Add all at once to the flour and whisk until well combined. Stir in the raisins (or currants), cranberries and candied peel.

   *Even though sugar might seem like a "dry" ingredient, in quick cakes it goes in with the liquids to dissolve so the batter is softer and easier to handle.*

   *If you are not fond of candied peel, replace that measurement with extra raisins or cranberries.*

4. **Divide the batter** evenly between the muffin cups.

5. **Bake the muffins** for 30 minutes for the extra-large muffins or 20 to 25 minutes for the regular-sized ones. Cool the muffins in their tins on a rack for 20 minutes. Transfer to a wire rack to cool completely before glazing.

6. **Make the glaze.** Whisk the icing sugar, water and meringue powder, if using, until smooth and the proper consistency for piping. To test the glaze, drizzle a little on a plate. If it spreads too much, add a little more icing sugar and whisk to combine. If it is too thick, loosen with a few droplets of water and whisk again. Spoon the glaze into a parchment paper cone and pipe a cross on the top of each muffin. Let the glaze set for an hour before serving.

   *The meringue powder helps the glaze set. If you make the glaze without it, let the muffins air-dry for an extra hour before storing them. And to make the muffins less seasonally specific, you can leave the crosses off or simply drizzle the glaze on top.*

**The muffins will keep in an airtight container at room temperature for up to 3 days.**

MAKES: one 9 × 5-inch (2 L) loaf (12 to 16 slices)

PREP TIME: 15 minutes
COOK TIME: 1 hour

**⚡ SIMPLE**

**BITES OF WISDOM:**
*Glossary of ingredients—Fruits, dried (p. 8), Glossary of ingredients—Molasses (p. 13)*

## INGREDIENTS

1 cup (150 g) pitted dates

⅔ cup (100 g) raisins

1 tsp baking soda

¾ cup (175 mL) boiling water

6 Tbsp (90 g) unsalted butter, at room temperature

¾ cup (150 g) packed dark brown sugar

¼ cup (65 g) fancy molasses

2 large eggs, at room temperature

1⅓ cups (200 g) all-purpose flour

1 tsp baking powder

½ tsp fine salt

½ tsp ground cinnamon

½ tsp ground ginger

## BONUS BAKE

### Sticky Toffee Loaf Cake with Warm Toffee Sauce

Turn this simple loaf cake into a plated sticky toffee dessert by serving it with a simple warm toffee sauce. In a medium saucepan, bring **1 cup (200 g) dark brown sugar, ¼ cup (60 g) butter** and **¼ cup (60 mL) whipping cream** to a boil over medium-high heat while stirring. Remove from the heat and add **a splash of whisky, rum or brandy** if you wish. Serve a slice of the cake on a plate and top with a ladleful of the warm sauce, and add a dollop of **Creme Frâiche** (p. 94) if you wish.

# Sticky Toffee Date Loaf

This easy loaf cake is inspired by memories of a date loaf I enjoyed at a friend's house when I was growing up and musings about why sticky toffee pudding is never served sliced but instead is most often a plated dessert. Soaked dates and raisins keep it moist and sweet.

1. **Preheat the oven** to 350°F (180°C). Lightly grease a 9 × 5-inch (2 L) loaf pan and use a piece of parchment to line the long sides and bottom of the pan, so that the paper comes just above the top of the pan.

2. **Soak the dates and raisins.** Chop the dates by hand as finely as possible and place in a bowl with the raisins and baking soda. Pour the boiling water overtop and let the fruit sit while making the batter.

   *Adding baking soda to the water helps to soften and break down the dates and raisins so they will add moisture to the loaf and be a more homogeneous part of the batter.*

3. **Beat the butter and brown sugar** by hand in a mixing bowl, then beat in the molasses, followed by the eggs, adding them one at a time and mixing well after each addition (switch to a whisk if you wish).

4. **Sift the flour, baking powder, salt, cinnamon and ginger** together in a separate bowl and add all at once to the batter, stirring until smooth. Add the dates and any remaining boiling water to the batter and stir until thoroughly combined—the batter will be very fluid.

5. **Bake the loaf.** Pour the batter into the prepared pan and bake for 50 to 60 minutes, or until a tester inserted in the centre of the cake comes out clean. Let the loaf cool in the pan on a rack for 20 minutes, then lift or tip it out to cool completely on the rack.

**The loaf will keep, well wrapped in plastic, at room temperature for up to 4 days.**

PREP TIME: under 10 minutes
COOK TIME: 35 minutes

❗ SIMPLE

BITES OF WISDOM:
*Preparing pans for baking—Lining with
parchment paper (p. 26), How acidity
works in baking (p. 66)*

INGREDIENTS

1 cup (200 g) granulated sugar

Zest of 1 lemon, lime or orange

½ cup (125 mL) plain kefir or regular
yogurt (not Greek)

⅓ cup (80 mL) extra-virgin olive oil

3 large eggs

1 tsp vanilla extract

¼ tsp almond extract (optional)

1 cup (150 g) all-purpose flour

½ cup (60 g) ground almonds

2 tsp baking powder

½ tsp fine salt

Citrus segments, for serving (optional)

Crème Fraîche, slightly sweetened
(p. 94) or Chantilly Cream (p. 95), for
serving (optional)

# Quick Kefir Citrus Cake

This brilliantly uncomplicated cake is perfect when you want a simple,
moist cake to go with fresh fruit. Whether you choose lemon, lime or
orange is up to you, even if the citrus you have in the fridge makes the
decision for you. Kefir is a fermented cow's milk beverage that is similar to
yogurt but tastes tangier and is fluid.

1. **Preheat the oven** to 350°F (180°C). Grease a 9-inch (23 cm) round or square
   pan and line the bottom with parchment paper.

2. **Whisk the sugar and citrus zest** together in a large mixing bowl.

   *When a cake is this simple, little steps like taking the time to draw out the citrus
   oils from the zest by whisking it into the sugar really make a difference. The
   citrus flavour will be more pronounced and even throughout the cake.*

3. **Add the wet ingredients.** Whisk in the kefir (or yogurt), olive oil, eggs,
   vanilla extract and almond extract, if using, until combined.

   *In this cake, the tart flavour of fermented dairy—the kefir (or yogurt)—mimics
   a citrus taste, no matter which of the three citrus fruits you choose.*

   *Using extra-virgin olive oil gives this cake a lovely depth of flavour. You can use
   vegetable oil if you'd prefer a milder cake, but I think the olive oil is much tastier.*

4. **Add the flour, almonds, baking powder and salt** and whisk again until just
   combined with no lumps visible.

5. **Bake the cake.** Pour the batter into the prepared pan and bake for 30 to
   35 minutes, until a tester inserted in the centre of the cake comes out clean.
   Cool in the pan on a rack for 20 minutes, then tip out onto the rack to cool
   completely. Serve slices of this cake on its own, or with citrus segments and
   a dollop of lightly sweetened Crème Fraîche or Chantilly Cream, as pictured.

   **The cake will keep, well wrapped in plastic, at room temperature for up to
   3 days.**

**MAKES:** one 9-inch (23 cm) torte
**SERVES:** 12 to 16

**PREP TIME:** 20 minutes, plus chilling
**COOK TIME:** 25 minutes

❗ **SIMPLE**
**BITES OF WISDOM:**
*How to melt chocolate (p. 41), How to whip egg whites (p. 34)*

**INGREDIENTS**

**12 oz (360 g)** dark baking/couverture chocolate

**⅔ cup (160 g)** unsalted butter, cut into pieces

**⅔ cup (140 g)** granulated sugar

**½ cup (60 g)** Dutch-process cocoa powder

**2 Tbsp (15 g)** cornstarch

**½ tsp** fine salt

**2 Tbsp (30 mL)** 2% milk

**4** large eggs, separated, at room temperature

# Flourless Chocolate Torta Tenerina

This dense and rich single-layer chocolate cake hails from Ferrara in the Emilia region of Italy, and it is for the true chocolate lover. Making this cake is similar to making a brownie, except that whipped egg whites are folded in before baking. The result is a cake that is more delicate and refined than a brownie but still intensely chocolaty, fulfilling to serve on its own or with a handful of fresh berries.

1. **Preheat the oven** to 350°F (180°C). Grease a 9-inch (23 cm) springform pan. Line the bottom of the pan with parchment paper and coat the sides of the pan with sugar, tapping out any excess.

2. **Melt the chocolate and butter** in a metal bowl placed over a pot of barely simmering water, stirring constantly until melted. Remove the bowl from the heat and allow to cool while preparing the other ingredients.

3. **Combine the dry ingredients.** Whisk the sugar, cocoa powder, cornstarch and salt together to remove any lumps in the cocoa. Using a spatula, stir this mixture into the melted chocolate followed by the milk. Add the egg yolks to the chocolate and stir again. The mixture will be a thick paste.

*In a recipe that includes flour, I typically sift the dry ingredients before adding them to the batter. Here the coarse granulated sugar easily breaks down any lumps in the cocoa powder when you whisk everything together. That means no sifting is needed—and there's one less tool to use and wash.*

4. **Whip the egg whites and fold into the batter.** Using a stand mixer fitted with the whip attachment, whip the egg whites on high speed until they hold a medium peak when the beaters are lifted. Fold the whites into the chocolate in two additions, folding well after each one. The egg whites will deflate a little as you fold them in. Scrape the batter into the prepared pan and gently spread to level the batter.

5. **Bake the cake** for 20 to 25 minutes, until the cake is set just an inch (2.5 cm) around the edge but is still very jiggly in the centre. Cool the cake completely in its pan on a rack; the centre of the cake will immediately begin to collapse. Chill the cake for at least 2 hours. Remove from the pan to serve.

*This cake collapsing in the centre as it cools is expected. After 20 minutes of baking, the centre of the cake will appear very fluid still, but don't be tempted to bake it any more than 5 minutes longer. If you do, the outside of the cake will be dry and crumbly once cooled. The large quantity of chocolate in the recipe needs time to cool and set, which is why the cake will seem underdone when you pull it from the oven.*

**The cake will keep, well wrapped, in the fridge for up to 4 days. Pull the cake from the fridge 30 minutes before you plan to serve it.**

**MAKES:** 18 madeleines

**PREP TIME:** under 10 minutes, plus chilling
**COOK TIME:** 12 minutes

❗ **SIMPLE**

**BITES OF WISDOM:**
*Glossary of ingredients—Chocolate & cocoa powder (p. 5)*

### INGREDIENTS

½ **cup (115 g)** unsalted butter, plus extra for greasing the pans

2 Earl Grey tea bags

2 large eggs

1 large egg white

10 **Tbsp (125 g)** granulated sugar

1 **tsp** honey

1 **tsp** finely grated lemon zest

1 **tsp** vanilla extract

1 **cup (150 g)** all-purpose flour

1 **tsp** baking powder

½ **tsp** cocoa powder

# London Fog Madeleines

These buttery shell-shaped little cakes are a staple in French patisseries, where they are judged not only by their flavour but also by the little peak in the centre of each one. That sign of a well-made madeleine is *la bosse*, literally translated as "the bump." Be sure to have proper madeleine pans for this recipe. The combination of Earl Grey tea and vanilla—popularly called London fog—gives these particular madeleines a subtle flavour that enhances their sweet, buttery character and makes them a lovely addition to an afternoon tea assortment. For a plated dessert, serve the madeleines with a scoop of Chocolate Crémeux (p. 317) or Creamy Mascarpone Mousse (p. 296) and a handful of fresh berries.

1. **Infuse the tea flavour.** Melt the butter in a small saucepan over low heat. Break open the tea bags into the butter and let steep on low for 5 minutes. Strain the butter into a bowl and cool for 10 minutes.

2. **Make the batter.** Whisk the eggs, egg white, sugar, honey, lemon zest and vanilla together by hand. Sift in the flour, baking powder and cocoa powder and whisk until smooth. Whisk in the butter. Cover and chill the batter for at least 2 hours and up to 24 hours.

   *The lemon zest and cocoa powder bolster the Earl Grey tea flavour, and the cocoa adds a little colour, giving the madeleines the same colour tone as a milky cup of tea.*

3. **Preheat the oven** to 400°F (200°C). Chill two madeleine pans for 10 minutes, then brush the pans with melted butter (the chilled pans help set the butter to prevent it from pooling in the pan). Freeze the buttered pans for 10 minutes.

   *As simple as these little cakes seem, I think I tested this recipe more times than any of the others in the book. I played with many flavour combinations before hitting on this one, but the trickiest part was making sure I got a bosse on each madeleine no matter what type of pan I used (stainless, non-stick or silicone). After much testing, I can say it's a fait accompli.*

4. **Scoop the batter** into 18 of the shell-shaped molds (a small ice cream scoop works best). Bake the madeleines for about 12 minutes, until browned at the edges. Immediately tap the madeleines out onto a rack to cool slightly. Serve them warm and freshly baked if you can.

   **If you must store madeleines, keep them in an airtight container at room temperature for a day at most, or freeze for up to 1 month. Thaw the madeleines on the counter and rewarm for 10 minutes in a 300°F (150°C) oven.**

**MAKES:** 24 little cakes

**PREP TIME:** 15 minutes, plus chilling
**COOK TIME:** 20 minutes

**SIMPLE**

**BITES OF WISDOM:**
*Glossary of baking tools—Baking pans (p. 21)*

**INGREDIENTS**

- **6 Tbsp (90 g)** unsalted butter
- **3** large egg whites
- **½ cup (100 g)** granulated sugar
- **½ cup (60 g)** ground almonds
- **⅓ cup (50 g)** all-purpose flour
- **¼ tsp** ground nutmeg
- Pink food colouring (optional)
- **12** Amarena or candied cherries, cut in half

# Brown Butter Cherry Financiers

Traditional financiers are dense, sweet cakes made with ground almonds and baked in individual bar-shaped pans. Their shape and buttery yellow colour are meant to resemble bars of gold, which may be how they got their name. This non-traditional version is baked in a mini-muffin pan and uses brown butter and a delicious, slightly sour Amarena cherry in the centre to deepen the flavour.

1. **Brown the butter.** Melt the butter in a small saucepan over high heat until it bubbles and the milk solids turn dark brown; the butter itself will turn amber. Set aside to cool for 15 minutes.

   *If the milk solids become black (and bitter), pour the butter through a coffee filter or fine-mesh sieve before adding it to the batter.*

2. **Mix the batter.** Whisk the egg whites and sugar together vigorously by hand for about 3 minutes until frothy and white, but not a meringue. Next, whisk in the almonds, flour and nutmeg until smooth. Slowly pour in the brown butter (still warm but not hot is ideal), whisking well. Stir in a little pink food colouring, if using. Chill the batter for at least an hour or up to a day before baking.

   *The brown butter causes these cakes to bake up with a warm honey colour instead of butter yellow. Adding a little pink food colouring gives them visual appeal, especially if they are part of an afternoon tea assortment, and references the cherry centre.*

3. **Preheat the oven** to 400°F (200°C). Grease a mini-muffin pan, financier pan or oval friand pan and chill for about 15 minutes before filling.

4. **Scoop the batter** into each pan using a portion scoop, filling each mold halfway. You will use about two-thirds of the batter. Press a cherry half into the centre of each cake and then top with the remaining batter (the cherries do not need to be fully covered).

   *Using a small scoop is the key to precise portioning. Dip your scoop into the batter and then scrape it against the top of the bowl to level so that each scoop is the same volume. With little cakes, even half a teaspoon more or less of batter can make one cake look significantly different from the others.*

5. **Bake the financiers** for about 15 minutes, until they brown around the edges and spring back in the centre when gently pressed. Cool the financiers in the pan on a rack for 15 minutes, then use a skewer to help lift them out of the pan to cool completely on a rack. Financiers are best the day they are baked, when the edges are still crisp.

**The little cakes will keep moist in an airtight container at room temperature for up to 4 days.**

**MAKES:** 8 little cakes

**PREP TIME:** 15 minutes, plus chilling
**COOK TIME:** 50 minutes

❗ SIMPLE

**BITES OF WISDOM:**
*Glossary of ingredients—Vanilla, p. 13*

**INGREDIENTS**

1 cup (250 mL) 2% milk

1 Tbsp (15 mL) vanilla bean paste or seeds from 1 vanilla bean

½ cup (100 g) granulated sugar

2 Tbsp (30 g) unsalted butter, plus extra for brushing the pan

1 large egg

1 large egg yolk

1 Tbsp (15 mL) amber or spiced rum

½ cup (75 g) all-purpose flour

# Cannelés

Hailing from the Bordeaux region of France, these little cakes are truly special. The batter is quite simple, very much like a sweeter crepe batter with vanilla and rum, but the magic happens as the cannelés bake. The cakes develop a deep brown caramelized crust and an airy yet custard-like interior. Cannelés are traditionally made in a special pan with 12 distinctively shaped cups or in individual fluted copper molds that are no more than 2 inches (5 cm) tall. The copper molds are beautiful but costly, so I recommend the non-stick metal cannelé pan for best results.

1. **Infuse the milk with vanilla.** In a small saucepan, heat the milk with the vanilla over medium-low heat, whisking often, for 15 minutes. If the milk has reduced in volume, top it up to 1 cup (250 mL) again.

2. **Mix the batter.** Remove the pan from the heat and whisk in the sugar and butter until the sugar has dissolved and the butter has melted. Whisk in the egg, egg yolk and rum, followed by the flour. Strain the batter through a fine-mesh sieve and chill for 12 to 24 hours.

   *Gently whisking the batter before and after chilling is the key to cannelés that bake well. If overmixed, the cakes can develop a "mushroom top" (the batter pushes up and out of the pan and spreads so the crown is wider than the base) or a "white butt" (the partially baked cannelés push away from the bottom of the pan and the base stays a pale white while the rest browns).*

3. **Preheat the oven** to 450°F (230°C). Chill the cannelé pan for 10 minutes, then generously brush the inside of each mold with butter and freeze the pan for 10 minutes.

   *Out of respect for the original method, I tested this recipe in classic copper fluted cannelé molds basted with butter and beeswax to help give the cannelés a shiny crust. A non-stick metal pan gave more consistent results. I don't recommend a silicone pan (which didn't brown the cannelés enough). A cannelé pan also bakes pretty muffins or individual pound cakes.*

4. **Portion the batter.** Give the batter a gentle whisk to recombine it (it will have separated during chilling) and pour into the pan, dividing it evenly between the holes.

5. **Bake the cakes** for 10 minutes at 450°F (230°C), then reduce the oven temperature to 375°F (190°C) and cook for another 35 to 40 minutes, until the tops are a deep, dark brown. Cool in the pan for 10 minutes, then tip the cakes out onto a rack to cool completely.

   *The long baking time is essential to get the dark brown, crispy exterior. Don't worry—the centre will still be soft and moist.*

**Cannelés are best enjoyed the day they are baked, but they can be stored, well wrapped, at room temperature for up to a day. Rewarm the cannelés in a 300°F (150°C) oven for 10 minutes to bring back the crisp crust.**

**MAKES:** about 3 dozen petits fours

**PREP TIME:** 1 hour, plus freezing and chilling
**COOK TIME:** 50 minutes

### ⦀⦀⦀ COMPLEX

**BITES OF WISDOM:**
*Glossary of ingredients—Molasses (p. 13),*
*How to melt chocolate (p. 41)*

### INGREDIENTS

**Gingerbread cake:**

⅔ cup (160 mL) vegetable oil

½ cup (100 g) granulated sugar

½ cup (100 g) packed light brown sugar

3 large eggs

2 Tbsp (12 g) finely grated fresh ginger

2 cups (300 g) all-purpose flour

2 tsp baking powder

¾ tsp ground cinnamon

¼ tsp ground cloves

¼ tsp ground allspice

¼ tsp ground nutmeg

½ cup (130 g) fancy molasses

½ cup (125 mL) maple syrup

1 cup (250 mL) ginger beer or sparkling water

1 tsp baking soda

**Icing & assembly:**

½ cup (125 mL) apricot jam

1 recipe Marzipan (p. 85) or 1 lb (450 g) store-bought

8 cups (1 kg) icing sugar, plus extra for dusting

¾ cup (175 mL) water

3 Tbsp (45 mL) corn syrup

2 tsp vanilla extract

2 oz (60 g) dark baking/couverture chocolate, chopped and melted

Orange and/or brown food colouring powder, paste or gel

Sprinkles, cinnamon or gold flake, for décor

# Gingerbread Petits Fours

Petits fours are little cakes served as part of an afternoon tea platter or with coffee after the main dessert during a formal meal. They are also the name for more formal little cakes that are covered with a poured fondant glaze, making them pretty and delicate. This gingerbread version is perfect for afternoon tea during the festive season: it's topped with apricot jam, covered with a sheet of marzipan and finished with a chocolate fondant icing that sets with a satin shine.

1. **Preheat the oven** to 350°F (180°C). Grease a 9 × 13-inch (23 × 33 cm) cake pan and line it with parchment paper so the paper comes up the sides.

2. **Make the gingerbread cake.** Whisk together the oil, granulated sugar, brown sugar, eggs and ginger. In a separate bowl, sift the flour, baking powder, cinnamon, cloves, allspice and nutmeg. Add the dry ingredients to the oil mixture and stir until blended. In a third bowl, whisk the molasses, maple syrup, ginger beer (or sparkling water) and baking soda (this will froth up). Add to the batter and beat vigorously until smooth—the batter will be very fluid. Pour into the prepared pan.

3. **Bake the cake** for 45 to 50 minutes, until a tester inserted in the centre of the cake comes out clean. Cool the cake in its pan on a rack.

   *This simple cake is lovely and delicious on its own. Dust it with icing sugar and serve squares with a dollop of Chantilly Cream (p. 95).*

4. **Assemble the petits fours.** Use the parchment paper to lift the cake from the pan. Spread an even layer of apricot jam over the top of the cake. Lightly dust a work surface with icing sugar and roll out the marzipan until it is a 9 × 13-inch (23 × 33 cm) rectangle. Carefully lift it onto the gingerbread cake and then gently rub the marzipan to smooth out any bumps. Freeze this cake for 2 hours. If freezing for longer and it becomes firm, you may need to thaw it in the fridge for 2 hours.

   *Gingerbread cake is moist and tender but can be very soft. Freezing the assembled cake for 2 hours makes it less sticky and easier to cut into precise shapes.*

5. **Cut the petits fours.** Line two baking trays with parchment paper and set a cooling rack on each one. Use a 1½-inch (4 cm) round cookie cutter to cut petits fours from the cake—try your best to cut straight down. Place the petits fours onto the racks (1).

   *Portioning these petits fours into perfect squares is more challenging than making round ones with a cutter. As you cut the petits fours, the jam can stick and make clean cuts more of a challenge. To solve this problem, rinse and dry your cutter occasionally between cuts.*

   *Chill any leftover cake trimmings and mix with Chantilly Cream (p. 95) to make a messy but delicious trifle.*

*CONTINUES*

6. **Make the fondant glaze.** Bring a pot of water to a gentle simmer over medium heat. Away from the heat but in a metal bowl that fits over the pot, whisk the icing sugar, water, corn syrup, vanilla and melted chocolate together. Add orange and/or brown food colouring to get the desired gingerbread colour. Place the bowl over the pot and warm to between 92°F (33°C) and 100°F (38°C). To test the consistency, ladle a little fondant over a scrap of gingerbread. If the fondant runs off too quickly and doesn't coat the cake, let the fondant cool to 92°F (33°C). If the fondant is too thick and sets too quickly, then warm it to 100°F (38°C).

*At the correct temperature, the glaze will seem ridiculously thick. You need it to slowly cascade down the sides of each petit four, coating it completely and evenly. Sticking to the temperature range is key. If the glaze gets warmer than 105°F (41°C), it can crystallize, which prevents it from setting up with a satiny shine.*

7. **Ladle the fondant** over each petit four and check that it fully covers the cake (2). After you've coated about six little cakes, add décor: sprinkles, cinnamon, or gold flake (3). Repeat the coating and decorating until all the petits fours are covered (4). Chill the cakes for at least 2 hours to set before nestling them into individual paper liners to pack and move.

*Be sure to check your petits fours from all angles as you ladle the fondant on top to make sure they are fully covered. If you are running low on fondant in the pot, scoop the fondant drips from the baking trays into the pot and reheat them to between 92°F (33°C) and 100°F (38°C).*

**The petits fours will keep in an airtight container in the fridge for up to 4 days.**

**MAKES:** 6 individual desserts

**PREP TIME:** 15 minutes, plus freezing and chilling

**COOK TIME:** 20 minutes

**SIMPLE**

**BITES OF WISDOM:**
*Glossary of ingredients—Chocolate & cocoa powder (p. 5), How to melt chocolate (p. 41)*

**INGREDIENTS**

7 oz (210 g) dark baking/couverture chocolate, chopped

6 Tbsp (90 g) unsalted butter, diced, plus extra for greasing

2 large eggs

2 large egg yolks

½ cup (100 g) granulated sugar

1 tsp vanilla extract

1 Tbsp (7 g) cocoa powder, plus extra for dusting

1 Tbsp (8 g) cornstarch

Pinch of fine salt

2 Tbsp (30 g) smooth peanut butter

2 Tbsp (30 mL) Dulce de Leche (p. 90) or store-bought

# Chocolate Peanut Butter & Dulce de Leche Lava Cakes

In my years as a restaurant pastry chef in the 1990s, no dessert menu was without a lava cake—a small dense flourless chocolate cake with a molten centre. Lava cakes went out of fashion for a while, but they are making a fierce comeback. This contemporary version combines salty peanut butter, sweet dulce de leche and the familiar warm dark chocolate centre.

1. **Prepare the dishes.** Grease six 5 oz (150 mL) ramekins and dust with cocoa powder to coat evenly, tapping out any excess.

2. **Melt the chocolate and butter.** Fill a pot with an inch (2.5 cm) of water and bring to a gentle simmer over medium heat. Set a metal bowl on top, add the chocolate and butter and stir gently until smooth. Remove from the heat to cool for 5 minutes.

3. **Whisk the eggs, egg yolks, sugar and vanilla** together by hand until combined, then whisk vigorously by hand for a minute more (1). This final minute builds in structure, but you won't see any visible difference.

4. **Whisk in the melted chocolate** followed by the cocoa powder, cornstarch and salt until combined (2).

5. **Portion part of the batter and freeze.** Divide half of the batter between the six ramekins and put them in the freezer for 15 minutes.

6. **Finish the filling.** Remove the ramekins from the freezer. Spoon 1 tsp each of the peanut butter and dulce de leche into the centre of each ramekin (3). Divide the remaining cake batter equally among the ramekins. Chill the lava cakes, uncovered, until ready to bake. (You can make lava cakes up to a day ahead.)

*If you want to avoid peanut butter, replace it with an extra spoonful of dulce de leche. (Or replace the dulce de leche with an extra spoonful of peanut butter, if you prefer.)*

7. **Preheat the oven** to 375°F (190°C).

8. **Bake the cakes.** Place the ramekins on a baking tray and bake for 20 minutes, until the cakes lose their shine on the surface. Let the cakes rest for 5 minutes. To serve, run a small palette knife around the inside edge of each ramekin. Place a small plate over one ramekin at a time and invert both together. Lift the ramekin off and serve immediately while warm.

*If you bake these cakes right after assembling them, bake for 18 minutes.*

**Unbaked lava cakes will keep, individually wrapped, in the fridge for up to 5 days. Baked lava cakes do not store well.**

**MAKES:** one 6-cup (1.5 L) dessert
**SERVES:** 6 to 8

**PREP TIME:** 15 minutes
**COOK TIME:** 45 minutes

❗ SIMPLE
**BITES OF WISDOM:**
*How to separate an egg (p. 32), How to whip egg whites (p. 34)*

**INGREDIENTS**

---

3 large eggs, separated, at room temperature

1½ cups (300 g) granulated sugar, divided

¼ cup (60 g) unsalted butter, at room temperature

Finely grated zest of **2** lemons

½ cup (75 g) all-purpose flour

½ tsp baking powder

¼ tsp fine salt

1½ cups (375 mL) milk

⅔ cup (160 mL) lemon juice

1 tsp vanilla extract

Icing sugar, for dusting

Fresh berries, for serving

# Warm Lemon Saucing Cake

This cake makes its own lemon curd at the bottom as it bakes, and is super lemony, while the top of the cake develops a tender caramelized crust. If you're making this cake ahead of time, prepare the batter up to 2 hours before and let it stand on the counter. Hold off on whipping the egg whites and folding them into the batter until right before you bake the cake.

1. **Preheat the oven** to 375°F (190°C) and lightly grease a 6-cup (1.5 L) shallow ceramic baking dish.

2. **Whip the egg whites** if you are ready to bake the cake. Using electric beaters or a stand mixer fitted with the whip attachment, whip the egg whites on high speed until foamy. Gradually pour in ¼ cup (50 g) sugar, continuing to whip until the egg whites hold a medium peak when the beaters are lifted. Set aside or, if using a stand mixer, transfer the whites to a separate bowl (no need to wash the stand mixer bowl).

3. **Make the base batter.** Using electric beaters or a stand mixer fitted with the paddle attachment, beat the butter, remaining 1¼ cups (250 g) sugar and lemon zest together on medium speed until combined. Add the yolks, scraping down the bowl if needed. Sift in the flour, baking powder and salt and mix until blended and smooth—the batter will be thick. Slowly pour in the milk while mixing, stopping to scrape the bowl occasionally. Add the lemon juice and vanilla and mix until combined (the batter will be very fluid).

4. **Fold in the egg whites.** Add a third of the egg whites to the batter and fold in. Add the remaining whites and fold in until no white streaks are visible. Pour the batter into the prepared pan.

5. **Bake the cake** for 40 to 45 minutes, until the top is an even rich golden brown and the sauce is bubbling at the sides. Let the cake cool for 10 to 20 minutes, then dust with icing sugar before bringing to the table to serve. Spoon into dishes and top with fresh berries.

*Although this style of dessert is typically served warm, I actually prefer it chilled. The sauce really takes on a lemon curd character and the cake stays soft and moist.*

**Leftover cake will keep, loosely covered, in the fridge for 2 days. Serve cold or rewarm in the microwave.**

**MAKES:** one 10-cup (2.5 L) dessert
**SERVES:** 8

**PREP TIME:** 15 minutes
**COOK TIME:** 1 hour

❢ **SIMPLE**

**BITES OF WISDOM:**
*Spirit & wine substitutes (p. 16)*

**INGREDIENTS**

**3 medium to large ripe bananas**, divided

**6 Tbsp (90 g)** unsalted butter, melted (still warm is OK)

**1½ cups (300 g)** packed light brown sugar, divided

**1 Tbsp (15 mL)** finely grated orange zest

**1 cup (250 mL)** 2% milk

**3 large eggs**, at room temperature

**6 Tbsp (90 mL)** amber or spiced rum, divided

**1 tsp** vanilla extract

**2 cups (300 g)** all-purpose flour

**2 tsp** baking powder

**¾ tsp** ground cinnamon

**½ tsp** fine salt

**1¼ cups (310 mL)** boiling water

**¼ cup (60 mL)** corn syrup

**Vanilla ice cream**, for serving

# Warm Bananas Foster Saucing Cake

Before I became a chef, I spent time as a server at a restaurant where making bananas Foster—bananas flambéed with rum—tableside was popular. The simple combination of butter, brown sugar, bananas and rum with a little orange and cinnamon is hard to resist. This cake is inspired by those flavours, with a warm caramel sauce that develops in the bottom of the dish.

1. **Preheat the oven** to 350°F (180°C) and lightly grease a 10-cup (2.5 L) shallow ceramic baking dish. Set the dish on a baking tray lined with aluminum foil or parchment paper.

2. **Make the cake batter.** Place one banana in a bowl and mash well with a fork. Whisk in the melted butter, followed by ¾ cup (150 g) brown sugar and the orange zest. Whisk in the milk, the eggs, 2 Tbsp (30 mL) rum and the vanilla until evenly combined. Sift the flour, baking powder, cinnamon and salt over the banana mixture and stir until combined. Pour the batter into the pan. Slice the remaining bananas into ¼-inch (6 mm) slices and arrange on top.

3. **Make the syrup.** Pour the boiling water over the remaining ¾ cup (150 g) brown sugar, the corn syrup and the remaining 4 Tbsp (¼ cup/60 mL) rum, and whisk until the sugar has dissolved. Pour over the cake.

4. **Bake the cake** for about an hour, until a tester inserted into the cake comes out clean of crumbs—the cake will soufflé and brown at the edges and will sink back down as it cools slightly. Let the cake cool for 10 minutes, then dust with icing sugar before bringing to the table to serve. Spoon into dishes and top with a scoop of vanilla ice cream.

**MAKES:** one 8-inch (20 cm) cake
**SERVES:** 8 to 10

**PREP TIME:** 15 minutes
**COOK TIME:** 30 minutes

❗ SIMPLE
BITES OF WISDOM:
*How cake bakes (p. 69)*

### INGREDIENTS

**4** large eggs

**⅔ cup (140 g)** granulated sugar

**1 tsp** vanilla extract or vanilla bean paste

**⅔ cup (100 g)** all-purpose flour

**⅓ cup (40 g)** Dutch-process cocoa powder

**½ tsp** fine salt

**2 Tbsp (30 g)** unsalted butter, melted (still warm is OK)

### BONUS BAKE

## Vanilla Sponge Cake

Just like the versatile chocolate sponge cake, this vanilla version can be served with cream and fruit on its own, but is also used in more elaborate desserts like the Vanilla Pear Chiboust Torte (p. 235). It makes a slightly larger 9-inch (23 cm) cake. Follow the method above, but **increase the vanilla to 2 tsp (10 mL)** and the **butter to 6 Tbsp (90 g), melted**. Omit the Dutch-process cocoa powder and the fine salt. Bake the cake for 35 minutes.

# Chocolate Sponge Cake

The cornerstone sponge cake of a baker's kitchen is the genoise, which contains butter and is leavened with beaten eggs. This simple single-layer chocolate sponge cake has multiple uses: top it with cream and fresh fruit or use it in an assembled torte, like the Torta Setteveli (p. 277).

1. **Preheat the oven** to 350°F (180°C). Line the bottom of a 9-inch (23 cm) springform pan with parchment paper but leave the sides of the pan unlined and ungreased.

   *The sponge batter grips the sides of the pan as it rises and bakes, which keeps the top of the cake level. If you were to grease the sides of the pan, the outside edge of the cake would slip down and the centre of the cake would end up higher than the sides, resulting in a domed top. This tip applies only to sponge cakes.*

2. **Warm the eggs in their shells.** Fill a bowl with hot tap water and add the eggs. Let them sit for 5 minutes, changing out the water at least once to make sure the eggs really warm up.

   *Warmed eggs whip to a greater volume than cold or even room-temperature eggs. The warmth allows the sugar to dissolve quickly and that is the key to building structure when whipping. If you're whipping eggs without sugar, warming them is less important.*

3. **Whip the eggs.** Using electric beaters or a stand mixer fitted with the whip attachment, whip the eggs with the sugar and vanilla on high speed until they triple in volume and hold a ribbon when the beaters are lifted, 5 to 8 minutes (1). Sift in the flour, cocoa powder and salt and quickly fold in by hand (2).

   *When folding in the flour, use a whisk or the whip attachment of your mixer. These tools pull the flour gently through the batter without deflating it. You can switch to a spatula for the final few folds to make sure you get right to the bottom of the bowl.*

4. **Mix in the butter.** Spoon about 1 cup (250 mL) of the batter into the bowl with the melted butter and stir to combine. Add this mixture back to the base batter and fold to incorporate. Pour the batter into the prepared pan (3).

5. **Bake the cake** for about 30 minutes, until the cake springs back when gently pressed. Place the cake pan on a rack to cool completely. To remove the cake from the pan, run a palette knife along the inside edge of the pan and remove the springform pan ring.

   **The cake will keep, well wrapped, on the counter for 2 days or frozen for up to 3 months.**

**MAKES:** one 9-inch (23 cm) torte
**SERVES:** 10 to 12

**PREP TIME:** 30 minutes, plus chilling

††† COMPLEX

**BITES OF WISDOM:**
*Specialty baking tools—Acetate (p. 24)*

**INGREDIENTS**

1 **recipe** Vanilla Sponge Cake (p. 232), baked and cooled

1 **recipe** Poached Pears (p. 88), including their syrup, chilled

**¾ cup (175 mL)** seedless raspberry or red currant jam

1 **recipe** Chiboust Cream (p. 99), freshly prepared

**2 Tbsp (30 mL)** pear brandy (Poire Williams)

Fresh raspberries, for décor (optional)

# Vanilla Pear Chiboust Torte

Delicate and airy, this cake combines many foundation elements of baking: a vanilla sponge base, tender poached pears and an ethereally light vanilla chiboust. The chiboust cream is the star of this torte, but the vanilla sponge cake and poached pears provide complementary flavours and textures.

1. **Prepare your pan.** Line the sides of a 9-inch (23 cm) springform pan with parchment paper or acetate.

2. **Line the pan with sponge cake.** Cut the vanilla sponge cake in half horizontally. Freeze or set aside the top layer for another use. Place the bottom cake layer into the prepared pan and brush it with some of the poached pear syrup.

3. **Spread the jam and arrange the pears.** Stir the jam and spread it over the cake in an even layer (1). Arrange six poached pear halves on top of the jam, with the narrow stem end of the pear pointed toward the centre (2).

4. **Top with chiboust cream.** Have the freshly made chiboust cream ready in a medium bowl. Stir in the pear brandy and pour the chiboust into the pan—it will cover the pears completely. If the top of the chiboust isn't smooth, give the pan a gentle jiggle or use a palette knife to smooth it out (3). Chill the torte for at least 4 hours.

5. **Decorate the torte.** Slice the remaining pear halves and fan over the torte, or top the torte with a few fresh raspberries.

**The torte will keep in an airtight container in the fridge for up to 4 days.**

**MAKES:** one 10-inch (25 cm) cake
**SERVES:** 12 to 16

**PREP TIME:** 20 minutes
**COOK TIME:** 50 minutes

❗ SIMPLE
**BITES OF WISDOM:**
*Glossary of ingredients—Flours (p. 7), How to separate an egg (p. 32), How to whip egg whites (p. 34)*

### INGREDIENTS

**10** large eggs, separated

**1¼ cups (250 g)** granulated sugar, divided

**1½ cups (195 g)** cake & pastry flour

**2 tsp** baking powder

**½ tsp** fine salt

**¾ cup (175 mL)** coconut milk

**½ cup (125 mL)** vegetable oil

**2 Tbsp (30 mL)** lime juice

**2 tsp** vanilla extract

**1 tsp** coconut extract (optional)

# Coconut Chiffon Cake

This fluffy cake seems to defy gravity. Whereas an airy angel food cake uses only whipped egg whites and has no added fat, a chiffon cake makes use of whole eggs, separated, and has added oil. The result is a moist, satisfying cake with a deeper flavour. This coconut version pairs perfectly with fresh tropical fruits like pineapple or mango.

1. **Preheat the oven** to 325°F (160°C) and have ready a 10-inch (25 cm) ungreased angel food cake pan.

   *An ungreased, straight-sided pan is essential for this chiffon cake recipe, which needs lots of space to rise. An angel food cake pan works well. Its straight sides make it easier to remove the cake from the pan after cooling, and the centre hole allows the heat to circulate through the batter evenly.*

2. **Whip the egg whites** using electric beaters or a stand mixer fitted with the whip attachment on high speed until they are foamy. Slowly pour in ½ cup (100 g) sugar while whipping, until a medium peak is reached. Set aside.

3. **Mix the dry ingredients and liquids.** In a separate bowl (or you can use the same bowl of the stand mixer), sift the flour, baking powder and salt. Add the reserved egg yolks, remaining ¾ cup (150 g) sugar, coconut milk, oil, lime juice, vanilla extract and coconut extract, if using. Whip at medium-high speed until the batter is well blended and smooth.

   *Cake & pastry flour has less protein than other flours, which keeps this batter from toughening up as it mixes. Don't worry about overmixing.*

4. **Fold a third of the whites into the batter,** folding until only a few streaks are visible. Add the remaining two-thirds and fold quickly but gently until combined. Pour the batter into the angel food cake pan and spread to level, if necessary.

5. **Bake the cake** for about 50 minutes, until the cake springs back when gently pressed. Invert the cake on a rack to cool, unless the cake has risen to the top of the pan or above it. In that case, set three or four ramekins on the rack and place the edges of the inverted cake pan on the ramekins so the top of your cake doesn't rest directly on the cooling rack.

   *Cooling a chiffon cake upside down is critical so that gravity can pull down the hot, fragile sponge mixture and keep the delicate air bubbles in the cake stretched until they are cool and stable. If cooled upright, the cake collapses somewhat and the texture becomes slightly dense rather than light and airy.*

6. **Remove the cake from the pan.** Run a palette knife along the inside edge of the outer ring of the cake (the centre ring will loosen itself, or you can help it along by dropping a bamboo skewer down the sides of the inner ring, but do not try to loosen with a palette knife). Give the bottom of the pan a not-so-gentle tap to pop the cake out onto the counter. Transfer to a serving plate.

*Don't be afraid to give the cake pan a good smack on the counter so it comes out in one piece—just make sure to do it on a counter or cutting board, not on your serving plate.*

**The cake will keep, well wrapped, on the counter for up to 3 days.**

**MAKES:** one 9-inch (23 cm) cake
**SERVES:** 12

**PREP TIME:** 15 minutes, plus resting
**COOK TIME:** 40 minutes

❗ **SIMPLE**

**BITES OF WISDOM:**
*Preparing pans for baking—Lining with parchment paper (p. 26)*

**INGREDIENTS**

5 large eggs, at room temperature or warmed in their shells (see p. 232, Chocolate Sponge Cake tip)

¾ cup (150 g) packed light brown sugar

2 tsp vanilla extract

½ cup (125 mL) 2% milk

6 Tbsp (90 mL) vegetable oil

2 cups (260 g) cake & pastry flour

2 Tbsp (24 g) custard powder or **2 Tbsp (15 g)** cornstarch

1 Tbsp (9 g) baking powder

½ tsp baking soda

¼ tsp fine salt

# Ma Lai Go (Cantonese Steamed Sponge Cake)

I have always loved going for dim sum, and although I eat more savoury dumplings than I intend to every time, I still leave space for dessert. Often it's a square of super-airy, often warm, steamed sponge cake. Steaming cake in a bamboo steamer instead of baking it in an oven adds moisture that allows for proportionately less sugar in the batter and a dessert that stays fresh for days.

1. **Prepare the pan.** Line the bottom of a 9-inch (23 cm) springform pan with parchment paper, but leave the sides of the pan unlined and ungreased.

2. **Whip the eggs, brown sugar and vanilla** using electric beaters or a stand mixer fitted with the whip attachment on high speed until more than doubled in size, about 5 minutes. The eggs should be thick and pale and the beaters will leave a ribbon of batter on top of the mixture when lifted.

   *You can't overwhip whole eggs with sugar, so if you are questioning whether you've whipped your eggs enough, let them whip a minute more. Brown sugar is coarser than granulated sugar and can take longer to whip.*

3. **Work the milk and oil into the batter.** Measure the milk and oil into a bowl. Spoon about 1 cup (250 mL) of batter into the milk and whisk to combine. Add this mixture back to the base batter and gently whisk in by hand to combine.

   *The cup of batter will deflate a fair bit when added to the milk—this is expected—but it gives the liquids some structure and makes them easier to fold into the base batter evenly and quickly.*

4. **Add the dry ingredients.** Sift the flour, custard powder (or cornstarch), baking powder, baking soda and salt into the batter and fold in by hand using a whisk to prevent lumps. Switch to a spatula to ensure that batter is well combined and smooth.

   *Custard powder is the secret to the yellow colour and distinctive vanilla flavour in some ma lai go. I like it, but if you don't have it or prefer to keep it simple, use cornstarch in its place.*

5. **Let the batter rest.** Pour the batter into the prepared pan and let sit on the counter for 30 minutes. You will see larger bubbles appear on the surface of the cake.

   *Usually we're told to quickly get batters with whipped eggs into the oven to bake, but the egg mixture here is stable enough to rest for a bit. This extra time allows the baking powder and baking soda to start activating and creates the multi-sized air bubbles that give the sponge its distinctive look.*

*CONTINUES*

6. **Steam the cake.** Fill the bottom of a wok or other wide pan with water and bring to a slow simmer (just a few bubbles breaking the surface) over medium heat. Place the rested cake in a large bamboo steamer and cover with the lid. If the lid doesn't fit snugly onto the base, wrap the outside of the steamer in foil to keep the steam in as the cake cooks. Place the steamer on the pot of simmering water and steam for about 40 minutes. Avoid checking the cake until at least 30 minutes. The cake is done when the centre of the cake springs back when gently pressed with a finger.

7. **Cool the cake** on a rack for at least 30 minutes before removing from the pan. Run a small palette knife around the inside edge of the pan and remove the springform ring. Peel away the parchment from the bottom of the cake and serve slices warm, or let the cake cool and serve at room temperature.

**The cake will keep, well wrapped, on the counter for up to 4 days.**

**MAKES:** one 10-inch (25 cm) dessert
**SERVES:** 8

**PREP TIME:** 20 minutes
**COOK TIME:** 20 minutes

⊪ **MORE INVOLVED**
**BITES OF WISDOM:**
*How to whip egg whites (p. 34)*

**INGREDIENTS**

**Swiss roll:**

¼ cup (60 mL) 2% milk

**1 Tbsp (15 mL)** matcha green tea
powder

**3** large eggs, separated, at room
temperature

**½ cup (100 g)** granulated sugar, divided

**⅓ cup (50 g)** all-purpose flour

**¼ cup (30 g)** cornstarch

Green food colouring gel, powder or
paste (optional)

Icing sugar, for dusting

**Raspberry cream:**

**1¼ cups (310 mL)** whipping cream,
divided

**2 tsp** cornstarch

**¼ cup (32 g)** icing sugar

**4 tsp** freeze-dried raspberry powder

**½ tsp** vanilla extract

# Matcha Swiss Roll with Raspberry Cream

This recipe is now my sister-in-law's official birthday cake forever. I gave Michino a taste when I was testing the recipe, and she has decided to have it every year. Swiss rolls and jelly rolls are sponge cakes that are shaped warm, while they are flexible. This makes them easy to unroll, fill with cream (Swiss roll) or jam or jelly (jelly roll) and then roll back up again without the cake cracking.

1. **Preheat the oven** to 350°F (180°C) and line the bottom of an ungreased 10 × 15-inch (25 × 38 cm) baking tray (jelly roll pan) with parchment paper.

2. **Heat the milk and matcha tea** in a small saucepan over low heat for 5 minutes, then set aside (it can be warm when used).

3. **Whip the egg whites** using electric beaters on high speed until frothy. Slowly pour in ¼ cup (50 g) sugar and continue to whip until the whites hold a stiff peak when the beaters are lifted. Set aside.

4. **Whip the egg yolks** with the remaining ¼ cup (50 g) sugar on high speed until they turn buttery yellow, thicken and hold a ribbon when the beaters are lifted. Whisk in the warm milk by hand. Sift the flour and cornstarch over the eggs and whisk in by hand.

5. **Fold in a third of the whipped whites** until almost incorporated and then add the remaining whites, folding gently but quickly until no streaks of the whites are visible. Add food colouring, if using. Scrape the batter into the prepared pan and spread the batter to make it as level as possible (1).

   *Matcha green tea gives the batter a pea-green colour. If you prefer a brighter green, add a drop or two of food colouring liquid or a little sprinkle of colour powder to the batter.*

   *Levelling the cake batter in the pan is important because this thin cake shows every detail and unevenness of the cake once rolled and sliced. When first spreading the batter in the pan, push the batter into the corners to get it to fasten to the edges, then use your palette knife to spread it evenly over the entire surface. Try not to lift your palette knife until you reach the edge of the pan, to keep the batter smooth and level.*

6. **Bake the cake** for 12 to 14 minutes, until the cake springs back when gently pressed. Cool the cake on a rack for 5 minutes.

   *The 5 minutes of rest allows the cake to cool a little, but not too much. If you rush to roll the cake directly from the oven, it might "sweat" when rolled in the tea towel, causing the surface of the cake to get sticky.*

*CONTINUES*

7. **Shape the cake while warm.** Run a palette knife around the inside edge of the pan to loosen the cake. Dust the surface of the cake with icing sugar and place a clean tea towel overtop. Place a cutting board or second baking tray on top of the towel and invert everything together. Remove the jelly roll pan (now on top) and peel away the parchment paper (2). Dust the cake with icing sugar and, using the tea towel to help, roll up the cake from a short side, rolling the towel in with it. Set the cake back on the rack to cool completely before filling.

*Add only a light sprinkling of icing sugar to the cake before covering with the tea towel and rolling. The icing sugar helps create a little barrier between the cake and the towel, but too much will just melt and stick.*

*When starting to roll the cake to shape it, lift the cake up a little as you coax it forward and over itself. That first roll is the most prone to cracking since it is the smallest part of the spiral and uses the outer edge of the cake, which might be drier than the centre.*

8. **Whip the cream with the cornstarch.** In a small saucepan over medium heat, whisk ¼ cup (60 mL) whipping cream with the cornstarch, whisking constantly until it thickens and just starts to bubble, under 2 minutes. Transfer the thickened cream to a dish to cool for 5 minutes (it can be warm).

*Thickening some cream with cornstarch and then adding it to a larger batch of whipping cream is a bakery technique that gives the cream more strength and structure than the skim milk powder technique (p. 95). In this recipe, the added step is worth it—your matcha roll will slice cleanly and the whipped cream will maintain its full volume.*

9. **Make the raspberry cream.** Whip the remaining 1 cup (250 mL) cream on high speed, and when it begins to thicken, add the thickened cream while whipping. Continue to whip until the cream holds a soft peak. Whip in the icing sugar, raspberry powder and vanilla.

*You can buy freeze-dried raspberry powder online or at specialty baking supply shops. It rehydrates when added to liquids like whipped cream and imparts its vibrant colour and concentrated flavour. If you don't have any of this powder, prepare the cream without.*

10. **Assemble the cake.** Carefully unroll the cooled cake (it will naturally curl up at the end that was in the centre of the spiral). Spread the cream over the cake, leaving about an inch (2.5 cm) uncovered at the flatter short side (3). Starting at the more curled short side, reroll the cake (4) and set the Swiss roll seam side down on a plate or platter. Wrap the Swiss roll well and chill until ready to serve. Dust the top with icing sugar and trim the ends before serving.

*If you prepared the cream without raspberry powder, spread it onto the cake and arrange fresh raspberries on top. Once the cake is rolled and sliced, you'll see lovely circles of fresh berries dotted within the cream.*

**The cake will keep, well wrapped in plastic, in the fridge for up to 3 days.**

**MAKES:** one 3-layer, 8-inch (20 cm) cake
**SERVES:** 10 to 12

**PREP TIME:** 30 minutes, plus chilling
**COOK TIME:** 35 minutes

🍴 **MORE INVOLVED**
BITES OF WISDOM:
*How to assemble a layer cake (p. 50)*

## INGREDIENTS

### Cake:

3 cups (390 g) cake & pastry flour

1¾ cups (350 g) granulated sugar

2½ tsp baking powder

½ tsp fine salt

Zest of 2 navel oranges

½ cup (115 g) unsalted butter, at room temperature and cut into pieces

4 large eggs, at room temperature

¾ cup (175 mL) fresh orange juice

¾ cup (175 mL) buttermilk

½ cup (125 mL) vegetable oil

1 Tbsp (15 mL) vanilla extract

1 tsp orange extract

Orange food colouring gel, powder or paste (optional)

### Frosting:

2 (8 oz/250 g) pkg cream cheese, softened

1 cup (225 g) unsalted butter, at room temperature

6 to 6½ cups (780 to 845 g) icing sugar, divided

2 tsp vanilla extract

2 tsp orange extract

Orange food colouring gel, powder or paste

# Creamsicle Cake

Orange and vanilla are the key flavours in this layer cake, which is also orange coloured. The cake is moist and not the least bit crumbly, and the cream cheese frosting handles easily and sets well, making this cake a manageable task for anyone new at assembling cakes (or for a family project with kids). It's perfect served right from the fridge and stable enough to transport to a party.

1. **Preheat the oven** to 350°F (180°C). Lightly grease and line the bottoms of three 8-inch (20 cm) round cake pans. Dust the sides of the pans with flour, tapping out any excess.

2. **Mix the dry ingredients and butter.** Sift the flour, sugar, baking powder and salt into a large bowl or the bowl of a stand mixer fitted with the paddle attachment. Add the orange zest and stir to combine. Add the butter and mix on medium-low speed until the mixture is crumbly, about 1 minute.

   *This cake-mixing method is known as the "reverse method." Originally this style of cake was made by beating the butter and sugar, adding the eggs and then alternately adding the flour and liquids. By working the butter into the flour and then adding the liquids and eggs all at once, the process is simpler and the results more consistent. It saves a few dishes too.*

3. **Add the liquids and eggs.** In a separate bowl, whisk the eggs, orange juice, buttermilk, oil and vanilla and orange extracts together. Add all at once to the flour. If using a stand mixer, switch to the whip attachment (hand beaters will still work fine) and mix first on low speed to combine. Increase the speed to medium and beat for 90 seconds, until the batter is thick and smooth. Add orange food colouring, if using. Divide the batter evenly among the pans. Give each pan a tap on the counter to knock out any air bubbles.

   *Chilling the batter reduces the intensity of the orange flavour, but adding 1 tsp natural orange extract helps to bolster it.*

   *When making a sponge cake, you want to avoid tapping or shaking the pans in order to keep all of the air you worked in by whipping the eggs. This creamsicle cake uses a thicker batter, and air bubbles can inadvertently work their way in when mixing or pouring the batter. Tapping the pans before baking helps to pop out the bubbles.*

4. **Bake the cakes for 30 to 35 minutes,** until a skewer inserted in the centre of the cake comes out clean. Cool the cakes in their pans for 20 minutes, then tip them out onto a rack to cool completely.

*CONTINUES*

5. **Make the frosting.** Using electric beaters or a stand mixer fitted with the paddle attachment, beat the cream cheese and butter on low speed to combine. Add 3 cups (390 g) icing sugar and beat on low speed, increasing to medium speed until combined. Stir in the vanilla and orange extracts. Add 3 cups (390 g) more of the icing sugar, beating at first on low speed and then increasing to medium. Beat for 2 minutes to build in structure. If the frosting seems too soft, add the remaining ½ cup (65 g) icing sugar and beat for another 2 minutes. Tint the frosting a pale orange colour.

*This recipe makes LOTS of frosting, in case you want to plan some elaborate piping. Any extra frosting can be frozen in an airtight container for up to 3 months. Thaw it to room temperature and rewhip before using.*

6. **Assemble the cake.** Place a cake layer onto a cake wheel or platter. Cover the top of the cake generously with frosting and spread to level it. Set the second cake layer on top and repeat, covering the top of it with frosting. Place the final cake layer on top. Cover the top of the cake with enough frosting to cover the cake in a level layer. Spread frosting on the sides of the cake to cover and fill in any gaps. The cake should not be visible through the frosting. Chill the cake for an hour before decorating.

7. **Decorate the cake.** Divide the remaining frosting into three bowls. Leave one as is. Tint one bowl a medium orange and the other a darker orange. Use an offset spatula to smear patches from all three bowls onto the side of the cake, leaving space between these smears. Use the same offset spatula or a cake or bench scraper to spread the frosting into a smooth layer while you spin the cake: blending the coloured patches will give the frosting a watercolour effect. If you wish, pipe any remaining frosting on top of the cake. Chill the cake for at least 2 hours before serving.

*Rice paper "sails" give this cake the appearance of movement. You will need three or four sheets of edible round rice paper (the type used in Vietnamese salad rolls), three or four sheets of parchment paper and some liquid or paste food colouring. Fill two to three pie plates with warm (not hot) tap water and add a few drops of liquid or paste food colouring to each. Crumple up a few pieces of parchment paper to give them height and structure and set them on baking trays or cooling racks. Submerge a sheet of rice paper in the water until it softens, about 30 seconds. Carefully lift the rice paper from the water and lay it across the crumpled parchment. Repeat with two to three more sheets. Allow the rice paper to air-dry, uncovered, on the counter for 24 hours, then peel away the parchment. Press the "sails" onto the decorated cake.*

**The cake will keep, with the cut portion covered, in the fridge for up to 4 days.**

**MAKES:** one 3-layer, 8-inch (20 cm) cake
**SERVES:** 12 to 16

**PREP TIME:** 40 minutes, plus chilling
**COOK TIME:** 45 minutes

### ⫯⫯⫯ COMPLEX

**BITES OF WISDOM:**

*Preparing pans for baking—Lining with parchment paper (p. 26), How to melt chocolate (p. 41), How to assemble a layer cake (p. 50)*

## INGREDIENTS

**Cake:**

¾ cup (175 mL) hot brewed coffee

3 oz (90 g) dark baking/couverture chocolate, chopped

2 cups (300 g) all-purpose flour

¾ cup (150 g) granulated sugar

½ cup (60 g) Dutch-process cocoa powder

1 tsp baking soda

¾ tsp baking powder

½ tsp fine salt

¾ cup (150 g) packed light brown sugar

¾ cup (175 g) unsalted butter, at room temperature and cut into pieces

¼ cup (60 mL) vegetable oil

¾ cup (175 mL) 2% milk

4 large eggs, at room temperature

2 large egg yolks

1 tsp vanilla extract

**Creamy truffle filling:**

3 oz (90 g) dark baking/couverture chocolate, chopped

3 Tbsp (45 g) unsalted butter, cut into pieces

⅔ cup (140 g) granulated sugar

6 Tbsp (45 g) Dutch-process cocoa powder

¼ cup (30 g) cornstarch

¾ cup (175 mL) water

¾ cup (175 mL) 2% milk

3 large egg yolks

2 tsp vanilla extract

# Black Velvet Chocolate Layer Cake

This cake is for the certified chocolate lover. A dense but rich and moist chocolate cake is layered with a thick chocolate pastry cream and then topped with chocolate ganache. In total, ¾ pound (over 350 g) of dark chocolate is needed for this recipe!

1. **Preheat the oven** to 350°F (180°C). Lightly grease three 8-inch (20 cm) cake pans. Line the bottoms with parchment paper and dust the sides with flour, tapping out any excess.

2. **Melt the chocolate.** Pour the hot coffee over the chocolate in a small bowl. Let sit for 1 minute and then whisk until the mixture is smooth. You can work with this chocolate while still warm.

   *Coffee is a common ingredient in chocolate cake batters because it adds moisture and intensifies the chocolate taste. If you prefer not to use coffee, use the same measure of hot water instead.*

3. **Mix the dry ingredients and cut in the butter.** Sift the flour, granulated sugar, cocoa powder, baking soda, baking powder and salt into a large mixing bowl or the bowl of a stand mixer fitted with the paddle attachment. Stir in the brown sugar. Add the diced butter and oil, working them in using electric beaters or the mixer on medium speed, until large pieces of butter are no longer visible, about 3 minutes.

4. **Add the liquid, eggs and chocolate.** Whisk the milk, eggs, egg yolks and vanilla together and add all at once to the flour mixture. Mix on low speed until combined, then increase the speed to medium and beat until smooth and thick, about a minute. Add the melted chocolate and mix again on medium speed until smooth, about 2 minutes. Divide the batter evenly between the pans and spread to level them, giving the pans a tap to knock out any air bubbles.

5. **Bake the cakes** for 30 to 35 minutes, until a tester inserted in the centre of a cake comes out clean. Cool the cakes in their pans on a rack for 15 minutes, then turn them out onto the rack to cool completely.

6. **Make the creamy truffle filling.** Place the chocolate and butter in a large bowl and set aside. In a medium saucepan, whisk the sugar, cocoa powder and cornstarch together. Whisk in the water, milk and egg yolks. Bring to a simmer over medium heat, whisking constantly, until the mixture thickens, turns glossy and a few bubbles just begin to break the surface, about 6 minutes. Scrape the filling into the bowl of butter and chocolate, whisking until both are melted. Stir in the vanilla. Place a piece of plastic wrap or parchment paper on the surface of the filling, cool for 1 hour on the counter and then chill for at least 4 hours before using.

   *This filling recipe follows the same method as making a pastry cream. For tips on making a pastry cream, refer to p. 96.*

*CONTINUES*

**Ganache topping & assembly:**

**6 oz (180 g)** dark baking/couverture chocolate, chopped

**½ cup (125 mL)** whipping cream

**2 Tbsp (30 g)** unsalted butter

7. **Make the ganache topping.** Place the chopped chocolate in a mixing bowl. Heat the cream and butter over medium heat until it comes to a simmer, pour it over the chocolate and let sit for a minute. Slowly whisk or stir the ganache until it is smooth. Let cool for 30 minutes and then chill for another 30 minutes until spreadable. (The ganache can also be made ahead, chilled and reheated over low heat to soften.)

*You can prepare the cake, filling and ganache 2 days before you plan to serve the cake. Assemble the cake a day ahead if you wish.*

8. **Assemble the cake.** Place a cake layer on a cake stand or cake wheel. Spread a generous quarter of the creamy filling evenly over the cake and top with a second cake layer. Spread another quarter of the filling over the cake and then top with the third cake layer. Spread most of the remaining filling over the top, making it as level as possible. Spread any remaining filling around the sides of the cake. If the ganache is still too fluid to set, chill the cake until ready.

9. **Spread the ganache** over the top of the cake, coaxing it down from the top edge and around the sides of the cake (it does not have to fully coat the sides). Spin the cake as you use an offset spatula to coax a bit of the ganache above the top edge of the cake, creating a ½-inch (1.2 cm) ruffled seam. Leave the top and sides of the cake smooth. Chill, uncovered, until ready to serve.

**The cake will keep, with the cut portion covered, in the fridge for up to 4 days.**

**MAKES:** one 3-layer, 8-inch (20 cm) cake
**SERVES:** 12 to 16

**PREP TIME:** 50 minutes, plus chilling
**COOK TIME:** 47 minutes

🍴 **MORE INVOLVED**
**BITES OF WISDOM:**
*Substitutions—In a pinch (buttermilk)*
*(p. 17), How to assemble a layer cake*
*(p. 50), How to use piping bags & tips*
*(p. 52)*

## INGREDIENTS

**Cake:**

2⅔ cups (350 g) cake & pastry flour

1¾ cups (350 g) granulated sugar

1 Tbsp (9 g) baking powder

½ tsp baking soda

½ tsp fine salt

¾ cup (175 g) unsalted butter, at room temperature and cut into pieces

1¼ cups (310 mL) buttermilk, at room temperature, divided

½ cup (125 mL) vegetable oil

5 large egg whites, at room temperature

1 Tbsp (15 mL) vanilla extract

**Boiled milk frosting & assembly:**

2 cups (500 mL) 2% milk

⅔ cup (100 g) all-purpose flour

2 cups (400 g) granulated sugar

½ tsp fine salt

2 cups (450 g) unsalted butter, at just below room temperature (65°F/18°C)

2 tsp vanilla extract

Food colouring gel, powder or paste

Sprinkles, for décor

Macarons (p. 390), for décor (optional)

# White Velvet Layer Cake

Sprinkles! It's a word that always brings a smile to people's faces—kids and grown-ups alike—and this beautiful white cake is decorated with lots of them. A white velvet cake is a vanilla cake made with unwhipped egg whites instead of whole eggs, so the cake has a pale colour. The boiled milk frosting, also known as ermine frosting, is silky and smooth with enough structure to hold piping detail. It sets well in the fridge but melts on the tip of the tongue faster than other styles of buttercream.

1. **Preheat the oven** to 350°F (180°C). Lightly grease three 8-inch (20 cm) round cake pans. Line the bottom of each pan with parchment paper and dust the sides with flour, tapping out any excess.

2. **Sift the dry ingredients and work in the butter.** Sift the flour, sugar, baking powder, baking soda and salt together into a large mixing bowl or into the bowl of a stand mixer fitted with the paddle attachment. Add the butter, working it in using electric beaters or the mixer on medium-low speed until no pieces of butter are visible, about 2 minutes.

3. **Add the liquids.** Whisk ¾ cup (175 mL) buttermilk and the oil together and add to the flour, mixing on low speed until combined. Whisk the remaining ½ cup (125 mL) buttermilk with the egg whites and vanilla, add at once to the batter and mix again on low speed until combined. Increase the speed to medium-high and beat well for about 3 minutes, until the batter is fluffy and thick. Divide the batter evenly between the pans and spread to level them, tapping the pans to knock out any air bubbles.

*Taking the extra moment to really whisk the egg whites and remaining buttermilk together will make for easier and more even blending once the mixture is added to the batter.*

4. **Bake the cakes** for about 40 minutes, until a tester inserted in the centre of a cake comes out clean. Cool the cakes in their pans on a rack for about 20 minutes before turning them out onto the rack to cool completely. Chill the cakes for at least 2 hours before assembling.

5. **Make the frosting.** Whisk the milk and flour together in a medium saucepan over medium heat until it thickens and just begins to bubble, about 4 minutes. Whisk in the sugar and salt and continue whisking over medium heat until the mixture begins to bubble again, about 3 more minutes. Pour the paste (it will look like a very pale pudding) into a dish and let cool, uncovered, until it reaches room temperature, 68°F to 70°F (20°C to 21°C).

*CONTINUES*

6. **Mix the butter into the frosting.** Check that your butter is just below room temperature (65°F/18°C). Using electric beaters or a stand mixer fitted with the paddle attachment, beat the butter at medium-high speed until fluffy. Add the cooled milk paste in three additions, mixing well after each addition. Add the vanilla. Add food colouring to your liking. You will need to use the frosting immediately.

*If the frosting doesn't appear smooth once you've added the butter, increase the speed to high and continue whipping. Often the warmth generated by the friction of the beaters warms the frosting enough to blend smoothly.*

7. **Assemble the cake.** Place one cake layer on a cake wheel or platter and top with a generous amount of frosting, spreading to level (1). Top with the second cake layer and spread with another generous amount of frosting, then top with the final cake layer (2). Spread a generous amount of frosting on the top of the cake, coaxing it to hang over the top edge. Spread more frosting to cover the sides of the cake, and use an offset spatula to smooth out the frosting, joining it to the frosting hanging over the top edge (3, 4).

*The outside of the cake will brown as it bakes. If you prefer to showcase the white of the cake against the coloured frosting and sprinkles, trim away the browned outside layer. Chill the cakes for at least 2 hours first and then use a serrated knife to shave away the brown layer from the top and sides as thinly as possible. Use a coarse rasp grater to shave away the brown around the top outside edge without compromising the round shape of the cake.*

8. **Decorate the cake.** Place the sprinkles in a pie plate or shallow dish and set it on the counter where you plan to work. Holding the cake by its base (or turning the cake wheel) with one hand, press sprinkles onto the bottom third of the cake, letting any extras fall back into the pie plate. Spoon any leftover frosting into a piping bag fitted with a decorative tip and pipe décor on the top of the cake. Chill the cake for at least 2 hours, then arrange evenly spaced macarons, if using, on top of the piping.

*For a rainbow twist of piping, first divide the frosting into bowls, colour each of them and spoon one colour into one side of the piping bag and the second colour into the opposite side. When you start piping, the two colours will twist together as you pipe a ring around the top edge of the cake.*

**The cake will keep, with the cut portion covered, in the fridge for up to 4 days.**

**MAKES:** one 3-layer, 8-inch (20 cm) cake
**SERVES:** 10 to 12

**PREP TIME:** 1 hour, plus chilling
**COOK TIME:** 35 minutes

**¦¦¦ COMPLEX**

**BITES OF WISDOM:**
*How to melt chocolate (p. 41), How to assemble a layer cake (p. 50), How to use piping bags & tips (p. 52)*

**INGREDIENTS**

**Cake:**

**4 oz (120 g)** dark baking/couverture chocolate, chopped

**¾ cup (175 mL)** boiling water

**1½ cups (300 g)** packed light brown sugar

**1 cup (250 mL)** buttermilk

**⅔ cup (160 mL)** mayonnaise

**2** large eggs

**1 tsp** vanilla extract

**2 cups (300 g)** all-purpose flour

**⅓ cup (40 g)** Dutch-process cocoa powder

**1 tsp** baking powder

**½ tsp** baking soda

**½ tsp** fine salt

**Peanut butter cream & assembly:**

**1 cup (250 g)** smooth peanut butter

**1 (8 oz/250 g) pkg** cream cheese, softened

**¾ cup (100 g)** icing sugar, sifted

**2 tsp** vanilla extract

**1 cup (250 mL)** whipping cream, whipped to soft peaks

**1 recipe** Chocolate Fudge Sauce & Filling (p. 91)

# Chocolate Peanut Butter Cream Cake

This cake is reminiscent of a peanut butter cup. It combines a mild but rich chocolate cake with an almost mousse-like peanut butter cream and an out-of-this-world double chocolate fudge frosting and filling. At once salty and sweet, airy and dense, this cake satisfies all of your cravings.

1. **Preheat the oven** to 350°F (180°C). Grease three 8-inch (20 cm) cake pans, then line the bottoms with parchment paper and dust the sides with flour.

2. **Melt the chocolate.** Place the chopped chocolate into a bowl and pour the boiling water overtop, letting it sit a minute. Whisk to melt the chocolate (don't worry if the mixture appears grainy). Set aside.

3. **Mix the cake batter by hand.** Whisk the brown sugar, buttermilk, mayonnaise, eggs and vanilla by hand in a large bowl until combined. Sift the flour, cocoa powder, baking powder, baking soda and salt into the bowl and whisk well until there are no visible lumps. Whisk in the chocolate mixture (the batter will be fluid) and divide evenly between the three prepared cake pans, tapping out any excess air bubbles.

*Mayonnaise is often an ingredient in chocolate cake recipes because it's an emulsion of eggs and oil that helps to make batters smooth. It also adds richness and moisture to cakes, keeping them nice and soft and a perfect match for the creamy fillings.*

4. **Bake the cakes** for about 30 minutes, until a tester inserted in the centre of a cake comes out clean. Allow the cakes to cool for 15 minutes, then turn them out onto a rack to cool completely.

5. **Prepare the peanut butter cream.** Beat the peanut butter and cream cheese until smooth. Beat in the icing sugar and vanilla, then fold in the whipped cream until smooth and evenly incorporated. Chill until ready to assemble.

*Making this filling is similar to making an easy mousse, but this chilled filling is actually creamier, which matches the rich cake and the fudge filling.*

6. **Assemble the cake.** Place the first cake layer on a platter. Spoon half of the peanut butter cream into one large piping bag (no tip needed) and half of the fudge filling into another. Pipe a ring of peanut butter cream around the outside edge of the cake layer. Pipe a ring of fudge filling just inside the peanut butter ring and keep repeating, alternating between the peanut butter and fudge fillings until you reach the centre. Place the second cake layer on top and repeat piping the rings, starting with the peanut butter and top with the third cake layer. Spread a layer of peanut butter cream on top and around the sides of the cake until smooth, then pull off some of the cream from the sides to reveal the cake layers ("naked style") or cover the sides of the cake completely. Chill the cake for 30 minutes to make decorating easier.

*CONTINUES*

7. **Decorate the cake.** Melt ¾ cup (175 mL) of the fudge filling over low heat until it is fluid but not runny. Pour into a small piping bag (no tip needed) or into a squeeze bottle. Holding the tip of the piping bag or bottle at the top edge of the cake, squeeze drips of the filling down as you rotate the cake, creating a drip effect—the drips should ideally run no more than halfway down the cake (1). Drizzle any remaining melted filling on top of the cake and use a palette knife to spread it and cover the top of the cake. Chill for 20 minutes.

8. **Finish the decorations.** Spoon the remaining peanut butter cream into a small piping bag (or multiple bags, with different tips) and spoon the remaining fudge filling into a small piping bag as well. Pipe dots and swirls of these frostings on top of the cake in a random pattern (2, 3). You can pipe a ring around the top edge of the cake or completely cover the top of the cake, if you wish. Chill the fully assembled cake for at least 2 hours before serving.

*I sometimes use pieces of Sponge Toffee (p. 363) to add a final, sweet and crunchy finish to this cake (4). If you'd like to do the same, add the sponge toffee up to 2 hours before serving (it will soften in the fridge if left on for too long).*

**The cake will keep in an airtight container in the fridge for up to 4 days.**

**MAKES:** one 9 × 13-inch (23 × 33 cm) cake
**SERVES:** 16 to 24 as a dessert

**PREP TIME:** 15 minutes
**COOK TIME:** 1 hour

❗ SIMPLE
**BITES OF WISDOM:**
*How cake bakes (p. 69)*

## INGREDIENTS

2 cups (300 g) all-purpose flour

1¾ cups (350 g) granulated sugar, divided

2 tsp ground cardamom

1 tsp baking powder

½ tsp ground cinnamon

½ tsp salt

¾ cup (175 g) unsalted butter, at room temperature and cut into pieces

3 large eggs

1 tsp vanilla extract

3 cups (300 g) fresh or frozen, thawed cranberries

# Cranberry Cardamom Tray Cake

Packed with cranberries, this rich cake can be portioned into larger squares as a dessert or cut into smaller bite-sized squares as part of a festive platter.

1. **Preheat the oven** to 325°F (160°C). Grease a 9 × 13-inch (23 × 33 cm) pan.

2. **Combine the dry ingredients and add the butter.** Sift the flour, ¾ cup (150 g) sugar, cardamom, baking powder, cinnamon and salt into a large mixing bowl or the bowl of a stand mixer fitted with the paddle attachment. Add the butter and blend the mixture on medium-low speed until the butter is no longer visible. You will have a rough crumble. Measure out ½ cup (125 mL) of this crumble and set aside. (If you used the stand mixer, tip the rest of the crumble into another bowl.)

   *Almost two cups may seem like a great deal of sugar for a single cake recipe, but you need the sweetness to balance the 3 cups (300 g) of very tart cranberries.*

3. **Whip the eggs and add the cranberries.** In a second bowl or in the bowl of the stand mixer fitted with the whip attachment, whip the eggs, remaining 1 cup (200 g) sugar and vanilla on high speed until the eggs have doubled in volume, about 3 minutes. Add the whipped eggs to the flour base and mix using the paddle or beaters on medium speed until combined, fluffy and smooth. Fold in the cranberries by hand. Spread the batter into the prepared pan and sprinkle the reserved crumble on top.

   *This cake batter is very dense, even with the whipped eggs added. As a cake bakes, cranberries have a tendency to float to the top of a more fluid batter, so the dense batter holds the cranberries in place. The baked cake is by no means heavy; it has a nice even crumb structure.*

4. **Bake the cake** for about an hour, until a skewer inserted in the centre of the cake comes out clean. Cool the cake in its pan on a rack to room temperature before serving.

   **The cake will keep for up to 3 days on the counter. It will also keep, well wrapped, in the fridge for up to a week or frozen for up to 3 months.**

**INGREDIENTS**

2 cups (300 g) all-purpose flour

1½ cups (300 g) granulated sugar,
  divided

1½ Tbsp (22 mL) finely grated lemon
  zest

1½ tsp baking powder

½ tsp fine salt

¾ cup (175 g) unsalted butter, at room
  temperature and cut into pieces

¾ cup (175 mL) sour cream

4 large eggs, separated, at room
  temperature

1 tsp vanilla extract

¾ cup (175 mL) Tart Lemon Curd
  (p. 100), chilled

1 recipe unbaked Almond Streusel
  (p. 82)

Icing sugar, for dusting

# Lemon Crunch-&-Cream Tray Cake

Crunchy almond streusel and tangy lemon curd provide the crunch and cream in this delicious tray cake. Adding lemon zest to the Almond Stresuel crumbled on top gives it an extra zip.

1. **Preheat the oven** to 325°F (160°C) and grease a 9 × 13-inch (23 × 33 cm) pan.

   *Be sure to use a ceramic or porcelain pan for a cake that bakes to a rich golden brown. A metal pan will result in a darker brown cake, though it will still be moist and tender.*

2. **Combine the dry ingredients and add the butter.** Sift the flour, 1 cup (200 g) sugar, lemon zest, baking powder and salt into a large mixing bowl or the bowl of a stand mixer fitted with the paddle attachment. Using electric beaters or the mixer on low speed, cut in the butter until the flour has an even, crumbly texture and large pieces of butter are no longer visible.

3. **Add the sour cream, egg yolks and vanilla** and mix on low speed until combined. Increase the speed to medium, beating well until the batter becomes pale and fluffy and has the consistency of buttercream frosting.

4. **Whip the egg whites and finish the batter.** In a separate clean mixing bowl, whip the egg whites on high speed until frothy, then slowly pour in the remaining ½ cup (100 g) sugar while whipping, until the whites hold a soft peak when the beaters are lifted. Fold a third of the whites into the batter until almost incorporated, then fold in the remaining two-thirds until fully incorporated. Spread the batter into the prepared pan. Dollop the batter with the lemon curd (1) and use a skewer or paring knife to swirl the curd into the batter a little, leaving it clearly visible (2). Crumble the streusel topping over the batter evenly (3).

   *To increase the lemon flavour even more, replace the cinnamon in the almond streusel with 1 Tbsp (15 mL) finely grated lemon zest.*

5. **Bake the cake** for 50 to 70 minutes, until a tester inserted in the centre of the cake comes out clean. Cool the cake in the pan on a rack before serving. Dust the top of the cake generously with icing sugar and cut into squares to serve.

   *The bake time depends on your pan. In a metal pan, the cake bakes in 50 to 60 minutes. In a ceramic pan, it takes 60 to 70 minutes.*

**The cake will keep, well wrapped, on the counter for up to a day or in the fridge for 3 days.**

**MAKES:** one 9 × 13-inch (23 × 33 cm) cake
**SERVES:** 16 to 20

**PREP TIME:** 35 minutes, plus chilling
**COOK TIME:** 70 minutes

### ♦♦♦ COMPLEX

**BITES OF WISDOM:**
*Glossary of baking tools—Baking pans
(p. 21), How to melt chocolate (p. 41)*

## INGREDIENTS

### Chocolate cake:

⅔ cup (160 g) unsalted butter, cut into pieces

5 oz (150 g) dark baking/couverture chocolate, chopped

¾ cup (150 g) packed dark brown sugar

⅓ cup (80 mL) water

⅓ cup (80 mL) sour cream

3 large eggs, at room temperature

1 cup (150 g) all-purpose flour

3 Tbsp (23 g) Dutch-process cocoa powder

1½ tsp baking powder

¼ tsp fine salt

### Vanilla cake:

1 cup (150 g) all-purpose flour

¾ cup (150 g) granulated sugar

1½ tsp baking powder

¼ tsp fine salt

6 Tbsp (90 g) unsalted butter, at room temperature and cut into pieces

½ cup (125 mL) buttermilk or plain kefir

2 large egg whites

1 tsp vanilla extract

### Chocolate marble glaze:

3 oz (90 g) dark baking/couverture chocolate, chopped

¾ cup (180 g) unsalted butter, at room temperature, divided

5 oz (150 g) white baking/couverture chocolate, chopped

1 (10 oz/300 mL) tin sweetened condensed milk

# Chocolate Swirl Tray Cake with Decadent Marble Glaze

Sometimes a marble cake can disappoint because it is a vanilla cake swirled with only a touch of chocolate. This very moist cake is an intense chocolate cake swirled with a separate vanilla cake. The batters are similar in consistency, so every delightful bite is a mix of vanilla and chocolate with a rich marble glaze that takes it to the next level.

1. **Preheat the oven** to 325°F (160°C) and grease a 9 × 13-inch (23 × 33 cm) baking pan.

2. **Make the chocolate cake portion.** Melt the butter and chocolate together in a medium saucepan over medium-low heat, stirring constantly with a spatula until smooth. Add the brown sugar and water, stirring together until smooth. Transfer to a large mixing bowl and cool for 5 minutes. Whisk in the sour cream by hand until smooth. Whisk in the eggs one at a time until blended in. Sift in the flour, cocoa, baking powder and salt and whisk just until smooth. Set aside.

3. **Make the vanilla cake portion.** Sift the flour, sugar, baking powder and salt into a large mixing bowl or into the bowl of a stand mixer fitted with the paddle attachment. Using beaters or the mixer on medium-low speed, cut in the butter until the flour has an even, crumbly texture. Add the buttermilk (or kefir), egg whites and vanilla to the flour, mixing at first on low to combine and then for a minute on medium speed until the batter becomes fluffy.

4. **Swirl the two cakes in the pan.** Ladle half of the chocolate batter into the prepared pan, leaving some space in between the spoonfuls (the batter will spread a touch; that's OK). Dollop half of the vanilla batter in between the gaps in the chocolate batter. Repeat with the remaining chocolate batter, ladling it over the vanilla dollops, then conversely dollop the remaining vanilla batter over the chocolate (1). Use a skewer or paring knife to swirl the two cake batters together, but not so much that you lose the distinction between them (2).

*Use a random swirling motion to create small and bigger circular swirls, so they don't look like a pattern once the cake is baked and sliced.*

5. **Bake the cake** for 40 to 60 minutes, until a tester inserted in the centre of the cake comes out clean. Cool the cake completely in its pan on a rack.

*The bake time depends on your pan. In a metal pan, the cake bakes in 40 to 50 minutes. In a ceramic pan, it takes 50 to 60 minutes.*

*CONTINUES*

6. **Make the marble glaze.** Place the dark chocolate and 6 Tbsp (90 g) butter in a metal bowl. Set over a pot filled with an inch (2.5 cm) of barely simmering water and stir gently until melted. Set aside. Place the white chocolate and remaining 6 Tbsp (90 g) butter in a separate bowl and melt over the water bath while stirring gently. Set aside. Heat the condensed milk over medium heat to about 115°F (46°C) while stirring. Measure about ⅔ cup (150 mL) into each bowl of chocolate and whisk until smooth. Use immediately.

*The white chocolate and butter, once melted, may take on a grainy appearance. Once you add the condensed milk and whisk, the ganache comes together smoothly. Heating the condensed milk makes the finished glazes more fluid and easier to swirl together.*

7. **Glaze the cake.** Ladle or pour some of the dark chocolate glaze onto the cake, letting it flow around the cake. Do the same with the white chocolate. Repeat with the remaining dark and white chocolate glazes (3) and use a skewer or paring knife to swirl the glazes together (4). Chill the cake for at least 2 hours to set the glaze, then serve at room temperature.

**The cake will keep, with the cut portion covered, in the fridge for up to 3 days.**

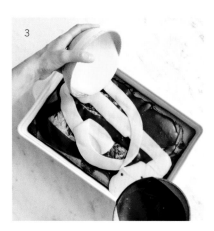

**MAKES:** one 9-inch (23 cm) cheesecake
**SERVES:** 12 to 16

**PREP TIME:** 15 minutes, plus chilling
**COOK TIME:** 40 minutes

❗ SIMPLE
**BITES OF WISDOM:**
*Glossary of baking tools—Springform pan
(p. 23)*

**INGREDIENTS**

**3 (8 oz/250 g) pkg** cream cheese,
   softened and cut into pieces

**1½ cups (300 g)** granulated sugar

**2 Tbsp (16 g)** all-purpose flour

**5** large eggs, at room temperature

**1** large egg yolk

**1½ cups (375 mL)** whipping cream

# Basque Cheesecake (Burnt Cheesecake)

This crustless cheesecake is for dairy lovers, and for those who don't want the stress of avoiding a cheesecake with cracks—this cheesecake is supposed to crack! The Basque region bordering Spain and France near San Sebastián is famous for its fine cuisine, and this cheesecake is all about simple contrasts. Custard-like at the centre and ricotta-like at the edges, the cake bakes with a deeply browned ("burnt") top that has a slightly caramelized flavour. No vanilla or lemon zest here!

1. **Preheat the oven** to 400°F (200°C). Lightly grease a 9-inch (23 cm) spring-form pan. Crumple two large pieces of parchment paper. Line the pan with the parchment, overlapping the sheets so that the sides of the pan are completely covered and the paper comes above the top of the pan.

   *The crumpled parchment is typical of this style of cheesecake and gives the cake its slightly uneven yet rustically appealing shape. The paper also holds the cheesecake in place while the cake rises significantly as it bakes and then collapses and sinks in the centre as it cools, and it helps you to remove the fragile cake from the pan.*

2. **Beat the cream cheese.** Using electric beaters or a stand mixer fitted with the paddle attachment, beat the cream cheese on medium-high speed until fluffy and smooth, scraping down the bowl well. Slowly add half of the sugar while mixing, pausing to scrape down the bowl at least once before adding the remaining sugar. Beat in the flour.

   *Scraping down the bowl often as you add the sugar to the cream cheese is the key to a smooth cheesecake. The firmer cream cheese can stick early on in the beating process, especially to the bottom of the bowl.*

3. **Add the eggs and cream.** Lightly whisk the eggs and egg yolk together in a small bowl. Add the eggs to the cream cheese mixture a little at a time on medium-low speed, stopping to scrape the bowl before adding more, until all have been incorporated. Keep mixing on medium-low speed as you pour in the cream slowly. The batter will be very fluid. Pour the cheesecake batter into the prepared pan.

4. **Bake the cheesecake** for about 40 minutes. It will soufflé and turn a deep brown on top but still quiver in the centre when the pan is gently moved. Let the cheesecake cool in its pan on a rack for at least 2 hours before chilling overnight.

   *Unlike North American cheesecake, this cake is baked at high temperature. It is expected to soufflé and then sink, and will turn a deep brown and crack as it bakes . . . and it is absolutely delicious!*

CONTINUES

5. **Serve the cheesecake in the parchment paper.** Remove the ring from the springform pan and use the parchment paper to lift the cheesecake onto a cutting board or serving platter (leave the parchment on the cake). Push down the paper to reveal more of the cheesecake and use a hot dry knife to cut slices.

*This cheesecake is typically enjoyed on its own, but you could serve it with fresh berries or with a drizzle of Pedro Ximénez, a sweet aged Spanish sherry with dried-fruit characteristics.*

**The cheesecake will keep, loosely covered, in the fridge for up to 2 days. Do not freeze.**

**MAKES:** one 9-inch (23 cm) cheesecake
**SERVES:** 12 to 16

**PREP TIME:** 45 minutes, plus chilling
**COOK TIME:** 55 minutes

🍴 **MORE INVOLVED**
**BITES OF WISDOM:**
*Glossary of ingredients—Milk & other dairy (p. 11)*

## INGREDIENTS

### Crust:

1½ **cups (190 g)** graham cracker crumbs

¼ **cup (25 g)** shredded coconut

⅓ **cup (75 g)** unsalted butter, melted

### Filling:

3 **(8 oz/250 g)** pkg cream cheese, softened

1 **(10 oz/300 mL)** tin sweetened condensed milk

½ **cup (125 mL)** coconut milk

3 **Tbsp (24 g)** cornstarch

2 large eggs, at room temperature

1 large egg yolk

1 **Tbsp (15 mL)** vanilla extract

### Toppings:

¾ **cup (175 mL)** Dulce de Leche (p. 90) or store-bought, divided (not dulce de leche–flavoured condensed milk)

½ **cup (50 g)** shredded coconut

1 **recipe** Chantilly Cream (p. 95)

6 **to 8** Alfajores (p. 389), cut in half, for décor

# Alfajor Cheesecake

This dense, creamy and rich North American–style cheesecake is made more decadent with flavours based on the South American dulce de leche–filled, coconut-dusted sandwich cookie known as the alfajor. If you love caramel, you will love this cheesecake and its graham crust and cream cheese filling. This recipe is perfect for mastering your cheesecake-making skills: avoiding a crack in the middle of a cheesecake is the biggest obstacle for bakers, and I include plenty of tips to ensure this won't happen to you.

1. **Preheat the oven** to 350°F (180°C). Grease a 9-inch (23 cm) springform pan well.

2. **Make the crust.** Stir the graham crumbs, coconut and melted butter together until combined. Press the crust into the base and halfway up the sides of the pan using the back of a spoon. Bake the crust for 10 minutes (there will be no visible change) and cool on a rack before filling.

   *You can use sweetened or unsweetened coconut here; the sweetness doesn't affect the recipe.*

3. **Beat the cream cheese with the milk.** Reduce the oven temperature to 300°F (150°C). Using electric beaters or a stand mixer fitted with the paddle attachment, beat the cream cheese on high speed. Scrape down the bowl once or twice as you go. Add the condensed milk in two additions and mix well, still on high speed, scraping the bowl between additions. Add the coconut milk and cornstarch and mix well, again scraping down the bowl.

   *Using silky-smooth condensed milk as the sweetener for this cheesecake seems to build in a texture that resists cracking.*

4. **Add the eggs to the filling.** Whisk the eggs, egg yolk and vanilla together and add all at once to the batter. Mix on medium-low speed until combined. Scrape the cheesecake filling into the prepared pan (it will fill the pan higher than the crust).

   *When you add the eggs to the batter, be sure to mix on a lower speed. If beaten too vigorously, the eggs may hold in air that will expand as the cheesecake cooks and then contract as the cheesecake cools, increasing the risk for a crack to develop.*

*CONTINUES*

5. **Bake the cheesecake** for about 45 minutes. The outside 2 inches (5 cm) of the cheesecake should be set, but the centre of the cheesecake will still be soft. Remove from the oven to a rack to cool. Let the cake cool for 15 minutes, then run a palette knife around the inside edge of the pan to prevent cracking as the cheesecake cools. Let the cheesecake cool in its pan on a rack for at least 2 hours before chilling overnight.

*Running a palette knife around the sides of the pan is a critical step. If the cheesecake is stuck to the pan and needs to contract, it will pull at the centre, creating the dreaded crack. If you loosen the cheesecake from the sides of the pan before it cools, it will contract from the outside edge slightly, leaving the centre intact. A second critical step is making sure to fully cool your cheesecake before chilling. It takes at least 2 hours for it to cool enough to chill. If the cake is too warm, the cold air in the fridge can cause it to contract and then . . . a crack develops!*

6. **Remove the cheesecake from its pan.** Run a palette knife around the inside edge of the pan again and remove the ring.

7. **Decorate the cheesecake.** Before you remove the base, spread ¼ cup (60 mL) dulce de leche around the sides of the cake in a sheer, even layer. Press coconut onto the sides of the cake all the way around. Slide your palette knife under the cheesecake to loosen it from the base and then slide the cake onto your serving plate. Spread the remaining ½ cup (125 mL) dulce de leche over the top of the cake, warming the caramel a little if needed to make it spreadable. Pipe Chantilly cream on top and decorate with alfajores. Chill the cheesecake until ready to serve.

*If you are using store-bought dulce de leche, be sure to buy a thick one that holds its shape when spread. Look for it in jars in the peanut butter and jam aisle of the grocery store. In South America, the thinner, lighter-coloured version is for spreading on toast, and the thicker, dark brown version is meant for desserts. Dulce de leche is also called manjar or arequipe in some countries or cajeta when made with goat's milk.*

*You should now have a beautiful, smooth cheesecake that's free of cracks (and tips that you can use with other cheesecake recipes). If a crack does develop, cover it with a little whipped cream.*

**The cheesecake will keep, loosely covered, in the fridge for up to 4 days.**

MAKES: one 8-inch (20 cm) torte
**MAKES:** one 8-inch (20 cm) torte
**SERVES:** 10 to 12

**PREP TIME:** 1 hour, plus chilling
**COOK TIME:** 40 minutes

🍴 **MORE INVOLVED**
**BITES OF WISDOM:**
*How to roll pastry doughs (p. 44), How to assemble a layer cake (p. 50)*

## INGREDIENTS

**Cake:**

½ cup (150 g) liquid honey

½ cup (115 g) unsalted butter

3¼ cups (487 g) all-purpose flour

⅔ cup (140 g) packed light brown sugar

1 tsp baking powder

1 tsp ground cinnamon

½ tsp fine salt

3 large eggs

2 tsp vanilla extract

**Honey cream frosting:**

⅓ cup (100 g) honey

2½ cups (625 mL) whipping cream, divided

1 cup (250 mL) Crème Fraîche (p. 94) or store-bought

# Medovik (Russian Honey Torte)

Ready to take on a project? This eight-layer Russian cake is distinctive because of the burnt honey in the cake batter and the frosting. The aromas of the honey and butter permeate the kitchen as you bake, building anticipation and appetite. Another distinctive feature is that the cake layers are made with a rolled-out dough and not from a pourable cake batter. These layers are crisp and biscuit-like when baked but soften once layered with the burnt honey frosting and chilled.

1. **"Burn" the honey for the cake.** Bring the honey and butter to a boil in a small saucepan over medium-high heat, stirring constantly. Cook the mixture, still stirring constantly, until the honey reaches 240°F (116°C), about 4 minutes. Remove the pan from the heat to cool for 15 minutes.

2. **Combine the dry ingredients and mix the dough.** Whisk the flour, brown sugar, baking powder, cinnamon and salt together in a large mixing bowl. Add the slightly cooled honey to the bowl and stir to combine. Whisk the eggs and vanilla in a small bowl, add to the dough and stir until evenly combined. Shape the dough into two discs, wrap and chill for an hour or up to a day.

   *This dough is softer to handle and work with than other pastry doughs because of the honey and melted butter. It will seem sticky when it first comes together, but chilling for an hour makes it easy to handle.*

3. **Preheat the oven** to 400°F (200°C). Line two baking trays with parchment paper.

4. **Roll out half of the dough.** Generously dust a work surface with flour. Cut the first disc of dough into four equal pieces. Roll out the first piece to a circle at least 8 inches (20 cm) across; it will be very thin (about ⅛ inch/3 mm). As you roll, be sure to lift and even flip the dough over to ensure it is not sticking. Use the bottom of an 8-inch (20 cm) cake pan or other pan to trace and cut an 8-inch (20 cm) circle from the dough. Carefully lift onto the baking tray and repeat with the remaining three pieces of dough, dusting the work surface as often as needed to prevent sticking. Save all of the dough scraps (keep them in their scrappy shapes).

   *To prevent the dough from sticking, keep the rolling surface well dusted and keep moving and rotating the dough as you roll it thinly. Alternatively, roll the dough between two sheets of unfloured parchment paper. After rolling, trim each circle to the right size and use the bottom sheet of parchment to lift up the pastry and flip it onto the baking tray, peeling away the paper.*

5. **Bake the layers** for 8 to 10 minutes, until lightly browned at the edges. Let the cake layers cool on the tray for 10 minutes before removing to cool on a rack.

*CONTINUES*

6. **Roll out the remaining dough.** While the first four layers are cooling, cut the second disc of dough into four pieces, roll them out and bake into four more layers.

7. **Bake the scraps.** After all eight layers are baked, arrange the scraps of pastry dough on a baking tray and bake for 8 to 10 minutes (1). Once cooled, pulse the scraps in a mini chopper or food processor until they are coarse crumbs and set aside (they will coat the sides of the cake).

*I love that old-school recipes like this one are designed not to waste anything. Many classic tortes are decorated using cake crumbs or crumbled cookies. Here, while the baked cake layers soften inside the torte, the baked crumbs on the sides hold some crunch and look lovely at the same time.*

8. **Cook the honey for the frosting.** Bring the honey to a boil in a small saucepan over medium heat. Boil, stirring occasionally, until the honey turns from amber to a dark caramel colour, about 5 minutes from when it begins to boil. Remove the pan from the heat and whisk in ¼ cup (60 mL) whipping cream. Set aside to cool to room temperature.

*Whereas cooking the honey for the pastry dough to 240°F (116°C) was about lending the right texture to the dough, cooking the honey to an amber to dark caramel colour for the filling/frosting is about developing an intense colour and flavour.*

9. **Add the cream to the frosting.** Whip the remaining 2¼ cups (560 mL) cream to a soft peak and whip in the crème fraîche. Add the cooled burnt honey and whisk in by hand.

10. **Assemble the torte.** Place a cake layer onto a cake wheel or cake platter. Spread an even layer of the honey cream about the same thickness as the cake overtop. Top with a second cake layer and another layer of honey cream (2). Repeat with the remaining cake layers. Spread an even layer of honey cream over the final cake layer, then spread the remaining cream around the sides of the cake. Press the baked pastry crumbs around the sides of the cake (3) and chill for at least 6 hours before serving.

*Decorate the top of the cake however you like. You can leave it flat and simple, pipe a birthday greeting or even add some little marzipan honeybees with sliced almonds for wings.*

*The cake layers soften and the flavours meld beautifully as the cake chills. While 6 hours is the minimum chilling time, assembling the cake a full day ahead is ideal.*

**The cake will keep, loosely covered, in the fridge for up to 4 days.**

**MAKES:** one 8-inch (20 cm) torte
**SERVES:** 8 to 10

**PREP TIME:** 50 minutes, plus cooling and chilling

**COOK TIME:** 17 minutes (if all layers are baked at once)

### ‖‖‖ COMPLEX

**BITES OF WISDOM:**
*Glossary of ingredients—Nuts & seeds (p. 11), How to whip egg whites (p. 34), How to make a parchment paper cone for piping (p. 54)*

### INGREDIENTS

**Almond hazelnut dacquoise:**

⅔ cup (80 g) ground almonds

⅔ cup (80 g) ground hazelnuts

⅓ cup (50 g) all-purpose flour

¼ tsp fine salt

8 large egg whites (240 g), at room temperature

1 tsp cream of tartar

1 cup (200 g) granulated sugar

**German buttercream:**

1 cup (225 g) unsalted butter, at room temperature

1 recipe Vanilla Pastry Cream (p. 96), made using 1 cup (250 mL) milk instead of 2 cups (500 mL), cooled to room temperature

2 Tbsp (30 mL) kirsch, orange liqueur or brandy (optional)

**Assembly & glaze:**

⅓ cup (80 mL) apricot jam

1½ oz (45 g) semisweet baking/ couverture chocolate, chopped

1½ cups (200 g) icing sugar

2 Tbsp (30 mL) hot water

2 tsp lemon juice

2 tsp vegetable oil

1 cup (110 g) lightly toasted sliced almonds

# Esterházy Torte

I absolutely love this torte. Although it was created in Budapest over 100 years ago and named for a Hungarian prince, this torte spread across the Austro-Hungarian Empire, which is why it is eaten across Central Europe. I remember eating it on a trip to Slovakia with my parents, who were visiting the country of their own grandparents for the first time. Many European tortes contain nuts, and this one features layers of dacquoise meringue (nut meringue) assembled with a German buttercream and topped with a sheer layer of apricot jam and a swirl of icing glaze. It's a truly delicious classic torte with an incredibly light taste and texture.

1. **Preheat the oven** to 350°F (180°C). Trace six 8-inch (20 cm) circles onto parchment paper, two circles per sheet. Place one sheet, marked side down, on each of three baking trays.

   *When I make and assemble this torte on the same day, I prepare the pastry cream before I make the dacquoise layers. By the time the dacquoise layers are baked and cooled, my pastry cream is cooled to room temperature and ready to be worked into the German buttercream.*

2. **Combine the ground nuts.** Whisk the ground almonds, ground hazelnuts, flour and salt together in a small bowl.

   *If you are grinding nuts from whole, weigh 2.8 oz (80 g) of each and pulse in a food processor with the full measure of the flour until finely ground.*

3. **Whip the egg whites and cream of tartar** using electric beaters or a stand mixer fitted with the whip attachment on high speed until they are frothy. While continuing to whip, slowly pour in the sugar and whip until the whites hold a stiff peak when the beaters are lifted.

4. **Fold the nuts into the whites.** Add half of the ground nut mixture to the whites and fold in gently but quickly. Repeat with the remaining nuts and fold in.

5. **Dollop the meringue onto the centre of each traced circle**, dividing it as evenly as you can. Use a palette knife to spread the meringue to fill in the circle and make it level. If you can't fit three trays into your oven, the third tray can sit out while the first two bake, without compromise.

   *While it might be tempting to measure and scoop out each portion of meringue, every extra contact deflates it. It's better to just dollop enough meringue to fill each circle from the bowl and then spoon a little from one circle to another if they look unequal.*

*CONTINUES*

6. **Bake the meringue layers** for 15 to 17 minutes; they will brown around the edges a little. Immediately after removing the trays from the oven, slide the parchment paper off the tray onto a cooling rack. Let the cake layers cool for 5 minutes, then use a palette knife to remove each dacquoise. Cool completely before assembling.

   *It is important for meringues to cool quickly when removed from the oven. Cooling them on a hot baking tray causes condensation to build up, adding moisture and making the dacquoise layers difficult to remove. If the dacquoises do stick to the paper, pop the parchment paper back in the oven for 3 more minutes to dry out the bottom. Cool for 5 minutes and try again. If the dacquoise layers are not perfectly round, trim the edges with a paring knife once they have cooled.*

7. **Make the German buttercream.** Beat the butter using electric beaters or a stand mixer fitted with the whip attachment on high speed until it is fluffy. Add a third of the cooled pastry cream to the butter and beat on medium speed, scraping the bowl. Add the remaining pastry cream in two additions, scraping after each. Increase the speed to medium-high and beat until fluffy. Beat in the spirits, if using, on low speed and set aside.

   *The pastry cream used as a base for this buttercream is very smooth and easy to work with. I also really like this buttercream because it is not as sweet or rich as an American (cupcake), Swiss or Italian buttercream.*

8. **Assemble the torte.** Place a dacquoise layer on a cake wheel or cake plate. Spoon about ⅔ cup (160 mL) buttercream into a small bowl and set aside for the sides of the torte. Dollop about ⅓ cup (80 mL) of the remaining buttercream onto the dacquoise layer and spread it to cover completely in an even layer. Set a second dacquoise layer on top and repeat with the buttercream and remaining dacquoise layers. Spread a thin layer of buttercream on the top of the cake and chill for 30 minutes.

9. **Spread the apricot jam** over the top of the cake. Place the chocolate in a metal bowl set over a pot filled with an inch (2.5 cm) of barely simmering water. Stir gently until the chocolate has melted, then pour into a small parchment cone for piping the finishing detail.

10. **Make the glaze.** Stir the icing sugar, hot water, lemon juice and oil together until it makes a thick paste. The glaze handles best at 80°F to 85°F (27°C to 29°C); if it is cooler than this, place the bowl over a pot of gently simmering water, stirring until it warms. If the glaze is too warm, set a piece of plastic wrap directly on the surface of the glaze and let it sit on the counter to cool.

11. **Pour the glaze** over the top of the cake, pouring right into the middle and letting gravity pull it to the outside edge; don't worry about how the sides of the cake look at this point. Once the top of the cake is completely covered and the glaze stops visibly moving, draw a spiral in the chocolate starting in the centre of the cake and spiralling outward. Use a skewer or paring knife to create a spider-web effect. First, pull the skewer through the glaze from the centre to the outside of the cake. Then move the skewer about an inch (2.5 cm) to the right and pull through the glaze in the opposite direction, from the outside edge to the centre. Continue around the cake, alternating directions.

*When decorating this cake, focus on the top of the cake before tackling the sides. Really let the glaze settle into place and stop moving before you pipe the spiral of chocolate and make the signature spiderweb pattern on top so that you know it will set nicely.*

12. **Finish decorating.** Use a palette knife to scrape away any glaze that spilled over the edge and to straighten the top edge of the cake. Use the reserved ⅔ cup (160 mL) buttercream to cover the sides of the cake completely and evenly. Press the sliced almonds into the side of the cake, covering the buttercream completely. Chill the cake for at least 2 hours before slicing.

*Pressing crumbs or nuts onto the side of a cake is traditional to many European tortes, just as it is for Medovik (p. 269). It hides uneven details and makes for a delicious, nutty finish.*

**The cake can be made and assembled a full day ahead of serving. It will keep, loosely wrapped, in the fridge for up to 5 days. Do not place wrap directly on the surface of the glaze.**

**MAKES:** one 9-inch (23 cm) cake
**SERVES:** 16 to 20

**PREP TIME:** 75 minutes, plus chilling
**COOK TIME:** 35 minutes

### ⦀⦀⦀ COMPLEX

**BITES OF WISDOM:**
*Specialty baking tools—Acetate (p. 24),*
*How to melt chocolate (p. 41), How to*
*assemble a layer cake (p. 50)*

## INGREDIENTS

### Hazelnut Bavarian cream:

1½ tsp (5.3 g) gelatin powder

2 Tbsp (30 mL) cold water

½ cup (125 mL) 2% milk

1½ cups (375 mL) whipping cream, divided

6 Tbsp (90 mL) hazelnut praline paste (see note below)

3 large egg yolks

3 Tbsp (37 g) granulated sugar

### Chocolate mousse:

¾ tsp (2.6 g) gelatin powder

1 Tbsp (15 mL) cold water

5 oz (150 g) semisweet baking/ couverture chocolate, chopped

1¼ cups (310 mL) whipping cream, divided

2 Tbsp (30 mL) hazelnut liqueur

### Simple syrup:

¼ cup (50 g) granulated sugar

¼ cup (60 mL) water

1 Tbsp (15 mL) hazelnut liqueur

### Chocolate mirror glaze & assembly:

One 8-inch (20 cm) Chocolate Sponge Cake (p. 232), cooled

¾ cup (115 g) Praliné Noisette (p. 85)

4 tsp (14 g) gelatin powder

3 Tbsp (45 mL) cold water

1 cup (200 g) granulated sugar

⅔ cup (80 g) Dutch-process cocoa powder

½ cup (125 mL) water

½ cup (125 mL) whipping cream

# Torta Setteveli

Setteveli means "seven veils" in Italian, and this seven-layer cake originated in Palermo, Sicily. The torte is made of two chocolate sponge cake layers, two hazelnut Bavarian cream layers, a chocolate mousse layer and a hazelnut praline layer, all enrobed in a chocolate mirror glaze. It is an expression of love for the time and effort involved, yet this one cake is a fantastic way to show off your skills making sponge cake, Bavarian cream and mousse and caramelizing sugar. If you are ready for this baking challenge, please review all of the sections relating to these separate baking skills beforehand to pick up some valuable extra tips. And pay close attention to the instructions about when to prepare each component.

1. **Make the hazelnut Bavarian cream** (1 to 3 hours ahead of assembling the torte). Start this by stirring the gelatin powder into the cold water to soften. Set aside.

2. **Heat the milk,** ½ cup (125 mL) cream and the hazelnut praline paste in a saucepan over medium heat until just below a simmer, whisking the paste into the milk.

   *Hazelnut paste (or hazelnut praline paste) is a sweetened nut butter found in European stores or stores that sell specialty baking ingredients. You can also make your own by pulsing 5 oz (150 g) Praliné Noisette with 2 Tbsp (30 mL) hazelnut liqueur or hazelnut oil in a mini chopper or food processor until it forms a paste.*

3. **Whisk the egg yolks and sugar** together in a bowl. Slowly pour the hot milk into the egg yolks while whisking constantly and then pour the entire mixture back into the pot. Continue whisking over medium heat, cooking for about 3 minutes until the custard has thickened and coats the back of a spoon. Remove the pot from the heat and whisk in the gelatin until dissolved. Transfer the custard to a bowl to cool, uncovered, to room temperature.

   *When you add the gelatin to the custard, it will appear to lose its thickened consistency a little—don't worry, the Bavarian cream will set up properly once cooled.*

4. **Fold the cream into the cooled custard.** Whip the remaining 1 cup (250 mL) cream to a soft peak and fold into the cooled custard in two additions. Chill the Bavarian cream until ready to assemble.

5. **Make the chocolate mousse** (immediately before assembling the torte). Stir the gelatin powder into the cold water to soften. Set aside.

   *Chocolate mousse is often made with gelatin when it will be used as a torte filling. When the mousse will be served as a dessert on its own, no gelatin is needed. Gelatin helps stabilize the mousse between the layers of cake so it doesn't leak out when the torte is sliced.*

*CONTINUES*

6. **Melt the chocolate.** Place the chocolate in a metal bowl set over a pot filled with an inch (2.5 cm) of barely simmering water. Stir gently until the chocolate has melted, then remove the bowl from the heat and set aside to cool for 10 minutes.

7. **Dissolve the gelatin.** Heat ¼ cup (60 mL) whipping cream with the softened gelatin in a small saucepan on medium-low heat, whisking until the gelatin has dissolved. Set aside to cool for 5 to 10 minutes.

8. **Finish the chocolate mousse.** Using electric beaters or a stand mixer fitted with the whip attachment, whip the remaining 1 cup (250 mL) cream on medium speed until it holds a soft peak. Add the cooled gelatin cream and the chocolate and mix until the chocolate is almost fully incorporated. Add the hazelnut liqueur and fold in by hand.

9. **Prepare the pan.** Prepare a 9-inch (23 cm) springform pan by lining the bottom and sides with parchment paper or acetate so that it comes up at least 2 inches (5 cm) higher than the top of the pan.

10. **Make the simple syrup.** Heat ¼ cup (50 g) sugar and ¼ cup (60 mL) water over medium heat, stirring until the sugar has dissolved. Remove the pan from the heat and stir in the hazelnut liqueur.

11. **Assemble the first layers of filling.** Spoon half of the chocolate mousse into a piping bag (no piping tip needed) (1) and spread the remaining half of the mousse into the bottom of the prepared pan, spreading to level it. Pipe a ring of chocolate mousse around the inside edge of the pan, about an inch (2.5 cm) tall. Give the hazelnut Bavarian cream a gentle stir to loosen it and spoon half of it into the pan, filling inside the chocolate mousse piping (2). Spread the Bavarian cream gently to make it level.

12. **Add the first layer of cake.** Cut the sponge cake in half horizontally. Place one layer of cake on top of the Bavarian cream and brush with the simple syrup (3). Pipe a ring of chocolate mousse around the cake (4), so that the mousse is level with the top of the cake, filling in any gaps. Now pipe another ring of mousse around the edge, leaving the centre for the remaining Bavarian cream.

13. **Assemble the second layers of filling and cake.** Spoon the remaining Bavarian cream into the pan, inside the mousse piping, and spread to level it. Sprinkle the praliné noisette over the top in an even layer (5). Place the remaining cake layer on top, brush with simple syrup and press in gently to secure (but not too hard or the Bavarian cream will ooze out). Use any remaining chocolate mousse to fill in the gaps around the cake (6). Cover and freeze for 2 hours, or chill for 6 hours.

*If you have extra Bavarian cream or chocolate mousse after assembling your torte, refrigerate them in an airtight container and use them to pipe detail on top of the mirror glaze after it has set.*

14. **Make the chocolate mirror glaze.** Stir the gelatin powder into the 3 Tbsp (45 mL) cold water to soften. Set aside. Whisk the sugar and cocoa powder together in a medium saucepan and then whisk in the ½ cup (125 mL) water and the whipping cream. Bring to a full boil over medium-high heat while whisking. Let boil for 30 seconds. Remove the pan from the heat and whisk in the gelatin to dissolve it. Transfer the glaze to a bowl and stir occasionally, letting the glaze cool to between 86°F and 90°F (30°C and 32°C) before pouring over the cake.

15. **Prepare your glazing area.** Line a baking tray with parchment paper and place a cooling rack over the top. Place a large ramekin or other dish with a flat surface on the cooling rack to rest the cake on.

16. **Unmold the frozen or chilled cake.** Remove the outer springform ring and peel away the parchment paper. Place a cake board on top of the cake and invert, resting the cake on the ramekin on the cooling rack. Lift off the bottom of the pan and peel away the parchment paper.

17. **Pour the glaze** over the cake in a single stream, being sure to check the sides to ensure coverage (7, 8). The excess glaze will run off the cake and collect on the baking tray. (You can pour this extra glaze into a bowl, chill and rewarm for other uses.) Use your palette knife to trim away any drips from the bottom of the cake and carefully lift the cake off its stand and onto your cake plate. Chill the cake until ready to serve.

*The shiny surface of a mirror-glazed torte is perfect for imaginative decoration. In addition to using any extra Bavarian cream or mousse to pipe detail, create a splashy starlight effect by mixing a little silver or gold pearl dust powder with a teaspoon of vodka. Dip a small paintbrush into the liquid and tap the brush against your hand near the cake, letting the pearlized liquid splatter onto the cake. The vodka will evaporate in a moment and the stardust splatter will remain.*

**The cake will keep, loosely wrapped, in the fridge for up to 4 days. Do not place wrap directly on the surface of the glaze.**

**MAKES:** one 9-inch (23 cm) cake
**SERVES:** 6 to 8

**PREP TIME:** 20 minutes
**COOK TIME:** 35 minutes

🍴 **MORE INVOLVED**
**BITES OF WISDOM:**
*How cake bakes (p. 69)*

**INGREDIENTS**

1½ cups (225 g) all-purpose flour

¾ cup (75 g) grated Parmesan cheese

3 Tbsp (24 g) cornstarch

1 Tbsp (12 g) granulated sugar

2 tsp dried oregano or herbes de Provence

1½ tsp baking powder

½ tsp fine salt

6 Tbsp (90 mL) sour cream

6 Tbsp (90 mL) 2% milk

2 large eggs

6 Tbsp + 1 Tbsp (105 g) unsalted butter, melted, divided

3 to 4 medium cooking onions

1 Tbsp (30 mL) extra virgin olive oil

# Onion, Herb & Parmesan Upside-down Cake

Looking for something different? This savoury upside-down cake is made the same way as sweeter fruit versions, but serve this fluffy Parmesan and herb cake in place of bread or potatoes as a side dish to a barbecue or a roast, or as a tasty starter course with a side salad.

1. **Preheat the oven** to 400°F (200°C). Have ready a 9-inch (23 cm) heavy-bottomed, ovenproof skillet ready. (If needed, you can use a skillet that's an inch/2.5 cm larger or smaller without changing the cook time too much, but the amount of onions used to cover the top may change.)

2. **Make the cake batter.** In a large bowl, stir together the flour, Parmesan, cornstarch, sugar, oregano (or herbes de Provence), baking powder and salt. In a separate bowl, whisk the sour cream, milk and eggs. Add the wet ingredients all at once to the flour, stirring just until combined. Stir in the 6 Tbsp (90 g) melted butter (the batter will be thick) and set aside.

   *Adding cornstarch helps to make the cake batter soft and tender. In sweet cakes, sugar stops protein from developing in the flour and making them tough. Here, cornstarch serves the same purpose.*

3. **Peel and cut the onions** into ½-inch (1.2 cm) thick slices and leave the rings intact (do not separate the rings of the onions).

4. **Cook the onions.** Heat the skillet over medium-high heat. Add the remaining 1 Tbsp (15 g) butter and oil and swirl to coat the pan. Once the butter stops bubbling, arrange the onions to completely fill the bottom of the pan, placing them as close together as you can without them overlapping. Let the onions cook for about 4 minutes, until the edge of the rings starts to brown.

5. **Top the onions with the cake batter.** Remove the pan from the heat and dollop the batter over the onions, using a spatula to gently spread the batter evenly over the onions to cover them. Put the pan in the oven and immediately reduce the temperature to 375°F (190°C).

6. **Bake the cake** for about 25 minutes, until a tester inserted in the centre of the cake comes out clean. Cool the cake in its pan for about 20 minutes before inverting the pan to tip the cake out onto a plate. Serve the cake warm or at room temperature.

**The cake will keep, well wrapped, at room temperature for up to 2 days.**

**MAKES:** one 3-layer, 8-inch (20 cm) cake
**SERVES:** 12 to 16

**PREP TIME:** 45 minutes, plus chilling
**COOK TIME:** 25 minutes

🍴🍴🍴 COMPLEX

**BITES OF WISDOM:**
*How acidity works in baking (p. 66), How to assemble a layer cake (p. 50)*

### INGREDIENTS

**Cornbread:**

2½ cups (375 g) all-purpose flour

1½ cups (250 g) cornmeal

1 cup (200 g) granulated sugar

2 Tbsp (18 g) baking powder

2 tsp chili powder

2 tsp fine salt

2 cups (500 mL) 2% milk

2 large eggs

½ cup (125 mL) sour cream

1 cup (225 g) unsalted butter, melted (still warm is OK)

**Chili cheese filling:**

2 cups (220 g) coarsely grated Cheddar cheese

¾ cup (175 mL) sour cream

4 green onions, thinly sliced

1 Tbsp (6 g) chili powder

**Guacamole frosting:**

3 large ripe avocados

1 (8 oz/250 g) pkg cream cheese, softened

6 Tbsp (90 mL) fresh lime juice

2 cloves garlic, minced

1 cup (250 mL) roughly chopped fresh cilantro leaves

2 green onions, sliced

Salt and pepper

**Assembly:**

1 cup (250 mL) store-bought tomato salsa, divided

2 cups (500 mL) shredded romaine or iceberg lettuce

# Nacho Cornbread Layer Cake

This surprising cornbread cake is layered with a chili cheese filling and salsa and then the entire cake is covered with a guacamole "frosting" with shredded lettuce on top. Every bite has all the flavours of a platter of nachos, but in a beautiful layer cake.

1. **Preheat the oven** to 400°F (200°C). Lightly grease three 8-inch (20 cm) cake pans and line the bottoms with parchment paper.

2. **Make the cornbread.** Whisk the flour, cornmeal, sugar, baking powder, chili powder and salt together in a mixing bowl to blend. Add the milk, eggs and sour cream and whisk until smooth. Whisk in the melted butter and pour the batter into the pan. Bake the cornbread for about 25 minutes, until a tester inserted in the centre of the bread comes out clean. Cool in the pan on a rack for at least 20 minutes before turning out to cool completely.

3. **Make the chili cheese filling.** Beat the Cheddar with the sour cream, green onions and chili powder until well bound (the grated cheese may break down a little). Set aside.

4. **Make the guacamole.** Cut the avocados in half, remove the pit and scoop out the flesh into a food processor. Add the cream cheese, lime juice, garlic, cilantro and green onions and pulse until smooth. Season to taste and set aside. If the guacamole seems soft, chill it for an hour before using.

*The lime juice and cream cheese in the guacamole prevent the avocados from discolouring quickly. This "frosting" also makes a delicious make-ahead dip on its own.*

5. **Assemble the cake.** Carefully place a cornbread layer on a platter or cake stand. Spread half of the cheese filling over the top, spreading to level it. Top with a third of the salsa, spreading it almost to the outside edge. Place the second cornbread layer on top and repeat with the remaining half of the cheese filling and a third of the salsa. Place the last cornbread layer on top and press gently to ensure the cake is level.

*Cornbread is more fragile than sweet cake layers, so handle the layers gently as you stack them.*

6. **Frost and decorate the cake.** Dollop and spread enough guacamole on the top of the cake to reach the sides, spreading to level it. If you wish, you can spread guacamole on the sides of the cake to cover the cake completely, or use a cake scraper to pull away excess guacamole, revealing the cornbread and cheese layers (naked cake style). Scoop some guacamole into a piping bag fitted with a plain tip and pipe décor detail around the top edge of the cake. Spread the remaining salsa within this piping and crown the top of the cake with the shredded lettuce. Chill the cake for at least 3 hours before serving.

**The cake will keep, loosely wrapped, in the fridge for up to 3 days.**

**MAKES:** 2 shareable waffle cakes (6 waffles)
**SERVES:** 4

**PREP TIME:** 45 minutes
**COOK TIME:** 40 minutes

🍴 **MORE INVOLVED**
*Bites of Wisdom:*
*How starch works in baking (p. 66)*

**INGREDIENTS**

**Easy Cheddar cheese sauce:**

**1 cup (250 mL)** 2% milk

**1 Tbsp (8 g)** cornstarch

**1 tsp** Dijon mustard

**2 cups (220 g)** grated Cheddar cheese

Salt and pepper

Sriracha sauce (optional)

**Zucchini Cheddar waffles:**

**4 cups (460 g)** grated zucchini (about 2 medium)

**½ tsp** fine salt

**3** large eggs

**1 cup (150 g)** all-purpose flour

**1 tsp** baking powder

**1 cup (110 g)** grated Cheddar cheese

**¼ cup (25 g)** finely grated Parmesan cheese

**2** green onions, thinly sliced

**Assembly:**

**4** strips smoked bacon

**4** large eggs

Chopped Italian parsley, for garnish

# Zucchini Cheddar Waffle Cake

This over-the-top brunch cake combines crispy warm zucchini Cheddar waffles with layers of bacon slices, fried eggs and a warm cheese sauce. Each waffle cake can be shared between two people, which makes it more manageable to make, assemble and serve than a larger waffle cake.

1. **Make the cheese sauce.** Whisk the milk, cornstarch and Dijon mustard together in a saucepan over medium-high heat, whisking until the milk simmers and thickens, about 4 minutes. Reduce the heat to medium and stir in the Cheddar until the cheese is melted and the sauce is smooth. Season to taste and stir in Sriracha, if using.

   *You can make the cheese sauce ahead of time and keep it on low heat, stirring occasionally. It will also keep in an airtight container in the fridge for up to 2 days. Reheat on low before using.*

2. **Make the waffle batter.** Stir together the zucchini and salt and let sit for 20 minutes. Squeeze out any excess liquid from the zucchini, discard the liquid and place the zucchini in a large mixing bowl. Whisk the eggs lightly and add them to the zucchini, stirring to combine. Add the flour and baking powder and stir in, followed by the Cheddar, Parmesan and green onions—the batter will be thick.

3. **Cook the waffles.** Preheat and grease your waffle iron and have ready a cooling rack set on a baking tray. Preheat the oven to 300°F (150°C). Drop ½ cup (125 mL) of the batter onto the centre of the waffle iron and press, cooking for about 4 minutes, or until browned. Set the cooked waffle onto the rack and hold in the oven while you cook the others. Repeat with the remaining batter. (You should have six waffles.)

   *The waffles can be made a day ahead, stored chilled and then rewarmed at 325°F (160°C) for 15 to 20 minutes.*

4. **Cook the bacon.** Cook the bacon in a skillet over medium heat, flipping it halfway through cooking, until crisp. Drain, transfer to the rack with the waffles and keep warm.

5. **Cook the eggs.** Depending on the size of your bacon skillet, crack two to four of the eggs into the pan and cook over medium heat for 4 to 5 minutes. If you prefer your eggs sunny-side down, flip them and cook for 30 to 60 seconds more. Repeat with the remaining eggs.

6. **Assemble the waffle cakes.** Place a waffle on a plate and arrange two fried eggs on top. Ladle a little of the cheese sauce overtop and arrange two bacon slices on top. Cover with a second waffle and repeat with two eggs, sauce and two slices of bacon. Place the third waffle on top, ladle cheese sauce overtop and sprinkle with parsley. Serve immediately.

   *If you prefer, skip the cake assembly and simply serve the warm waffles on a plate with bacon, eggs and cheese sauce, almost like eggs Benedict.*

# Custards & Creams

# Recipes at a Glance

Custards and creams are a great place to start a baking journey. They can often be enjoyed as a simple dessert or combined with other components to create a more elaborate dessert. Although pastry creams (pp. 96 to 99) are the most versatile of custards, eggs and dairy can be combined in baking in many ways. The result can be rich and simple like a crème brûlée, tart and vibrant like a lemon curd, or airy and ephemeral like a mousse or soufflé.

I've divided this chapter into sections that reflect various techniques for thickening and aerating eggs, milk and cream. Each of these recipes relies on carefully cooking the eggs so they do not curdle or separate, and following the recommended cooling and chilling times carefully so the custards set.

## Puddings

Puddings come first in this chapter because they rely more on cornstarch than eggs to thicken them, so they are easier and less delicate to make than other custards. If you are new to making custards, puddings are an ideal place to start because you can watch them transform from thin liquids to thick, rich puddings in moments as you stir them on the stove.

## Mousses

Light and airy and uncomplicated, well-made mousses deliver plenty of flavour and a creamy melt-on-your-tongue texture. Although the flavour bases can vary, most mousses are made by folding in whipped cream to aerate the final dessert.

## Soufflés

Soufflés are often surrounded by mystery, perhaps because their shining moment is so fleeting. Except for twice-baked versions, soufflés must be assembled immediately before baking and served within moments of pulling them from the oven. They get their airiness from whipped egg whites folded into a sweet or savoury base. This section will ensure that all of your soufflés fully rise to the occasion!

## Crème Brûlées

Rich, silky custards that are just barely set, crème brûlées are baked or set in their serving dishes. Their crowning glory is a crunchy top of caramelized sugar. Once you crack the crust with a spoon to reveal the custard beneath, and each bite is heavenly.

## Crèmes Anglaise

Custards made by cooking egg yolks into cream to thicken them are known as crèmes anglaise, and they are most commonly used as sauces with chocolate or fruit desserts. But they are also a foundation for other creams such as crémeux and Bavarian cream (crème bavaroise).

## Pastry Creams

These grandes dames of custards make smooth and silky fillings or excellent foundations for other cream fillings and frostings. The Pineapple & Pink Peppercorn Pavlova (p. 322) and Parisian Vanilla Flan (p. 325) showcase two different uses of these very versatile classic creams.

# Lemon Curds

Curds are custards with maximum citrus flavour in
every creamy yet tangy bite. Butter is the key to
a curd's smooth texture, and the lemony colour doesn't
come from the lemons, but the egg yolks in the recipe.

**Creamy Chocolate Pudding**
Page 292

**Maple Butterscotch Pudding**
Page 295

**Creamy Mascarpone Mousse**
*(plus Bonus Bake: Coconut Chiffon
& Strawberry Trifle)*  Page 296

**Milk Chocolate Orange Mousse**
Page 299

**Lemon Mousse**
Page 300

**Chocolate Soufflé**
Page 303

**Strawberry Rhubarb Soufflé**
Page 304

**Classic Cheese Soufflé**
Page 306

**Twice-baked Brie & Mushroom Soufflé**
Page 308

CRÈME BRULÉES ▶

**Classic Vanilla Bean Crème Brûlée**
Page 310

**Banoffee Crème Brûlée**
Page 313

**Parmesan Rosemary Crème Brûlée**
Page 314

CRÈME ANGLAISE ▶

**Poires Belle Hélène with Chocolate Crémeux**  Page 317

**Îles Flottantes (Oeufs à la Neige)**
Page 318

**Jasmine Tea Bavarian Cream Pots**
Page 321

**Pineapple & Pink Peppercorn Pavlova**
Page 322

**Parisian Vanilla Flan**
Page 325

**Lemon Bostock Bread Pudding**
Page 326

**Pink Lemonade Eton Mess**
Page 328

**SERVES:** 6

**PREP TIME:** under 15 minutes, plus chilling
**COOK TIME:** under 10 minutes

❗ **SIMPLE**

**BITES OF WISDOM:**
*Glossary of ingredients—Chocolate &
cocoa powder (p. 5)*

### INGREDIENTS

½ cup (100 g) granulated sugar

3 Tbsp (24 g) cornstarch

2 Tbsp (15 g) cocoa powder, sifted

1¼ cups (310 mL) 2% milk

1 cup (250 mL) whipping cream

2 large egg yolks

2 oz (60 g) dark baking/couverture
chocolate, chopped

½ tsp vanilla extract

¼ tsp fine salt

Chantilly Cream (p. 95), for serving

Sprinkles, for décor (optional)

# Creamy Chocolate Pudding

This chocolate pudding is just right, meaning that it's the perfect balance of sweet and rich chocolaty flavour without being too dense and intense. Once you've mastered this basic recipe, start getting creative by adding orange zest, mint or espresso powder. Or keep it simple like I do with a dollop of Chantilly Cream (p. 95).

1. **Make the custard.** Whisk the sugar, cornstarch and cocoa powder together in a medium saucepan. Whisk in the milk, cream and egg yolks. Bring to a simmer over medium-high heat while whisking constantly. Once the pudding begins to bubble, whisk a little more vigorously until the pudding is evenly thickened and looks glossy.

   *Whisking the dry ingredients together works out any lumps in the cocoa and distributes the cornstarch so that you will have a smooth pudding.*

   *Once cornstarch reaches 212°F (100°C), it turns glossy and reaches its full thickening power. Wait until you see a few bubbles break the surface of the pudding, not just one, before you pull it off the heat. To test if it is cooked enough, taste it. If the mixture tastes at all chalky, then cook it a little more.*

2. **Add the flavours.** Remove the pan from the heat and whisk in the chocolate, vanilla and salt until the chocolate has melted.

3. **Cool and chill the pudding.** Transfer the pudding to a bowl to cool. Place a sheet of plastic wrap directly on the surface of the pudding to prevent a skin from forming. Let cool for an hour on the counter, then chill for at least 2 hours. Serve the pudding in individual dishes topped with a dollop of Chantilly cream and top with sprinkles (if using).

   **The pudding will keep in an airtight container in the fridge for up to 4 days.**

**SERVES:** 6

**PREP TIME:** 20 minutes, plus chilling
**COOK TIME:** 15 minutes

❗ **SIMPLE**

**BITES OF WISDOM:**
*How to cook & caramelize sugar (p. 38)*

**INGREDIENTS**

2 Tbsp (30 mL) water

1 tsp lemon juice

½ cup (100 g) granulated sugar

¼ cup (60 mL) maple syrup

1 cup (250 mL) whipping cream

1 cup (250 mL) 2% milk

3 Tbsp (24 g) cornstarch

2 large egg yolks

2 Tbsp (30 g) unsalted butter

1 Tbsp (15 mL) rum (optional)

1 tsp vanilla extract

½ tsp salt

Chopped Praliné Noisette (p. 85), for décor (optional)

# Maple Butterscotch Pudding

Finding the perfect balance of rich caramelized flavour and sweetness can be tricky, yet it's the key to a delicious butterscotch. Maple syrup is the secret and really gives this pudding its own identity.

1. **Make the caramel.** Measure the water and lemon juice into a small saucepan and then add the sugar and maple syrup. Bring to a full boil over high heat without stirring, then boil until the sugar turns a rich amber colour, about 6 minutes. Remove the pan from the heat and slowly and carefully whisk in the whipping cream (it will steam and bubble initially). If the caramel does not fully dissolve into the cream, return the pan to medium heat and whisk until smooth. Remove the pan from the heat but leave it nearby.

2. **Make the pudding.** Whisk the milk, cornstarch and egg yolks together in a medium saucepan. Slowly whisk in the still-warm caramel. Bring the pudding to a full simmer over medium-high heat, whisking constantly until it has thickened and becomes glossy, about 7 minutes. Remove the pan from the heat and whisk in the butter, rum (if using), vanilla and salt, until the butter melts.

   *Some people claim that the "scotch" in butterscotch refers to Scotch whisky, but rum is the more common addition to this pudding. Either spirit is fine, or omit the alcohol completely if you prefer. To more closely replicate the flavour of butterscotch pudding made from a mix, add 1 tsp rum extract when you add the vanilla.*

3. **Cool and chill.** Transfer the pudding to a bowl and place a sheet of plastic wrap directly on the surface so it doesn't form a skin. Let the pudding cool on the counter for an hour and then chill for at least 2 hours before serving. Sprinkle the pudding with praliné noisette right before serving (if using).

**The pudding will keep in an airtight container in the fridge for up to 4 days.**

**MAKES:** about 3 cups (750 mL)
**SERVES:** 6

**PREP TIME:** under 10 minutes

❦ **SIMPLE**
**BITES OF WISDOM:**
*How to repair overwhipped cream (p. 56)*

**INGREDIENTS**

**1 cup (235 g)** good-quality mascarpone cheese

**½ cup (65 g)** icing sugar

**1 cup (250 mL)** whipping cream

Spiced Plums (p. 86), for serving

Chopped lightly toasted unsalted shelled pistachios, for serving

**BONUS BAKE**

## Coconut Chiffon & Strawberry Trifle

Use this mascarpone mousse as the creamy base for an easy and delicious summertime trifle.

Cut half of a Coconut Chiffon Cake (p. 236) into 1-inch (2.5 cm) slices and use a third of them to line the bottom of an 8- to 10-cup trifle or other glass bowl. Sprinkle the cake with a **generous tablespoonful (20 mL) of orange liqueur**. Spread a third of the prepared mascarpone mousse over the cake, followed by **1¼ cups (200 g) sliced fresh strawberries**. Repeat this layering of cake, mousse and strawberries twice more, topping the trifle with **¼ cup (40 g) strawberries**. Chill until ready to serve. (You can assemble this trifle up to 4 hours ahead of serving.)

# Creamy Mascarpone Mousse

Cream on cream. This silky mousse is the height of simplicity: the natural sweetness of fresh mascarpone cheese enhanced with a bit of sugar and folded into light and airy whipped cream. The flavour is pure, natural dairy, so use only the best-quality mascarpone and cream you can find.

1. **Cream the mascarpone** in a bowl by hand to smooth it out, then stir in the icing sugar.

   *I like Italian-made mascarpone cheese with a fat content of 40% or higher. Take care not to beat or whip the mascarpone, as it might curdle and split. The aim is simply to smooth out any lumps or bubbles.*

2. **Whip and fold in the cream.** Using electric beaters or a stand mixer fitted with the whip attachment, whip the cream on high speed until it holds a soft peak. Fold a quarter of the cream into the mascarpone until combined, then fold in the remaining cream. Chill until ready to serve. Dollop a spoonful of the mousse into individual bowls. Place a spoonful of the spiced plums beside the mousse and sprinkle with pistachios.

   *You can also serve this mousse in place of clotted cream with Classic English Scones (p. 158), along with a little jam. Or dollop the mousse on a plate of Almond Streusel (p. 82), fresh berries and/or figs and a drizzle of Pedro Ximénez sweet sherry. Or stir in ½ tsp espresso powder and 1 Tbsp (15 mL) rum to make a tiramisu mousse to serve with a slice of sponge cake and a grating of dark chocolate on top.*

**The mousse will keep in an airtight container in the fridge for up to 2 days.**

**MAKES:** six 6 oz (180 mL) desserts

**PREP TIME:** 15 minutes, plus chilling

**COOK TIME:** 5 minutes

❗ SIMPLE

**BITES OF WISDOM:**

*Gelatin powder or sheet substitutes (p. 16), How to melt chocolate (p. 41), How to repair overwhipped cream (p. 56)*

## INGREDIENTS

**10 oz (300 g)** milk baking/couverture chocolate, chopped

**½ tsp (1.8 g)** gelatin powder

**½ cup (125 mL)** cold 2% milk

Finely grated zest of **1** orange

**1 cup (250 mL)** whipping cream

**2 Tbsp (30 mL)** orange liqueur

White chocolate shavings, for décor (optional)

# Milk Chocolate Orange Mousse

A milk chocolate mousse is mild and creamy and takes on other flavours well. If chocolate and orange as a pairing is your thing (like it is mine), then you will adore this simple mousse recipe. Because of the gelatin, it also has a nice set should you choose to use it as a filling for a cake. I like to serve this mousse in individual footed glasses.

1. **Melt the chocolate** in a metal bowl placed over a pot filled with an inch (2.5 cm) of barely simmering water, stirring gently until smooth. Remove the chocolate from the heat.

2. **Soften the gelatin and combine with the chocolate.** Sprinkle the gelatin over the cold milk in a saucepan and whisk in to soften. Add the orange zest and heat the milk on medium-low, whisking until the gelatin dissolves and the milk is warm. Gently whisk the warm milk into the melted chocolate, until combined. Set aside to cool to room temperature.

   *Milk chocolate has more cocoa butter and sugar than dark chocolate, so it sets up less firmly than dark chocolate—hence the gelatin in this recipe. The texture of this mousse will still be soft and melt in your mouth at each bite.*

3. **Whip and fold in the cream.** Using electric beaters or a stand mixer fitted with the whip attachment, whip the cream on high speed to a soft peak. Fold the cream into the chocolate in two additions. Fold in the orange liqueur—the mousse will be fluid. Pour or ladle the mousse into dessert coupes or other serving glasses and chill for at least 3 hours. Top with a few white chocolate shavings (if using) right before serving.

**The mousse will keep, covered with plastic wrap, in the fridge for up to 3 days.**

**MAKES:** about 3 cups (750 mL)
**SERVES:** 4

**PREP TIME:** under 15 minutes, plus chilling
**COOK TIME:** 10 minutes

🍴 SIMPLE

**BITES OF WISDOM:**
*Gelatin powder or sheet substitutes
(p. 16), How to repair overwhipped cream
(p. 56)*

**INGREDIENTS**

---

**1 tsp (3.5 g)** gelatin powder

**2 Tbsp (30 mL)** cold water

**4** large eggs

**6 Tbsp (75 g)** granulated sugar

Zest of **1** lemon

**¼ cup (60 mL)** fresh lemon juice

**2 Tbsp (30 mL)** sour cream

**½ cup (125 mL)** whipping cream

# Lemon Mousse

This ultra-airy mousse gets its volume not only from whipped cream but also from a sabayon: eggs whipped with sugar and lemon juice over a water bath. Lemon juice and zest give the mousse a big citrus kick.

1. **Soften the gelatin** in the cold water and set aside.

2. **Make the sabayon.** Whisk the eggs, sugar, lemon zest and juice together in a metal bowl placed over a pot filled with an inch (2.5 cm) of gently simmering water. Whisk until the mixture is frothy and doubled in volume (it should reach 150°F/65°C), about 10 minutes.

*The acidity of the lemon juice prevents the eggs from coagulating and overcooking as you whip them.*

3. **Stir in the gelatin and let cool.** Remove the bowl from the heat, whisk in the softened gelatin until it is no longer visible, then whisk in the sour cream. Set the bowl aside to cool to room temperature.

*Adding the sour cream at this stage helps to cool the sabayon down, so you won't have to wait too long to fold in the whipped cream. Don't be tempted to whisk the sabayon as it cools; it might break down the volume you just added to it.*

4. **Fold in the cream.** Using electric beaters or a stand mixer fitted with the whip attachment, whip the cream on high speed until it holds a soft peak. Fold the cream all at once into the cooled lemon mixture. Pour the mousse into serving dishes and chill for at least 3 hours before serving.

**The mousse will keep, covered with plastic wrap, in the fridge for up to 3 days.**

**MAKES:** six 8 oz (250 mL) soufflés

**PREP TIME:** 20 minutes
**COOK TIME:** 22 minutes

**❗ SIMPLE**
**BITES OF WISDOM:**
*How to whip egg whites (p. 34), How to repair overwhipped egg whites (p. 55)*

**INGREDIENTS**

---

½ cup (125 mL) 2% milk

½ cup (8 Tbsp/100 g) granulated sugar, divided, plus extra for the soufflé dish

2 tsp cornstarch

1 tsp vanilla extract

5 oz (150 g) bittersweet baking/couverture chocolate, chopped

2 Tbsp (30 g) unsalted butter

10 large egg whites, at room temperature

½ tsp cream of tartar

# Chocolate Soufflé

When most of us think of a sweet soufflé, the chocolate version comes to mind instantly. The balance between warm chocolate intensity and airy lightness is why chocolate soufflé is so beloved, and it's relatively straight-forward to make. I bake individual chocolate soufflés to serve on their own or with warm Salted Butter Caramel Sauce (p. 89) or chilled Crème Anglaise (p. 318). Invite guests to take a bite from the middle of their soufflé and then pour the sauce into that warm, soft centre.

1. **Preheat the oven** to 400°F (200°C). Lightly butter six 8 oz (250 mL) soufflé or other 1-cup (250 mL) straight-sided baking dishes. Sprinkle the inside of the cups with sugar and tap out any excess. Place the dishes onto a baking tray and chill until ready to fill and bake.

2. **Make the chocolate base.** Whisk the milk, 2 Tbsp (25 g) sugar, the cornstarch and the vanilla in a small dish and set aside. Melt the chocolate and butter in a small saucepan over low heat, stirring constantly until melted. Stir in the milk mixture in two additions, whisking until evenly blended. Keep this base warm over very low heat while you prepare the egg whites. (You can prepare this base ahead of time, refrigerate and warm over low heat before baking the soufflés.)

*After adding the milk, the chocolate mixture will be a thick paste and may look a little grainy. Don't worry—it will smooth out after the whipped egg whites are folded in.*

3. **Whip the egg whites** and cream of tartar using electric beaters or a stand mixer fitted with the whip attachment on high speed until they are foamy. Slowly pour in the remaining 6 Tbsp (75 g) sugar and whip until the whites hold a soft peak when the beaters are lifted. Transfer the warm chocolate base to a larger bowl.

*You might think that soufflés involve whipping your egg whites to a stiff peak, but this isn't always the case. A soft peak is easier to fold into the chocolate base and has more air bubbles within it to expand in the heat of the oven. As well, a stiff peak is trickier to achieve successfully since it is seconds away from overwhipped whites, which will collapse and fall if baked.*

4. **Fold a third of the whites** into the warm chocolate quickly but gently—they will deflate quite a bit, but this is expected. Fold in the remaining two-thirds of the egg whites until incorporated. Pour this mixture into the prepared soufflé dishes.

5. **Bake the soufflés** for 15 to 18 minutes, until the tops take on a dull look (they will rise well above the top of the soufflé dishes). Serve immediately.

**♨ MORE INVOLVED**

BITES OF WISDOM:

*How to whip egg whites (p. 34), How to repair overwhipped egg whites (p. 55)*

---

**INGREDIENTS**

---

**Strawberry rhubarb purée (makes about 2 cups/500 mL):**

2 cups (250 g) diced fresh or frozen, thawed rhubarb

2 cups (330 g) sliced fresh strawberries

⅔ cup (140 g) granulated sugar

**Soufflé:**

1½ Tbsp (12 g) cornstarch

3 Tbsp (37 g) granulated sugar, divided, plus extra for the soufflé dish

1 cup (250 mL) Strawberry Rhubarb Purée (above)

5 large eggs, separated, at room temperature

Icing sugar, for dusting

# Strawberry Rhubarb Soufflé

I love the sweet and tart combination of strawberries and rhubarb in a pie, so I was curious whether the full flavour and colour would come through in a warm soufflé . . . and they do! Half of the fruit base for this soufflé becomes a sauce to pour over the fluffy, warm baked dessert.

1. **Make the fruit purée.** Simmer the rhubarb, strawberries and sugar together in a large saucepan over medium heat, stirring often, until the fruits are very soft and the syrup takes on a rich red colour, about 15 minutes. Purée the fruits and chill until ready to make the soufflé.

   *I prefer fresh strawberries for this recipe because frozen ones can be watery and less colourful. Rhubarb has such a brief season that using fresh or frozen is fine, and frozen does not change the consistency or colour of the purée.*

2. **Preheat the oven** to 400°F (200°C). Butter six 10 oz (300 mL) soufflé dishes generously with butter. Sprinkle the dishes with sugar, ensuring it coats every inch and tapping out any excess. Chill the dishes until ready to fill.

3. **Finish the soufflé base.** Whisk the cornstarch with 1 Tbsp (12 g) sugar. Pour the strawberry rhubarb purée into a large bowl (1), then whisk in the cornstarch mixture followed by the egg yolks.

   *Some fruit soufflés are made using a pastry cream as the base, but this method produces a lighter soufflé with brighter fruit flavour and the cornstarch thickens the fruit as the soufflé bakes.*

4. **Whip the egg whites** using electric beaters or a stand mixer fitted with the whip attachment on high speed until foamy. Slowly pour in the remaining 2 Tbsp (25 g) sugar and continue to whip until the whites hold a soft peak when the beaters are lifted. Fold a third of the whites into the fruit base, folding gently but quickly—the whites don't have to be fully incorporated. Add the remaining whites and continue to fold until combined (2). Pour the soufflé mix into the prepared dishes and spread to level it. Use your thumb to trace around the edge of the dish at the top of each soufflé (3)—this will help it rise level.

5. **Bake the soufflés** for 18 to 20 minutes (try not to open the oven door until 15 minutes have passed) until the tops are an even brown. Dust the soufflés with icing sugar and serve immediately. Serve the remaining strawberry rhubarb sauce on the side so guests can pour a little into the centre of their soufflé after the first spoonful.

   *The sugar on the top and sides of these soufflés will brown as they bake, but when you spoon into the centre, the pretty pink colour and fruity aroma will be revealed.*

**The strawberry rhubarb purée can be made up to a day ahead of time and stored in an airtight container in the fridge.**

**PREP TIME:** 20 minutes
**COOK TIME:** 45 minutes

🍴 **MORE INVOLVED**

**BITES OF WISDOM:**
*How to whip egg whites (p. 34), How to repair overwhipped egg whites (p. 55)*

**INGREDIENTS**

---

**5 Tbsp (75 g)** unsalted butter, plus extra for the dish

**5 Tbsp (45 g)** all-purpose flour

**1 cup (250 mL)** 2% milk

**10 Tbsp (150 mL)** whipping cream

**¼ tsp** ground nutmeg

**¼ tsp** fine salt

**¼ tsp** ground white or black pepper

**¾ cup (82 g)** coarsely grated Emmenthal cheese

**¾ cup (75 g)** finely grated Parmesan cheese, plus extra for the dish

**6** large eggs, separated, at room temperature

# Classic Cheese Soufflé

If you haven't had a cheese soufflé lately (or ever), I encourage you to try this recipe. The contrast between rich melted cheese and the gravity-defying lightness of the soufflé itself are a delight served as a starter course.

1. **Preheat the oven** to 400°F (200°C). Generously rub the inside of a 5¼-cup (1.25 L) soufflé dish with butter and then sprinkle it with Parmesan cheese, ensuring the cheese coats every inch and tapping out the excess. Wrap the outside of the soufflé dish in a sheet of parchment paper that is 4 inches (10 cm) taller than the top of the dish and secure it in place with a piece of butcher's twine. Chill the dish until ready to fill.

   *The 5¼-cup (1.25 L) size is a standard-sized dish for soufflés. If you bake the soufflé in a larger-volume or oval ceramic dish, you may not get the same "lift," but you will still get the airy texture and creamy taste.*

   *The parchment paper collar around the dish coaxes the soufflé to bake with straight sides and a level top. You can bake the soufflé without a collar, but it will look more like a chef's hat with a billowy top. However it looks, it will still be delicious.*

2. **Make the soufflé base.** Melt the butter over medium heat in a medium saucepan. Add the flour, and using a wooden spoon, stir the roux, cooking until it bubbles and smells like almonds, about 4 minutes. Slowly whisk in the milk and cream in three additions, ensuring the mixture is smooth after each one. Add the nutmeg, salt and pepper and continue to whisk until the sauce bubbles and thickens, about a minute. Scrape the sauce into a large bowl to cool for about 10 minutes. Use this time to get your soufflé dish ready.

   *This soufflé base is a béchamel sauce, a creamy sauce commonly used in savoury cooking. This sauce holds the cheese and whipped whites well, resulting in a super-creamy yet fluffy soufflé.*

3. **Add the cheese.** Stir the Emmenthal and Parmesan cheeses into the slightly cooled sauce—the cheese will melt a little but not completely into the sauce. Stir in the egg yolks.

   *It is very important that the added cheese not melt fully into the sauce. If it does, the base sauce becomes heavy and your soufflé won't rise as high as it could. As well, letting the cheese melt as the soufflé bakes results in strings of melted cheese that make the soufflé more delectable and fun to eat.*

4. **Whip the egg whites** using electric beaters on high speed until they hold a medium peak when the beaters are lifted.

   *While sweet soufflés use egg whites whipped to a soft peak, this cheesy béchamel needs egg whites whipped to a medium peak to stand up to the thicker sauce as they are folded in and then baked.*

5. **Fold a third of the whites** gently but quickly into the soufflé base, then fold in the remaining two-thirds of the egg whites. Pour the batter into the prepared dish and put it into the oven quickly.

6. **Bake the soufflé** for 40 minutes without opening the oven to peek—the top should be an even golden brown. Have everyone ready to eat, remove the parchment collar and serve immediately after baking.

*Your cheese soufflé will have a soft, saucy centre to it, so there is no need to pour in an additional sauce.*

**MAKES:** one 9-inch (23 cm) soufflé
**SERVES:** 8

**PREP TIME:** 35 minutes
**COOK TIME:** 75 minutes

### ♦♦♦ COMPLEX

**BITES OF WISDOM:**
*How to whip egg whites (p. 34), How to repair overwhipped egg whites (p. 55)*

### INGREDIENTS

**4 Tbsp (60 g)** unsalted butter, divided, plus extra for greasing the pan

**⅓ cup (43 g)** dry breadcrumbs, for the pan

**½ lb (225 g)** cremini mushrooms, sliced

**1 clove** garlic, minced

**7 oz (210 g)** single or double cream Brie

**½ cup (125 mL)** whipping cream, plus extra for brushing

**5 large eggs**, separated

**¼ cup (37 g)** all-purpose flour

**1 cup (250 mL)** 2% milk

**Pinch** of ground nutmeg

**¼ tsp** fine salt

**3 Tbsp (45 mL)** finely chopped chives

# Twice-baked Brie & Mushroom Soufflé

This savoury soufflé is a lovely alternative to a quiche and can be prepared ahead of time and then reheated to serve so it doesn't come with the drama of a freshly assembled soufflé. While it does collapse after its first baking, it retains an essential lightness that reminds you it is a soufflé. Its buttery rich Brie and mushroom flavours make a fantastic starter for a meal, or a light lunch with a side salad.

1. **Prepare the pan.** Generously grease a 9-inch (23 cm) springform pan or other 8 to 10 cup (2 to 2.5 L) ovenproof dish with butter and sprinkle in the breadcrumbs to coat the bottom and sides, tapping out any excess. Chill the pan until ready to fill and bake.

2. **Cook the mushrooms.** Melt 1 Tbsp (15 g) butter in a sauté pan over medium heat. Add the mushrooms and sauté until tender and any liquid has evaporated, about 5 minutes. Add the garlic, stir for a minute more and remove the pan from the heat to cool a little.

3. **Blend the cheese and mushrooms.** Cut the Brie into pieces but leave the rind on. Place 5 oz (150 g) Brie along with the cream, egg yolks and slightly cooled mushrooms into a food processor or blender and pulse until combined—the mixture will not be smooth. Set aside.

   *A soft, ripe single or double cream Brie is best for this recipe because of its natural mushroom flavour. A triple cream Brie, while tempting, is too mild and melts too fluidly to be used in this recipe.*

4. **Make the sauce base.** Melt the remaining 3 Tbsp (45 g) butter in a saucepan over medium heat, then add the flour, making a roux. Use a wooden spoon to stir the roux for about 3 minutes, until it smells a little like toasted almonds but does not colour. Switch to a whisk and pour in half of the milk, whisking until smooth and thickened before adding the rest, along with the nutmeg—this is a béchamel sauce. Bring to a simmer and then transfer the béchamel to a large bowl to cool for 10 minutes.

5. **Preheat the oven** to 400°F (200°C).

6. **Finish the base.** Once the béchamel has cooled to lukewarm temperature, whisk in the mushroom mixture until combined (but do not melt the cheese).

7. **Whip the reserved egg whites** with the salt using electric beaters or a stand mixer fitted with the whip attachment on high speed until they hold a soft peak when the beaters are lifted. Fold a third of the whites into the soufflé base until almost combined, add the chives and then fold in the remaining whites quickly but gently until fully combined. Stir in the remaining 2 oz (60 g) diced Brie. Pour the filling into the chilled pan, spreading gently to ensure it is level.

8. **Bake the soufflé** for about 45 minutes (do not open the oven for the first 20 minutes), until the soufflé is puffed up and golden brown on top. Remove from the oven and let cool for at least 15 minutes before removing from the pan to serve, or let it cool completely in the pan if baking a second time. If baking twice, the soufflé will keep, wrapped in the pan, in the fridge overnight.

9. **Bake the soufflé a second time.** Lower the oven temperature to 350°F (180°C). Bake the soufflé for 15 to 20 minutes to warm through and toast the top. Serve immediately, sliced into wedges.

**The soufflé will keep, well wrapped, in the fridge for up to 3 days.**

**MAKES:** six 5 oz (150 mL) desserts

**PREP TIME:** 15 minutes, plus chilling
**COOK TIME:** 35 minutes

❘ **SIMPLE**
**BITES OF WISDOM:**
*How to separate an egg (p. 32), How to temper eggs (p. 33)*

### INGREDIENTS

2¼ **cups (560 mL)** whipping cream

**1** vanilla bean or **1 Tbsp (15 mL)** vanilla bean paste

**6** egg yolks

**6 Tbsp (75 g)** granulated sugar, plus extra for the brûlée topping

# Classic Vanilla Bean Crème Brûlée

This crème brûlée recipe is adapted from a version in *Bake with Anna Olson*. It is less sweet and has a softer, creamier set.

1. **Preheat the oven** to 325°F (160°C) and place six 5 oz (150 mL) flat crème brûlée dishes or ramekins in a large pan where the sides of the pan are higher than the ramekins.

2. **Heat the cream** in a medium saucepan over medium-low heat with the scraped seeds of the vanilla bean pod (and the pod, too, if you wish). If using vanilla bean paste, whisk it into the cream and heat. Heat the cream for about 5 minutes, watching so that it doesn't boil over.

   *Heating the cream for 5 minutes draws out and enhances the vanilla bean flavour since the custards bake for only a short time.*

3. **Whisk the egg yolks and sugar** together in a small bowl. Whisk in the hot cream slowly, whisking constantly (but not overly vigorously) until all has been added. Strain through a fine-mesh sieve into a clean bowl and then ladle or pour into the ramekins.

   *If any small bubbles appear on the surface of the custards, use the corner of a paper towel to dab them off (bubbles will prevent the brûlée from browning easily and evenly).*

4. **Prepare the hot water bath and bake.** Pour boiling water carefully around the brûlée dishes in the pan, so that the water comes just past halfway up the dishes. Carefully place the pan in the oven. Bake the custards for about 20 minutes for flat dishes and about 30 minutes for regular ramekins, until they are set around the edges but still jiggle a little when gently moved. Transfer the pan to a cooling rack and let the custards cool in the water bath for 10 minutes. Remove them using an oven mitt to cool completely on the rack.

   *If the crème brûlées are in regular ramekins, use a jar lifter to remove them from the water bath. Jar lifters are sold with canning tools (they are used to lift jam or pickle jars out of the water after water processing them).*

5. **Chill the custards** for at least 3 hours before serving.

6. **Caramelize the tops with sugar.** Sprinkle each custard with a thin layer of sugar. Carefully ignite a kitchen butane torch and caramelize the sugar by moving the torch back and forth over the custard, about an inch or two away from the top. Sprinkle another thin layer of sugar over the first layer and torch it, repeating another two times or until the caramel layer is to your liking. Adding the sugar in small amounts results in a more evenly melted and caramelized top. Serve immediately.

**The brûlées will keep without the caramelized sugar layer, uncovered, in the fridge for up to 2 days.**

**MAKES:** six 5 oz (150 mL) desserts

**PREP TIME:** 20 minutes, plus chilling
**COOK TIME:** 12 minutes

⏸ **MORE INVOLVED**
**BITES OF WISDOM:**
*How to separate an egg (p. 32), How to temper eggs (p. 33)*

### INGREDIENTS

1 cup (250 mL) Dulce de Leche (p. 90) or store-bought, divided

2 bananas, divided

1½ cups (375 mL) whipping cream

¼ tsp ground cinnamon

6 large egg yolks

1 Tbsp (15 mL) rum or ½ tsp rum extract

Granulated sugar, for caramelizing

# Banoffee Crème Brûlée

All the flavours of a banoffee tart—bananas, caramel, cream, cinnamon and a hint of rum—are found in this crème brûlée. Rather than baking the custard as I would for a traditional crème brûlée, I cook it on the stove like a crème anglaise. This method produces a thicker and richer custard that sets up like a baked crème brûlée and keeps the sliced bananas at the bottom of each dish tender. The result: a delicate and flavourful chilled crème brûlée.

1. **Line the ramekins with dulce de leche.** Have ready six 5 oz (150 mL) ramekins or other dishes. Warm the dulce de leche in a small saucepan over low heat to make it fluid but not hot. Spoon 2 Tbsp (30 mL) dulce de leche into each ramekin. Slice one banana and arrange the slices to cover the top of the caramel in each dish.

   *If you can, use heatproof glass ramekins to showcase the layers of caramel, banana and custard.*

2. **Make the custard.** Heat the cream and cinnamon in a medium saucepan over medium heat to just below a simmer. Whisk the remaining ¼ cup (60 mL) dulce de leche with the egg yolks in a small bowl. Slowly pour the hot cream into the yolks while whisking them and then return this mixture to the pot. Continue to whisk the cream until it thickens, about 4 minutes. Immediately strain the custard into a pitcher and stir in the rum (or rum extract).

   *The custard is cooked when it coats the back of a spoon, when you can use a spoon to draw a line through the custard and the line stays intact, or when the temperature reaches 165°F (74°C) and no higher than 180°F (83°C) on a thermometer.*

3. **Chill the custard.** Divide the custard equally among the ramekins and chill, uncovered, until set, at least 3 hours.

4. **Caramelize the tops with sugar.** Slice the second banana and arrange the slices on top of each chilled custard. Sprinkle with a thin layer of sugar. Carefully ignite a kitchen butane torch and caramelize the sugar by moving the torch back and forth over the custard, about an inch or two away from the top. Sprinkle another thin layer of sugar over the first layer and torch it, repeating another two times or until the caramel layer is to your liking. Serve immediately.

**MAKES:** four 5 oz (150 mL) crème brûlées

**PREP TIME:** 20 minutes, plus chilling
**COOK TIME:** 40 minutes

**⏍ MORE INVOLVED**
**BITES OF WISDOM:**
*How to separate an egg (p. 32), How to temper eggs (p. 33)*

### INGREDIENTS

**Frico (makes 8):**

**1 cup (40 g)** freshly grated Parmesan cheese (see note)

**1 tsp** finely chopped fresh rosemary

**Parmesan crème brûlée:**

**1 cup (250 mL)** whipping cream

**1 cup (250 mL)** half-&-half cream

**1** shallot, peeled and thinly sliced

**2 Tbsp (30 mL)** coarsely chopped fresh rosemary

**2 oz (60 g)** chunk Parmesan cheese or **4 oz (120 g)** Parmesan rinds

**4** large egg yolks

**1** large egg

# Parmesan Rosemary Crème Brûlée

Why serve crème brûlée only for dessert? This savoury version makes a decadent appetizer. Instead of a crunchy top made from caramelized sugar, I make frico—a crisp of baked Parmesan cheese. The frico is so thin and crispy, you'll still get that satisfying "crack" as you break into it to get to the creamy and cool cheese custard beneath.

1. **Preheat the oven** to 375°F (190°C) and line a baking tray with parchment paper or a silicone baking mat.

2. **Make the frico.** Toss the grated Parmesan with the rosemary. Use a 2½-inch (6.5 cm) round cookie cutter to help portion the cheese. Place the cutter onto the baking tray and spoon 2 Tbsp (30 mL) into the centre of the cutter, spreading it to the edges. Lift up the cutter. Repeat with the remaining cheese, leaving at least 2 inches (5 cm) in between each portion. (You should have eight fricos.) Bake for about 5 minutes, until a light golden brown. To add a curve to the frico, use a palette knife to gently lift the hot frico onto a rolling pin or other curved surface to cool.

*Use only freshly grated Parmesan in this recipe. For a really nice lacy frico, grate a chunk of fresh Parmesan (or Parmigiano-Reggiano, if you can) against the side of your box grater with the small holes. You will have extra frico, so pick the prettiest ones for your crème brûlées and reserve the rest in case one breaks—or just eat them as a snack (which I inevitably do).*

3. **Prepare the dishes.** Arrange four 5 oz (150 mL) ramekins or flat crème brûlée dishes in a large pan where the sides of the pan are higher than the ramekins.

4. **Infuse the cream.** Heat the whipping cream, half-&-half, shallots, rosemary and Parmesan chunks (or rinds) in a medium saucepan over medium-low heat for 15 minutes. Do not let the cream simmer or reduce—this step is to infuse the flavour into the cream.

*You can use any rinds and old bits of Parmesan you have tucked in the back of your fridge for this step. Flavouring the cream is key, not the freshness or texture of the cheese.*

5. **Make the custard.** Whisk the egg yolks and whole egg together in a bowl. Strain the cream into a separate bowl or pitcher. Pour the hot cream over the eggs, whisking constantly until combined. Ladle or pour the custard into the ramekins.

6. **Prepare the hot water bath and bake.** Pour boiling water carefully around the brûlée dishes in the pan, so that the water comes no higher than the level of the custard. Carefully place the pan in the oven. Bake the crème brûlées for 15 to 18 minutes (or a few minutes longer for regular ramekins), until the custard no longer jiggles when gently tapped. Transfer the pan to a cooling rack and let the crème brûlées cool in the water bath for 10 minutes. Remove the crème brûlées from the water bath to cool on the rack completely.

7. **Chill the crème brûlées** for at least 2 hours before serving.

8. **Place a frico on top** of each crème brûlée and serve.

Both the fricos and the crème brûlées can be prepared a day ahead. Store the fricos in an airtight container and the crème brûlées, uncovered, in the fridge overnight.

SERVES: 4

PREP TIME: 20 minutes, plus chilling
COOK TIME: 10 minutes

! SIMPLE

BITES OF WISDOM:
*How to temper eggs (p. 33), How to toast nuts (p. 36)*

## INGREDIENTS

### Crème anglaise (makes 2 cups/500 mL):

1½ cups (375 mL) half-&-half cream

1 vanilla bean or 1 Tbsp (15 mL) vanilla bean paste

4 large egg yolks

6 Tbsp (75 g) granulated sugar

### Chocolate crémeux (makes about 1 cup/250 mL):

4 oz (120 g) dark baking/couverture chocolate, chopped

1 cup (250 mL) freshly made Crème Anglaise (above), still warm

### Assembly:

1 recipe Poached Pears (p. 88)

½ cup (55 g) lightly toasted sliced almonds

# Poires Belle Hélène with Chocolate Crémeux

This timeless dessert has been around for more than 100 years and is still a staple in France, especially on quick weekday prix fixe lunch menus. Who's to argue with poached pears served with a chocolate sauce and crème anglaise? In this recipe I've replaced the chocolate sauce with chocolate crémeux, a chocolate cream with crème anglaise as a base; it is softer and less intense than a chocolate ganache.

1. **Make the crème anglaise.** Heat the cream in a small saucepan over medium heat, along with the scraped seeds and the vanilla pod (or the vanilla bean paste), until it just begins to come to a simmer. Remove the vanilla pod. Whisk the egg yolks and sugar in a small bowl. Slowly pour the hot cream into the egg mixture, whisking constantly, then return the mixture to the pot. Switch to a wooden spoon and stir the cream (still over medium heat) until it coats the back of the spoon, about 4 minutes. Pour the crème anglaise through a fine-mesh strainer into a clean bowl.

2. **Make the chocolate crémeux.** Place the chopped chocolate in a medium bowl. Measure 1 cup (250 mL) of the hot crème anglaise and pour over the chocolate. Whisk until smooth.

   *To make a creamy crémeux outside of this recipe, heat ¾ cup (175 mL) half-&-half cream over medium heat until it just comes to a simmer. Whisk two egg yolks and 3 Tbsp (37 g) sugar in a small bowl. Slowly pour the hot cream into the egg mixture and then return to the heat, stirring constantly, until it coats the back of a spoon. Strain and serve with warm London Fog Madeleines (p. 216).*

3. **Chill the creams.** Allow both the crème anglaise and crémeux to cool on the counter, uncovered, to room temperature. Cover and chill both for at least 2 hours.

4. **Assemble the poires.** Spoon some of the crème anglaise into a flat-bottomed bowl (such as a pasta bowl). Use a warmed spoon to scoop a quenelle of the chocolate crémeux and set on top of the crème anglaise. Arrange two drained pear halves near the crémeux. Sprinkle the dish with almonds and serve. Repeat with the remaining pears.

**The crème anglaise and crémeux will keep, stored separately in airtight containers, in the fridge for up to 3 days. Plate the components immediately before serving.**

**MAKES:** 16 meringues
**SERVES:** 8

**PREP TIME:** 25 minutes, plus chilling
**COOK TIME:** 20 minutes

🍴 **MORE INVOLVED**

**BITES OF WISDOM:**
*How to whip egg whites (p. 34), How to repair overwhipped egg whites (p. 55), How to temper eggs (p. 33), How to cook & caramelize sugar (p. 38)*

**INGREDIENTS**

**Meringues & crème anglaise:**

**2 cups (500 mL)** 2% or whole milk, plus about ¾ cup (175 mL) extra to top up

**1 Tbsp (15 mL)** vanilla bean paste or seeds from 1 vanilla bean

**6** large eggs, separated

**1 cup (200 g)** granulated sugar, divided

**1 tsp** cornstarch

**Caramelized sugar:**

**1 Tbsp (15 mL)** water

**1 tsp** lemon juice

**⅓ cup (70 g)** granulated sugar

Lightly toasted sliced almonds, for sprinkling

# Îles Flottantes (Oeufs à la Neige)

These "floating islands" or "eggs in the snow" are pillows of meringue floating on a bed of crème anglaise with just a hint of caramelized sugar. Îles flottantes is rarely found on fine-dining menus these days, but like Poires Belle Hélène with Chocolate Crémeux (p. 317), it does pop up on prix fixe menus at cafés in France. While it is soft and soothing to eat, this dessert relies on some professional baking techniques, including the method for poaching the meringues in the milk.

1. **Heat the milk.** Pour the milk into a wide saucepan and whisk in the vanilla bean paste (or seeds). Heat on medium-low.

   *This dessert is very efficient in its use of ingredients. Whole eggs are separated, and the whites are used to make the meringue and the yolks to thicken the crème anglaise. Even the milk is used twice: once to poach the meringues and then again to make the sauce.*

2. **Whip the egg whites** using electric beaters or a stand mixer fitted with the whip attachment on high speed until the whites are frothy. Slowly pour in ⅔ cup (140 g) sugar while whipping. Continue to whip until the whites hold a medium peak when the beaters are lifted. Fold in the cornstarch.

3. **Poach the meringues.** Make sure that the milk is hot but not bubbling at all. Use two large spoons to shape and drop ovals of meringue into the hot milk, leaving space between the meringues. Poach the meringues, uncovered, for 2½ minutes, then gently flip them over and cook for another 2½ minutes. Use a slotted spoon to lift the meringues onto a dish to cool. Poach the meringues in batches until all of the eggs have been used. (You should have 16 meringue portions.) Chill, uncovered in the dish, until ready to serve.

4. **Make the crème anglaise.** Strain the milk through a fine-mesh sieve into a clean medium saucepan. Top up the milk to equal 2 cups (500 mL) and heat on medium to just below a simmer. Whisk the egg yolks in a bowl with the remaining ⅓ cup (70 g) sugar. Slowly pour all the hot milk into the bowl while whisking constantly. Return this mixture to the pot and stir with a wooden spoon over medium heat until the custard coats the back of a spoon. Strain the custard into a clean bowl and place a piece of plastic directly on the surface of the custard to prevent it from forming a skin. Cool to room temperature, then chill completely before serving.

5. **Spoon the crème anglaise into eight flat dishes** and top each serving with two meringues.

6. **Caramelize the sugar.** Combine the water and lemon juice in a small saucepan and measure in the sugar. Bring to a full boil over high heat, without stirring but occasionally brushing down the sides of the pan with water. Cook until caramelized, about 2 minutes. Remove the pan from the heat and let cool a moment.

*The caramelized sugar will cool and set as soon as it meets the chilled sauce and meringue. As an alternative to caramelizing the sugar to order, you can sprinkle the desserts with chopped Praliné Noisette (p. 85), made ahead of time.*

7. **Finish the desserts.** Drizzle the caramelized sugar over the meringues and custard. Sprinkle with sliced almonds and serve immediately.

**The meringues and crème anglaise can be made and chilled up to 8 hours ahead, but assemble the dessert immediately before serving.**

**MAKES:** about 3 cups (750 mL)
**SERVES:** 6

**PREP TIME:** 20 minutes, plus chilling
**COOK TIME:** 15 minutes

❗ SIMPLE
**BITES OF WISDOM:**
*How to temper eggs (p. 33)*

**INGREDIENTS**

**1 cup (250 mL)** half-&-half cream

**4** jasmine green tea bags

**1 tsp** finely grated lemon zest

**1½ tsp (5.3 g)** gelatin powder

**2 Tbsp (30 g)** cold water

**4** large egg yolks

**5 Tbsp (62 g)** granulated sugar

**1½ tsp** vanilla bean paste or vanilla
extract

**1¼ cups (310 mL)** whipping cream

**2 tsp** icing sugar (optional)

Fresh berries, for décor

# Jasmine Tea Bavarian Cream Pots

Bavarian cream (crème bavarois) is a derivative of crème anglaise made by adding a little gelatin while warm and then, once cooled, folding in whipped cream. It might be compared to a mousse but is typically less rich tasting. Use the cream as part of a larger dessert (such as the Hazelnut Bavarian Cream in Torta Setteveli, p. 277) or on its own. Bavarian cream takes on flavour well, and jasmine tea makes these individual dessert pots a joy to eat.

1. **Heat the cream** with the tea bags and lemon zest in a small saucepan over medium-low heat for about 10 minutes, stirring occasionally, to infuse the cream. Remove the tea bags, squeezing them out well. Increase the heat to medium and bring the cream to just below a simmer.

   *Of course, any tea flavour can be infused into the milk to suit your tastes.*

2. **Soften the gelatin** in the cold water and set aside.

3. **Make the crème anglaise.** Whisk the egg yolks, sugar and vanilla bean paste (or extract) in a bowl. Slowly pour the hot cream into the yolks while whisking them, until all the cream has been added. Return the cream to the pot and whisk over medium heat, cooking for about 3 minutes, until the custard coats the back of a spoon. Remove the pot from the heat and whisk in the softened gelatin. Strain the crème anglaise into a bowl and let cool to room temperature on the counter (this can take 30 to 60 minutes).

4. **Whip the cream** with electric beaters on high speed until it holds a soft peak when the beaters are lifted. Set aside ¾ cup (175 mL) whipped cream to top the chilled dessert. Fold the remaining cream into the cooled crème anglaise in two additions, using a whisk at first and then switching to a spatula. The cream will deflate as you fold it in, and the result will be a thick but pourable Bavarian cream.

5. **Pour the Bavarian cream into six serving glasses** and chill for at least 2 hours before serving. Top each portion with a dollop of the reserved whipped cream (sweeten it with icing sugar if you like) and a fresh berry.

   *This dessert makes a pretty addition to an afternoon tea selection. Pour the Bavarian cream into smaller dishes and serve topped with cream, a berry and a small spoon.*

**MAKES:** one 8-inch (20 cm) dessert
**SERVES:** 6 to 8

**PREP TIME:** 15 minutes
**COOK TIME:** 90 minutes

**☕ MORE INVOLVED**

**BITES OF WISDOM:**
*How to whip egg whites (p. 34), How to repair overwhipped egg whites (p. 55)*

**INGREDIENTS**

**Pavlova:**

**1 cup (200 g)** granulated sugar

**4** large egg whites, at room temperature

Zest of **1** lime

**1 Tbsp (8 g)** cornstarch

**1 tsp** white vinegar

**1 tsp** cracked pink peppercorns

**1 tsp** vanilla extract

**Assembly:**

**½ recipe** Vanilla Pastry Cream (p. 96), chilled

**1½ cups (22 5 g)** diced fresh pineapple

**½ cup (63 g)** fresh raspberries

**½ tsp** cracked pink peppercorns

# Pineapple & Pink Peppercorn Pavlova

Don't let the simplicity of this meringue dessert fool you. While a pavlova is a basic meringue slowly baked, simply adding cornstarch and vinegar creates a soft marshmallow-like centre and a crisp outer shell. I adore pavlova served with tropical fruits and the subtle heat of cracked pink peppercorns which has its own fruity character.

1. **Preheat the oven** to 250°F (120°C). Trace an 8-inch (20 cm) circle onto a sheet of parchment paper and place it marker side down onto a baking tray.

2. **Pulse the sugar** in a mini chopper or food processor to make it finer.

   *The key to success is making sure the sugar dissolves into the whipped egg whites, which is why you want to pulse the sugar and make sure those egg whites are definitely at room temperature. You can use ¾ cup + 2 Tbsp (200 g) superfine sugar and skip the step of pulsing it.*

3. **Whip the egg whites** using electric beaters or a stand mixer fitted with the whip attachment on high speed until they turn frothy. Slowly pour the sugar into the egg whites, whipping continuously until the whites hold a stiff peak when the beaters are lifted.

4. **Finish and shape the meringue.** Quickly but gently fold in the lime zest, cornstarch, vinegar, pink peppercorns and vanilla. Dollop the meringue onto the baking tray and use your spatula to shape it within the traced circle, making the top level or even giving it a little divot in the centre (to hold the cream and fruits).

   *Cornstarch absorbs moisture but doesn't dissolve or liquefy below the boiling point. When I realized that adding cornstarch was the difference between a meringue that stayed soft in the centre and one that would crisp up all the way through, I wondered if this trick would work for cookies too. Turns out it really helps a chocolate chip cookie stay tender and soft in the centre, which is why my signature chocolate chip cookie recipe contains cornstarch.*

5. **Bake the meringue.** Place the meringue in the oven and immediately turn down the temperature to 225°F (107°C). Bake for about 90 minutes, until the pavlova loses its shine and develops small cracks. The meringue should not brown at all. If it starts to brown, crack the oven door open for 15 minutes and then close it to complete baking. Completely cool the meringue on the tray on a rack.

6. **Assemble the pavlova** immediately before serving. Place the meringue on a serving plate. Top with the pastry cream and then the pineapple and raspberries. Sprinkle with cracked pink peppercorns and serve.

*Serve the pavlova with Chantilly Cream (p. 95) instead of pastry cream to save on time.*

*Pink peppercorns are softer than black peppercorns, and you will find them easy to crush using a mortar and pestle or the bottom of a pot.*

**Unassembled pavlova will keep for 6 to 8 hours, uncovered, at room temperature. Assembled pavlova is best enjoyed immediately after assembling.**

**MAKES:** one 8-inch (20 cm) springform pan
**SERVES:** 8 to 10

**PREP TIME:** 35 minutes, plus chilling
**COOK TIME:** 70 minutes

🍴 **MORE INVOLVED**
**BITES OF WISDOM:**
*Glossary of ingredients—Vanilla (p. 13),*
*How to roll pastry doughs (p. 44), How to*
*separate an egg (p. 32)*

## INGREDIENTS

**Thick vanilla pastry cream:**

**2 cups (500 mL)** 2% milk

**¾ cup (175 mL)** whipping cream

**1** vanilla bean or **1 Tbsp (15 mL)** vanilla
bean paste

**⅔ cup (140 g)** packed light brown sugar

**6 Tbsp (45 g)** cornstarch

**6** large egg yolks

**Assembly:**

**½ recipe** Classic Pie Dough (p. 108)

**¼ cup (60 mL)** apple jelly or strained
apricot jam, for glazing (optional)

# Parisian Vanilla Flan

This was the very first recipe I started playing with for this book because I was determined to recreate the flan I remembered from past trips to Paris. To make it tall and sliceable, this delectable tart uses a thicker, richer pastry cream than the standard Vanilla Pastry Cream (p. 96). It then gets baked for quite some time to brown the top. That contrast between the pastry cream and its caramelized top is almost reminiscent of a crème brûlée.

1. **Infuse the milk.** Measure the milk and cream into a medium saucepan and scrape the seeds of the vanilla bean into the pot (or add the vanilla bean paste). Heat over medium heat, whisking occasionally, for 15 minutes, to infuse the vanilla flavour into the milk. Set aside to cool completely to room temperature (or infuse the milk a day ahead and chill).

   *If you have neither a vanilla bean nor vanilla bean paste, use vanilla extract instead but skip this step of heating the milk. Add 1 Tbsp (15 mL) extract immediately after you have cooked and thickened the pastry cream on the stovetop.*

2. **Line the pan with pastry.** Dust a work surface lightly with flour. Roll out the pie dough into a circle just under ¼ inch (6 mm) thick. Lightly dust an 8-inch (20 cm) removable-bottom fluted tart pan with flour. Line the bottom and sides of the pan with the dough, taking time to press into the edges, then trim away any excess dough from the top of the pan. Chill the pie shell for at least 30 minutes.

   *You can also bake this tart in a 9-inch (23 cm) springform pan, but trim the pastry to 2 inches (5 cm) from the bottom of the pan; the pastry cream will not fill the larger pan entirely, and any pie dough above the fill line will burn in the hot oven.*

3. **Preheat the oven** to 350°F (180°C).

4. **Make the pastry cream.** Whisk the brown sugar and cornstarch together in a medium saucepan and whisk in the cooled milk followed by the egg yolks. Bring to a simmer over medium heat, whisking constantly until the custard has thickened and bubbles begin to break the surface. The custard will be thick.

5. **Fill the dough and bake.** Immediately pour the hot custard into the chilled pastry-lined pan and spread to level it. Place the pan on a baking tray and bake for about 45 minutes, until the top of the custard browns extensively. Cool the flan in its pan on a cooling rack (this step can take up to 2 hours) and then chill for at least 3 hours.

6. **Glaze the tart.** To add a shine that highlights the browned custard, melt the apple jelly (or strained apricot jam) in a small saucepan over low heat. Brush the top of the flan with the jelly and chill until ready to serve.

**The flan will keep in an airtight container in the fridge for up to 4 days.**

**MAKES:** one 6-cup (1.5 L) pudding
**SERVES:** 8 to 10

**PREP TIME:** 20 minutes
**COOK TIME:** 1 hour

🍴 **MORE INVOLVED**

**BITES OF WISDOM:**
*Glossary of baking tools—Baking pans*
*(p. 21)*

**INGREDIENTS**

**Bread pudding:**

**4 cups (1 L)** cubed brioche (like Brioche Loaf p. 440) or white bread, cut into 1½-inch (4 cm) pieces

**2** large eggs

**6 Tbsp (75 g)** granulated sugar

**1 cup (250 mL)** half-&-half cream

**1 cup (250 mL)** 2% milk

Zest of **1** lemon

**1 tsp** vanilla extract

**Frangipane & assembly:**

**1 cup (130 g)** Tant pour Tant (p. 82)

**¼ cup (60 g)** unsalted butter, at room temperature

**1** large egg

**¼ tsp** almond extract (optional)

**½ cup (125 mL)** Tart Lemon Curd (p. 100)

# Lemon Bostock Bread Pudding

Bread pudding has long been a staple homespun dessert that makes use of day-old bread by soaking and baking it in a simple milk-based custard. This version is dressed up a bit with dollops of lemon curd and a frangipane topping that adds a layer that crisps up on top—just like bostock, the jam-filled, frangipane-topped toast that French bakeries sell to use up their own day-old bread.

1. **Preheat the oven** to 350°F (180°C). Grease a 6-cup (1.5 L) baking dish.

2. **Toast the bread.** If the bread is less than 2 days old, spread it out on a baking tray and toast for about 10 minutes to dry it out a touch. Let it cool for 15 minutes before using. If the bread is stale, use it as is.

3. **Mix the custard and soak the bread.** Whisk the eggs with the sugar in a large mixing bowl until combined. Whisk in the cream, milk, lemon zest and vanilla until blended. Add the cubed bread and stir to coat. Let the mixture sit for 10 minutes to soak in, stirring once or twice.

   *It's important to let the bread soak before baking to ensure it really absorbs the custard, which will cause it to soufflé as the pudding bakes.*

4. **Prepare the frangipane.** Pulse the tant pour tant, butter, egg and almond extract, if using, in a mini chopper or food processor until well combined and a thick but smooth paste. Set aside.

5. **Assemble the pudding.** Pour the bread pudding into the prepared baking dish. Dollop the lemon curd on top. Dollop the frangipane over the pudding. Both will spread as the pudding bakes.

6. **Bake the pudding** for 50 to 60 minutes, until a tester inserted in the centre of the pudding comes out clean and the pudding soufflés. Let the pudding cool on a rack for at least 30 minutes before serving.

   *Because of the eggs in the custard, the pudding will soufflé toward the end of baking but immediately begin to sink as you remove it from the oven. Don't feel you have to rush the pudding to table—it would be too hot to enjoy at that point, and the pudding still stays fluffy even when it falls.*

SERVES: 6

PREP TIME: under 15 minutes
COOK TIME: 40 minutes

❗ SIMPLE
BITES OF WISDOM:
*How to whip egg whites (p. 34)*

## INGREDIENTS

**Meringue:**

2 large egg whites, at room temperature

½ tsp cream of tartar

½ cup (100 g) granulated sugar

Pink food colouring

**Assembly:**

1 recipe Chantilly Cream (p. 95)

½ cup (125 mL) Tart Lemon Curd
(p. 100)

2 cups (500 mL) fresh berries (raspberries, sliced strawberries or a mix)

# Pink Lemonade Eton Mess

Celebrate strawberry season with this stepped-up strawberries-and-cream dessert. Berries and shards of crisp, pink meringue are folded into Chantilly cream with swirls of tart lemon curd to add a little sparkle.

1. **Preheat the oven** to 250°F (120°C) and line a baking tray with parchment paper.

2. **Make the meringue.** Whip the egg whites and cream of tartar using electric beaters or a stand mixer fitted with the whip attachment on high speed until they become foamy. Slowly pour in the sugar, whipping continuously on high speed until the whites hold a stiff peak when the beaters are lifted. Stir in a few drops of pink food colouring. Spoon the meringue onto the prepared baking tray and spread it out to a thin, level layer that fills the tray.

3. **Bake the meringue** for about 40 minutes. If the meringue shows signs of browning, crack the oven door open and continue to bake. Remove the tray of meringue to a wire rack to cool. The meringue will crisp up as it cools, but if you notice that the centre still seems soft, return the meringue to the oven for another 5 to 10 minutes to dry out (even if the meringue has cooled completely). Cool the meringue completely.

*You can make the meringue a day ahead. Keep it, broken into large pieces, in an airtight container at room temperature.*

4. **Mix the cream, curd and berries.** Spoon the Chantilly cream into a large bowl. Dollop the curd onto the cream and sprinkle the berries overtop. Gently fold the curd and berries into the cream a few times, but do not fully combine them (1).

*If you really want to bring on the pink, add a few drops of pink food colouring to the Chantilly cream. You can assemble the cream, curd and berries a day ahead and chill until ready to serve.*

5. **Add the meringue** immediately before serving. Crumble the meringue over the lemon cream and fold in gently but quickly (2, 3). Spoon this mixture into a large serving bowl or divide into individual glasses or dessert coupes and serve immediately.

**Do not try to keep an assembled Eton mess—within an hour you will have a literal hot mess of soft meringue and weeping berries.**

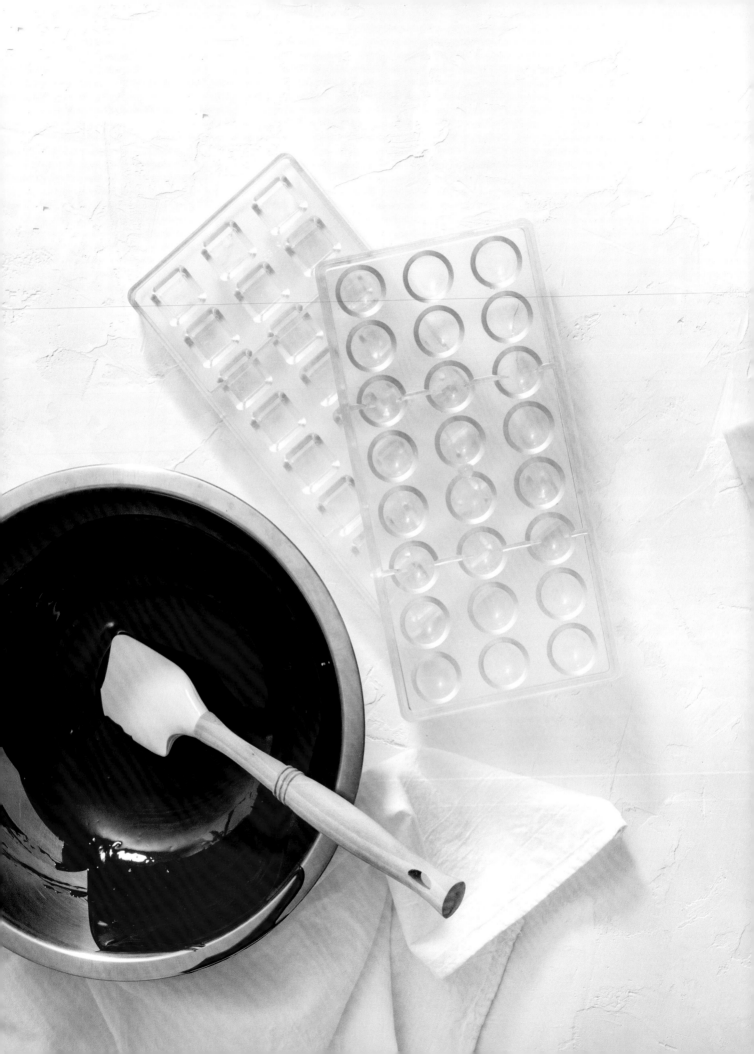

# Confections

# Recipes at a Glance

Candies may not seem like baking, but they are simply the same ingredients—sugar, chocolate, nuts, etc.—combined using methods and even some tools that are unique to making confections. The keys to shiny filled bonbons, chewy salt water taffy and elegant nougat are temperature and mastering a few basic techniques. Using the right sugar for the right application is important too. If you're new to confectionery, or even if you're not, begin by reading about the properties of different sugars (p. 12), tips on how to cook and caramelize sugar (p. 38) and tips on how to melt chocolate (p. 41) and how to temper chocolate (p. 42).

The sections in this chapter highlight different ways of working with caramelized sugar, whether mixed with gelatin or cream or cooked to precise temperatures, and with tempered chocolate. Soon you'll be confidently boiling and shaping taffies and candy canes and turning out gorgeous batches of chocolates with shine and a good "snap."

## Fruit Candies

Fruit candies stand out from a confectionery platter because of their vibrant colours, which are also a clue about their flavour. Soft and chewy candies like Raspberry Jelly Candies (p. 336) and Peach Raspberry Salt Water Taffy (p. 339) are often popular with kids, but be sure to choose your flavours wisely so everyone gets their favourite.

## Sugar Candies

Hard candies are made from sugar cooked to the hard crack stage (300°F to 310°F/149°C to 154°C) so they hold their shape without any surface stickiness. You will definitely want to use a candy thermometer or instant-read digital thermometer for accuracy. These confections last well and can be colourful and playful, like Cranberry Lollipops (p. 359) and Candy Canes (p. 355).

## Chocolates

All set confectionery chocolate is tempered, melted, cooled and warmed again to specific temperatures—so it is stable and strong and sets up quickly and with a satiny shine for candy making. Tempering takes a bit of practice, but once you get the hang of it, the possibilities for styles and flavour pairings are nearly endless. Plus, a box of well-made chocolates makes a great gift for friends or someone special.

## Caramels

If you keep boiling sugar past its hard crack stage (300°F to 310°F/149°C to 154°C) until it develops a rich amber colour, you get caramel. Deeply caramelized sugar has a subtle hint of bitterness and a familiar rich, toasty sweetness, and soft or crunchy caramels are almost as popular as chocolates. Vary the flavours by using golden corn syrup, honey or brown butter and play with texture, such as in Buttercrunch Toffee (p. 364).

## Nut Candies

Adding nuts to chocolate or caramelized sugar often cuts a candy's sweetness, adds crunch and provides a rich buttery flavour. Use only fresh nuts and toast them to bring out their best flavour, then play around with different combinations until you find your favourites. The Mixed Nut Brittle (p. 352) is an easy place to start.

## Meringue Candies

We think of meringue folded into cakes and frostings to aerate them, but this blend of whipped egg whites and sugar is also the foundation for fluffy, light candies like soft and squishy Maple Marshmallows (p. 369) and crisp and crunchy Giant Chocolate Meringues (p. 367).

**FRUIT CANDIES ▶**

Raspberry Jelly Candies (Pâte de Fruits) *(plus Bonus Bake: Jelly-filled Macarons)* Page 336

Peach Raspberry Salt Water Taffy
Page 339

**CHOCOLATES ▶**

Chocolate Elderflower Truffles
Page 341

Chocolate Mendiants
Page 345

Butter Ganache Bonbons
Page 346

**NUT CANDIES ▶**

Almond Rochers
Page 351

Mixed Nut Brittle
Page 352

**SUGAR CANDIES ▶**

Candy Canes
Page 355

Sour Lemon Drops
Page 356

**Cranberry Lollipops**
Page 359

CARAMELS ▶

**Sea Salt Caramel Candies**
Page 360

**Sponge Toffee (Honeycomb Toffee)**
Page 363

**Buttercrunch Toffee**
Page 364

MERINGUE CANDIES ▶

**Giant Chocolate Meringues**
Page 367

**Maple Marshmallows**
Page 369

**Montélimar Nougat**
Page 371

**MAKES:** 3 dozen candies

**PREP TIME:** 20 minutes, plus setting

**COOK TIME:** 15 minutes

⚡ **SIMPLE**

**BITES OF WISDOM:**

*Glossary of ingredients—Sugars (p. 12)*
*How to cook & caramelize sugar (p. 38)*

### INGREDIENTS

½ cup (125 mL) raspberry purée (puréed and strained frozen raspberries work best)

⅓ cup (80 mL) unsweetened applesauce

⅔ cup (160 mL) white corn syrup

1¼ cups (250 g) granulated sugar

1 (2.7 oz/80 mL) pouch liquid pectin

Granulated sugar or cornstarch, for coating

### BONUS BAKE

## Jelly-filled Macarons

Make stunning-looking Macarons (p. 390) filled with this raspberry jelly instead of a buttercream. Prepare the jelly recipe as above but set it in a 9-inch (23 cm) square pan so that the jellies are a bit flatter. Use a 1½-inch (4 cm) round cutter to cut out discs of jelly but do not coat them in sugar or cornstarch. When assembling the macarons, drop a round jelly into the centre of each one. Without the sugar coating, the jelly-filled macarons can be refrigerated.

# Raspberry Jelly Candies
## (Pâte de Fruits)

Even as a kid I was drawn to fruit jelly candies of all types, and when I joined the world of pastry I was thrilled to discover that pâtes de fruits are held in high regard. After you've made these jellies once, your candy-making confidence will soar and you'll be ready to try your own flavours and styles of presentation.

1. **Prepare the pan.** Lightly grease an 8-inch (20 cm) square baking pan and line it with parchment paper.

2. **Cook the fruit purée and sugars.** In a medium saucepan, whisk the raspberry purée and applesauce and bring to a simmer over medium heat. Add the corn syrup and sugar and bring to a gentle but even simmer, still over medium heat, whisking constantly. Keep simmering the liquid, stirring constantly, until it reaches 225°F (107°C), 8 to 10 minutes.

*Acidic fruit purées and juice will work very well here without changing the recipe ratio. For example, try ½ cup (125 mL) fresh orange juice in place of the raspberry purée. Add a few drops of orange food colouring, and I add a little orange blossom water to my orange jellies too.*

*While corn syrup and glucose syrup are both invert sugars (see p. 13), corn syrup is thinner than glucose syrup and they are not always interchangeable. Use corn syrup in this recipe.*

3. **Add the pectin.** Remove the pan from the heat, pour in the pectin and whisk. Return the mixture to the heat, let it come to a simmer and then immediately pour into the prepared pan. Let this jelly cool until set, uncovered, about an hour.

*Jelly candies rely on cooked sugar and pectin to set them. Pectin is found naturally in many fruits, especially in their skins and seeds (think how cranberries set on their own = pectin), and it's sold in liquid or powder form to set jams and jellies. It needs sugar and acidity to fully activate. Here the pectin helps the jelly candies hold their shape and remain tender to bite into.*

4. **Cut and coat the jellies.** Turn the jellies out onto a clean cutting board, peel off the parchment paper and cut into 36 squares. Roll the jellies in granulated sugar or cornstarch to keep them from sticking to each other. Let them air-dry for 2 hours, then pack between layers of parchment in an airtight container.

**These jellies will keep at room temperature for up to a week.**

**MAKES:** about 4 dozen candies

**PREP TIME:** 30 minutes, plus cooling
**COOK TIME:** 5 minutes

🍴 **MORE INVOLVED**
**BITES OF WISDOM:**
*How to cook & caramelize sugar (p. 38)*

## INGREDIENTS

3 Tbsp (45 mL) water

1 cup (200 g) granulated sugar

¾ cup (175 mL) white corn syrup

¼ cup (60 g) unsalted butter

½ tsp fine sea salt

½ tsp peach candy flavouring

½ tsp raspberry candy flavouring

Peach and pink food colouring powder, paste or gel

# Peach Raspberry Salt Water Taffy

These soft, sweet and flavourful chewy candies are fun to make with kids, and you might want to invite a friend to help, especially when it comes time to pull and stretch the taffy.

1. **Have ready a baking tray** lined with a silicone baking mat on a cooling rack.

2. **Cook the sugar.** Pour the water into a pot, followed by the sugar and corn syrup. Cover the pot and bring to a full boil over high heat. Uncover the pot and stir in the butter. Continue to cook, constantly stirring, until the candy reaches 245°F (118°C) on a candy thermometer, about 4 minutes. Remove the pan from the heat, stir in the salt and pour the candy onto the baking mat. Let cool to about 84°F (29°C) or until you can lift it with your hands and it pulls away from the mat, 10 to 30 minutes (1).

   *In candy making, the cooling temperature is just as important as the cooking temperature. Developing the right structure plus the ease in handling are key to getting the right texture.*

   *Always add salt at the end of the recipe or directly after cooking; otherwise, it can interfere with how the sugar cooks. Add flavourings after the sugar has cooled to prevent heat from evaporating or breaking them down.*

3. **Flavour and colour the taffy.** Divide the taffy into two pieces on the silicone mat. Drizzle peach flavouring and peach colouring onto one half, and raspberry flavouring and pink colouring onto the second half. With clean hands, start pulling and stretching the peach taffy. Some of the extracts or colour may drip out as you start pulling, but you can dab it up as you stretch and reshape the taffy. Continue to stretch and reshape the taffy for about 15 minutes (2), until it becomes a pale colour and holds its shape when set down on the mat.

   *Buy concentrated candy flavourings at stores that sell baking and candy-making supplies. They are very concentrated, so you need only a little. Give these raspberry jellies a sweet and sour kick by adding ½ tsp ascorbic acid powder (or a product like Fruit-Fresh) to each of the flavoured taffies.*

   *Taffy becomes lighter in colour as you stretch and aerate it. Keep that in mind when choosing your colours. If you're stretching the taffy on your own for this recipe, alternate between the two flavours. Stretch the peach for 5 minutes, then the raspberry. Go back and forth until both have been pulled for about 15 minutes each.*

*CONTINUES*

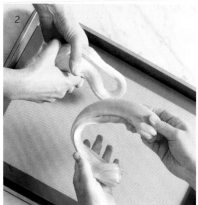

4. **Stretch the two flavours together.** For the final stretch, stack the peach taffy on top of the raspberry taffy. Give them three or four pulls and twists to intertwine them without fully combining them (3).

*If you prefer, make all peach or all raspberry taffy candies and skip the final twisting.*

5. **Portion the taffy.** Grease a pair of scissors and snip the taffy into four dozen pieces on the silicone mat (4). Wrap each candy in a small square of parchment or taffy paper.

*Look for candy/taffy paper wrappers where you buy candy flavourings. Wrapping the soft, tender taffies individually prevents them from losing their shape and sticking together (plus it's another reason to have a friend help you with this project).*

**The taffies will keep in an airtight container at room temperature for up to 10 days.**

**MAKES:** about 2½ dozen truffles

**PREP TIME:** 1 hour, plus setting and chilling
**COOK TIME:** under 5 minutes

🍴 **MORE INVOLVED**
**BITES OF WISDOM:**
*How to melt chocolate (p. 41), How to temper chocolate (p. 42)*

**INGREDIENTS**

**Ganache:**

**7 oz (210 g)** dark baking/couverture chocolate, chopped

**6 Tbsp (90 mL)** whipping cream

**2 Tbsp (25 g)** glucose syrup

**2 Tbsp (30 g)** unsalted butter, softened

**2 Tbsp (30 mL)** elderflower liqueur (St-Germain)

**Truffle assembly:**

**9 oz (270 g)** tempered dark baking/ couverture chocolate (p. 42)

Cocoa powder or icing sugar, for rolling

# Chocolate Elderflower Truffles

Chocolate truffles are iconic chocolate confections. Whereas bonbons have a molded shell into which you pipe a filling (of just about any flavour) before allowing them to set, truffles are pieces of ganache that are shaped and then dipped in tempered chocolate. When you bite into that thin outer shell, the chocolate ganache centre should melt away on the tip of your tongue . . . heavenly.

1. **Make the chocolate ganache.** Place the chopped chocolate in a metal bowl. Bring the cream and glucose syrup to a full simmer in a medium saucepan over medium-high heat, stirring in the syrup to dissolve it. Pour the hot cream over the chocolate and stir (not whisk) gently until the chocolate has melted and the ganache is smooth. Transfer to a pie plate and place a sheet of plastic wrap directly on the surface. Let the ganache cool to room temperature (this can take 30 minutes to an hour).

   *When stirring butter or cream with melting chocolate, always stir slowly and gently and use a spatula, not a whisk. Vigorous stirring can separate the fat from the chocolate and dairy, and you'll end up with a greasy, separated mass. While adding a few droplets of water can fix split chocolate in a baked recipe, this solution is less effective with truffles because the chocolate could split again after chilling, resulting in less creamy or even grainy truffles.*

2. **Work in the butter.** Beat the butter in a bowl to soften it. Add a few tablespoons of the cooled ganache and stir to combine. Add the remaining ganache and the elderflower liqueur and stir well to combine. Gently stir for a minute to help crystallize the chocolate so it holds its shape when piped.

3. **Pipe the truffles.** Have ready a baking tray lined with parchment paper or a silicone baking mat. Transfer the ganache to a piping bag fitted with a medium plain tip. Pipe truffles about an inch (2.5 cm) in diameter onto the tray (1). Let set for 20 to 30 minutes at room temperature or chill for 10 minutes.

   *Be patient getting the set consistency of your truffles just right before you dip them. If you chill the truffles too much, they will set the tempered chocolate coat too quickly and too thickly. If the truffles are too warm when dipped, they won't hold their round shape. After their 10-minute chill, the truffles should be easy to lift off the tray but still soft enough to dent if handled too roughly. Let the truffles warm or chill a few minutes longer before you fully dive into dipping all of them.*

*CONTINUES*

4. **Dip the truffles.** Using truffle forks or a skewer, dip each truffle in the tempered chocolate (2), tapping the forks or skewer gently on the side of the bowl to shake off excess chocolate. Place the truffle back on the baking tray and continue with the remaining truffles. Chill the truffles for 20 minutes to finish setting the chocolate. Remove from the tray, roll in cocoa powder (or icing sugar) (3, 4) and pack in an airtight container.

**The truffles will keep in the fridge for up to 10 days. Let them sit out for 30 minutes before eating.**

*The ideal temperature for storing chocolate truffles and bonbons is between 58°F and 68°F (14°C and 20°C). Although few of us have a dedicated chocolate fridge like professional chocolatiers, keeping the chocolates in your fridge is better than storing them at room temperature.*

**MAKES:** about 3½ dozen chocolates

**PREP TIME:** 20 minutes

**SIMPLE**

**BITES OF WISDOM:**

*How to melt chocolate (p. 41), How to temper chocolate (p. 42), How to make a parchment paper cone for piping (p. 54)*

**INGREDIENTS**

**6 oz (180 g)** tempered dark, milk or white baking/couverture chocolate (p. 42)

**1 oz (30 g)** unsalted shelled pistachio halves

**1 oz (30 g)** dried cherries or cranberries

**1 oz (30 g)** crystallized rose petals or violets

# Chocolate Mendiants

While many chocolate bonbons hide their fillings, chocolate mendiants put their toppings on display. Easy to make and easy to eat, these little discs of decorated tempered chocolate make a lovely host gift when bundled. I usually make mendiants at the end of a chocolate-making day to use up any leftover tempered chocolate and goodies I have around.

1. **Line two baking trays with parchment paper** or silicone baking mats.

2. **Spoon the tempered chocolate** into a parchment paper cone. Have the toppings ready.

   *The toppings are up to you, but the key is to balance flavour, colour and texture. Make sure your ingredients are dried or toasted because any moisture will spoil the mendiants. Consider the following combinations: toasted hazelnut half, dried apricot slice, crystallized ginger slice; large toasted coconut flake, dried mango slice, salted peanut; cacao nibs, dried blueberry, freeze-dried raspberry powder.*

   *If your dried cherries or cranberries are large, cut them in half and use both halves on each mendiant.*

3. **Pipe the chocolate into discs.** Pour the chocolate into a parchment paper cone or a piping bag fitted with a small plain tip. Pipe discs about ¾ inch (2 cm) wide onto half of the first baking tray, leaving a little space between them for the chocolate to spread. Arrange a pistachio half, a dried cherry (or cranberry) and a crystallized flower petal or two onto each mendiant. Continue to fill the tray and decorate the mendiants. Chill the first tray while you pipe mendiants onto the second. Remove the first tray from the fridge and chill the second tray for 5 minutes.

4. **Pack the mendiants** between sheets of parchment in an airtight container.

   **The mendiants will keep in a cool place out of direct sunlight for up to a week. (Refrigerate them only if you can't store them in a cool place.)**

**MAKES:** about 4 dozen chocolates

**PREP TIME:** 90 minutes, plus setting and chilling

**COOK TIME:** under 5 minutes

### ⫲⫲⫲ COMPLEX

**BITES OF WISDOM:**
*How to melt chocolate (p. 41), How to temper chocolate (p. 42), How to use piping bags & tips (p. 52)*

### INGREDIENTS

---

#### Ganache:

**4 oz (120 g)** milk baking/couverture chocolate, chopped

**4 oz (120 g)** dark baking/couverture chocolate, chopped

**¾ cup (175 mL)** whipping cream

**2 Tbsp (30 mL)** corn syrup

**6 Tbsp (90 g)** unsalted butter, cool, cut into pieces

#### Bonbon assembly:

Cocoa butter colours (optional)

**12 oz (360 g)** tempered dark baking/ couverture chocolate (p. 42)

Pearl dust powder (optional)

# Butter Ganache Bonbons

The first time I made molded bonbons I was covered in chocolate, and so was my kitchen, but I felt so proud of my tiny, beautiful morsels of chocolate. Making properly molded bonbons takes a sincere commitment of time and tools. They cannot be rushed, and each step of molding, filling and setting is timed, so don't let yourself get distracted with other projects. The butter ganache filling in this recipe is fluffier than a chocolate truffle filling, which is why it needs to be set into a tempered chocolate shell. For glossy, perfectly shaped bonbons, invest in polycarbonate chocolate molds, or use flexible silicone ones if you want to be less precise. Learning a skill like this one is worthy of eating as many chocolates as you wish!

1. **Make the ganache.** Place the milk and dark chocolates together in a bowl. Bring the whipping cream to a full simmer in a small saucepan over high heat, then pour over the chocolate. Let this mixture sit for a minute and then gently and slowly whisk or stir the chocolate until the mixture is smooth, shiny and evenly combined. Stir in the corn syrup and set the ganache aside to cool to room temperature.

   *To infuse flavour into the ganache, add orange zest, tea, instant espresso powder, cinnamon or other spices when you heat the whipping cream. Strain the cream to get rid of any solids before you pour it over the chocolate.*

   *To add spirits to the ganache, stir no more than 1 Tbsp (15 mL) into the warm ganache before it cools.*

2. **Beat the butter into the ganache.** Using electric beaters or a stand mixer fitted with the whip attachment, whip the ganache on medium speed to aerate it a little. Add the butter, whipping continuously, and then increase the speed to high and continue to whip until the butter is fully incorporated and the ganache takes on a light milk chocolate colour.

   *The butter ganache is best used at room temperature. You can prepare it ahead of time and keep it chilled, but let it soften on the counter to room temperature and rewhip before using.*

3. **Prepare and decorate your molds.** Line a baking tray with parchment paper. Use a microfibre cloth to polish each cavity of the chocolate molds well (1) (this step promotes a shiny surface for each bonbon). Use a small brush or a gloved fingertip and dip into the cocoa butter colour, if using. Paint patterns onto the cavities of the chocolate molds (2). Layer the colours if you wish or keep it simple with one. Place the molds on the lined baking tray to set.

   *Cocoa butter colours are different from regular food colouring, which is water- or alcohol-based and could split the chocolate. If the colours are preblended, you can simply dip and brush away. If not, melt a bit of pure cocoa butter and stir the powdered food colouring into it.*

*CONTINUES*

4. **Line the chocolate molds.** Pour the tempered chocolate into a new piping bag (no tip) and keep the bowl you used to temper the chocolate handy. Snip a small opening at the end of the piping bag and pipe chocolate into each cavity of the mold to fill it to the top (3). Quickly invert the filled mold over the bowl and let all of the excess chocolate run out. Tap the side of the mold to draw out more chocolate but keep the mold fully upside down (4).

*I used to ladle chocolate into my molds, until master chocolatier Rachel McKinley showed me that piping uses less chocolate and is tidier. While ladling is faster in the moment, you spend more time scraping and cleaning your mold afterward.*

*As you move from cavity to cavity with the piping bag, pinch the bottom of the bag to close it off so you will make less of a mess.*

5. **Clean the molds.** Use your palette knife (or putty knife, if you table tempered your chocolate) and, keeping the mold upside down, scrape away any chocolate from the top of the mold. Place the molds upside down onto the tray and chill for 10 minutes.

*A clean top to the mold will make it easier to pop out the finished chocolates, and their edges will be tidy.*

6. **Fill the bonbons.** Fill a small piping bag with the soft butter ganache and snip the tip off. Pipe chocolate into each cavity, leaving an ⅛-inch (3 mm) gap at the top (5). Give each chocolate mold a gentle tap to push out any air bubbles and level the ganache filling. Chill the chocolate shells for 10 minutes—you may have to retemper your chocolate at this point.

*This step is by far the trickiest in making bonbons. If the bonbons are overfilled, you won't be able to seal them with the final coating of chocolate and the filling will leak out. And if they are underfilled, you will have a bonbon with too thick of a chocolate base. Definitely do not rush this step, and if you think you have overfilled any bonbons, use a small spoon or even a bamboo skewer to scoop out a little of the filling.*

*Once you have mastered the basic technique, you can experiment with different fillings, such as Roasted White Chocolate Ganache (p. 92), Salted Butter Caramel Sauce (p. 89) or jelly. Simply bear in mind two things: 1) keep the filling temperature below 82°F (28°C) or you run the risk of melting the tempered chocolate mold; and 2) leave a little extra space when filling bonbons with caramel or other fluid fillings. Chocolate contracts when it chills, so to prevent leaks you can make the final chocolate layer a touch thicker.*

7. **Cover the bonbons with chocolate and chill.** Using a ladle, cover the top of each chocolate mold completely with chocolate (6). Give the molds a shake to let out any air bubbles and then use your palette knife or putty knife to scrape the excess chocolate off the top as you hold the molds over your chocolate bowl (7). The bonbons will be completely covered in chocolate, and the space around each cavity should be clean and clear of chocolate. Chill the bonbons for an hour.

*Ladling is the best way to thoroughly coat the bonbons at this point. With the mold upright, you can really check that the top of the mold is clean and that every bonbon is filled.*

8. **Unmold and dust the bonbons.** Remove the molds from the fridge and take them off the baking tray. One at a time, invert the molds and firmly smack them onto the baking tray—the bonbons should pop out onto the tray (8). If there are any chocolates left in the mold, clear away the other bonbons and smack the tray again. Use a dry brush to dust the bonbons with pearl dust powder, if using. Transfer the bonbons to an airtight container and refrigerate until ready to package or serve.

*If you smack the mold and no bonbons pop out, either the bonbons haven't chilled long enough or the chocolate was not properly tempered and didn't contract enough to loosen from the mold. All is not lost—pop the chocolate mold into the freezer for 15 to 20 minutes and try again. The chocolates should release just fine.*

**The bonbons will keep in the fridge for up to 10 days. Let them sit on the counter at room temperature for 30 minutes before serving.**

🍴 **MORE INVOLVED**

**BITES OF WISDOM:**
*Glossary of ingredients—Nuts & seeds (p. 11)*

**INGREDIENTS**

**2 cups (220 g)** slivered almonds

**1 Tbsp (8 g)** icing sugar

**1 Tbsp (15 mL)** orange liqueur

**Pinch** of ground cinnamon

**Pinch** of fine salt

**5 oz (150 g)** tempered dark baking/couverture chocolate (p. 42)

# Almond Rochers

The word *rocher* may mean "rock" in French, but these clusters of sweet toasted almonds bound with chocolate are anything but rocky. You can also make these using other chopped or slivered nuts, such as hazelnuts, pistachios or peanuts (leave the peanuts whole) or even a mixture.

1. **Preheat the oven** to 350°F (180°C) and line a baking tray with parchment paper.

2. **Toast the almonds.** Toss the almonds with the icing sugar, orange liqueur, cinnamon and salt and spread onto the baking tray. Bake for about 15 minutes, stirring once halfway through baking, until the nuts are a light golden brown. Cool the almonds on the tray to just above room temperature.

   *The almonds should be slightly warm, but not hot, so that once they are stirred into the chocolate, the rochers do not set too quickly and become more chocolate than nuts. If you need time to get organized or to temper your chocolate, you can warm the almonds in a 300°F (150°C) oven for 3 minutes. Be sure to check their temperature before adding them to the tempered chocolate—they should be no warmer than 82°F (28°C).*

3. **Coat the almonds with chocolate.** Line two baking trays with parchment paper and have your tempered chocolate ready in a bowl. Pour half of the almonds into a clean bowl and add half of the chocolate, stirring well to coat. Work as quickly as you can and drop teaspoonfuls of the almond mixture onto the baking trays, ensuring the almonds are in a tidy stack. Repeat with the remaining almonds and chocolate.

   *Working in batches gives you time to portion out the rochers before the entire bowl of chocolate has set.*

4. **Chill the rochers.** After the rochers have started to set, pop the trays in the fridge to fully set for 10 to 15 minutes. Pack the rochers in an airtight container.

   **The rochers will keep in a cool place for 3 to 4 days or in the fridge for up to 10 days.**

**MAKES:** about one 12 × 16-inch (30 × 41 cm) piece
**SERVES:** 16 to 20

**PREP TIME:** 15 minutes, plus cooling
**COOK TIME:** 10 minutes

❗ SIMPLE
**BITES OF WISDOM:**
*How to toast nuts (p. 36), How to cook & caramelize sugar (p. 38)*

**INGREDIENTS**

¼ **cup (60 mL)** water

1½ **cups (300 g)** granulated sugar

½ **cup (125 mL)** white corn syrup

2 **Tbsp (30 g)** unsalted butter

1 **tsp** baking soda

1 **tsp** vanilla extract

1½ **cups (375 mL)** lightly toasted unsalted nuts, such as peanuts, cashews and/or pistachios

**Pinch** of coarse sea salt

# Mixed Nut Brittle

Peanut brittle might be the most familiar version of this candy made with caramelized sugar and nuts, but I like to use a mix of nuts when I make mine. I particularly love crushing any brittle to sprinkle on top of ice cream or dipping it in tempered chocolate to give as a gift.

1. **Prepare the pans and ingredients.** Line a baking tray with parchment paper and lightly grease it, or line with a silicone baking mat. Have all of the ingredients ready before you start to cook the sugar.

   *Once the sugar caramelizes, you have to move quickly. Put the butter, baking soda and vanilla in one dish, ready to add to the sugar all at once.*

2. **Cook the caramel.** Bring the water, sugar and corn syrup to a boil in a medium saucepan over high heat. Boil, uncovered but occasionally brushing down the sides of the pot with water, until the caramel is a light amber colour.

3. **Add the nuts.** Remove the pot from the heat and immediately stir in the butter, baking soda and vanilla. Be careful of the steam. Stir in the nuts and spread the mixture on the prepared baking tray, dispersing the nuts evenly. Sprinkle the brittle with sea salt and let cool completely to room temperature. Roughly break into pieces before eating or using.

   *As soon as you add the baking soda, the sugar mixture will froth up, and once that cool air gets into the sugar, you need to work quickly. The tiny air bubbles set into the sugar make nut brittle more tender and easier to eat than it would be if you stirred the nuts into a large mass of straight caramelized sugar.*

**The brittle will keep in an airtight container at room temperature for up to a week.**

**MAKES:** about 24 candy canes

**PREP TIME:** 20 minutes, plus cooling
**COOK TIME:** 5 minutes

⫰⫱ **MORE INVOLVED**
**BITES OF WISDOM:**
*How to cook & caramelize sugar (p. 38)*

**INGREDIENTS**

½ cup (125 mL) water

2 cups (400 g) granulated sugar

½ cup (125 mL) white corn syrup

1 tsp peppermint extract

Red food colouring gel, paste or powder

# Candy Canes

It's true that candy canes are inexpensive to buy and in every store at Christmastime, so why make them? Because it's so much fun! Between twisting the red and white colours together and creating original shapes beyond the typical cane, you can make truly special gifts from the kitchen.

1. **Preheat the oven** to 200°F (93°C). Line two baking trays with silicone baking mats or parchment paper.

2. **Boil the sugar.** Measure the water into a medium saucepan, followed by the sugar and corn syrup. Bring to a full boil over high heat without stirring, and continue to boil until the sugar reaches 300°F (149°C) on a candy thermometer. Remove the pan from the heat and stir in the peppermint extract.

   *The hard crack stage of cooking sugar is between 300°F and 310°F (149°C and 154°C), which is the temperature you need for the candy canes to fully set up. I pull the sugar off the heat as soon as it reaches 300°F (149°C) because it is then easier to handle for longer than if you let it cook to 310°F (154°C).*

   *Peppermint may be the classic flavour for candy canes, but you can add ½ tsp of another candy flavouring, such as cherry, raspberry or even root beer or peach. Feel free to switch up the colour while you're at it, to match the flavour.*

3. **Colour half of the sugar.** Pour half of the melted sugar onto one baking tray. Add red food colouring to the remaining sugar in the pot, stir and pour onto the second baking tray. Let the sugar cool enough that you can handle it with your bare hands (it will pull away from the mat or parchment without sticking). If it sets too much, pop the trays in the oven to soften up the sugar.

4. **Stretch the cooked sugar.** Start with the clear sugar, pulling and stretching it until it turns an opaque white colour, about 3 minutes. When it becomes too tough to pull, twist it into a log about an inch (2.5 cm) across, return to the tray and keep warm in the oven so it stays pliable. Repeat this pulling, stretching and shaping with the red sugar and add it to the tray already in the oven.

5. **Shape the candy canes.** Working in batches, use a pair of scissors to snip a 2-inch (5 cm) piece of each coloured sugar log and keep the rest warm. The candy will be warm but not hot and should be pliable. Shape both pieces to roughly the same length and width, stack one piece on top of the other and stretch into a rope. Roll the rope on the counter or a baking tray (see note) to create a shiny, smooth surface, then twist it to create the candy cane stripe. For typical 4-inch (10 cm) candy canes, cut the rope into 6-inch (15 cm) pieces and curl one side over. Set on the baking tray to cool. Repeat until all of the sugar has been used.

   *To give yourself a few more minutes when rolling and shaping your candy canes, line a second baking tray with a silicone baking mat and keep it warm in the oven. Roll your candies on this surface to keep the sugar pliable longer.*

   **The candy canes will keep between sheets of parchment paper in an airtight container at room temperature for up to a week.**

**MAKES:** about 3 dozen lemon drops

**PREP TIME:** 10 minutes, plus cooling
**COOK TIME:** 10 minutes

❢ SIMPLE

BITES OF WISDOM:
*How to cook & caramelize sugar (p. 38)*

**INGREDIENTS**

⅓ cup (80 mL) water

1 cup (200 g) granulated sugar

2 Tbsp (40 g) glucose syrup

1 tsp citric acid

½ tsp lemon extract

Yellow food colouring liquid or gel

# Sour Lemon Drops

These tart and tangy hard lemon candies look very pretty when set in a silicone mold—but don't feel you need to stick with a lemon shape for these. A flower, heart or other small shape will look just as sweet.

1. **Prepare the pans.** Place two to three silicone candy molds onto a baking tray.

   *Flexible silicone baking molds are the ideal tool to shape and release the lemon drops. Make sure they are very clean with no oil residue on them, which can dull the finish of your candies.*

2. **Boil the sugar.** Measure the water, sugar and glucose syrup into a large saucepan and bring to a boil over high heat. Boil, uncovered and without stirring, until the sugar reaches 300°F (149°C) on a candy thermometer, about 8 minutes.

3. **Let the sugar cool a little.** Remove the pot from the heat and gently stir in the citric acid, lemon extract and food colouring. Keep stirring gently to let the syrup stop boiling and any bubbles dissipate.

   *Letting the bubbles subside is the key to clear hard candies. Be patient—the hot sugar will be fluid and pourable for a good 10 minutes. If the sugar does start to set, reheat it over low heat but avoid stirring it vigorously.*

4. **Let the candies set and harden.** Transfer the syrup to a heatproof pitcher or ladle the syrup into the silicone molds. Let the lemon drops set for at least an hour before unmolding. Wrap the lemon drops individually in parchment paper or candy wrap paper, or store them between layers of parchment paper.

   **The lemon drops will keep in an airtight container at room temperature for up to 3 weeks.**

**MAKES:** 8 to 10 lollipops

**PREP TIME:** 20 minutes, plus cooling
**COOK TIME:** 10 minutes

**⟁ SIMPLE**

BITES OF WISDOM:
*How to cook & caramelize sugar (p. 38)*

**INGREDIENTS**

2 to 3 cups (260 to 390 g) icing sugar

8 to 10 wooden lollipop sticks

½ cup (125 mL) cranberry juice

¼ cup (60 mL) water

1 cup (200 g) granulated sugar

¼ cup (60 mL) white corn syrup

Sprinkles, for decorating

# Cranberry Lollipops

For this recipe, you don't need special molds. By making impressions in icing sugar on a baking tray, the sugar finds its shape just fine.

1. **Create the lollipop mold.** Line a baking tray with parchment paper. Sift the icing sugar onto the tray and spread gently into an even layer about ½ inch (1.2 cm) thick. Use a flat-bottomed water glass roughly 2 inches (5 cm) across and press into the icing sugar at intervals, making sure the impression is level (if you make a mistake, you can always loosen the icing sugar and start again). Place one end of a lollipop stick into each depression.

   *Get creative with your shapes here—find everyday items that can leave an unusual pattern. A fluted dish could make a flower or petal shape. Try a geometric shape or the side of your fist and add touching fingerprints for a foot pattern. Cookie stamps can also work, provided they are deep enough.*

2. **Reduce the juice to concentrate the flavour and colour.** Place the cranberry juice in a small saucepan over high heat and reduce it to just 2 Tbsp (30 mL). Set aside to cool.

   *Purple or white grape juice also work well, if you prefer purple or clear lollipops. Or skip this step altogether and add candy flavouring after you cook the sugar (no need to replace this 2 Tbsp/30 mL of liquid if you add candy flavouring instead).*

3. **Boil the sugar.** Place the water, sugar and corn syrup in a medium saucepan and bring to a boil over high heat without stirring. Occasionally brush the sides of the pan with water to prevent any sugar splashes from sticking and crystallizing. Cook the sugar until it reaches 300°F (149°C) on a candy thermometer.

4. **Add the juice.** Remove the pan from the heat and stir in the reduced cranberry juice.

5. **Quickly but carefully fill the lollipop molds** by ladling the hot sugar into each depression so that it fills it and covers the lollipop stick. Decorate the lollipops with sprinkles. Let the lollipops cool completely.

   *You can decorate lollipops that have set just as you would sugar cut-out cookies. Add a drizzle of tempered chocolate or royal icing, and add sprinkles, coloured sanding sugar or other edible décor.*

6. **Unmold the lollipops.** Lift the lollipops out of the icing sugar and gently tap off any icing sugar stuck to them. Use a damp paper towel (cool water) to wipe the icing sugar side of the lollipop and then immediately dry that side with a dry paper towel. Wrap the lollipops individually in cellophane bags if you wish.

**The lollipops will keep, well wrapped, at room temperature for up to a month.**

**MAKES:** 3½ to 4 dozen candies

**PREP TIME:** 15 minutes, plus cooling
**COOK TIME:** 15 minutes

🍴 **MORE INVOLVED**

**BITES OF WISDOM:**
*How to cook & caramelize sugar (p. 38)*

**INGREDIENTS**

1½ **cups (300 g)** granulated sugar

¼ **cup (50 g)** packed dark brown sugar

1 **cup (250 mL)** evaporated milk

½ **cup (125 mL)** whipping cream

Seeds from ½ vanilla bean

⅔ **cup (160 mL)** white corn syrup

1 **Tbsp (15 g)** unsalted butter

½ **tsp** fine sea salt

1½ **tsp** flaked sea salt, for finishing

# Sea Salt Caramel Candies

If you've ever made a caramel sauce (such as Salted Butter Caramel Sauce, p. 89), then you can make caramel candies. The method for these soft candies is virtually the same: what differs is when you add the ingredients to get the caramel candies to set.

1. **Prepare the pan.** Grease and line an 8-inch (20 cm) square pan with parchment paper on the bottom and sides.

2. **Start the sugar boiling and add the corn syrup.** Place the granulated sugar, brown sugar, evaporated milk, cream and vanilla seeds into a large saucepan. Have the corn syrup, butter and fine sea salt measured and nearby. Bring the mixture to a boil over medium-high heat, whisking well and switching to a long-handled spatula or wooden spoon as the caramel begins to steam. When the mixture reaches a full boil, add the corn syrup. Stir constantly, still over medium-high heat, until the mixture reaches 242°F (116°C) on a candy thermometer, 8 to 10 minutes. It will be a pale peanut butter colour and will darken as it sets.

   *Evaporated milk contains less water than fresh milk so it is more stable when cooked at a high temperature and adds an extra level of creaminess to the completed caramel candies.*

   *If you don't have a vanilla bean, use 1½ tsp vanilla extract instead. Stir it in when you add the butter and salt.*

3. **Add the butter and salt.** Remove the pan from the heat and quickly stir in the butter and fine sea salt, then pour the caramel into the prepared pan. Sprinkle the surface with flaked sea salt and let cool on a wire rack for at least 4 hours (it takes a while to set.)

4. **Portion the caramels.** Before cutting the caramels, chill the pan for about 90 minutes to make it easier to slice the caramels precisely. Once the caramels are cut into squares, line an airtight container with a sheet of parchment paper. Arrange the caramels on top in a single layer.

**The caramels will keep at room temperature for up to 2 weeks.**

**MAKES:** 2 to 3 dozen pieces

**PREP TIME:** 5 minutes, plus cooling
**COOK TIME:** 15 minutes

## ⚔ MORE INVOLVED
**BITES OF WISDOM:**
*How to cook & caramelize sugar (p. 38)*

## INGREDIENTS

1½ Tbsp (30 g) honey

5 tsp (20 g) baking soda

½ tsp (1.5 g) cream of tartar

1 cup (250 mL) water

3½ cups (700 g) granulated sugar

1½ cups (375 mL) golden corn syrup

# Sponge Toffee (Honeycomb Toffee)

Sponge toffee is crazy fun to make because it more than quadruples in size when you add the baking soda and cream of tartar. It may be hard to imagine, but the taste of that small amount of honey really does come through in this crisp yet tender confection.

1. **Prepare the pan.** Grease and line a 9 × 13-inch (23 × 33 cm) pan with parchment paper so that the paper comes up an inch (2.5 cm) higher than the sides.

2. **Prepare all of your ingredients.** Have the honey measured in one dish and stir the baking soda and cream of tartar together in another dish. Have these on hand, along with a sieve, by the stove before you start to cook the sugar.

   *Timing is key when making sponge toffee because you can't leave a pot of boiling sugar unattended even for a moment. Have everything measured and on hand.*

3. **Start cooking the sugar and corn syrup.** In a small pasta pot, combine the water (water first allows the sugar to dissolve evenly), sugar and corn syrup and bring the mixture to a boil over high heat, stirring just once or twice to ensure everything is dissolving evenly. Continue boiling, without stirring, until the mixture reaches 284°F (140°C) on a candy thermometer, about 8 minutes.

   *A 10- to 12-quart (10 to 12 L) pasta or other high-sided pot is best so the sponge toffee has room to grow.*

4. **Add the honey.** Stir in the honey and continue boiling until the mixture reaches 300°F (149°C). The sugar will be pale amber but not caramelized fully.

   *Although it looks like the sugar for this toffee recipe is not fully caramelized, it is cooked to the hard crack stage and will set up firmly.*

5. **Add the baking soda and cream of tartar.** Remove the pot from the heat and, using a wooden spoon, quickly sift in the baking soda mixture, stirring quickly and vigorously to make sure it is fully incorporated. Quickly scrape the frothing mass (it will keep growing and growing!) into the prepared pan and let it set (do not spread it) until cool, up to 2 hours. The toffee will continue to grow a little more before it sets.

   *This toffee keeps growing for minutes after you've added the baking soda. Once the baking soda is fully incorporated, stop stirring or the sponge toffee will start to deflate.*

6. **Portion the toffee.** Crack the toffee with a rolling pin to break into bite-sized pieces.

   **The toffee will keep in an airtight container at room temperature for up to 1 month.**

**MAKES:** 2 to 3 dozen bite-sized pieces

**PREP TIME:** 15 minutes, plus cooling
**COOK TIME:** 20 minutes

### ⫙⫙⫙ COMPLEX

**BITES OF WISDOM:**
*How to cook & caramelize sugar (p. 38),
How to temper chocolate (p. 42), How to
toast nuts (p. 36)*

### INGREDIENTS

1 cup (225 g) unsalted butter

1¼ cups (250 g) granulated sugar

3 Tbsp (45 mL) water

1½ tsp vanilla extract

½ tsp fine salt

12 oz (360 g) tempered dark baking/
couverture chocolate (p. 42)

1 cup (160 g) medium-toasted unsalted
whole almonds (skins on)

Flaked sea salt, for sprinkling

# Buttercrunch Toffee

This toffee is my kryptonite, and whenever I make a batch I have to give most of it away or else I end up eating it all myself. Buttery, crunchy thin sheets of toffee are coated on both sides with chocolate and then sprinkled with sliced almonds and salt. You see why it's so hard to resist?

1. **Line a baking tray** with parchment paper and set aside.

2. **Boil the butter and sugar.** Melt the butter in a medium saucepan over medium-high heat, swirling the pan to coat the sides with melted butter. Add the sugar and water and bring to a boil (still over medium-high heat), stirring often with a wooden spoon or silicone spatula. Once the mixture comes to a boil, lower the heat to medium and stir constantly but slowly, and without scraping the sides of the pot, until the mixture reaches 300°F (149°C) on a candy thermometer (it will be a pale amber rather than caramel coloured), about 16 minutes.

   *Swirling the butter around the pan to coat the sides helps to prevent the sugar from crystallizing as you cook it. As the sugar cooks, the butter is browning within it and adding to the distinctive toffee taste.*

3. **Finish and pour the toffee to set.** Remove the pan from the heat and stir in the vanilla and salt, then quickly pour the mixture onto the prepared tray (do not spread it around). Let the toffee set until completely cooled, about 2 hours.

4. **Prepare the toffee for coating.** Gently wipe the top of the buttercrunch with a paper towel to remove any excess oil that could prevent the chocolate from sticking properly. Have ready a second baking tray lined with parchment paper.

5. **Coat the toffee with chocolate.** Pour half of the chocolate over the toffee and spread to cover evenly and as close to the edges as possible. Sprinkle the chocolate with half of the almonds and a light sprinkling of sea salt. Once set (about 3 minutes), place the second baking tray over the buttercrunch and carefully invert them together. (The chocolate-coated side should be on the bottom.) Peel away the parchment and wipe the buttercrunch with a paper towel. Pour the remaining half of the chocolate over the toffee and spread evenly, finishing with the remaining almonds and a little sea salt.

6. **Set and portion the toffee.** Once the chocolate is almost set, pop the tray into the fridge for just 3 to 4 minutes to set the chocolate. Remove the chocolate from the fridge, crack into pieces and store in an airtight container in a cool, dark place.

   *Store the buttercrunch out of direct sunlight. Whereas chocolate truffles and bonbons are stored chilled, toffees and caramels cannot be because the sugar will eventually liquefy and lose its shape.*

**The toffee will keep in an airtight container in a cool, dark place for up to a week.**

**PREP TIME:** under 15 minutes
**COOK TIME:** 2 hours

**❗ SIMPLE**

**BITES OF WISDOM:**
*How to whip egg whites (p. 34)*

**INGREDIENTS**

**5** large egg whites

**1½ cups (300 g)** granulated sugar

**Pinch** of fine salt

**2 Tbsp (15 g)** Dutch-process cocoa powder

# Giant Chocolate Meringues

These fluffy dollops of swirled chocolate meringue are just like the ones you see in pastry shop windows. What sets confectionery meringues apart from the ones used in other desserts like the Pineapple & Pink Peppercorn Pavlova (p. 322) is the amount of sugar. These ones are sweeter, and the additional sugar helps the outside of the meringue set up crisp yet tender, yielding to a slightly chewy, soft centre.

1. **Preheat the oven** to 225°F (107°C) and line a baking tray with parchment paper.

2. **Heat the egg whites and sugar.** Whisk the egg whites, sugar and salt together in a metal bowl placed over a pot filled with an inch (2.5 cm) of gently simmering water. Warm the eggs to no more than 98°F (37°C), which helps the sugar to dissolve better as you whip the meringue.

   *Warming the egg whites with the sugar fully dissolves the sugar, which gives the meringue its structure.*

3. **Whip the egg whites.** Transfer the warmed egg whites and sugar to a stand mixer fitted with the whip attachment or use electric beaters to whip the whites to a stiff peak on high speed. Sift the cocoa powder overtop (1) and fold it into the meringue, but only partly—you want to see streaks and ribbons of the cocoa powder and not have it fully mixed in (2).

   *Because these crisp meringues have a high sugar-to-egg ratio (sugar is double the weight of the eggs) it takes longer for the whites to reach a stiff peak and you really can't overwhip them. Sugar stabilizes a meringue, so resist any temptation to reduce the amount of sugar in the recipe—any less sugar and the meringues may collapse or crumble.*

4. **Portion and bake.** Use two large kitchen spoons to make six big dollops of meringue on the baking tray (3). Bake the meringues for 2 hours, until they lift easily away from the parchment paper. Cool the meringues on the tray on a rack.

   **The meringues will keep in an airtight container at room temperature for 1 week.**

**MAKES:** 30 large marshmallows

**PREP TIME:** 30 minutes, plus setting

**COOK TIME:** 6 minutes

🍴 **MORE INVOLVED**

**BITES OF WISDOM:**
*Gelatin powder or sheet substitutes (p. 16)*

**INGREDIENTS**

1½ Tbsp (12 g) gelatin powder

6 Tbsp (90 mL) cold water

1 Tbsp (5 g) meringue powder

1½ cups (375 mL) pure maple syrup

2 tsp vanilla extract

¼ tsp fine salt

Equal parts icing sugar and cornstarch mixed together, for dusting

# Maple Marshmallows

Homemade marshmallows are lighter, fluffier and more flavourful than store-bought, and I love that the natural flavour of maple syrup really comes through in these ones. Enjoy them plain as a confection, dip them in tempered chocolate and give them as a gift, or melt them into s'mores.

1. **Prepare the "molds."** Have ready two cardboard paper towel tubes. Cut two sheets of parchment paper long and wide enough to fit inside the tubes. Using a piece of paper towel, lightly grease the parchment paper with vegetable oil and slide one piece inside each tube to line it.

2. **Soften the gelatin and meringue powder.** Stir together the gelatin powder and cold water in a large heatproof mixing bowl or in the bowl of a stand mixer fitted with the whip attachment. Let sit for 2 minutes and then stir in the meringue powder.

   *Meringue powder is simply dried and powdered egg whites mixed with corn-starch and other stabilizers. When I make marshmallows, I prefer this powder to fresh eggs because the marshmallows set better and stay fresh longer without any liquid from the egg.*

3. **Cook the maple syrup.** Measure the maple syrup into a large saucepan over high heat and bring to a full boil. Boil the syrup, without stirring, until it reaches 237°F (114°C) on a candy thermometer, about 6 minutes.

   *Be sure to use a large saucepan because the maple syrup will bubble up quite a bit as it cooks. It may also appear to let off puffs of smoke as it cooks, but don't worry, it is not burning . . . keep cooking until the syrup reaches 237°F (114°C).*

   *Although most of the maple syrup for sale is amber coloured, use dark maple syrup if you can. Either will work just fine, but darker syrup has a deeper colour and a more intense maple flavour.*

4. **Carefully add the hot syrup to the gelatin mixture.** With the mixer set on medium-high speed, slowly pour the sugar down the side of the bowl into the gelatin mixture. Once all of the syrup has been added, increase the speed to high and whip until the meringue cools to almost room temperature, about 4 minutes. Stir in the vanilla and salt.

*CONTINUES*

5. **Shape and cool the marshmallows.** Spoon the cooled marshmallow into a piping bag without a piping tip. Cut the opening to the piping bag about 1 inch (2.5 cm) across. Pipe enough marshmallow into the paper towel tubes to fill them completely. Allow the marshmallow to cool until completely set, about 2 hours.

*To make squares instead of cylinders, line an 8-inch (20 cm) square pan with parchment paper so that it comes up the sides. Using a piece of paper towel, lightly grease the parchment paper with vegetable oil. Scrape the marshmallow into the prepared pan and spread to level. Sift a layer of the icing sugar/cornstarch mixture overtop. Let the marshmallow set, about 2 hours. When set, gently invert the pan onto a cutting board and cut the marshmallow into squares.*

6. **Cut the marshmallow into rounds.** When the marshmallow has set, peel away the cardboard and parchment paper and dust the marshmallow with the icing sugar/cornstarch mixture. Use a paper towel to rub some vegetable oil onto a chef's knife and cut into individual rounds, wiping your knife after each cut.

7. **Finish the marshmallows.** Place the icing sugar mixture in a wide shallow bowl. Carefully roll each marshmallow in the sugar to coat all sides, then pack the marshmallows into an airtight container.

**The marshmallows will keep in an airtight container at room temperature for up to 10 days.**

**MAKES:** one 8 × 11-inch (20 × 28 cm) nougat (3 to 4 dozen pieces)

**PREP TIME:** 20 minutes, plus cooling
**COOK TIME:** 10 minutes

### ||| COMPLEX

**BITES OF WISDOM:**
*How to cook & caramelize sugar (p. 38),*
*How to whip egg whites (p. 34)*

### INGREDIENTS

1 cup (160 g) unsalted whole almonds, toasted

1 cup (135 g) whole hazelnuts, toasted and peeled

1 cup (125 g) unsalted shelled whole pistachios

1 cup (130 g) dried apricots, each one cut into 4 strips

½ cup (70 g) dried cherries or cranberries

½ cup (75 g) dried blueberries

¼ cup (60 g) cocoa butter or virgin coconut oil, melted

2 cups (400 g) granulated sugar, divided

2 tsp meringue powder

2 large egg whites

6 Tbsp (90 mL) water

½ cup (120 g) glucose syrup

¾ cup (225 g) honey

2 (8 × 11-inch/20 × 28 cm) sheets edible rice paper

# Montélimar Nougat

Nougat is a confection of nuts (and sometimes fruits) in a sugar paste, and it has been made in the town of Montélimar in the east of France since the 19th century. Shops in this region and nearby Provence specialize in only this style of nougat, which is traditionally made with almonds and flavoured with honey. Honey is still a key flavour ingredient, but the fruits and nuts can vary. The set meringue is light with a gentle "chew" to it, but nothing that will stick in your teeth.

1. **Preheat the oven** to 250°F (120°C). Toss the almonds, hazelnuts, pistachios, apricot slices, cherries (or cranberries) and blueberries together in a pan or pie plate and keep warm in the oven. Place the melted cocoa butter (or coconut oil) in a separate dish and keep warm in the oven.

   *The cocoa butter or coconut oil, glucose syrup and edible rice paper can be purchased at a specialty baking supply store or online.*

   *Warming the fruits and nuts makes them easier to fold into the nougat and then spread into the pan. Adding room-temperature items to the nougat would immediately start to set it.*

2. **Prepare the meringue ingredients.** Stir 2 Tbsp (25 g) sugar together with the meringue powder. Add this mixture and the egg whites to the bowl of a stand mixer fitted with the whip attachment or a large heatproof bowl if using electric beaters.

   *As with the Maple Marshmallows (p. 369), using meringue powder is about managing water content. Here, a mix of meringue powder (dried egg whites) and fresh egg whites strikes the perfect balance.*

3. **Combine the sugar and glucose.** Measure the water, remaining 1¾ cups + 2 Tbsp (375 g) sugar and the glucose into a medium saucepan and set aside.

4. **Cook the honey.** Measure the honey into a second medium saucepan and bring to a boil over high heat, uncovered and without stirring, until it reaches 226°F (108°C). At this point, start whipping the egg whites on high speed.

   *Orange blossom or chestnut honey is commonly used to make nougat in Provence. Both have a beautiful aroma when heated. Regular wildflower honey is just as delicious.*

   *Cooking the sugar and honey separately makes for a fluffy yet sliceable nougat that holds its shape. The sugar cooks to the hard crack stage, ensuring the candy will set fully. The honey cooks to the thread stage, ensuring the nougat will be pliable and easy to eat.*

CONTINUES

5. **Add the honey to the meringue but keep cooking the sugar.** Continue cooking the honey to 248°F (120°C)—this will take only a minute. Immediately remove the honey from the heat and carefully pour it into the egg whites while they whip. Keep the whites whipping while you bring the pot with the sugar to a full boil over high heat, uncovered and without stirring. Cook the sugar until it reaches 311°F (155°C). Immediately yet carefully pour the sugar down the side of the bowl into the whipping meringue and continue to whip for about 3 minutes, just to cool it down a little.

6. **Pour the warm melted cocoa butter (or coconut oil) into the whipping nougat.** The mixture may appear to separate a little at first, but keep whipping and the cocoa butter will blend in.

7. **Stir in the nuts and fruits by hand,** coating them fully (2). Place a sheet of the rice paper onto a baking tray. Spoon the nougat on top of the rice paper and spread to level it as much as possible, keeping within the boundaries of the paper as best as you can. Place the second rice paper sheet on top of the nougat and press gently so it adheres (3).

8. **Let the nougat cool for at least 2 hours** before cutting. Use a sharp chef's knife to slice the nougat into pieces. Place the nougat between layers of parchment paper in an airtight container or wrap the nougat pieces individually to store.

**The nougat will keep at room temperature for up to 3 weeks.**

# Cookies
# & Bars

# Recipes at a Glance

Who doesn't like cookies and bars? Whether they are round, rectangular or square, involve a great deal of mastery to make (Macarons, p. 390) or very little (Chewy Brownie Cookies, p. 381), these small bites are a source of comfort for many of us. They're among the first recipes we learn to make when we're kids, and they're the ones we go to again and again for snacks, last-minute desserts or impromptu gifts. They bring back memories and they create new ones.

The recipes in each of the following sections are arranged from simplest to complex.

## Drop Cookies

These cookies earn their title because of the way their batter is dropped by spoonfuls onto the baking tray, melting and baking into flat round cookies from that initial shape.

## Shaped or Filled Cookies

Taking the time to cut, shape or assemble filled cookies elevates them, making this style of cookie ideal for the holiday cookie tin or sharing. This doesn't mean that making these cookies takes much longer than drop cookies, but the presentation is a little more polished.

## Fancy Cookies

Making a specialty cookie can be as involved as making an elaborate pastry. The technique and presentation factor into the effort required, but the result is fantastic. Macarons are the epitome of fancy cookies, with their colourful shells and inventive fillings, and the lacy, delicate Florentine is as delicious as it is beautiful. These two recipes definitely fit into the "fancy" category, but although the way they're made is dramatically different, the satisfaction you get is identical.

## Bars & Squares

These sweet treats are very versatile—they can fit into a holiday cookie tin, they can be cut into large portions and served as a dessert or they can be cut into dainty portions to serve with tea or coffee. Flavours and styles can be everything from tart and lemony to rich and chocolaty, but what squares and bars share is that they are baked in a pan (rather than on a baking tray) and then portioned after baking.

**Sugar Cookies with Sprinkles**
Page 378

**Chewy Brownie Cookies**
Page 381

**Peanut Butter Banana Cookies**
Page 382

**MAKES:** about 2 dozen cookies

**PREP TIME:** 15 minutes
**COOK TIME:** 12 minutes

❧ **SIMPLE**

**BITES OF WISDOM:**
*How to melt chocolate (p. 41)*

**INGREDIENTS**

---

**1 cup (250 mL)** candy sprinkles, for decorating

**2 oz (60 g)** white baking/couverture chocolate, chopped

**½ cup (115 g)** unsalted butter, at room temperature

**½ cup (100 g)** granulated sugar

**½ cup (65 g)** icing sugar

**1** large egg

**2 tsp** vanilla extract

**1⅔ cups (250 g)** all-purpose flour

**2 Tbsp (15 g)** cornstarch

**1 tsp** baking soda

**½ tsp** fine salt

# Sugar Cookies with Sprinkles

These classic sugar cookies are guaranteed to brighten anyone's day. They're easy to make, and the colourful sprinkles provide a little crunch and a whole lot of joy.

1. **Preheat the oven** to 350°F (180°C) and line two baking trays with parchment paper. Place the candy sprinkles in a wide shallow dish.

2. **Melt the white chocolate** in a metal bowl set over a pot of barely simmering water, stirring gently until melted. Set aside to cool (but using it while still a little warm is OK).

   *The white chocolate adds sweetness and moisture to this cookie, keeping the centre nice and soft.*

3. **Cream the butter, granulated sugar and icing sugar** together until smooth. Add the egg and vanilla, beating well. Stir in the white chocolate.

   *The batter won't be smooth after you add the egg, but once you stir in the white chocolate, the batter will smooth out.*

4. **Sift in the flour, cornstarch, baking soda and salt** and stir until well blended. Scoop a tablespoonful of dough and roll between your palms to form a ball. Roll each ball in sprinkles to coat it completely and set it on the baking tray. Repeat with the remaining dough, leaving 2 inches (5 cm) between each cookie.

   *Most sprinkles are designed to hold their shape and colour in the oven, but some do bleed or melt. You might want to test-bake a cookie to see how the sprinkles behave before rolling them all.*

5. **Bake the cookies** for about 12 minutes, until they are lightly browned on the bottom. Remove the trays from the oven and immediately smack them against the counter, to collapse the cookies. Cool the cookies on their trays on a rack.

**The cookies will keep in an airtight container at room temperature for up to 3 days.**

**MAKES:** 24 cookies

**PREP TIME:** 15 minutes, plus chilling
**COOK TIME:** 10 minutes

❗ SIMPLE

**BITES OF WISDOM:**
*How to melt chocolate (p. 41)*

## INGREDIENTS

---

**8 oz (240 g)** dark baking/couverture chocolate, chopped

**¼ cup (60 g)** unsalted butter, diced

**2** large eggs

**½ cup (100 g)** granulated sugar

**½ cup (100 g)** packed light brown sugar

**1 tsp** vanilla extract

**½ cup (75 g)** all-purpose flour

**¼ cup (30 g)** Dutch-process cocoa powder

**¼ tsp** baking powder

**¼ tsp** fine salt

**½ cup (85 g)** chocolate chips (white, milk or semisweet)

# Chewy Brownie Cookies

These moreish cookies have a lovely crackled satin surface that looks just like a well-made pan of chocolate brownies, and they have a chocolate flavour that's just as intense. Get that glass of cold milk ready!

1. **Preheat the oven** to 375°F (190°C) and line two baking trays with parchment paper.

2. **Melt the chocolate and butter** in a small metal bowl placed over a pot of barely simmering water, stirring gently until smooth. Set aside (but the chocolate can be used still warm).

   *You can use semisweet baking/couverture chocolate if you'd like a sweeter taste or bittersweet chocolate if you'd prefer a more intense chocolate flavour. The overall texture of the cookies will not change.*

3. **Whisk the wet ingredients.** In a large bowl, vigorously whisk the eggs, granulated sugar, brown sugar and vanilla by hand for a minute, until paler in colour. Whisk in the melted chocolate.

4. **Sift in the flour, cocoa powder, baking powder and salt** and stir to combine. Stir in the chocolate chips. The batter will be quite fluid, but if you let it rest for a minute or two, it will thicken up on its own. Scoop the cookies onto the trays, leaving 2 inches (5 cm) between them.

   *How long it takes the batter to thicken will depend on what kind of chocolate you use and how hot it was when melted. Let the batter cool long enough that you can scoop it easily, but don't chill it or the chocolate will set up and make the batter difficult to scoop.*

   *You can also make a crinkle cookie version of this recipe by rolling each cookie in icing sugar before placing onto the baking tray. The bake time remains the same.*

5. **Bake for 8 to 10 minutes,** until the cookies appear crackled on the surface. Remove from the oven and cool on the trays, on cooling racks, for 10 minutes. Lift the cookies onto the racks to cool completely.

   **The cookies will keep in an airtight container at room temperature for up to 5 days.**

**MAKES:** about 3 dozen cookies

**PREP TIME:** 15 minutes
**COOK TIME:** 12 minutes

❙ **SIMPLE**
**BITES OF WISDOM:**
*Glossary of baking tools—Ice cream scoops (p. 25)*

**INGREDIENTS**

---

½ **cup (115 g)** unsalted butter, at room temperature

¾ **cup (150 g)** packed light brown sugar

¼ **cup (50 g)** granulated sugar

¾ **cup (187 g)** smooth peanut butter

1 **cup (250 mL)** mashed very ripe banana (2 medium bananas)

1 **tsp** vanilla extract

2 **cups (300 g)** all-purpose flour

1 **Tbsp (8 g)** cornstarch

1 **tsp** baking soda

½ **tsp** fine salt

1 **cup (175 g)** chocolate chips (any flavour)

# Peanut Butter Banana Cookies

If you love the salty sweetness of peanut butter cookies, adding mashed banana to the batter takes them to the next level. Make this recipe if you have two ripe bananas sitting on your counter—they may not be enough for banana bread, but they're the perfect amount for a batch of these soft cookies.

1. **Preheat the oven** to 350°F (180°C) and line two baking trays with parchment paper.

2. **Cream the butter, brown sugar and granulated sugar** together by hand in a large mixing bowl. Beat in the peanut butter followed by the banana and vanilla.

   *Because of the moisture and structure from the bananas and the leavening from the baking soda, this cookie recipe has no eggs, but be sure that your bananas are very ripe in order to get the full banana flavour.*

3. **Stir the flour, cornstarch baking soda and salt** together and add to the batter, stirring until combined. Stir in the chocolate chips. Drop spoonfuls of batter onto the baking trays, leaving 2 inches (5 cm) between each cookie.

   *With peanut butter–based cookies, any chocolate chip or combination of flavoured chips will work: dark or white chocolate, peanut butter, butterscotch, sea salt caramel or toffee chips.*

   *I like to use a portion scoop (ice cream scoop) to get perfectly round cookies.*

4. **Bake the cookies** for about 12 minutes, until lightly browned at the edges. Remove from the oven and cool on the tray on a cooling rack.

   **The cookies will keep in an airtight container at room temperature for up to 3 days.**

**MAKES:** about 3½ dozen cookies

**PREP TIME:** 15 minutes
**COOK TIME:** 20 minutes

❗ SIMPLE

**BITES OF WISDOM:**
*Glossary of ingredients—Chocolate &
cocoa powder (p. 5)*

**INGREDIENTS**

1 cup (225 g) unsalted butter, at room
temperature

½ cup (65 g) icing sugar, plus extra for
dusting

2 Tbsp (30 mL) espresso coffee, cooled

2 tsp vanilla extract

2¼ cups (337 g) all-purpose flour

¼ cup (30 g) cocoa powder

¼ tsp fine salt

Granulated sugar, for coating

# Mocha Sablé Slices

I have been making these cookies for decades, and they always make it
onto my holiday baking list. Don't limit them to the holidays, though.
A variation of shortbread, they are tender, soft and rich without being
overly sweet—perfect with a cup of tea or coffee at any time.

1. **Preheat the oven** to 325°F (160°C) and line two baking trays with parchment
   paper.

2. **Beat the butter and icing sugar** together by hand or using electric beaters on
   medium speed. Stir in the espresso and vanilla.

3. **Sift in the all-purpose flour, cocoa powder and salt** and mix until the dough
   comes together.

   *While I prefer the flavour of Dutch-process cocoa powder for certain cakes and
   other chocolate recipes and the way it reacts (or doesn't) with leavenings,
   regular cocoa powder will work well in this recipe too.*

4. **Shape and slice the dough.** Lightly dust a work surface with icing sugar.
   Divide the dough into two pieces and shape them into logs about 12 inches
   (30 cm) long. Flatten each log with your hand, then use a sharp knife to cut
   each log on an angle into ½-inch (1.2 cm) slices. Stand the cookies upright on
   the baking trays, leaving at least an inch (2.5 cm) between them.

5. **Bake the cookies** for 20 minutes, until they lose their shine and can be lifted
   easily from the baking tray.

6. **Coat the cookies in sugar.** Place the granulated sugar in a wide shallow bowl.
   Gently toss the warm cookies, two at a time, in the sugar and transfer them to
   a wire rack to cool.

   **The sablés will keep in an airtight container at room temperature for up
   to 5 days.**

**MAKES:** about 4 dozen cookies

**PREP TIME:** 20 minutes, plus chilling
**COOK TIME:** 20 minutes

🍴 SIMPLE
**BITES OF WISDOM:**
*Glossary of ingredients—Nuts & seeds (p. 11)*

**INGREDIENTS**

---

**1⅔ cups (170 g)** untoasted walnut halves

**1⅔ cups (250 g)** all-purpose flour, divided

**1 cup (225 g)** unsalted butter, at room temperature

**½ cup (65 g)** icing sugar, plus extra for rolling the cookies

**2 tsp** vanilla extract

**½ tsp** fine salt

# Walnut Snowball Cookies

Sometimes called Russian tea cakes or Mexican wedding cookies, these tender and buttery little shortbread cookies are made with finely ground nuts. The cookies are shaped into balls and rolled in icing sugar, ensuring a snowstorm of powdered sugar on the front of your shirt with every bite.

1. **Pulse the walnuts** with ⅔ cup (100 g) flour in a food processor or mini chopper until the nuts are finely ground. Set aside.

   *Pulsing the nuts with flour will prevent the nuts from turning into a paste. You can certainly use the same measure of pecan halves or unsalted shelled pistachios if you wish.*

2. **Beat the butter and sugar.** Using beaters or a stand mixer fitted with the paddle attachment, beat the butter for a minute to fluff it up. Add the icing sugar, beating well on medium-high speed until fluffy again, scraping the bowl often. Beat in the vanilla.

3. **Add the dry ingredients.** Add the nut mixture, remaining 1 cup (150 g) flour and the salt and mix on low speed until the dough comes together.

4. **Portion the cookies.** Turn the dough out onto a work surface, knead into a ball and flatten it slightly. Cut the dough into four pieces and then divide each quarter into 12 little pieces. Shape each piece of dough into a ball between your palms and place onto a plate or tray. Chill the cookies for at least an hour before baking.

   *Chilling the cookie dough will help to ensure the cookies remain round when baked.*

5. **Preheat the oven** to 325°F (160°C) and line two large baking trays with parchment paper. Arrange the chilled cookies on the trays, leaving an inch (2.5 cm) between them.

6. **Bake the cookies** for about 20 minutes, until there is just a hint of browning on the bottom of the cookies. Let the cookies cool on the baking trays on a wire rack.

7. **Roll in icing sugar.** Place some icing sugar in a wide shallow bowl. After the cookies are completely cooled, roll them in the sugar to coat them generously.

   *Make sure the cookies have cooled completely before rolling them in the icing sugar, otherwise the sugar will melt and the surface of the cookies will be sticky. Do not roll the baked cookies in the sugar if you plan to freeze them. (Roll them in sugar after you've thawed them.)*

**The cookies will keep in an airtight container at room temperature for up to 2 weeks.**

**MAKES:** about 2 dozen filled cookies

**PREP TIME:** 40 minutes, plus chilling
**COOK TIME:** 10 minutes

🍴 **MORE INVOLVED**
**BITES OF WISDOM:**
*How to roll pastry doughs (p. 44)*

**INGREDIENTS**

1 cup (225 g) unsalted butter, at room temperature

¾ cup (150 g) granulated sugar

2 tsp finely grated lemon zest

4 large egg yolks

1 tsp vanilla extract

1⅓ cups (200 g) all-purpose flour

1 cup (120 g) cornstarch

1 tsp baking powder

½ tsp fine salt

½ cup (50 g) unsweetened shredded coconut

1¼ cups (310 mL) store-bought or 1 (10 oz/300 mL) tin Dulce de Leche (p. 90)

# Alfajores

These sandwich cookies are well known throughout South America, where there are a few variations. The tender discs of delicate shortbread joined by sweet Dulce de Leche (p. 90) and dusted with shredded coconut are especially typical in Argentina. Once you've tried one, you'll know exactly why they are so popular. Be sure to use a thicker, darker dessert version of dulce de leche for the filling.

1. **Beat the butter and sugar together.** Using electric beaters or a stand mixer fitted with the paddle attachment, beat the butter with the sugar and lemon zest until smooth and fluffy. Add the egg yolks and vanilla and beat in well.

2. **Add the flour, cornstarch, baking powder and salt** and mix on low speed until fully combined. Shape the dough into two discs, wrap and chill until firm, at least an hour or up to 3 days.

*The cornstarch in most alfajor dough recipes is the secret to the delicate and tender cookies.*

3. **Preheat the oven** to 325°F (160°C) and line two baking trays with parchment paper.

4. **Roll and cut the cookies.** Lightly dust a work surface with flour. Gently knead the first disc of dough to soften it. Roll out the dough to just under ¼ inch (6 mm) thick, then use a 2-inch (5 cm) round cookie cutter to cut rounds from the dough. Transfer these cookies to the baking trays, leaving an inch (2.5 cm) between them. Repeat with the remaining disc of dough, rerolling any scraps.

5. **Bake the cookies** for about 10 minutes, until the bottoms just barely turn brown (be careful when lifting them; they are delicate). Let the cookies cool on their trays on a rack before filling.

6. **Assemble the cookies.** Fill a wide shallow bowl with the coconut. Spread about 2 tsp dulce de leche on the bottom of one cookie, spreading it almost to the edges. Set a second cookie onto the filling, pressing gently. Gently spread a little extra dulce de leche, or any drips that may squeeze out from the filling, around the sides of the alfajor. Roll this outside edge in the coconut and set on a tray or plate to dry. Repeat with remaining cookies. Allow the alfajores to air-dry for 2 hours before packing them into a cookie tin or airtight container.

*These cookies soften a little after they sit for a day in a cookie tin because of the moisture of the dulce de leche.*

**Assembled cookies will keep in an airtight container at room temperature for up to 5 days, in the fridge for 2 weeks and frozen for 3 months. Thaw before serving.**

**MAKES:** 3 dozen macarons (6 dozen individual cookies)

**PREP TIME:** 40 minutes, plus cooling
**COOK TIME:** 15 minutes

||| COMPLEX
**BITES OF WISDOM:**
*How to whip egg whites (p. 34), How to use piping bags & tips (p. 52)*

**INGREDIENTS**

---

**Macaron shells:**

**250 g** Tant pour Tant (p. 82)

**50 g** icing sugar

**125 g** egg whites (about 4)

**100 g** granulated sugar

Food colouring powder or paste

**French buttercream filling:**

**3 Tbsp (45 mL)** 2% milk

**3 Tbsp (37 g)** granulated sugar

**2** large egg yolks

**½ cup (115 g)** unsalted butter, at room temperature

**1 tsp** pure vanilla extract

Flavours and colours (optional)

# Macarons

Making perfect macarons takes patience and practice. Over the years I've tried many methods to obtain round tender almond meringues with a smooth satin top and a ruffled "foot" below. I began with the French method of simply whipping egg whites and sugar together, and then I found more consistent results with the Italian method of cooking sugar and pouring it into the egg whites to stabilize the meringue. My go-to these days is the Swiss method, which produces flawless macarons every time. By warming the sugar and egg whites together before whipping, similar to making a Swiss buttercream, I get a meringue that's strong and flexible and gives me more control as I fold, stir, pipe and bake the macaron shells. Even though I use the Swiss method for making the macaron shells, I fill them with a French buttercream.

While macarons call for few ingredients, precise measurement is key, which is why this recipe lists the measurements only in grams, and does not also include volume measures or imperial weights.

1. **Prepare three baking trays.** Cut one sheet of parchment paper for each baking tray and one longer sheet for a piping template. The extra length gives you a "handle" with which to pull this sheet out from beneath your top parchment after you've piped your macarons. On this template parchment, use a marker to trace circles 1½ inches (4 cm) across and at least 1 inch (2.5 cm) apart. Place this sheet on a baking tray and cover it with one of the smaller sheets of parchment.

   *If you plan to make macarons regularly, invest in silicone baking mats with the macaron template printed on them. They will save you time tracing and sliding the parchment paper around.*

2. **Make the macaron base.** Pulse the tant pour tant and icing sugar in a mini chopper or food processor until well combined. Set aside.

   *I learned about tant pour tant while researching the Swiss method for making macarons, and now it is one of my pantry staples. Pulsing the tant pour tant and the extra icing sugar is the key to a macaron shell with a smooth top and a soft centre.*

3. **Make the Swiss meringue.** Bring an inch (2.5 cm) of water to a gentle simmer over medium heat in a small pot. Whisk the egg whites and granulated sugar together in a metal bowl and set it over the pot, whisking constantly but not vigorously until the meringue reaches 150°F (65°C). Remove the bowl from the heat. Using electric beaters or a stand mixer fitted with the whip attachment, whip the egg whites on high speed until they hold a stiff peak but are still warm (this does not take too long).

   *Warming the sugar and egg whites together dissolves the sugar and loosens the proteins in the egg whites, allowing them to whip to full volume. The result is a stable and well-structured meringue with movement, which is essential for the macaronage step that follows.*

*CONTINUES*

Fillings: French buttercream,
and Raspberry Jelly Candy
(p. 336)

4. **Fold the macaron base into the meringue.** Sprinkle a third of the almond mixture over the whites and fold in well (1, 2, 3). Add the remaining almonds in two additions, folding well after each. Stir in just a touch of food colouring if desired (4) and continue to fold (the macaronage) until the batter flows off your spatula in a sheet (5).

*When making macarons, use food colouring powders and concentrated pastes rather than liquid food colouring, which can change the consistency of the batter. Note that the colours become more intense as the batter sits.*

*The macaronage (folding) is the most challenging step because experience is your best guide (not helpful if this is your first try at macarons). The best advice I can give is to fold the batter a few times, stop and lift your spatula to see how the batter falls off it. "Sheeting" is the term to describe the consistency of the perfect macaron batter: the batter should slide off the spatula in a sheet but not appear runny, and it should build up onto itself in the mixing bowl and not disappear into a flat mass of batter. If it falls off in big bits, then fold two to three more times and check again. As you get close to the batter flowing off in a sheet, it will become glossier.*

5. **Pipe the macaron shells.** Spoon the batter into a piping bag fitted with a ½-inch (1.2 cm) plain tip. Using the template as a guide, hold the tip of the piping bag straight down and quite close to the parchment and completely fill each circle just to its edge with batter (6). Once you've finished piping the first tray, gently slip the template from beneath the sheet of macarons. Set the template on the second tray, cover it with the remaining sheet of parchment paper and continue piping. Repeat with the third tray.

*When piping, hold the tip and the bag perpendicular to the tray to let gravity do the work. The batter should flow without you having to apply much pressure to the piping bag. When you move from piping one macaron to the next one, quickly lift the tip up and at least 90 degrees from the tray to stop the batter flowing.*

6. **Dry the macaron shells.** Let the almond meringues set for 45 minutes to 1 hour to develop a "skin" on their surface. Touch the top of the macarons gently with your finger; the surface will be losing its lustre slightly, going from shiny to satin, and it should not be sticky.

7. **Preheat the oven** to 325°F (160°C).

8. **Bake the macarons** for 12 to 15 minutes, until you can gently but easily loosen and lift them from the baking tray. Remove them from the oven, and carefully lift the parchment paper from the pan and set it on a wire rack to let the macarons cool completely. Once cooled, gently peel the macarons from the paper. Discard the parchment paper. If you are not using the macarons immediately, store them, unfilled, in an airtight container at room temperature (do not refrigerate).

*My late dear friend and extraordinarily talented pastry chef Philippe Corbière told me that at Lenôtre in Paris, which is famous for its macarons, the bakers run cold water between the parchment paper and baking tray when the macaron shells come out of the oven, to stop the cooking. That notion terrifies me because a drop of water on the wrong side of the paper could ruin the whole batch, but quickly pulling the macaron shells off the baking tray and onto a rack helps them cool without becoming sticky.*

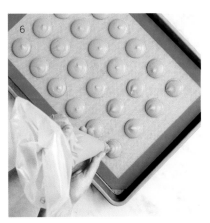

9. **Make the custard base for the buttercream.** Place the milk, sugar and egg yolks in a small saucepan over medium heat. Gently whisk until the milk thickens and coats the back of a spoon, about 5 minutes. Remove the pan from the heat and pour the custard through a fine-mesh sieve into a bowl. Place a piece of plastic wrap directly on the surface of the custard to prevent a skin from forming and let cool completely to room temperature. (If you make the custard ahead and chill it after cooling, be sure to bring it back to room temperature before completing the buttercream.)

10. **Finish the buttercream.** Once the custard has cooled, use electric beaters or a stand mixer fitted with the whip attachment to beat the butter on high speed to soften it. Reduce the speed to medium and add the custard gradually, stopping occasionally to scrape down the sides of the bowl. If the buttercream looks curdled, simply increase the speed to high after all the custard has been added and the buttercream will smooth out (this could take 1 to 3 minutes). Once smooth, stir in the vanilla, and any other flavourings or colourings as desired.

*Add flavourings using extracts, freeze-dried powders or citrus zest. You can even fill the macarons with piped butter ganache (p. 346) or a disc of Raspberry Jelly Candy (p. 336). The colour of the macaron shells often hints at the flavour inside, but that's certainly not a rule.*

11. **Assemble the macarons.** Spoon the buttercream into a small piping bag fitted with a ½-inch (1.2 cm) plain tip. Pipe a dot of buttercream (about 1½ tsp) onto the flat side of a macaron shell and gently press a second one, flat side down, onto the buttercream to make a "sandwich." To avoid crushing the delicate macarons, try to hold them by their edges rather than pressing down on their tops. Chill the macarons until ready to serve.

**The macarons will keep in an airtight container in the fridge for up to a week. Allow them to come to room temperature to serve. They can also be frozen for up to 3 months, but are very fragile, so pack them carefully.**

**MAKES:** about 4 dozen cookies

**PREP TIME:** 50 minutes
**COOK TIME:** 16 minutes

♨ **COMPLEX**
**BITES OF WISDOM:**
*How to cook & caramelize sugar (p. 38)*

**INGREDIENTS**

---

**1½ cups (165 g)** untoasted sliced almonds

**¼ cup (35 g)** finely chopped dried cranberries or dried cherries

**2 tsp** finely grated orange zest

**½ cup + 2 Tbsp (125 g)** granulated sugar

**¼ cup (75 g)** honey

**⅓ cup (80 mL)** whipping cream

**5 oz (150 g)** tempered dark baking/couverture chocolate (p. 42) (optional)

# Classic Florentine Cookies

Although the batter for these lacy almond and dried-fruit cookies seems more candy-like, Florentines are baked into their perfect round shapes like a cookie. The added step of brushing the bottoms with tempered chocolate makes the cookies more durable (and tasty), but it is not essential.

1. **Preheat the oven** to 350°F (180°C). Line a baking tray with a silicone baking mat.

2. **Prepare the fillings.** Place the sliced almonds in a resealable bag and crush them a little using a rolling pin or even your hands. Toss them with the dried cranberries (or cherries) and orange zest and set aside.

*Because the Florentines bake so flat, the almonds are exposed to the heat of the oven and toast up as the cookies bake, so there is no need to pretoast them.*

3. **Cook the sugar batter.** Place the sugar, honey and whipping cream in a small saucepan and bring to a full boil over high heat while stirring. Boil and stir until the mixture reaches 244°F (118°C) on a candy thermometer, 3 to 4 minutes. Remove the pot from the heat, stir in the almond mixture and transfer to a bowl to cool for about 15 minutes, until the batter is no longer fluid.

4. **Portion the Florentines.** Have a bowl of cool water on hand as well as a 2½-inch (6.5 cm) round cookie cutter. Drop small teaspoonfuls of the almond batter onto the prepared baking tray, leaving at least 3 to 4 inches (7.5 to 10 cm) in between (1). With wet fingers, press down the almond batter a little.

*Test-bake a single Florentine to get a sense of how much the batter expands as the cookie bakes. You may be surprised at how much barely 1 tsp of batter can spread—over two inches (5 cm)! Adjust the portion size and spacing of your scoops of batter accordingly.*

5. **Bake the Florentines** for about 12 minutes, until they have flattened and browned evenly (you may find rotating the pan halfway through baking promotes even browning). Let the Florentines sit for 1 to 2 minutes to set a little (but not fully).

6. **Shape the cookies.** Dip the cookie cutter in the cool water and press it into each cookie to cut a precise circle (2). Allow the cookies to cool fully on the baking tray. When cool, use a palette knife to gently lift the cookies off the tray, carefully pulling away the trimmings (3). Repeat with the remaining batter (and keep the cookie trimmings to sprinkle over ice cream or stir into a cheesecake batter).

7. **Coat with chocolate.** Line a baking tray with parchment paper. Use a pastry brush to brush an even layer of the tempered chocolate onto the back of each Florentine and place on the lined tray to set. Pop the tray in the fridge for 3 to 5 minutes for a final "cure" or set. Pack the Florentines between layers of parchment paper in an airtight container and store in a cool place.

**The Florentines will keep at room temperature for up to a week. Do not freeze.**

**MAKES:** one 9-inch (23 cm) square pan (16 to 25 squares)

**PREP TIME:** under 15 minutes
**COOK TIME:** 30 minutes

**SIMPLE**
BITES OF WISDOM:
*Portioning baked goods—Bars (p. 74)*

**INGREDIENTS**

1 cup (225 g) unsalted butter, melted and cooled

1 cup (200 g) packed light brown sugar

½ cup (100 g) granulated sugar

2 large eggs

2 tsp vanilla extract

2¼ cups (337 g) all-purpose flour

¼ cup (30 g) cornstarch

¾ tsp baking soda

¾ tsp fine salt

1½ cups (263 g) chocolate chips

# Chewy Chocolate Chip Cookie Bars

I love these bars when you want to fill a CCC (chocolate chip cookie) need but you don't have the time, patience or volunteers to help you scoop cookies. Super chewy, these bars are easy to slice and they freeze fantastically well, too.

1. **Preheat the oven** to 350°F (180°C). Lightly grease and line a 9-inch (23 cm) square pan with parchment paper so that the paper comes up the sides.

2. **Combine the butter and sugar.** Whisk the melted butter with the brown and granulated sugars. Whisk in the eggs and vanilla.

3. **Sift in the flour, cornstarch, baking soda and salt** and stir until evenly combined. Stir in the chocolate chips. Scrape the batter into the prepared pan and spread to level it.

   *Cornstarch is the secret to the chewy centre of my signature chocolate chip cookies, and it also keeps these bars nice and chewy.*

4. **Bake the square** for about 30 minutes, until it starts to rise at the edges. Cool in the pan on a rack, then use the parchment paper to lift the square out of the pan and cut into squares.

   **The bars will keep, well wrapped, in the fridge for up to 5 days or frozen for up to 3 months.**

**MAKES:** one 8-inch (20 cm) square pan
(16 to 25 squares)

**PREP TIME:** under 15 minutes, plus chilling
**COOK TIME:** 45 minutes

⌀ **SIMPLE**
**BITES OF WISDOM:**
*Portioning baked goods—Bars (p. 74)*

### INGREDIENTS

**1 double recipe** Almond Streusel (p. 82),
unbaked

**1½ cups (375 mL)** of your favourite fruit
jam: raspberry, strawberry, apricot or
other

Icing sugar, for dusting

# Almond Streusel Jam Squares

The versatility of the Almond Streusel (p. 82) continues. Not only is it used as a topping for tarts and cakes, it can also be the foundation for squares. Here the streusel is both pressed into the pan to make a sliceable but sturdy base for these jam squares and sprinkled over the top as a crumbly topping.

1. **Preheat the oven** to 325°F (160°C). Lightly grease and line an 8-inch (20 cm) square pan with parchment paper so that the paper comes up the sides.

2. **Assemble the square.** Spoon two-thirds of the almond streusel into the pan and press into the corners and the base. Spread the jam over the base to cover evenly. Crumble the remaining streusel overtop, covering the jam completely.

   *I love to make these squares in the spring, when I realize that I have to use up last year's stash of homemade jam before the new fruit season begins.*

3. **Bake the square** for about 45 minutes, until the streusel is a light golden brown.

4. **Cool the square** in the pan on a rack completely and then chill for at least 2 hours before dusting with icing sugar and slicing the pan into squares.

   **The squares will keep in an airtight container in the fridge for up to a week.**

**MAKES:** one 9 × 13-inch (23 × 33 cm) pan (24 brownies)

**PREP TIME:** 15 minutes
**COOK TIME:** 30 minutes

❙ **SIMPLE**
**BITES OF WISDOM:**
*How to melt chocolate (p. 41), Portioning baked goods—Bars (p. 74)*

**INGREDIENTS**

10 oz (300 g) dark baking/couverture chocolate, chopped

1 cup (225 g) unsalted butter, cut into pieces

6 large eggs, at room temperature

2 cups (400 g) granulated sugar

1 cup (150 g) all-purpose flour

⅔ cup (80 g) Dutch-process cocoa powder

¾ tsp fine salt

¾ cup (187 g) peanut butter

½ cup (125 mL) raspberry or strawberry jam

# Peanut Butter & Jam Chocolate Brownies

I have created a fair number of brownie recipes over the years, and it seems that whichever is the most recent becomes my favourite. So true to form, this brownie recipe is my new top pick. Rich, dense and fudgy, these brownies are made more decadent by swirls of peanut butter and jam throughout.

1. **Preheat the oven** to 375°F (190°C). Grease a 9 × 13-inch (23 × 33 cm) pan and line it with parchment paper so that the paper comes up the sides.

2. **Melt the chocolate and butter** together in a small pot over low heat, stirring until melted. Set aside to cool slightly while preparing the other ingredients.

3. **Whip the eggs and sugar** using electric beaters or a stand mixer fitted with the whip attachment until the mixture holds a ribbon when the beaters are lifted, about 5 minutes.

   *Most brownie batters are mixed by hand to keep the brownies dense and moist. In this recipe, I whip the eggs and sugar to balance the weight of the peanut butter and jam that I swirl in before baking. You can still expect a dense and chewy brownie with a nicely crackled top.*

4. **Add the chocolate and dry ingredients.** Pour the melted chocolate into the batter and whisk in by hand. Sift the flour, cocoa powder and salt overtop and fold in with a spatula until evenly combined. Scrape the batter into the prepared pan and spread to level it.

5. **Swirl in the peanut butter and jam.** Stir the peanut butter and dollop over the brownies. Stir the jam to loosen it and dollop it on top. Use a butter knife to swirl the peanut butter and jam throughout the batter. Don't be afraid to really pull the knife through the brownie batter, not just over the surface.

6. **Bake the brownie** for about 30 minutes, until it begins to rise at the edges. Cool the brownie completely in the pan. When cool, use the parchment paper to lift the brownie onto a cutting board and slice into 24 bars.

**The brownies will keep, well wrapped, at room temperature for up to 5 days.**

**MAKES:** one 9-inch (23 cm) square pan (24 bars)

**PREP TIME:** 20 minutes, plus chilling
**COOK TIME:** 50 minutes

🍴 **MORE INVOLVED**
**BITES OF WISDOM:**
*Glossary of ingredients—Citrus (p. 6), Portioning baked goods—Bars (p. 74)*

**INGREDIENTS**

**Crust:**

**1½ cups (225 g)** all-purpose flour

**6 Tbsp (48 g)** icing sugar

**2 tsp** finely grated lemon zest

**½ tsp** fine salt

**½ cup (115 g)** unsalted butter, cold

**Filling:**

**1¼ cups (250 g)** granulated sugar

**¼ cup (37 g)** all-purpose flour

**1 Tbsp (15 mL)** finely grated lemon zest

**⅔ cup (160 mL)** fresh lemon juice

**⅓ cup (80 mL)** sour cream or Crème Fraîche (p. 94)

**4** large eggs

**¾ cup (95 g)** fresh blueberries

Icing sugar, for dusting

# Lemon Blueberry Bars

I love a pucker-worthy lemon bar, and the addition of fresh blueberries is a magical match for the creamy yet tart lemon filling. These bars can definitely be served in larger portions as a dessert.

1. **Preheat the oven** to 350°F (180°C). Lightly grease a 9-inch (23 cm) square pan and line it with parchment paper so the paper comes up the sides.

2. **Make the crust.** Stir the flour, icing sugar, lemon zest and salt together in a mixing bowl. Use a box grater to grate in the cold butter and use a pastry cutter or your fingertips to work the butter into the dry ingredients until you have a fine, sandy mixture. Alternatively, you can pulse the butter into the flour using a food processor. Tip the crust mixture into the pan, and using the back of a spoon, press it into the bottom and up against the sides just a little. Bake the crust for about 20 minutes, until it begins to brown a bit at the edges.

3. **While the crust bakes, prepare the filling.** Whisk the sugar, flour and lemon zest together in a medium bowl. Whisk the lemon juice and sour cream (or crème fraîche) in a small bowl to combine, then add to the sugar, whisking well. Whisk in the eggs until smooth and evenly combined.

4. **Pour the filling onto the hot crust.** When the crust comes out of the oven, pour the filling over the still-hot crust.

   *I find that pouring the filling onto the hot crust starts to cook the filling immediately, which helps prevent it from leaking around the edges (a common issue with lemon bars) and softens the base ever so slightly so that, once cooled, the bars slice without crumbling.*

   *Fresh blueberries are definitely preferred over frozen or dried in this recipe, to retain their shape and colour during baking. Of course, you can omit the blueberries for a classic plain lemon bar.*

5. **Bake the bar** for 15 minutes and then sprinkle the blueberries overtop. Continue baking for an additional 10 to 15 minutes, until the filling is set when the pan is gently jiggled. If the filling rises up at the edges, turn down the oven temperature to 325°F (160°C). Cool in the pan on a rack and then chill for at least 4 hours before cutting into bars.

**The bars will keep in an airtight container or loosely wrapped in the fridge for up to 4 days.**

# Breads

# Recipes at a Glance

Yeasted baked goods provide fulfillment on multiple levels: the bread maker gets the satisfaction of coaxing the yeast dough to life and kneading and shaping it. And everyone in the house gets to enjoy the unmistakable slightly sweet and toasty smell of bread baking followed by the first warm slices fresh from the oven.

All of the breads in this chapter are yeast breads. Some are savoury, some sweet, some earthy and wholesome; others are rich with butter and eggs; and a few are even served as dessert. Learning about yeast and the steps involved in rising dough are key to all of these recipes, so once you master one, you can take on the others with confidence.

## Slow-rise Breads

These "lean" doughs are based on water, yeast and flour. Allowing them plenty of time to ferment helps to develop a deep flavour and a crackling or richly browned crust once baked.

## Enriched Breads

Bread doughs made with dairy, eggs and sometimes sugar are soft, tender and often very fluffy. These enriched doughs are easier to handle than lean yeast doughs and they are forgiving if under- or over-kneaded. The end result is a tender, golden-brown crust that yields to a soft, finely bubbled crumb within.

## Babas & Savarins

The one-of-a-kind dough used to make babas and savarins is rich in eggs and butter. It is an extremely soft dough with a lot of yeast, so it proofs and bakes with a tremendously airy texture. These breads are meant to be soaked in a syrup before filling and serving.

## Brioches

Like the baba dough, brioche dough is made with lots of butter and eggs, but the proportion of these two ingredients is far greater. Making brioche dough is almost like making a cake batter, except yeast gives brioche its bread-like texture. This style of bread is remarkably versatile: it can be baked up as a simple loaf or burger buns, filled with fruit and glazed like a pastry or laminated like a croissant dough. One of my favourite brioche recipes, the Fougasse Aigues-Mortes (p. 444), brings back memories of visits to the south of France, where the dough is accented with orange blossom water and sprinkled with sugar, much to my (and hopefully your) delight.

SLOW-RISE BREADS ▶

**Farmhouse Oat & Whole Wheat Loaf**
Page 410

**Robert's Rhubarb Rye Bread**
Page 413

**Stromboli**
Page 416

**Ricotta, Dill & Onion Buns**
Page 419

ENRICHED BREADS ▶

**Foundation: Soft Egg Dough**
Page 420

**Soft Cinnamon Knots**
Page 423

**Apple Cinnamon Pull-apart Bread**
Page 424

**Garlic Cheese Pull-apart Bundt Bread**
Page 427

**Swedish Semlor**
Page 428

**Holiday Stollen**
Page 431

BABAS & SAVARINS ▶

**Rum Babas**
Page 433

**Icewine Berry Savarins**
Page 437

BRIOCHES ▶

**Foundation: Classic Brioche Dough**
Page 438

**Brioche Loaf** (*plus Bonus Bake: Brioche Buns*)  Page 440

**Chocolate Hazelnut Laminated Brioches with Cardamom & Orange**
Page 441

**Fougasse Aigues-Mortes**
Page 444

**MAKES:** 1 large farmhouse boule or 2 smaller loaves

**PREP TIME:** under 15 minutes, plus proofing and cooling

**COOK TIME:** 1 hour

🍴 **MORE INVOLVED**

**BITES OF WISDOM:**
*Glossary of ingredients—Yeast (p. 11), Glossary of ingredients—Flours (p. 7), Glossary of baking actions—Proof (p. 31), How to troubleshoot other common baking issues—Breads (p. 60), Glossary of baking tools—Banneton (p. 25)*

### INGREDIENTS

1½ cups (150 g) regular rolled oats

1⅔ cups (250 g) whole wheat flour, divided

1¾ cups (425 mL) boiling water

¾ cup (175 mL) 2% milk, at room temperature

2 Tbsp (30 mL) vegetable oil

1 Tbsp (18 g) honey

2 cups (300 g) bread flour

1 (2¼ tsp/7 g) pkg instant dry yeast

1½ tsp fine sea salt

# Farmhouse Oat & Whole Wheat Loaf

Earthy but not at all heavy, this 100% wholegrain loaf is ideal for toasting, making sandwiches and especially for eating, still warm and slathered with butter and a sprinkle of salt. You can bake this bread as one giant round loaf (boule) in a cast-iron pot, but it is equally delicious baked as two smaller loaves on a baking tray.

1. **Soak the oats.** Combine all of the oats and ⅔ cup (100 g) whole wheat flour in a large mixing bowl or in the bowl of a stand mixer fitted with the hook attachment. Pour the boiling water over the grains and stir well—this will make a thick, stodgy paste (like porridge). Set aside to cool for 20 minutes.

   *This bread is delicious made with walnuts. Add 1 cup (100 g) walnut halves to the soaking liquid to soften them.*

2. **Mix and knead the dough.** Add the milk, oil and honey and mix until roughly combined. Add the bread flour, remaining 1 cup (150 g) whole wheat flour, yeast and salt and mix until the dough comes together. If using the mixer, continue to knead the dough on medium-low speed until it becomes elastic and pulls away from the sides of the bowl, about 5 minutes. If kneading by hand, lightly dust a work surface with flour (see tip), turn the dough out onto it and knead the dough until elastic, about 7 minutes.

   *The key to successfully kneading dough by hand is to not add too much flour when kneading. The dough will naturally be sticky when you start because the flour hasn't had time to absorb the water, nor have the proteins in the flour developed. When combining the dough, I hold back ⅓ cup (50 g) of the whole wheat flour listed in the ingredient list, and then I use that flour to dust my kneading surface. That trick makes the dough easier to knead and I know I am not adding extra flour. Halfway through kneading, the dough will start to become more taut and less sticky.*

3. **Proof the dough for 90 minutes.** Transfer the dough to an ungreased bowl and cover the bowl tightly. Let sit on the counter until doubled in size, about 90 minutes.

4. **Shape the loaves and proof for 30 minutes.** Lightly flour a work surface, then turn the dough out onto it. Knock the dough down and shape it into a ball. If you prefer two loaves, divide the dough in half and shape into two balls or roll out into two ovals. Place the dough onto a square of parchment paper not much bigger than the width of the dough itself, or place onto the baking tray. Cover the dough and let it rest for 30 minutes.

   *After shaping your loaves, place them seam side down onto the tray so that the taut top surface will rise and bake evenly.*

*CONTINUES*

*If using a banneton (p. 25) to proof your shaped dough, flour it generously before setting the dough inside and covering it. When it's time to bake, uncover the dough and gently tip it out onto a sheet of parchment paper so you can lift the dough to the pot without damaging the pattern. Do not score the bread before baking.*

5. **Preheat the oven** to 425°F (220°C) and place a large Dutch oven inside to heat, or line a baking tray with parchment paper instead.

6. **Score the dough.** Uncover the dough and use a sharp paring knife or a bread lame (see p. 25) to score the top of the bread. If using the Dutch oven, carefully remove the pot from the oven and lift the lid. Carefully place the loaf on its parchment paper in the bottom of the pot and cover the pot. Place the Dutch oven (or baking tray) in the oven.

7. **Bake the bread** for 30 minutes, remove the lid of the pot and then bake for another 30 minutes (two smaller loaves on a tray will take a total of 50 minutes). Immediately remove the bread from the oven and transfer it from the pot or tray to a rack to cool for at least 30 minutes before slicing.

*Baking bread in a Dutch oven gives it great lift and a crunchy crust. The oven heats the pot, which directly transfers heat to the bread.*

**The bread will keep, well wrapped, at room temperature for 3 days or frozen for up to 3 months.**

**MAKES** 1 large round loaf or 2 smaller loaves

**PREP TIME:** 20 minutes, plus proofing and cooling

**COOK TIME:** 1 hour

⏸ **MORE INVOLVED**

**BITES OF WISDOM:**
*Glossary of baking tools—Banneton (p. 25), How bread bakes (p. 70), How to troubleshoot other common baking issues—Breads (p. 60)*

## INGREDIENTS

### Starter:

**1 cup (125 g)** finely diced fresh or thawed frozen rhubarb

**1 cup (250 mL)** warm water (115°F/46°C)

**1 cup (120 g)** light rye flour

**½ cup (75 g)** bread or all-purpose flour

**Pinch** of instant dry yeast

### Bread:

**1 cup (125 g)** finely diced fresh or thawed frozen rhubarb

**2 Tbsp (36 g)** honey

**2 Tbsp (30 mL)** sour cream or plain Greek yogurt

**1½ cups (180 g)** light rye flour

**1½ cups (225 g)** bread or all-purpose flour

**1½ tsp** instant dry yeast

**1½ tsp** coarse salt

# Robert's Rhubarb Rye Bread

This recipe is a shout-out to my publisher and dear friend Robert McCullough, who has often reminded me that on the first day we spent baking together, decades ago, I was playing around with a rhubarb starter for rye bread. The result was a bread with a deliciously fruity sour taste because of the rhubarb and the rye flour. Although this bread does begin with a starter, it is not a sourdough bread (not all starter-based breads are sourdoughs). Instead, the starter allows the rhubarb flavour to permeate the dough. Plan to make the starter a day ahead of when you expect to bake the loaf.

1. **Prepare the starter a day ahead.** Stir the rhubarb, water, rye flour, bread (or all-purpose) flour and yeast together in a bowl; it will be a thick paste (1). Cover the bowl tightly and let sit on the counter for 12 to 24 hours (2).

   *Both fresh and thawed frozen rhubarb work well in this recipe. If using frozen rhubarb, save the juices that result from thawing to replace some of the 1 cup (250 mL) water for the starter.*

2. **Simmer the rhubarb** for the bread with the honey in a medium pot over medium heat for 6 to 8 minutes, stirring often, until completely softened. Remove the pan from the heat and stir in the sour cream (or yogurt) to cool the rhubarb down to around 115°F (46°C).

   *The only water in this bread dough is the water for the starter. The rest of the liquid comes from the stewed rhubarb, and that fruity flavour permeates the dough.*

3. **Mix, knead and proof the dough for 2 hours.** Measure the flours, yeast and salt into a large mixing bowl or the bowl of a stand mixer fitted with the hook attachment. Add the starter and the slightly cooled stewed rhubarb. If mixing by hand, stir the ingredients together until it becomes too difficult to do so. Lightly dust a work surface with flour and then turn the dough out onto the counter and continue to knead by hand until elastic, about 7 minutes. Try to avoid adding too much extra flour as you knead; the dough will pull away from your hands more easily as you knead. If using the mixer, process on low speed until the ingredients are combined. Increase the speed by a step or two and continue to knead the dough until it comes away from the sides of the bowl and feels elastic, about 5 minutes. Transfer the dough to an ungreased bowl, cover the bowl well and let rise for 2 hours, until doubled in size (3).

   *Rye flour contains much less gluten than wheat flour, and if used on its own in a bread recipe can result in a dense and heavy loaf. Using a blend of two flours solves that problem. The wheat flour provides structure and the rye flour delivers an earthy, tangy flavour. I prefer light rye flour because it yields a slightly fluffier loaf. If you use dark rye flour, expect a denser loaf with a more intense rye taste.*

*CONTINUES*

4. **Shape and proof the dough for 45 minutes.** Lightly dust a work surface with flour and turn the dough out onto it. Knock the dough down and shape it into a ball. If you prefer two loaves, divide the dough in half and shape into two balls or roll out into two ovals. Place the dough onto a square of parchment paper not much bigger than the width of the dough itself, or place onto the baking tray. Cover the dough and let it rest for 45 minutes.

*If you have a banneton (see p. 25), place the shaped loaf, seam side up, into the flour-dusted basket. Cover and allow to finish rising. The banneton is breathable, which helps the dough to rise evenly, and it leaves a lovely pattern. When it's time to bake, tip the loaf out onto your tray or into the pot, so that the pattern is on top.*

5. **Preheat the oven** to 400°F (200°C) and place a large Dutch oven inside to heat, or line a baking tray with parchment paper instead.

6. **Score the dough.** Uncover the dough and use a sharp paring knife or a bread lame (see p. 25) to score the top of the bread. If using the Dutch oven, carefully remove the pot from the oven and lift the lid. Carefully place the loaf on its parchment paper in the bottom of the pot and cover the pot. Place the Dutch oven (or baking tray) in the oven.

7. **Bake the bread** for 40 minutes, remove the lid of the pot and then bake for another 20 minutes (two smaller loaves on a tray will take a total of 50 minutes). Immediately remove the bread from the oven and transfer it from the pot or tray to a rack to cool for at least 30 minutes before slicing.

**The bread will keep, well wrapped, at room temperature for up to 3 days or frozen for up to 3 months.**

**MAKES:** 1 stromboli

**SERVES:** 4 as a main course, or 6 to 8 as a snack or lunch

**PREP TIME:** 30 minutes, plus proofing
**COOK TIME:** 30 minutes

🍴 **MORE INVOLVED**

**BITES OF WISDOM:**
*Glossary of ingredients—Yeast (p. 11),*

**INGREDIENTS**

**Dough:**

2½ cups (375 g) "00" flour

1 (2¼ tsp/7 g) pkg instant dry yeast

1 tsp fine salt

1 cup (250 mL) warm water (around 115°F/46°C)

2 Tbsp extra-virgin olive oil

**Fillings:**

¾ cup (175 mL) prepared tomato sauce or pizza sauce

5 oz (150 g) thinly sliced Black Forest ham or prosciutto cotto (Italian cooked ham)

2 oz (60 g) thinly sliced hot Genoa or Calabrese salami

2 oz (60 g) thinly sliced capicola

¼ cup (32 g) roughly chopped pitted kalamata olives (optional)

2 cups (500 mL) loosely packed fresh spinach leaves

2⅓ cups (250 g) coarsely grated mozzarella cheese

Medium egg wash (see p. 33)

¼ cup (25 g) finely grated Parmesan cheese

# Stromboli

Imagine making a pizza, topping it with sauce, meats and cheese and then rolling it up to bake . . . that's stromboli! An American creation, stromboli's inclusion of tomato sauce inside makes it different from the pocket-shaped Italian calzone, which is served with tomato sauce on the side.

1. **Make and proof the dough.** Stir the flour, yeast and salt together in the bowl of a stand mixer fitted with the hook attachment. Add the water and olive oil and mix on low speed until the flour is worked in. Increase the speed a few levels to knead for about 4 minutes, until the dough is elastic and comes away from the sides of the bowl. If mixing by hand, combine the ingredients until it becomes too difficult to stir in a bowl; turn the dough out onto the counter and knead until it feels elastic, about 5 minutes. Place the dough in an ungreased bowl, cover the bowl and let rise on the counter for an hour, until doubled in size.

   *This recipe also makes a delicious pizza dough, enough for two medium pizzas. You can make this dough ahead of time, let it rise for an hour and then knock it down before wrapping well in plastic and freezing it for up to 3 months. Thaw it in the fridge overnight to use it the following day, or thaw it on the counter for about 4 hours.*

2. **Roll and top the dough.** Lightly dust a work surface with flour and roll out the risen dough to a rectangle about 12 × 20 inches (30 × 50 cm). Spread the tomato sauce (or pizza sauce) over the dough (1), leaving an inch (2.5 cm) bare around the edge. Layer the ham, salami and capicola on top of the sauce. Sprinkle the olives over, if using, followed by the spinach. Sprinkle the cheese overtop.

   *Sliced deli meats are typical to a stromboli, making it almost sandwich-like. That said, use whichever fillings you prefer. Do make sure they are fully cooked and well drained before placing them on the dough.*

3. **Roll up the stromboli.** Line a baking tray with parchment paper. Fold the short sides of the dough over the filling by an inch (2.5 cm). Starting from a long side, roll up the dough and filling (like a cinnamon bun) (2, 3). When you reach the end, pinch the end of the dough into the roll and carefully lift the stromboli onto the baking tray. Cover loosely and let the stromboli rise for 30 minutes.

4. **Preheat the oven** to 400°F (200°C).

5. **Finish the stromboli.** Brush the stromboli with egg wash and sprinkle with Parmesan cheese. Use a paring knife to make cuts at 2-inch intervals on the top, to allow steam to escape.

6. **Bake the stromboli** for about 30 minutes, until an even golden brown. Cool for 10 minutes before slicing. Serve warm or at room temperature.

   **The stromboli will keep, well wrapped, in the fridge for up to 2 days. Rewarm in a 325°F (160°C) oven for about 20 minutes before serving.**

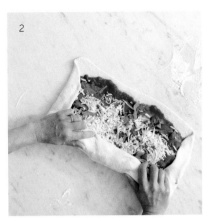

**MAKES:** 12 sandwich buns

**PREP TIME:** 20 minutes, plus proofing
**COOK TIME:** 35 minutes

🍴 **MORE INVOLVED**
**BITES OF WISDOM:**
*How to portion unbaked batters & doughs
(p. 49)*

## INGREDIENTS

1 Tbsp (15 mL) extra virgin olive oil

1 medium onion, finely diced

**4 cups (600 g)** all-purpose or bread flour

**2 Tbsp (25 g)** granulated sugar

**1 Tbsp (15 mL)** dried dill or **2 Tbsp (30 mL)** chopped fresh dill

**1 (2¼ tsp/7 g)** pkg instant dry yeast

**2 tsp** fine salt

**1 cup (225 g)** creamy ricotta cheese

**1 cup (250 mL)** warm water (115°F/46°C)

**¼ cup (60 mL)** extra-virgin olive oil

**2 large eggs,** at room temperature

Medium egg wash (see p. 33)

# Ricotta, Dill & Onion Buns

I love making these buns for holiday meals, not just to serve with the meal but also to have on hand after everyone has gone home. The buns make a mean sandwich with the leftover meats from roasted ham, turkey or beef.

1. **Cook the onions.** Heat the oil in a sauté pan over medium heat and cook the onions until translucent, about 5 minutes. Remove the pan from the heat to cool a little.

   *You need to cook the water out of the onions before adding them to your dough, otherwise this moisture will cook out as the buns bake, leaving air pockets surrounded by spongy dough.*

2. **Mix and proof the dough for 90 minutes.** Combine the remaining ingredients except the egg wash in a large mixing bowl or in the bowl of a stand mixer fitted with the hook attachment. Mix the dough by hand or on low speed until it starts to come together, then add the slightly cooled onions and mix in. If mixing by hand, lightly dust a work surface with flour, and once the dough becomes too difficult to mix with a spoon, turn it out onto the counter and knead until smooth, about 5 minutes. If using a mixer, knead the dough on low for 3 minutes more once it has come together. Place the dough in an ungreased bowl, cover well and let rise at room temperature until almost doubled in size, about 90 minutes.

   *Bread doughs with a lot of dairy can take longer to ferment and rise than doughs made with water, because milk ingredients are more alkaline (higher pH) than water. Dairy-laden doughs are also less temperature-sensitive, which makes them more forgiving if your ingredients are warmer or cooler than expected.*

3. **Shape and proof the dough.** Lightly dust a work surface with flour and grease a 9 × 13-inch (23 × 33 cm) baking pan. Turn the dough out onto the counter and divide into 12 pieces. Shape the dough into balls and arrange them in the pan. Cover with a tea towel and let rise at room temperature for 45 minutes.

4. **Preheat the oven** to 350°F (180°C).

5. **Bake the buns.** Uncover the buns, brush with the egg wash and bake for about 35 minutes, until they are a rich golden brown on top. Cool the buns on a rack before serving.

   **The buns are best eaten within a day of baking, but they will keep, well wrapped, at room temperature for up to 2 days or frozen for up to 3 months. Thaw at room temperature before serving.**

**MAKES:** just over 2.2 lb (1 kg) dough

**PREP TIME:** 10 minutes, plus proofing

❗ **SIMPLE**

**BITES OF WISDOM:**
*Glossary of ingredients—Yeast (p. 11),
How to troubleshoot other common
baking issues—Breads (p. 60)*

### INGREDIENTS

**3¾ cups (560 g)** all-purpose flour

**2 Tbsp (25 g)** granulated sugar

**1 (2¼ tsp/7 g)** pkg instant dry yeast

**1 tsp** fine salt

**½ cup (125 mL)** hot water (hot from
the tap)

**½ cup (125 mL)** 1% or 2% milk, cold

**2** large eggs, at room temperature

**½ cup (115 g)** unsalted butter, at room
temperature, cut into pieces

# Soft Egg Dough

This basic egg dough is fluffy, tender and perfect for fillings. Twist it into Soft Cinnamon Knots (p. 423) or layer and fold it into pull-apart breads. The dough itself isn't sweet, so you can tailor it for sweet or savoury bakes. Once you become comfortable making this simple dough, you can get creative with your own fillings and shapes.

1. **Combine the dry ingredients.** Measure the flour, sugar, yeast and salt in the bowl of a stand mixer fitted with the hook attachment.

2. **Add the liquids and mix.** In a separate bowl, stir together the hot water and milk (the hot water and cold milk should result in a liquid of about 115°F/46°C). Add the milk mixture and the eggs to the bowl and start the mixer on low, letting it go for a minute or two until the dough is almost combined. With the motor running, add the butter, a few pieces at a time. Increase the speed one level and continue to mix until the dough looks smooth (it will be very soft), about 6 minutes.

   *You can mix this dough by hand but you won't be able to turn it out onto the counter to knead it—it is too soft. Instead, keep stirring the dough vigorously by hand using a large wooden spoon until the dough starts to feel stretchy and elastic, about 8 minutes.*

3. **Let the dough rise.** Transfer the dough to an ungreased bowl, cover with plastic wrap and let sit on the counter for about 90 minutes, until doubled in size.

   *You can make this dough a day ahead, cover the bowl and let it proof in the fridge overnight. It is very easy to work with chilled, since the butter will have set, but add an extra 30 minutes to the final rising time before you bake.*

**MAKES:** 12 knots

**PREP TIME:** 20 minutes, plus proofing
**COOK TIME:** 25 minutes

❗ SIMPLE

**BITES OF WISDOM:**
*How bread bakes (p. 70)*

**INGREDIENTS**

---

¼ **cup (60 g)** unsalted butter, at room temperature

½ **cup (100 g)** packed light brown sugar

**1 Tbsp (6 g)** ground cinnamon

**1 recipe** Soft Egg Dough (p. 420), proofed on the counter for an hour or in the fridge overnight

Medium egg wash (see p. 33), for brushing

# Soft Cinnamon Knots

Literally a "twist" on the cinnamon bun, these buttery knots are twisted before being baked into muffin cups rather than rolled and cut like cinnamon buns.

1. **Make the filling.** Beat the butter by hand to smooth it out, then add the brown sugar and cinnamon, beating well.

   *While these knots are on the simpler side, you can still get inventive and add your own extra flavourings in addition to the cinnamon—try adding the zest of a lemon or orange, 2 tsp of vanilla extract or 1 tsp of almond extract. Or replace the cinnamon with the same measure of pumpkin pie spice.*

2. **Spread the filling.** Lightly dust a work surface with flour. Roll the risen dough into a rectangle about 12 × 18 inches (30 × 46 cm). Spread the filling over half of the rectangle, covering a 9 × 12-inch (23 × 30 cm) surface. Fold the uncovered half of the dough over the covered part. Use your rolling pin to press the halves in place to work out any air pockets, rolling the dough into a 12-inch (30 cm) square. Trim away the rough and open edges.

   *Twist any leftover scraps together and bake them as a separate "bonus" knot.*

3. **Shape the knots.** Grease a muffin tin well and set it on a baking tray. With the folded edge toward you, cut the dough into 12 (1-inch/2.5 cm) strips, ensuring that each strip has a folded end. To create the knots, grasp a strip of dough at either end and twist in opposite directions as much as it will go, stretching the dough a little but not enough to tear. Fold the twist in half, grasp the ends and twist again. Tie the twisted dough into a knot and place into a muffin cup, pressing down gently to make sure it snuggles into the hole. (See the photo on the cover of this book and on p. 421 to illustrate the process.) Repeat with the remaining strips of dough. Cover the muffin tin with a tea towel and let the knots rise for 30 minutes.

4. **Preheat the oven** to 350°F (180°C).

5. **Bake the knots.** Brush the knots with the egg wash and bake for about 25 minutes, until they are a rich golden brown. Cool the knots in their pan on a rack for 20 minutes, then transfer them from the tin to the rack to cool further before enjoying.

   **The knots are best enjoyed the day they are baked. They will keep in an airtight container at room temperature for up to 2 days. Reheat in the microwave for 30 to 60 seconds or in a 325°F (160°C) oven for 10 minutes to refresh them.**

**MAKES:** one 9 × 5-inch (2 L) loaf
**SERVES:** 8

**PREP TIME:** 20 minutes, plus proofing
**COOK TIME:** 45 minutes

**❚❚ MORE INVOLVED**
**BITES OF WISDOM:**
*Glossary of baking actions—Proof (p. 31)*

**INGREDIENTS**

**Bread:**

1½ cups (260 g) peeled and diced
apples, cut into ½-inch (1.2 cm) dice

⅔ cup (140 g) packed light brown sugar

2 Tbsp (30 g) unsalted butter, melted

2 tsp ground cinnamon

½ tsp ground nutmeg

½ recipe Soft Egg Dough (p. 420),
proofed on the counter for an hour or
in the fridge overnight

**Glaze:**

1 cup (130 g) icing sugar

2 Tbsp (30 mL) 1% or 2% milk

½ tsp vanilla extract

# Apple Cinnamon Pull-apart Bread

Layers of cinnamon and diced apples are nestled between folds of soft egg dough, so that each portion can be easily pulled away from the loaf.

1. **Make the filling.** Toss the apples with brown sugar, melted butter, cinnamon and nutmeg to coat well. Set aside.

   *Feel free to add 1 cup (90 g) coarsely grated Cheddar cheese to the mix to give this loaf a good salty and sweet flavour.*

2. **Prepare the pan.** Grease a 9 × 5-inch (2 L) loaf pan and line the tin with parchment so that the paper comes up and over the long sides of the pan.

3. **Roll the dough.** Lightly dust a work surface with flour. Roll the risen dough into a 15-inch (38 cm) square.

4. **Fill and fold the dough.** Spoon a third of the apples in a strip over the middle third of the dough. Fold one side of the dough over the apples to cover them and spoon a third of the apples on top of this piece of dough. Fold the opposing strip of dough over to cover the apples (you may have to stretch the dough a little) and top with the remaining apples. (You will now have a rectangle of three layers of dough with three layers of filling.)

5. **Trim the dough and fill the tin.** Trim the dough on the long sides so that the edges are all now open (and can be pulled apart once baked). Cut the loaf along the longer side into three equal pieces, each about 5 inches (12.5 cm) square, and then cut these squares into triangles, like you would a sandwich. Carefully lift each triangle section up and place one half of the "sandwich" into the pan so that it sits upright against the short side of the pan and the right angle is nestled in the bottom to one side. Overlap the second half of the "sandwich" over the first, with its right angle nestled against the opposite bottom side. Repeat with the remaining portions. Cover the pan loosely and let sit on the counter to rise for 30 minutes.

6. **Preheat the oven** to 350°F (180°C).

7. **Bake the loaf.** Uncover the pan and bake for about 45 minutes, until the bread turns a rich golden brown. Cool the bread in its pan on a rack for at least 30 minutes before removing to glaze.

8. **Make the glaze.** Whisk together the icing sugar, milk and vanilla and drizzle on top of the slightly cooled bread. Cool for another 20 to 30 minutes before serving.

**The bread is best served the day it's made.**

MAKES: one 10-cup (2.5 L) Bundt loaf
SERVES: 12

PREP TIME: 25 minutes, plus rising
COOK TIME: 1 hour

🍴 MORE INVOLVED
BITES OF WISDOM:
*How to portion unbaked batters & doughs (p. 49)*

**INGREDIENTS**

½ cup (115 g) unsalted butter, melted, plus extra for the pan

1 clove garlic, minced

8 oz (240 g) mozzarella or Monterey Jack cheese

¾ cup (75 g) finely grated Parmesan cheese, plus extra for the pan

1 recipe Soft Egg Dough (p. 420), with 3 cloves of minced garlic and 1 cup (250 mL) finely chopped green onions added to the dough, proofed on the counter for an hour or in the fridge overnight

# Garlic Cheese Pull-apart Bundt Bread

If garlic cheese bread is your kryptonite, then beware—this bread is deliciously and decadently tempting. Individual balls of dough are filled with cheese and then dipped in garlic butter before being layered in a Bundt pan to bake. Make sure you eat this pull-apart bread warm while the cheese is still melted. A side of warm marinara sauce for dipping is strongly recommended.

1. **Prepare the pan.** Brush a 10-cup (2.5 L) Bundt pan with melted butter and coat with Parmesan cheese, tapping out any excess.

2. **Get the garlic butter and cheese ready.** Place the ½ cup (115 g) melted butter in a small bowl, stir in the garlic and set aside. Dice the mozzarella (or Monterey Jack) cheese into 32 cubes, about ½ inch (1.2 cm) across. Place the Parmesan cheese in a bowl.

3. **Divide the dough.** Lightly dust a work surface with flour. Turn the risen dough (with garlic and green onions worked into it) onto the counter and divide into 32 pieces.

4. **Stuff the bread pieces with cheese and proof.** Hold a piece of dough in one hand and press a cheese cube into the centre of it, bringing the edges together and pinching to seal the cheese inside. Dip the dough ball into the garlic butter to coat and then roll it in Parmesan. Place in the Bundt pan and repeat with the remaining dough. Once you fill the bottom of the pan with dough balls, sprinkle a little extra Parmesan on top and begin a new layer. You should get about three layers. Cover the Bundt loosely and let rise for 45 minutes on the counter.

*You can assemble the bread up to this point a day ahead and, instead of proofing on the counter for 45 minutes, cover and refrigerate. Let the bread warm up at room temperature for 90 minutes before baking.*

5. **Preheat the oven** to 350°F (180°C).

6. **Bake the bread** for 50 to 60 minutes, until the top is a rich golden brown. Cool the bread in the Bundt pan on a rack for 15 minutes before turning it out of the pan on the rack. Serve immediately, while the cheese inside is still hot.

**The bread is best enjoyed warm and freshly baked. Leftovers will keep, loosely wrapped, in the fridge for up to 2 days, but should be reheated to serve. Reheat in a 325°F (160°C) oven for 20 minutes before serving.**

**MAKES:** 12 buns

**PREP TIME:** 40 minutes, plus proofing
**COOK TIME:** 25 minutes

🍴 **MORE INVOLVED**

**BITES OF WISDOM:**
*How to portion unbaked batters & doughs*
*(p. 49), How to use piping bags & tips*
*(p. 52)*

**INGREDIENTS**

**Buns:**

**3 cups (450 g)** all-purpose flour

**3 Tbsp (37 g)** granulated sugar

**1 (2¼ tsp/7 g) pkg** instant dry yeast

**2 tsp** ground cardamom

**1 tsp** baking powder

**1 tsp** fine salt

**1 cup (250 mL)** 2% milk, heated to
lukewarm

**6 Tbsp (90 g)** unsalted butter, melted

Medium egg wash (see p. 33)

**Filling:**

**2 cups (500 mL)** whipping cream

**2 Tbsp (25 g)** granulated sugar

**1 tsp** vanilla extract

**3 oz (90 g)** Marzipan (p. 85) or
store-bought

**2 cups (130 g)** crumbs from scooping
out baked buns

**¼ cup (60 ml)** 2% milk

Icing sugar, for dusting

# Swedish Semlor

These cream buns are traditionally a Lenten treat in Sweden, but I think they are worth making year-round. Cardamom-spiced soft buns are baked, hollowed and then filled with marzipan and a cream thickened with some of the fresh crumbs. I love that semlor are simple yet frilly at the same time.

1. **Mix and proof the dough.** Stir the flour, sugar, yeast, cardamom, baking powder and salt together in the bowl of a stand mixer fitted with the hook attachment. Add the milk and melted butter and blend on low speed to combine. Increase the speed by a level, and continue to knead the dough until it pulls away from the bowl with an elastic stretch. The dough will be soft yet dense. Cover the bowl and let the dough rise for 90 minutes (it will not double in size).

   *This dough is enriched with milk and butter but doesn't contain any eggs, so it might feel denser yet stretchier than other soft doughs you've made. It handles easily and really holds its shape well when proofed and baked.*

2. **Shape and proof the dough.** Line a baking tray with parchment paper and lightly dust a work surface with flour. Turn the dough out onto the counter and divide the dough into 12 equal portions. Shape each piece into a ball and place on the lined baking tray. Cover the tray with a tea towel and let the buns rise for an hour until risen by 50%.

3. **Preheat the oven** to 350°F (180°C).

4. **Bake the buns.** Brush the buns with egg wash and bake for about 25 minutes, until they are an even golden brown. Transfer the buns from the tray to a rack to cool completely before filling.

5. **Prepare the buns to be filled.** Use a paring knife to cut a 1½-inch (4 cm) circular opening in the top of each bun. Pop the "lid" off each bun and use a melon baller or your fingers to scoop out most of the soft bread at the centre of each bun without breaking the outer surface (1). Save 2 cups (130 g) crumbs for the filling. Set aside the lids to place on top of the buns after filling.

6. **Make the filling.** Using electric beaters or in a stand mixer fitted with the whip attachment, whip the cream to a soft peak on high speed. Whip in the sugar and vanilla and set aside (or chill if making more than an hour ahead). In a separate bowl, use electric beaters to soften the marzipan. Add the reserved crumbs and the milk, beating until the mixture is soft and well combined. Fold in the whipped cream in two additions, ensuring that the filling is well combined.

   *The crumbs will soften and break down in the cream so that the filling is easy to pipe.*

7. **Fill the buns.** Spoon the cream filling into a large piping bag fitted with a large star tip. Fill each bun so that the cream spirals up and above the lip of the bun (2). Gently place the cap on the buns (3) and dust with icing sugar. Store the semlor in the fridge until ready to eat.

   **The buns are best enjoyed within a day of assembling. Semlor will keep, loosely covered, in the fridge for up to 2 days.**

**MAKES:** three 9-inch (23 cm) loaves

**PREP TIME:** 45 minutes, plus proofing
**COOK TIME:** 1 hour

### ⫼ COMPLEX
**BITES OF WISDOM:**
*Glossary of ingredients—Fruits, dried (p. 8), and Nuts & seeds (p. 11)*

## INGREDIENTS

**Fruit & nut mixture:**

2 cups (300 g) raisins

1½ cups (165 g) sliced or slivered almonds

1 cup (150 g) diced candied orange peel

1 cup (140 g) coarsely chopped dried cherries or cranberries

½ cup (125 mL) spiced rum

1 tsp ground cardamom

½ tsp ground cinnamon

½ tsp ground nutmeg

¼ tsp ground cloves

¼ tsp ground allspice

**Sponge starter:**

1 cup (250 mL) 2% milk, heated to lukewarm

1 cup (150 g) bread flour

1 (2¼ tsp/7 g) pkg instant dry yeast

**Dough:**

½ cup (125 mL) 2% milk, heated to lukewarm

4 cups (600 g) bread flour

½ cup (100 g) granulated sugar

1 large egg

2 egg yolks

Finely grated zest of **1** orange

1 tsp fine salt

¾ cup (175 g) unsalted butter, cut into pieces, at room temperature

**Assembly & glaze:**

8 oz (240 g) Marzipan (p. 85) or store-bought

½ cup (100 g) granulated sugar

⅓ cup (80 mL) water

¼ cup (60 g) unsalted butter

1 cup (130 g) icing sugar

# Holiday Stollen

This dense, rich sweet bread is dotted with dried fruits and nuts, but what stands out is the marzipan centre. Like a festive fruitcake, stollen can be made well ahead of time and frozen to serve over the holidays or give as a gift. Start by steeping the dried fruits in rum the day before you plan to serve this bread, and give yourself a bit of time to complete each step.

1. **Steep the fruit a day ahead.** Toss the raisins, almonds, candied peel and dried cherries (or cranberries) with the rum in a large bowl, then stir in the cardamom, cinnamon, nutmeg, cloves and allspice. Cover the mixture well and let sit on the counter for a day, stirring occasionally.

2. **Make the sponge starter.** Stir the milk, flour and yeast together by hand in a large mixing bowl or in the bowl of a stand mixer. Let sit for 30 minutes, uncovered.

3. **Make the stollen dough.** Add the milk, flour, sugar, egg, egg yolks, orange zest and salt to the sponge starter. If using a mixer, combine on low speed with a dough hook. With the motor running, add the butter and then increase the speed by one level and knead until the dough looks elastic and pulls away from the sides. It should still be soft and stick a little to your hands when touched. If mixing by hand, stir the dough (including the butter) with a wooden spoon until the flour is no longer visible. Lightly dust a work surface with flour and then tip the dough out onto the counter and knead by hand until elastic. Add no more than ¼ cup (37 g) flour as you knead, to prevent the dough from becoming too tight and dry. Place the dough in an ungreased bowl, cover the bowl tightly and let rise for an hour (it won't rise too noticeably).

4. **Add the fruits and nuts.** Uncover the dough and add the fruits and nuts. Use your hands to work the dried fruits into the dough—don't be afraid to really get in there to mix it. Cover the bowl again and let the dough rise for 20 minutes.

5. **Shape and fill the stollen.** Line two baking trays with parchment paper and lightly dust a work surface with flour. Turn the dough out onto the counter and divide it into three pieces. Roll the first piece into an oval about 9 inches (23 cm) long and 7 inches (18 cm) wide. Divide the marzipan into three pieces, knead it to soften and roll each piece into an 8-inch-long (20 cm) long rope. Place one piece of marzipan slightly left of centre on the rolled-out dough (1). Fold the dough from the left side over the marzipan, pressing down to create a seam to cover it (2). Fold the dough from the right side to meet this seam and press down again. Coax the stollen back into a tidy oval if it has shifted and place on the lined baking tray. Repeat with the two remaining pieces of dough and marzipan. (You should be able to fit two stollen on a tray.) Cover the trays with tea towels and let sit for 30 minutes.

*The marzipan does more than add a surprise at the centre of the stollen. It helps keep the bread moist, which is why stollen will keep for a week on the counter.*

*CONTINUES*

*If you are planning to give the stollen as gifts, or want to freeze and have smaller ones to serve later, divide the dough into four pieces and shape. Bake the smaller stollen for 10 minutes less, but keep the proof times the same.*

6. **Preheat the oven** to 350°F (180°C).

*Before baking the stollen, pick out any raisins that have broken through the surface of the dough—they have a tendency to burn.*

7. **Bake the stollen.** Uncover the stollen and bake for 50 to 60 minutes, until the loaves are an even rich golden brown.

8. **Glaze the stollen.** While the stollen are baking, make the glaze. In a small pot, bring the granulated sugar and water to a simmer over medium heat, stirring until the sugar dissolves. Turn off the heat and stir in the butter until melted. After the stollen have been out of the oven for 10 minutes, reheat the glaze on low heat. Use a tea towel to hold a loaf in one hand, then brush the glaze all over the outside of the stollen and place on a wire rack to cool completely (3). Once cooled, generously dust each stollen with icing sugar (4).

**The stollen will keep, well wrapped in plastic, at room temperature for 1 week or in the fridge for up to 3 months.**

## ⁘ MORE INVOLVED

**BITES OF WISDOM:**

*Glossary of baking actions—Proof (p. 31),
How to use piping bags & tips (p. 52)*

## INGREDIENTS

**Baba dough:**

1 cup (150 g) all-purpose flour

1 Tbsp (12 g) granulated sugar

1 (2¼ tsp/7 g) pkg instant dry yeast

3 large eggs, at room temperature

6 Tbsp (90 g) unsalted butter, at room
temperature

**Syrup:**

½ cup (100 g) granulated sugar

½ cup (125 mL) water

½ cup (125 mL) spiced rum

# Rum Babas

Traditional rum babas are baked in a dariole mold, a muffin-style tin
with deeper, narrower cups that allow the babas to rise over the top edge,
giving them their signature mushroom-like look. If you don't have
a dariole mold, a regular muffin tin will do but you will need to double
the recipe for the syrup.

1. **Make the baba dough.** Stir the flour, sugar and yeast together in a mixing
bowl and add the eggs and butter. Stir with a wooden spoon or spatula until
the dough is stretchy (it will be very sticky). Really work the dough with your
spoon, stretching it and slapping it against the side of the bowl, to make it
even more elastic (1, 2). Cover the bowl and let the dough rise for 30 minutes
(the dough will rise a little, but not dramatically).

*The proportionately higher amount of yeast relative to the flour makes baba dough
one of the quickest yeast doughs to proof. And this quick and active fermentation
makes the baked babas very airy, leaving lots of room for syrup to soak in.*

2. **Pipe the baba dough.** Lightly grease a silicone or metal dariole pan (see recipe
introduction) and set it on a baking tray. Use a spatula to knock down the
sticky dough and spoon it into a piping bag fitted with a large plain tip. Pipe
the dough into each cup, filling it two-thirds full. Set aside, uncovered, for
30 minutes, until the babas rise to the top of the pan (3).

*This dough is so soft and pliable that it pipes easily into the mold.*

3. **Preheat the oven** to 375°F (190°C).

4. **Bake the babas** for 15 to 18 minutes, until golden brown on top. Remove
from the oven and cool the babas in the pan for 5 minutes, then transfer to
a wire rack to cool completely (4).

*You can make and bake the babas ahead of time to this point. Transfer to an
airtight container and store at room temperature for up to a day or freeze until
ready to assemble. Thaw on the counter before filling.*

5. **Make the syrup.** Bring the sugar and water to a full simmer in a small
saucepan over high heat, stirring occasionally, and cook just until the sugar has
dissolved. Remove the pan from the heat and stir in the rum.

*If you don't have spiced rum, add one cinnamon stick and four cloves to the
syrup when simmering.*

*Babas baked in a muffin tin will soak up much more syrup than babas baked in
a dariole mold because the muffin-tin babas are wider. Make double the syrup to
be sure you have enough.*

*CONTINUES*

6. **Dip the babas in the syrup.** Line a baking tray with parchment paper or a muffin tin with paper liners. Using tongs, dip the babas in the syrup one at a time and let the syrup soak in completely (the babas won't fall apart). As you lift them out of the syrup, give them a gentle squeeze so they are moist but not soggy. Set the babas on the tray or in the tin and chill until ready to serve.

*Rum babas can be served plain, but I like to make a plated dessert. Place a baba on each plate, dollop or pipe a little Chantilly Cream (p. 95) on the side and serve with fresh peach slices. You can even reduce any extra rum syrup to make a glaze and drizzle it over the peaches.*

**The babas will keep in an airtight container in the fridge for up to 3 days.**

**MAKES:** 4 savarins

**PREP TIME:** 20 minutes, plus proofing
**COOK TIME:** 18 minutes

🍴 **MORE INVOLVED**
**BITES OF WISDOM:**
*How to use piping bags & tips (p. 52)*

### INGREDIENTS

**1 recipe** Baba Dough (p. 433), freshly made and risen for 30 minutes

**¾ cup (175 mL)** icewine

**½ cup (100 g)** granulated sugar

**½ cup (125 mL)** water

**2 Tbsp (36 g)** honey

**1 Tbsp (15 mL)** fresh lemon juice

**2 cups (500 mL)** Chantilly Cream (p. 95)

**2 cups (500 mL)** mixed fresh berries (raspberries, blueberries, blackberries)

Icing sugar, for dusting

# Icewine Berry Savarins

Made with the same dough as the Rum Babas (p. 433), savarins are piped into doughnut-like ring molds before baking. The savarin rings are soaked in a flavoured syrup and then filled with cream and fruits, making them a refreshingly cool dessert to end a summer meal.

1. **Pipe the dough.** Lightly grease four 4½-inch (11.5 cm) savarin molds and place on a baking tray. Spoon the dough (still very sticky) into a piping bag fitted with a large plain tip and pipe into each ring, filling it up halfway. Set aside, uncovered, for 30 minutes to rise.

   *Doughnut molds work perfectly well for baking savarins too. The centre hole of a doughnut mold is a little smaller, so you will get eight savarins. Bake them for 12 to 15 minutes and stack a few more berries on top of each other when you assemble the desserts.*

2. **Preheat the oven** to 375°F (190°C).

3. **Bake the savarins** for 15 to 18 minutes, until golden brown on top. Let the savarins cool for 5 minutes, then remove them from the molds to cool completely.

   *You can make and bake the savarins ahead of time to this point. Transfer to an airtight container and store at room temperature for up to a day or freeze until ready to assemble. Thaw on the counter before filling.*

4. **Make the syrup.** Bring the icewine, granulated sugar, water, honey and lemon juice to a full simmer in a small saucepan over high heat, stirring occasionally and cooking just until the sugar has dissolved. Remove the pan from the heat.

   *If you don't have icewine, any sweet dessert wine like a late-harvest Riesling or Sauternes will work fine.*

5. **Dip each savarin in the syrup.** Using tongs, dip the savarins in the syrup one at a time and let the syrup soak in completely (the savarins won't fall apart). As you lift them out of the syrup, give them a gentle squeeze so they are moist but not soggy. Set the savarins on a tray or plate and chill until ready to assemble.

6. **Assemble the savarins.** Place each savarin on a dessert plate. Pipe Chantilly cream into the centre of each one and top with the fresh berries. Dust the savarins with icing sugar and serve.

**Assembled savarins will keep, uncovered, in the fridge for up to 6 hours. You may need to dust them again with icing sugar before serving.**

# Classic Brioche Dough

Making brioche dough is virtually the same as making Soft Egg Dough (p. 420), but the brioche contains more eggs and butter.

**MAKES:** about 2.6 lb (1.2 kg) brioche dough

**PREP TIME:** 15 minutes, plus proofing and chilling

❕ SIMPLE

**BITES OF WISDOM:**
*How to portion unbaked batters & doughs (p. 49)*

## INGREDIENTS

4 **cups (600 g)** all-purpose flour

2 **Tbsp (25 g)** granulated sugar

1 **(2¼ tsp/7 g)** pkg instant dry yeast

1½ **tsp** fine salt

¾ **cup (175 mL)** 2% milk, warmed to 115°F (46°C)

5 large eggs, at room temperature

¾ **cup (175 g)** unsalted butter, diced, at room temperature

1. **Mix the dough.** Stir the flour, sugar, yeast and salt together in the bowl of a stand mixer fitted with the hook attachment. Add the milk and eggs and blend on low speed until the ingredients are almost fully combined. With the motor running, add the butter in pieces. Increase the speed one level and knead for about 8 minutes, until the dough looks stretchy and elastic as it pulls from the side of the bowl to the hook.

   *Because of all the room-temperature butter, this dough is extremely soft when you mix it—more like a batter than a dough. Don't be tempted to add extra flour. Once you chill the dough, the butter will set and the dough will be much easier to handle.*

   *You can mix this dough by hand but you won't be able to turn it out onto the counter to knead it—it is too soft. Instead, keep stirring the dough vigorously by hand using a large wooden spoon until it starts to feel stretchy and elastic, about 8 minutes.*

2. **Let the dough rise and then chill.** Transfer the dough to an ungreased bowl and cover the bowl well. Let the dough sit for an hour and then chill for at least 8 hours, or overnight before using.

Brioche Loaf, (p. 440)

**MAKES:** two 9 × 5-inch (2 L) loaves

**PREP TIME:** 10 minutes, plus proofing
**COOK TIME:** 45 minutes

⚔ **MORE INVOLVED**
**BITES OF WISDOM:**
*How bread bakes (p. 70)*

*Photos on p. 409 and 439*

**INGREDIENTS**

1 recipe Classic Brioche Dough (p. 438)

Medium egg wash (see p. 33)

Sesame or poppy seeds, for sprinkling
(optional)

**BONUS BAKE**

## Brioche Buns

Instead of making loaves, you can use the same classic brioche dough (p. 438) to make 16 buns to use for burgers or sandwiches. Divide the chilled dough into 16 pieces and shape them into balls. Place them well-spaced on 2 parchment-lined baking trays, cover with tea towels and let them rise on the counter for 90 minutes. Brush the buns with egg wash, sprinkle with **poppy seeds or sesame seeds** if you wish and bake for about 25 minutes at 350°F (180°C) until a rich golden brown. Let the buns cool on the tray on a rack.

# Brioche Loaf

Because of the butter, a baked brioche loaf stays fresh for a few days and toasts up marvellously. It also freezes very well. Or use it to make the Lemon Bostock Bread Pudding (p. 326).

1. **Shape the dough.** Grease two 9 × 5-inch (2 L) loaf pans. Lightly dust a work surface with flour and divide the dough into 16 pieces. Using your palm, roll each piece of dough on the counter to form it into a ball. Place eight balls in a single layer in each loaf pan, cover with a tea towel and let rise at room temperature for 2 hours.

2. **Preheat the oven** to 350°F (180°C).

3. **Bake the brioches.** Brush the tops of the loaves with egg wash. Sprinkle them with sesame (or poppy) seeds, if using. Bake the loaves for about 45 minutes, until the tops are a rich golden brown. Let the loaves cool in the pans on a rack for only 10 minutes, then tip out onto the rack to cool completely.

**The brioches will keep, well wrapped, on the counter for up to 2 days or frozen for up to 3 months.**

PREP TIME: 45 minutes, plus chilling and proofing

COOK TIME: 45 minutes

||| COMPLEX

BITES OF WISDOM:
*How to toast nuts (p. 36)*

## INGREDIENTS

½ **recipe** Classic Brioche Dough (p. 438), risen and chilled overnight but unbaked

1 **cup + 6 Tbsp (315 g)** unsalted butter, at room temperature, divided

¾ **cup (115 g)** toasted and peeled hazelnuts

6 **Tbsp (75 g)** granulated sugar

Finely grated zest of **1** orange

2 **tsp** ground cardamom

1 **tsp** ground cinnamon

3 **oz (90 g)** dark baking/couverture chocolate, chopped

# Chocolate Hazelnut Laminated Brioches with Cardamom & Orange

When you want a croissant-like pastry with crisp, flaky layers on the outside and a soft, buttery centre in a fraction of the time it takes to make puff pastry or croissant doughs, laminating chilled brioche dough with butter is a simple solution. Adding a filling of toasted hazelnuts and chocolate spiked with cardamom and orange really takes these brioches to a patisserie level of sophistication in taste and technique.

1. **Laminate the brioche dough.** Lightly dust a work surface with flour. Turn the chilled dough onto the counter and roll it out to a 12-inch (30 cm) square. Beat 1 cup (225 g) butter to soften it and spread evenly over the brioche. Roll up the brioche like a cinnamon bun. Press the roll flat with your hands and cut in half crosswise to make two 6-inch (15 cm) pieces. Stack these two pieces on top of each other, flatten and roll out to a 12-inch (30 cm) square. Roll up the brioche and flatten again. Wrap and chill for at least 30 to 60 minutes, but up to 4 hours (or even overnight) is ideal.

*Rather than achieving many, many layers like a puff pastry or croissant dough, this simplified lamination method aims to create distinct layers in an already butter-rich dough. This method results in a pastry that bakes up a deep golden brown with a crisp surface and a soft, fragrantly filled centre.*

2. **Make the filling.** Grease six 8 oz (250 mL) ramekins and place on a baking tray. Pulse the hazelnuts, remaining 6 Tbsp (90 g) butter, sugar, orange zest, cardamom and cinnamon together in a food processor or mini chopper to form a coarse but well-blended paste.

3. **Assemble the brioches.** Roll out the laminated dough to a 12 × 14-inch (30 × 35 cm) rectangle and spread with the filling. Sprinkle the chocolate over the filling (1). Fold the dough in half, bringing the short sides together, and roll the dough lightly to push out any air bubbles (2).

*CONTINUES*

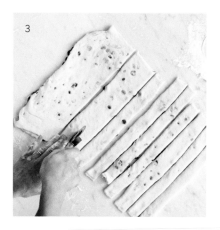

4. **With the folded edge toward you,** cut the dough into 12 (1-inch/2.5 cm) strips, ensuring that each strip has a folded end (3). To create each knot, place two strips of dough on top of each other and twist in opposite directions, stretching the dough a little but not enough to tear (4, 5). Twist the dough into a tight spiral and place into a ramekin, pressing down gently to make sure it snuggles into the hole (6). Repeat with the remaining strips of dough. Cover the tray with a tea towel and let the brioches rise for 90 minutes.

5. **Preheat the oven** to 350°F (180°C).

6. **Bake the brioches** for 40 to 45 minutes, until the tops are an even rich golden brown. Cool the brioches in the ramekins on a rack for 10 minutes, then carefully loosen and tip them out onto the racks to cool completely.

*Some of the filling may escape to the bottom of the ramekins as the brioches bake. Once you've removed the brioches, spoon out any filling left behind and spread it over the pastries (or save it to dress up regular toast).*

**The brioches are best enjoyed the day they are baked, but filled and rolled brioches will keep in an airtight container in the fridge for up to 2 days before baking or frozen for up to 3 months. Thaw overnight in the fridge before baking.**

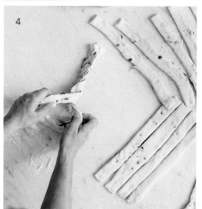

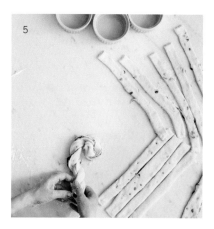

**MAKES:** one 9-inch (23 cm) round bread

**PREP TIME:** 20 minutes, plus proofing
**COOK TIME:** 35 minutes

🍴 **MORE INVOLVED**
**BITES OF WISDOM:**
*Glossary of baking actions—Proof (p. 31)*

## INGREDIENTS

**Dough:**

**2 cups (300 g)** all-purpose flour

**3 Tbsp (37 g)** granulated sugar

**1 (2¼ tsp/7 g)** pkg instant dry yeast

**1 tsp** fine salt

**¼ cup (60 mL)** Crème Fraîche (p. 94) or store-bought, or full-fat sour cream

**¼ cup (60 mL)** 2% milk

**3** large eggs

**1 Tbsp (15 mL)** orange blossom water

**6 Tbsp (90 g)** unsalted butter, at room temperature

**Sugar crackle:**

**¼ cup (50 g)** granulated sugar

**3 Tbsp (45 g)** unsalted butter, melted

**4 tsp** orange blossom water

# Fougasse Aigues-Mortes

Aigues-Mortes is an ancient walled city near the Camargue salt flats in the south of France. The specialty brioche of the town—and, in fact, the region—is fougasse Aigues-Mortes, an airy and sweet brioche that is almost cake-like with its crackled sugar top. Traditionally served as a holiday dessert, it is now popular year-round. Orange blossom water in the dough and sugar crackle gives it a distinct perfumed aroma that brings back delicious travel memories. And now I can recreate the feeling of walking through the region at home! Serve the fougasse sliced into wedges or squares on their own, with tea or coffee, or with rich or strong cheeses.

1. **Make the dough.** Stir the flour, sugar, yeast and salt together in a stand mixer fitted with the hook attachment. In a small saucepan, heat the crème fraîche and milk together over low heat until they reach 115°F (46°C). Pour the hot milk over the dry ingredients, add the eggs and orange blossom water and blend on low speed until the ingredients are almost fully combined. With the motor running, add the butter in pieces. Increase the speed one level and knead for about 5 minutes, until the dough looks stretchy and elastic as it pulls from the side of the bowl to the hook. The dough will be very sticky and soft, as much like a batter as a dough.

   *Some orange blossom products are meant for scenting soaps and potpourri but not for eating, so be sure to buy food-grade orange blossom water for cooking. Look for it online or in specialty grocers.*

2. **Proof the dough in its pan.** Grease a 9-inch (23 cm) round baking pan and line the bottom with parchment paper. Scrape the dough into the prepared pan and use your spatula to spread it evenly. Cover the pan loosely with a tea towel and let the dough rise for 90 minutes, until almost doubled in size.

3. **Preheat the oven** to 350°F (180°C).

4. **Bake the fougasse.** Using well-floured fingertips, make indentations like dimples in the dough. Bake for 20 minutes. Prepare the sugar crackle while the bread bakes.

   *Dimpling the fougasse with your fingers is similar to the method for making Italian focaccia. This step deflates the dough just enough that it won't rise up unevenly or develop big air pockets when it bakes.*

5. **Make and pour the sugar crackle.** Stir the sugar, melted butter and orange blossom water together in a small bowl. After the 20 minutes of baking, pull the fougasse from the oven and quickly pour the sugar mixture over it, using a pastry brush to cover completely. Return the fougasse to the oven to bake for another 10 to 15 minutes, until the bread is a light golden brown. Cool the fougasse in its pan on a wire rack for 30 minutes, then remove from the pan and cool completely.

**The fougasse will keep, well wrapped, at room temperature for up to 2 days.**

# Acknowledgements

Baking wisdom, in real life and in this book, does not happen alone. The influences and expertise of many make the transition from knowledge to wisdom possible, and it is to all these people that I offer my sincere thanks.

My maternal grandmother, Julia Hajzak, likely never realized what a significant impression she made upon me. She expressed her love for family through baking, and I carry my memories of time spent in the kitchen with her in a special place in my heart. It was her love of baking as a form of self-expression that made it important in my life, and I find it equally fulfilling to share my love of baking with others.

You, gentle readers, are my baking "family," and I create recipes with you in mind. My success as a cookbook author hinges on your success in making my recipes, and that feeling of wanting to deliver to you delicious, precise and fulfilling recipes that excite you to bake and develop your own baking wisdom inspires me every day. Thank you for reading and sharing these dishes.

I would not be writing these pages without the wisdom and talents of the wonderful professionals I work with. Publisher Robert McCullough and editorial director Lindsay Paterson keep my eye on the big picture: they have the vision to see how I can best connect with you and remain true to myself and my baking style. Lisa Rollo and Amy Pelley test my recipes with immense commitment, and their help with the photographs is invaluable. Janis Nicolay photographed all of these stunning images with patience and a good few laughs. And photo stylist Catherine Therrien made sure each baked good was beautifully framed to be the star of the photo. Thank you to this entire team and to the home bakers, such as Mark McGraw, who tested and enjoyed many of these recipes, and to countless other taste testers too.

Thanks once again to Lucy Kenward for her astute editing skills and for frank and open conversations on the sides of the pages as we edited the recipes and supporting text. And thank you to copy editor Lana Okerlund and proofreader Eva van Emden for all the attention to detail that is so crucial in putting together a book of this complexity. Emma Dolan provided the gorgeous design that makes this book appealing to browse through and the recipes easy to follow, and ideally will have you returning to the book time and again. Thank you to the entire team at Penguin Random House Canada who worked so hard to make this book available to you.

And lastly, thank you to my dearest Michael for always being my support. You are treasured. The recipes for this book were developed during an unforgettable time in our history, and it feels so good to have something positive result from such a challenging period. That time has also made me appreciate my family more, especially my mom and dad, Mi, Mika, John and now little Esmae. I hope I can share with her my baking wisdom and love of baking in the same way that my grandmother did with me. And, dear reader, I hope you develop your own memories and baking wisdom through many hours in the kitchen with those you love—making these recipes and your own family favourites.

# Index

# References

Dairy Farmers of Canada, www.dairyfarmers
    ofcanada.ca.
Davidson, Alan. *The Penguin Companion to
    Food*. Penguin Books, 2002. Previously
    published as *The Oxford Companion to
    Food*.

Egg Farmers of Canada, www.eggs.ca.
Egg Farmers of Ontario, www.getcracking.ca.
Farrimond, Stuart. *The Science of Cooking*.
    DK Penguin Random House, 2017.
McGee, Harold. *On Food and Cooking*. Rev.
    ed. Scribner, 2004.